DOMINICAN WOMEN

A TIME TO SPEAK

KATHLEEN BONER OP

Cluster Publications
2000

ISBN 1-875053-14-X

First published in 2000.

Published by Cluster Publications
P. O. Box 2400
Pietermaritzburg
3200

Printed by The Natal Witness Printing and Publishing Company (Pty) Ltd.

For my sisters
with respect and amazement.

Contents

List of illustrations		vi
Abbreviations		vii
Acknowledgments		viii
Preface		ix
Introduction		xi

1	A Time to Search	1
2	Women in the Church	6
3	A Time to Plant: The Irish Foundations	18
4	Cabra to Cape Town, 1863-1920	31
5	Sion Hill to Port Elizabeth, 1867-1918	64
6	Dominican Missionary Women: The Quest for Perfection	89
7	The Professionals	112
8	The Professionals: Deaf Education	135
9	Dominican Missionary Women: The Lay Sisters	157
10	The Debate: Crisis of Identity	183
11	The Union	204
12	The Visit	239
13	St Rose's Congregation, 1938-1974	269
14	The Congregation	291
15	The Struggle: Senzenina?	315
16	A Time to Change	344

Appendix I:	Oral evidence and personal records	374
Appendix II:	Higher superiors and Councils, SA	376
Appendix III:	Sisters in the Region of SA	385
Appendix IV:	Sisters who have worked in SA	389
Appendix V:	Obituaries	390
Notes		397
Select Bibliography		426
Index		435

List of Illustrations

1   St Mary's Dominican Convent, Cabra, Dublin, during the nineteenth century. (Opposite page 21.)

2   Mother Dympna Kinsella OP (1828-1903), foundress of the Dominican foundation in Cape Town in 1863. (Opposite page 41.)

3   St Dominic's Church, Springfield, Wynberg, Cape. (Opposite page 52.)

4   Dominican Convent, Sion Hill, Dublin. (Opposite page 67.)

5   Foundresses of Holy Rosary Convent, Port Elizabeth. Mother Rose Whitty is seated second from the right. (Opposite page 72.)

6   Novices at St Dominic's Priory, Walmer, Port Elizabeth, 1926. Back row, from left: Sisters Dominic Wilson, Lucy Maher, Elizabeth Oldham, Monica Carr, Evangelist Raleigh, Vincent Drew. Front row, from left: Sisters Alphonsus Cummins, Emily O'Keeffe, Margaret Mary Hogan, Bernard Mackesy, Benvenuta Ivers. (Opposite page 97.)

7   The chapel at St Dominic's Priory, Port Elizabeth. (Opposite page 261.)

8   The *Salve* procession at the end of *Compline*, at Springfield Convent, Wynberg, Cape, in the early 1950's. (Opposite page 295.)

9   Dominican sisters of the Western Cape taking part in an Eucharistic procession through the streets of Cape Town in 1951. (Opposite page 302.)

10 Sister Marian O'Sullivan, Regional Vicar in South Africa, 1977-1986; Prioress General of Cabra Dominicans 1986-1998. (Opposite page 354.)

List of Abbreviations

Archives:

CA	State Archives, Cape Town
CAC	Catholic Archives, The Chancery, Cape Town
DAC	Dominican Archives, Regional House, Cape Town
DCA	Dominican Archives, Cabra, Dublin
DAG	Dominican Archives, General, Dublin
DGA	Dominican Archives, Galway
DAP	Dominican Archives, Holy Rosary Convent, Port Elizabeth
DPA	Dominican Archives, St Dominic's Priory, Walmer, Port Elizabeth
DAS	Dominican Archives, Sion Hill, Blackrock, Co Dublin
DAW	Dominican Archives, Wittebome, W Cape

Other:

AWR	Association of Women Religious
CMRSSA	Congress of Major Religious Superiors, South Africa
CT	Cape Town
ECAR	Education Council of Associations of Religious
EP	Eastern Province, Cape
HRC	Holy Rosary Convent, Port Elizabeth
KB	Kathleen Boner
OP	Order of Preachers
MAKB	Master of Arts Dissertation, Kathleen Boner
PE	Port Elizabeth
SACBC	Southern African Catholic Bishops' Conference
SACC	South African Council of Churches
SACES	South African Catholic Education Survey
WP	Western Province, Cape

Acknowledgments

I wish to acknowledge permission to reproduce the following copyrighted material:

Cover picture: St Dominic receiving the first nuns into the Order. Detail from a stained glass window in the Dominican Convent, Tokyo, Japan. © Albert Carpentier OP.

Austin Flannery OP, (General editor), *Vatican Council II: The Conciliar and Post Conciliar documents*, © Harry J Costello and Austin Flannery OP, 1975.

William A Hinnebusch, OP, *The History of the Dominican Order*, © Society of St Paul, Staten Island, New York, 1966.

Gerard Huyghe, *et al*, *Religious orders in the modern world*, © Geoffrey Chapman Ltd, London, Dublin, 1965.

Jerusalem Bible, © Darton, Longman and Todd Ltd, and Doubleday and Company, Inc, 1966.

Assumpta O'Hanlon, OP, *Dominican pioneers in New South Wales*, © Dominican Nuns, Strathfield, 1949.

The Religious woman, minister of faith, A Compilation of addresses given at the First International Assembly Consortium Perfectae Caritatis, © Consortium Perfectae Caritatis, 1974.

Simon Tugwell, OP, *Saint Dominic*, © Editions du Signe, Strasbourg, 1995.

Preface

In the one hundred and thirty-five years since the six young Irish Dominican sisters set out on the sailing vessel, the *Saxon*, for the Cape of Good Hope, virtually everything in life has changed and changed radically. Politically the Cape Colony had to go through many transformations before the first free elections in 1994 led to the establishment of a Government of National Unity under President Mandela. In 1863 the Catholic Church in the Cape Colony consisted of approximately 3 000 Catholics, mostly European immigrants, with a very small minority of indigenous converts. In the entire Cape Colony there were only two Vicars Apostolic, one in Cape Town and one in Grahamstown in the Eastern Cape. Today the Catholic Church is growing so rapidly, that three million may be a conservative estimate and official ecclesiastical gatherings reflect a rainbow nation. In the second half of the nineteenth century religious life was lived under strict discipline in a patriarchal church and society. Today many of the values of that era are being challenged. The cultural revolutions following two world wars and the related reforms of Vatican II, have transformed and liberated members of religious communities, but have also weakened the appeal of religious life. During the one hundred and thirty-five years since the first foundation of the Irish Dominicans in Cape Town hundreds of young Irish women have left their homes in order to minister to the people in this beautiful and challenging country. Some returned home enriched, having given the best years of their lives to the mission. Most stayed and were joined by South Africans, and all of these through their educational apostolate, contributed to the growth of the church in the sub-continent.

Our understanding of the meaning of mission has changed. In the past missionaries, going out from Europe, saw themselves as bringing salvation to those who did not know the God of Jesus Christ. Their religious faith and values were firmly rooted in European culture and it was assumed that both faith and culture would benefit those who were privileged to share them. Developments in theology, missiology and cultural anthropology challenge us today to recognise God's presence and action in people of all faith traditions and in every culture. Does this mean that there is no need to be in mission? Not at all. The gospel has to find expression in every culture and in every generation even though no culture can do justice to the fullness of the gospel message. The history of the Dominican sisters told in these pages illustrates their readiness "to discern in faith the real needs of the people through an understanding of their faith and culture".[1]

The role of women in society and in the church has also changed significantly. Well-educated and professional though the women in this story were, they accepted without much question, the subordinate position assigned to them by their ecclesiastical superiors. This historical study of the first Dominican sisters in South Africa, *Dominican women: A Time to speak*, goes some way towards recognising their worth and makes an important contribution to women's history. Kathleen Boner OP and her research assistant, Caitríona Owens OP, have spent years in patient research, taking oral evidence, as well as classifying, restoring and binding thousands of documents which form the basis of this work, and are now accessible to other researchers. Kathleen tells the story with affection and even tenderness, but with the same rigorous scholarship and commitment to truth that she brought to her work as Professor of History and one-time Vice-Principal of the University of Bophuthatswana, (now the University of the North West). The story belongs not only to the Congregation of Dominican Sisters, Cabra, but also to Ireland and South Africa, to the Irish Missionary Movement and to the Women's Movement. And those of us who follow in the footsteps of these women are filled with gratitude to them and with renewed courage for the future.

Marian O'Sullivan OP
Prioress General
Congregation of Dominican Sisters, Cabra
Dublin, 13 April 1998.

Introduction

A definitive history of the life and work of the Dominican sisters of Cape Town and Port Elizabeth has never before been written, and this despite the rich documentary resources available in state, church and convent archives. Sister Marian O'Sullivan, Prioress General of the Congregation of Dominican Sisters, Cabra, recognising the need for such a study, commissioned me to carry out the work of research in Ireland and in South Africa, and to write the history of the missionary foundations in Southern Africa. This involved mutual consultation and exchange of ideas and of documentary resources with Sisters Cecile Diamond and Rose O'Neill, who were collaborating in work on the history of the Cabra Dominicans in Ireland and Portugal. Sister Rose O'Neill has already completed *A Rich inheritance: Galway Dominican nuns, 1644-1994*, the history of the Galway community from its foundation to its amalgamation with the Congregation of Dominican Sisters, Cabra in 1971.[1] This excellently documented study has been a valuable resource and at the same time a challenge to the historian to present another view of Dominican life, in a missionary context and without the securities of unimpeachable Dominican provenance, such as that enjoyed by the Galway foundation. Sister Cecile Diamond in her organisation and leadership of pilgrimages to Lisbon and St Dominic's country, promoted interest in the history of the Order. She did not live to complete her research on the Convent of Bom Successo in Lisbon. This task is being done by other members of the Congregation in Ireland and its completion is eagerly awaited. Another Cabra publication, *From silence to speech: Fifty years with the deaf*, written in autobiographical style by Sister Nicholas Griffey OP, is a clear and absorbing account of the development of deaf education.[2] In the absence of any definitive publication on Dominican work for the deaf in Southern Africa, this has been a valuable source of information, as well as clear indication of the value of the biographical approach, used with such skill in this book. Studies such as those written by Sisters Nicholas Griffey and Rose O'Neill, are an incentive to others who in the future will be challenged to take up the task of community historian.

A further incentive is the present keen interest in the history of the Catholic Church and its institutions in Southern Africa. Interest in the history of Dominican women is not however merely local. Sisters in Australia and New Zealand, as well as those in

South Africa, who are heirs of the nineteenth century Irish Dominican missionary diaspora, are becoming involved in a process of research and academic interaction in an attempt to rediscover the life and work of women of the Order, and their apostolic role in the Church. Assumpta O' Hanlon OP was one of the earliest historians to study the status question. For her book, *Dominican pioneers in New South Wales*, she has used material from Irish Dominican archives, including those of Cabra and Dun Laoghaire. Her history of the status debate relies heavily on the papers of Cardinal Moran, and her analysis has been of great help in this present study.[3] The latest publication in South Africa, *Being driven forward*, which recounts the history of the Newcastle Dominicans, is rich in unedited documentary material and provides new evidence on the questions and debates of the early and mid-1920's.[4]

The preparation for the writing of the history of the Dominican Region of South Africa, has been an expensive task involving time, travel and extensive research. This was made possible by the generous funding provided by Marian O'Sullivan OP, Prioress General of the Cabra Dominicans, worldwide, together with her Council in Ireland. In 1991 the long study leave granted by the University of Bophuthatswana, (the North West), made it possible for me to carry out research in Ireland and South Africa. While the present history claims to be neither definitive, nor indeed complete, it is based on documentary and oral evidence, the latter representing a wide variety of disparate opinions. Appendix 1 records the names of those who contributed either to individual interviews, face to face or telephonically, or in group discussions. Sincere thanks must also be given to those sisters whose names, for one reason or another, are not included either in the text or in the appendix.

For the remoter past greater dependence has been placed on written evidence in all its forms. The documentary resources are abundant and varied. In respect of manuscript collections, access to the Dominican Regional Archives, Cape Town, the General Archives of the Congregation in Dublin, convent archives in Southern Africa, and those of Cabra and Sion Hill, supplied documentation essential for every period of the history of the South African Dominican communities which have their roots in Ireland. The official records held in these collections are among the main sources of information in respect of daily life in the convent. They cover interaction with ecclesiastical superiors, financial affairs, professional commitments and the more dramatic incidents that disturbed the normal tenor of convent life. Written records and annals of the Irish Dominican nuns do not cover the full life-span of this group of women whose history dates back to the mid-seventeenth century, but those which are available are remarkable both for what they freely reveal and the events and personal divergence of opinion and action they attempt to conceal.

Because of the extensive collection of documentary resources, it has been necessary to analyse and compile material into categories and to identify bound sets of documents by subject, block number and archival source/s. For reference purposes block and page numbers are printed in italics, while each document in the block reflects its own archival source. This resource material should facilitate further research and perhaps inspire those who use it to preserve and submit to archives, personal or congregational records that would help the next generation to understand its inheritance. Since the present study is no more than a tentative first step in the compilation of the complex history of Dominican women with their roots in Cabra, Ireland, it is hoped that these classified resources, for the first time available in 340 bound volumes of documents, will enable the professional as well as the amateur historian to find more readily, the evidence needed for further studies in Dominican history.[5] Each house, each convent, each person, has a story, and while it would not be possible to record the full history of every foundation, or of each woman in relatively large communities, those with greater professional knowledge or biographical skills, can find in these collections of documents a starting point for the investigation and writing of specialised monographs in the field of Dominican women, their lives and their history.

To the Dominican archivists, Sister Rose O'Neill of the Galway community, Sister Rosemary Graham of Sion Hill, Sister Bertranda Flynn of Cabra and Sister Dominique Horgan, General Archivist, who made available the documentary resources of the archives under their control, our sincere thanks is due. This project was also given unstinting support by Sister Raymunda Brennan and her Council, who in 1991 gave us hospitality, free access to the Regional Archives, and every facility to promote the collection of essential data. Margaret Kelly OP, Regional Vicar and Sally Young OP, Regional Councillor have patiently assisted us in the search for contemporary material and for this we are sincerely grateful. We remember with gratitude the sisters in Sion Hill who welcomed us, and by their interest, encouragement, and valuable oral evidence, increased our understanding of the complexities of Irish Dominican history. Deserving of special memory is the late Sister Sabina Fahey, who gave us free access to her office and all of its facilities, and welcomed us as full family members of the Dominican Congregation. Among the brethren in South Africa, the assistance of the Vicar Provincial, Father Bernard Connor OP, deserves our sincere thanks. He helped, with his journalistic expertise, to select, scan, lay-out and film photographs and other illustrations for the book.

Most of those engaged in the history of Dominican women recognise that neither dates of events, nor records of new foundations form the heart of Dominican history. It is a story about people, religious women, whose lives have been hidden for centuries under a virtually impenetrable veil of anonymity, enclosure, loyal silence and sacred convention. This study is an attempt to bring to light something of the more recent history of a formidable body of nuns who, over a period of 350 years, survived political dispersal, foreign exile, penal law, and voluntary emigration to distant missions. They too endured discrimination and moral domination, the common lot of women in an essentially male-dominated Church. The history of these Dominican women also records the pain and insecurity suffered by members of Cabra and its foundations, at home and abroad, during the nineteenth and early twentieth centuries, when both their status and their membership of the Dominican Order were put into question by their own brethren. One of the problems for the historian is the temptation to interpret the lives and achievements of these Dominicans in a politically correct and permissible manner, that is for the edification of the reader. But history and hagiology are not synonymous, nor would it be worthy of Dominican tradition to sacrifice truth to hagiographical conceits.

Before the history of this missionary community can begin, certain obstacles to objectivity must be acknowledged. It is not easy to be altogether objective about one's own family. Blood counts, but in this case the spirit has a more pressing claim. To analyse the history of one's own community and to give due weight to the negative as well as the positive aspects is not a task for the fainthearted nor one that might inspire confidence in the historian herself. Ideally, to achieve this demands great honesty and a willingness to view the sacred and familiar with critical detachment. It also requires great confidence in one's Dominican sisters, and the support of much consultation and honest discussion and debate. It necessitates the imposition of strict discipline and integrity in the use and interpretation of sources and a willingness to acknowledge that this is not the final word on all or any of the contentious historical topics that, up to the present, have been given little serious attention by historians. It is a first attempt to tell something of what happened, and even more important, why it happened in one specific way and not another. And wherein lay the secrets and the mystery surrounding these women and their lifestyle.

The history which follows, though it has been written by one hand, is the result of a long period of co-operation with Caitríona Owens OP who volunteered for this work in 1990. Since then she has participated fully and creatively in every aspect of the research; in the search and retrieval, as well as in the analysis and preparation of documents, and as collaborator in every step in the planning and writing process. She has read and reviewed every sentence in the text and has observed with critical detachment the unfolding of a study of the life of a group of Dominican women, and consequently she can well echo the words of the Sage: "One last thing, my sister, be warned that writing books involves endless hard work, and that much study wearies the body".[6] It also enriches the spirit and develops skills in detection, and as the story unfolds, in the critical analysis of documentary and oral evidence. However when the final page is written there remains a firm conviction that this is no more than a first assay into the history of specific groups of religious women who in their lives, aspirations, ambitions and impact on society, within and outside the cloister, represent a microcosm of the world in which they, as women, lived.

Chapter One

A Time to Search

The basic primary evidence for the history of the Irish Dominican women is to be found in state and convent archives and in other ecclesiastical records. The religious and legal aspects of the daily life of nuns are recorded in constitutions, annals, minutes, diaries, personal memoirs, account books, journals, private and official letters and other personal documents. Formal conventual records are usually impersonal and consequently often lack any sense of the human experience of life in a convent, where daily interaction in a close-knit community presents its own challenges. The stereotypes of religious life, and more specifically of the life of cloistered nuns have persisted for centuries. This is reflected in official convent records and in the laws of the Church which control the lives of vowed women religious throughout the world. For this reason the relevant ecclesiastical laws which over the centuries have found expression in written *Constitutions*, form an important resource for this study. Equally significant are the *Directories* or *Customaries* which spelt out in precise detail, the daily application of the minutiae of the law as laid down in the *Constitutions*.

Since women had no voice in the formulation of laws governing their own lives in the cloister, the image of consecrated women, who became an integral and formative part of the society in which they worked and prayed, was all too often narrow, shadowed and diminished. This has been the result not only of the ecclesiastical laws that controlled them, but also of the silence of nuns and sisters themselves. Consequently women religious must share the responsibility for the historical misconceptions that persisted about the life, characteristics and virtues of the ideal nun. She accepted, often without question, the limited role imposed on her by the hierarchy, and superiors and subjects alike saw the ideal nun as holy, humble, meek, totally detached, silent in the face of reproach or correction, and with human emotions under strict control. In a hierarchical society she was expected to be uncritically law-abiding and appropriately dependent on clerical guidance for the solution of spiritual and temporal problems. Women who committed themselves by vow to the service of God were expected to strive for perfect holiness. Indeed until the teaching of Vatican Council II brought new light to bear on religious life in the modern world, the quest for personal perfection was accepted as the supreme end of consecrated, conventual life.

That the ideal does not reflect the reality of the situation, is clear to those who themselves chose a cloistered life. It is contrary to available evidence to conclude that the majority of cloistered women were spineless, subservient, and incapable of strong, even passionate opinions, or the ability to follow such passion through into action. Independence of thought and action, powerful leadership, stubborn adherence to personal opinion, sound judgement, a spirit of adventure and a profound spiritual life, essentially Dominican in character, are not the monopoly of post-amalgamation nuns, or indeed of those post-Vatican II Dominican women, who from the vantage point of South Africa during the last years of the twentieth century, trace their origins back to a Dominican foundation in seventeenth century Galway. There is abundant evidence to prove that the picture today is very different, less edifying perhaps, but full of human interest and human pain, and that kind of stalwart endurance familiar to women of every age and culture, and in every walk of life.

Human endeavour cannot be fathomed in a purely chronological narrative because chronology defies context and out of context there can be little historical truth. The Dominican women who are the subject of this story lived through over three centuries of political violence, social unrest, religious persecution, extreme poverty and forced or voluntary dispersal. In all this time their choice of religious life was a free one, far freer indeed than that of many of their contemporaries, women, married or single who endured the pressures of social and economic control in a society where women were legal minors and male control was accepted as ordained by God. In this nuns too were part of their own age, sharing the pain of excessive paternalism, not the less burdensome for being imposed by ecclesiastical law and with the blessing and authority of the Church. Any institution, and particularly one subject to external political pressure and acting in the name of God, demands loyalty and support, and in this the Church and her institutions are not exceptions. Where membership is essentially voluntary, where obedience is an integral condition of acceptance and where love is the guiding principle, it is not surprising that often, to the detriment of truth, a misplaced loyalty interprets life in idealistic, but often unrealistic terms. It has been widely acknowledged, especially in the last 25 years, that the religious life of nuns, in respect of the positive as well as the negative aspects of conventual life, has been hedged around and shielded from public scrutiny, by some of the best kept secrets in human society. For the historian who ventures into this field of research, the humanness of the women concerned, their pain and disillusionment, but also their capacity for love, their joyful celebration of life, their political acumen, professionalism, creativity and spiritual strength, speak for themselves. Nor are their weaknesses, individual and corporate unrecorded.

In the past, when enclosure ensured that individual nuns gained little public acclaim, their praises could be sung only after their death. Obituaries to be found in the Dominican Archives, Cape Town, provide good examples of hagiographical writing, and include two manuscript collections, newspaper cuttings and transcripts of sermons. It is evident that these documents idealise the lives of ordinary women who committed themselves by vows to the service of God, and who had lived what were outwardly, very uneventful lives. However they also provide clues as to the ordinary activities of the individual sister, and of the community of which she was a part, and they serve to emphasise the attributes and gifts that were perceived by the nuns to be a reflection of the perfect fulfilment of a life dedicated to God. In addition they give new insights into the writer, her expectations, her role in the community and her attitude to those with whom she has lived, and about whom she writes. The sisters who have shared the same life style and have worked together, are aware of the human person behind the conventional words of praise, and that is what they remember. And for the Dominican historian, while she may not always find it possible or even expedient to tell the whole truth, at least in relation to her own sisters she can confidently subscribe to the adage *de mortuis nil nisi veritatem*. Who would question the good?

However a more realistic insight into the lives of the real Dominican women, the subject of this study, can be gained from the personal journals and letters, the diaries and official visitation reports and admonitions, and the records of conventual crises. The detailed answers to questionnaires, analysed and presented to General Chapters in the post-Vatican II era, are forthright, sometimes harsh in their judgement, and they reveal the influence of a new age where individuals, even consecrated women religious, were not afraid to express negative judgements on a wide variety of subjects. As the available evidence indicates, this study cannot take the form of a simple chronology of the two foreign missions established in the Cape Colony by Cabra and Sion Hill during the third decade of Queen Victoria's reign. It is more than that. It is an attempt to look critically at the origins of these communities, to consider the laws to which they were subject, the historical environment which brought them to birth, the training, spiritual and professional they received, and the spiritual, social, and the cultural and political influences that shaped their lives. But while these may help to constitute the context, the real and fundamental interest lies with the people, who as individual women, and as members of a corporate body, are the actors in this drama. Their ventures, their successes and failures and the ideals which they expressed in their lives, these are the ultimate goal of this history. In the quest for clarity about the life and work of a close-knit community the most important resource is the person. However a span of history that stretches over 350 years does not permit of personal face to face interaction and the mutual exchange of opinion with the majority of the cast. But for the contemporary period this has been possible and the value of oral evidence has far outweighed the time and patience demanded of those involved in the sharing and recording of personal opinion and data.

Many sisters in Ireland and South Africa willingly took part in the search for historical clarity. They have freely contributed their knowledge and perceptions of Dominican life and the way in which it evolved in the twentieth century.[1] Personal interviews and informal group discussions on very specific topics and areas of interest have been conducted, and the twentieth century witnesses to the life and people of the communities under discussion gave evidence that was open, objective and free from rancour. Where conflicting evidence came to light this was corroborated both from living witnesses and from documentary sources.[2] A significant number of sisters, as part of larger and often informal discussion groups, made valuable contributions to the project. Some of the witnesses were prepared to have their evidence recorded on tape, others willingly sat through long hours of discussion on a wide variety of relevant topics, and permitted the taking of written records. All freely assented to the use of their evidence for the projected history, while a few requested that their identity be withheld, and this has been respected.[3]

While oral evidence revealed a treasury of anecdote on many aspects of conventual life, this was not the main aim or value of the process. The search focused on past actions and events, on personalities and policies, and on the historical reasons for the divisions that made unification difficult. Serious discussion revealed deep insights into many aspects, positive and negative, of conventual life. It gave substance to those clerics and Dominican women, conservatives and liberals, who in the past had played leading roles in the processes of change in the communities subject to them. In addition it clothed the dry bones of chronology in living flesh and placed the lives of these women in an authentic historical context, giving valuable insights into past events and opening up new avenues of thought and debate. When the discussions were informal, over meals, or during walks in the country, or on the beach, it became possible to enter into the minds both of women of the past and of those contemporaries, many of whom are well versed in the field of Dominican history. A wide range of opinions were expressed on a variety of subjects, ranging from the theology of religious life and the meaning and implications of the vows, to the perceived indignities of novitiate experience, the intransigence of clerics and the petty tyrannies or the generous tolerance of superiors. Strong opinions were voiced on government, including the vexed questions of shared leadership, and the principles involved for the Congregation and for those individuals who, while formally assigned to a convent, choose to live alone.

The collection, analysis and use of such oral evidence, constitutes a deliberate attempt to discover the living voice of those women, who at all levels of the community have knowledge and opinions on matters relevant to this study, opinions which seldom find a place in politically correct histories of religious congregations. Canonised conventions die hard and while in the past many sisters did not hesitate to air their views in private, the majority were reluctant to share these opinions with superiors. The open debate on the revision of constitutions in the period following Vatican Council II, made the analysis of every aspect of religious life not only permissible, but imperative, and this is reflected in the interviews and informal discussions which provide valuable resource material for this project. In all the ramifications of oral evidence collected there is little direct stress placed on the role of women in society at large, and more specifically of consecrated women in the modern church. However it is clear that many Cabra Dominicans support women's movements and in their daily apostolic life, look for opportunities to live out their Dominican vocation fully and without the artificial restraints based on outmoded social norms. In respect of the Church, the freedom of women, secular or religious has a chequered history, and past practices have easily assumed the status of hallowed tradition.

Chapter Two

Women in the Church

The Dominican sisters who left Ireland to work in South Africa, together with the members of the Irish communities from which they trace their origin, represent in microcosm a host of women who, under the authority of the Catholic Church, in every age from the beginning of the Christian era, committed their lives to the service of God and the spread of his kingdom. In a male-dominated paternalistic society, religious women trod a precarious path. Although they were revered for their vowed consecration and for their dedication and service to society, they were confined by laws and petty restrictions both as to their life-style and in their work. Women of strength and determination, of prudence and administrative ability, were seldom encouraged to participate in public life in the Church, and especially not by the hierarchy. A definitive history of women in the church is still to be written, but a brief survey of the position and role of nuns through the ages will shed light on the story of the Dominican sisters who have lived and worked in South Africa for over 130 years.[1]

While in principle the teaching of Jesus Christ affirms the equality of people, women and men, in practice the attitude of the hierarchy, exclusively male, has dominated the authority roles in the Church with varying degrees of determination and success from the apostolic age until the present. Women followed Jesus and shared in an evangelising partnership with the apostles and with Paul. While in theory, in terms of the Kingdom, equality of the sexes was preached, ecclesiastical regulations were applied that placed the man as head over his wife, and in line with social norms of the secular society, reduced the role of women to that of domestic subservience in the home. What held for secular society could be applied with equal success in the Church and in the cloister. The effect of and reaction to this diminution of the role of women both in the domestic and in the apostolic spheres did not remain static, but differed from age to age and from place to place.

In the second century AD some women, forbidden by the Church to teach or preach, formed heretical sects which gave them an outlet for the exercise of apostolic zeal. Others accepted the opportunity for supreme witness to their evangelising fervour by martyrdom, where in the face of death, the equality of Christian men and women was publicly acknowledged. By the fourth century, as the clerical state became more and more professional, women were excluded from higher office in the Church though for a time retaining that of deaconess. In this position however their ministry was limited to women. How could they express their call to spread the gospel of Jesus Christ when hierarchical authority balked their efforts? It was no consolation to be taught, as did the Fathers of the Church, that from the point of view of morality women were equal to men. For the woman who wanted to be totally committed to God and at the same time play a significant if subservient religious role, the choice most acceptable to the church was that of consecrated virginity. Despite the fact that the married state was regarded as necessary and deserving of honour, for the Fathers of the Church the brides of Christ, consecrated virgins, held a place of high regard. The monastic opportunity for women of the fourth century, while it won little public acclaim in the Church, nevertheless did provide limited spiritual and apostolic opportunities. This was especially the case during the sixth and seventh centuries, when both monks and nuns evangelised the pagan Germanic peoples beyond the frontiers of the Christian world. In this situation abbots and abbesses wielded equal authority, and in the case of the latter, only a queen in her court would have exercised like power. Women were now sharing directly and with authority in the spread of Christian civilisation. At the same time they were carrying out the normal daily tasks within their monasteries, where they also applied those skills typical of women in the social milieu into which they had been born. They did not act as rivals to their male counterparts but in a period of political and social chaos, as participants in an apostolic task of great magnitude.

With the founding of double monasteries during the seventh and eighth centuries in the English and Frankish Kingdoms, the abbess was usually the head of the community and work roles, male and female, were delegated according to physical and mental strength, and ability. This form of monastic life established certain expectations in the relationship between men and women religious, both in the material sphere and in the spiritual and sacramental life of the nuns. While nuns could and did promote apostolic fervour, cultural development, art, sound administration and law within the vast territories under their control, they did not have priestly powers. Because they could neither administer the sacraments to their own communities nor to those among whom they exercised their apostolic zeal, they remained dependent on ordained priests who were often the subjects, within the monastic community, of the reigning abbess.

However during the Carolingian age the educational work of nuns placed them in a unique position to influence and civilise the young men and women destined for positions of authority in society and in the Church. Both monks and nuns educated boys and girls. The role of women as educators of men was not normal at the time but necessary in the missionary situation, especially on the frontiers of the Empire. By the ninth century women were not permitted to hold positions of leadership over men, consequently double monasteries were no longer acceptable. A further restraint was imposed on women religious. They were placed under the strict control of bishops who now usurped the powers formerly held by the abbess, that of the admission and formal reception of candidates to the community, and their admission to religious profession. This led to the growing dependence of women religious on the hierarchy, a form of control that did not decrease in later centuries.

Another field of apostolic endeavour was closed to women religious. The nuns were forbidden to teach boys, the sons of nobles who were to be the future administrators and leaders in a violent society. This meant that young men of good family were deprived of the civilising influence of a sound literary education formerly available in monastic schools where as teachers, consecrated women held an equal place with men. In the two centuries following the reign of Charlemagne many schools had been established by women religious. Nuns and canonesses had studied the liberal arts and they themselves contributed to literature in its many forms. They and other notable women of their day were also skilled in law, politics, diplomacy and administration. The post-Carolingian era was a period of political disintegration and the development of the feudal system. This first feudal age, towards the end of the ninth century, restored to women powers that had been lost in more stable times. During the tenth and eleventh centuries women played powerful political roles in society, as landowners, judges within their manors and as owners of churches over which they had the power, within their jurisdiction, of ecclesiastical appointment. The use of such power by abbesses did not go unnoticed or without criticism by the clergy. It was too powerful a tool to be left in any hands other than those of the bishops. This diminution of the power of women in the Church was not limited to nuns. By the middle of the eleventh century some married women outside the monastic system were also to lose their pastoral opportunity within the local church. This was the result of the gradual imposition of celibacy on the clergy, a move made possible around 1050 AD both by the more settled political situation and by the growing power of the hierarchy. The wives and daughters of priests had formed a vital part of the apostolic unit of the parish. Not only did the wife bring with her a dowry, but in many cases also her skills in management and pastoral care. These she could apply for the smoother running of the parish. In addition her spiritual input was complementary to that of her husband, the priest. The imposition of celibacy on the clergy brought to an end the service of wives and daughters of priests in parochial administration and in pastoral service to the people. This was not the only change that limited the role of women. Nuns, for whom the education of the young had become an integral part of their monastic work, soon found their opportunities curtailed. With the concentration of church leadership and power in Rome, the authority of bishops gradually replaced that of Abbots, and cathedral schools and universities now took over the educational role of monasteries. Since the new urban educational institutions excluded women either as students or as household staff, there was no formal role for the woman with intellectual aspirations and no female influence in the academic environment. Even on the domestic level all offices involving household management were held by men. Nuns however continued to educate girls and to contribute to all art forms. In addition the mystics among them expressed in their writings a pure and sublime spiritual vision that placed them in the forefront as mystical writers.

The year 1171 saw the birth of Dominic Guzman, founder of both the first Dominican convent of women around 1206, and of the Order of Preachers, which received final papal approval in 1217. The moving force behind this foundation for cloistered nuns, made at Prouille in the Province of Langeudoc in Southern France, a land rife with heresy, reflects the political and spiritual problems of the early decades of the thirteenth century.[2] According to Dominican tradition these young women, Dominic's first recruits, were snatched from the danger of heresy and formed into a religious community. This was done both for the safety of their own lives and so that they might serve as a spiritual third force in the battle against heresy. Dominic regarded his nuns, whose main task was to pray for the work of the preaching brethren, as powerful intercessors in the battle for truth against the inroads of heresy. There is no direct evidence that the nuns made education one of the main thrusts of their apostolate, but teaching as a part of their Dominican apostolate cannot be ruled out in their regard. However their link with the Dominican Order and their relationship with the three other convents for women founded directly by Dominic implied that the community life, contemplation, liturgical prayer and work of these women was to be an essential part of the web and weave of the Order.

While like their sisters, the Dominican men were obliged to conform to the rigours of community life and discipline, egress and mobility for apostolic purposes gave them freedom to fulfil the fullness of the Dominican vocation of preaching and teaching. The nuns on the other hand were subject to the Benedictine ideal of stability, their field of active apostolic endeavour limited to their cloister and those who made contact with them there. For those women who sought the purely contemplative life, this was an ideal situation, but for others who saw the Dominican vocation as an active involvement in the *vita apostolica*, it was a second best choice imposed by law. That this limitation was the result of contemporary attitudes and laws concerning women is clear when the structure of the Order is considered. Although he was an innovator in religious life, there is no evidence that Dominic intended to found enclosed, contemplative convents of clerics or even lay brothers to serve as a spiritual force behind the preachers of the Order. His preachers were not monks, they were active preachers, who in an age of political turmoil and rampant heresy would go out into the market place and bring the word of God to the people.

There is little evidence that Dominic Guzman considered religious women, nuns of his own foundation, as active participants in his apostolic work of teaching and preaching, except in an indirect and restricted way. It is however difficult to believe that some of these women failed to express a strong desire to carry out the fulness of the Dominican vocation, the public apostolate of teaching and preaching. The historical precedent was there for women, as it had also been in the case of men. The bands of peripatetic preachers, the *perfectae*, whose mode of operation served as a model for Dominic's own Order, included women as well as men, and history does not underrate the missionary zeal or preaching ability of the former. However in the founding of Prouille and other convents, the force of tradition prevailed over the spirit of innovation and in the absence of direct evidence to the contrary, it would do violence to history to portray these thirteenth century Dominican nuns as discontented with their enclosed monastic life or with the role of the brethren in their lives.

The assignment of clerics, including Dominic's own brother Mannes, to provide spiritual and temporal help to his nuns, was not a sign of male condescension. In the historical context this was a normal division of responsibilities within mixed apostolic groups. Dominic had placed his first nuns under the care of his followers nearly ten years before his Order was given formal papal recognition, and the first clerics to whom he entrusted the spiritual and temporal welfare of his nuns were not in the strict sense of the word, Dominicans. Indeed they could not claim to be the first offspring of Dominic's apostolic zeal. That position belonged then, as it still does today, to the women of the Order. In practice and in the absence of a formalised and ecclesiastically recognised body of brethren, the nuns were Dominic's great support and consolation. However, even in an age of heretical strife which demanded a new and creative approach to evangelisation, it was not considered appropriate or orthodox for women consecrated by vows and living in convents, to participate outside the cloister in the office of public preaching or active evangelisation.

The mendicant friars, Franciscans and Dominicans, like their contemporaries the migrant workers and the heretical *perfectae*, had the freedom to move from place to place, following the ideals of the *vita apostolica*. They met and challenged heretics on their own ground. With papal approval these clerics and brothers could take to the open roads, while consecrated women on the other hand, must remain in the convent with its protective enclosure and its dependence on clerical support. For the newly formed Order of Preachers the cloister and monastic observances, common to both clerics and nuns, formed a bulwark against the intrusion of the secular world. The convent also ensured an environment for study, regular life, the solemn celebration of the sacred liturgy and the contemplative life of prayer. It was on these that the brethren found strength and inspiration for their mission of preaching and teaching. And for the Dominican nuns it provided the physical and spiritual protection, seen to be essential for survival in a violent society. However the monastic way of life was not the only alternative for women desiring to dedicate their lives to the service of God, and at this time, when women were rated as a surplus commodity, perhaps not the most effective solution.

With the growth of princely power, the role of women was curtailed in the political as well as in the ecclesiastical sphere. They had been pushed to the background in church matters so that for those who longed for the fullness of the *vita apostolica* and a life of voluntary poverty outside the monastic system, the choice was often heresy. Women of the *perfectae* preached, administered the sacraments and in many cases lived ascetical lives of service and sacrifice. These apostolic movements, sometimes orthodox, more often heretical, proliferated throughout society. They found a fertile environment in the rapidly growing urban centres where the market economy was creating great wealth and providing challenging opportunities for women as well as for men. For some the lure of money was interpreted as a sign that Satan was active in society, and new and ardent witnesses were needed to combat the powers of evil. For others, including women of spiritual strength and moral stature who were a part of secular society, the marketplace, with its vibrant life, economic opportunities and social injustices, presented a spiritual as well as an economic challenge.

One form of feminine response to this challenge, the Beguine movement, was gradual and involved neither a formalised plan of action nor ecclesiastical legislation.[3] The Beguines did not emulate the wandering bands of the *perfectae* but chose a stable way of life while seeking the fulness of their Christian vocation outside the restraints of the cloister. They set up house, often in the vicinity of a church, which guaranteed their sacramental life, spiritual guidance and physical safety. They attracted into their company women old and young, some widowed and others unmarried, all of whom had in common the desire to follow Christ in the midst of a secular society. Such a choice also ensured economic independence and apostolic opportunity. While this way of life provided a practical solution to the needs of women for protection and mutual support, it was also a means of promoting their spiritual life and Christian interaction with society, outside the legal limits of the monastic system. The older, wiser and more experienced guided the younger women in the spiritual life as in the practical details in matters of house-keeping, the trades, marketable skills and social responsibility. The Beguines were to find their field of missionary endeavour in the vibrant urban markets and in the workplaces where the exploitation of the poor was the norm rather than the exception. Those Beguines who were both skilled in business and deeply involved in social reform, became a challenge and reproach to their male counterparts especially those employers in the cloth trade who exploited their workers. In an age in which the status of women was low, the Beguines proved that women could dedicate their lives to God's service and the good of His people in every sphere of secular life. Indeed it was one way in which orthodox groups of women living in close proximity in the vicinity of a church, could live an intense spiritual life while retaining their place in secular society. At the same time they could follow the *vita apostolica* among the poor in the work-place. At the outset the very informality of the association of the groups of Beguines and the measure of *gravitas* provided by the older women who guided the younger, unmarried members, safeguarded them from negative ecclesiastical attention. Clergy, sympathetic to their aims and edified by their spiritual efforts, gave them the support they needed. The Beguines had their own form of spirituality, they fasted and prayed, and by their life-style provided a ministry to women from about 1150 to the last decades of the thirteenth century, the period that saw the founding and early growth of the Dominican Order.

The success with which the Beguines carried out their mission can be inferred by the opposition they met from two main sources, the church and the business world. To the ecclesiastical authorities their ascetical way of life and their independence were both a reproach and a challenge, and to the merchants their business prowess and support of the oppressed workers a hindrance to male economic power and development. When the Church began to apply pressure on the Beguine way of life and to see their freedom from cloister and formal vows outside clerical control, as a challenge to orthodoxy, the day of these women was drawing to a close. The application of their apostolic ideal of life and service to society was a reproach to the clergy, and the Second Council of Lyons (1274) made it clear that the place for religious women was in the convent, behind grilles and under firm male, ecclesiastical control. Once again the only recourse for women seeking the full apostolic life was in formal communities under clerical guidance. This meant in practice that religious women including groups of Beguines, in order to procure the temporal guidance and spiritual support essential for recognition by the Church, had to seek affiliation with a male Order.

While women had proved themselves to be able and willing to pursue their own business, spiritual, social and economic, the imposition of monastic life with strict enclosure placed insuperable restraints on their movements and activities. In the case of the Beguines their dependence on clerics did not derive from inborn feminine weakness or incompetence, as they had proved in over a century of their existence, but was ultimately the result of restrictive ecclesiastical laws. This was especially the case in urban centres, where the force of law could be applied with ease and where it could be argued that the environment was more dangerous and a greater source of temptation to women than that in more rural environments. As growing bands of women sought affiliation with religious bodies, including the Dominican Order, the clergy concerned claimed, not without justification, that the temporal and spiritual administration of convents of women hindered their apostolic work. That the brethren tried to rid themselves of this burden, placed on them by Dominic himself, is well-attested in Dominican history, and in this matter they did not escape with honour. However the growing number of communities of women seeking affiliation for the sake of gaining ecclesiastical approval grew rapidly, and as a consequence of this, groups of Dominican Tertiaries added their claims on the brethren to those of the nuns of the Second Order. This process of affiliation led through the centuries, to the establishment of bodies of Dominican sisters who found their links with the Order tenuous, and their claim to Dominican orthodoxy and membership matters of law rather than of family relationship and spirit.

The enclosed Dominican nuns of the Second Order became in time the elite among the women of the Order. They represented in the eyes of the brethren and more especially in their own view, the cream of female membership. It would appear that despite the strength of their own personal and corporate humility, their claims to Dominican authenticity and superiority of status were often expressed in terms of undue pride. The founding branch of the Dominican nuns in Ireland was in this regard, a relevant case in point. For the many groups of cloistered women, Tertiaries affiliated to the Order, their status was often in question. In the case of the contemplative nuns, the "real Dominicans" and spiritual successors of the Prouille foundation, these lived under the direct jurisdiction of the Order and their status was not normally challenged. However even these, as women of the Second Order, had no voice in General Chapters and consequently did not participate in the democratic processes of legislation even when it applied to their own lives. This remained the exclusive privilege of the male branch. This is particularly interesting in the context of the history of the nineteenth century Cabra and Sion Hill foundations and their missionary offshoots in South Africa. For almost a century and a half the questions of status, orthodoxy, the practice of true Dominicanism and the right to spiritual privileges of the Order were a matters of debate, sometimes acrimonious. Indeed it remained a burning issue until well beyond the mid-twentieth century and hence forms a vital part of this study.

Notwithstanding these inequalities and whatever the status of the various categories of Dominican women in the first centuries of the Order, their numbers multiplied. Wherever the vanguard of Preachers ventured, women found in the ideals of the Order the inspiration to follow a vocation at once contemplative and apostolic. And where devotion to these *ideals* was weak, the need for protection, spiritual support and papal approval gave impetus enough to inspire religious groups to seek affiliation. In many respects there was little to choose in practice between the nuns and the cloistered Tertiaries in terms of public apostolic opportunity. In 1566 in the Constitution, *Circa Pastorales*, Pius V, the Dominican Pope, closed the gap between the two categories of consecrated women, at least in respect of enclosure and vows. This law decreed that all nuns with solemn vows were bound to enclosure, and to tidy up the less constrained female religious, all Tertiaries including "those who are called of the penance" were obliged to take solemn vows and accept enclosure.[4] This implied that religious women whatever the public or social nature of their apostolate, would be cut off from the world, even from those whom they had been founded to serve. Happily the imperative of service overcame the narrow Roman view of religious life for women, and despite the law new congregations which defied enclosure, emerged. The evident value of the good works being done by these bodies won papal approbation before the institutions were given formal approval by the Church.

In practice this imposition of universal enclosure on women religious, while it was a neat method of control, would have made social service to the people virtually impossible. In the sixteenth century Angela Merici founded a *company* of women because she saw enclosure, the habit, public vows and common life as a hindrance to women's apostolate to the family. St. Vincent de Paul, when in the seventeenth century he founded the Sisters of Charity, did not want them to be religious subject to enclosure. This is clear from his exhortation to the women who offered themselves for a life of service to the people: "For monasteries you have the houses of the poor, for cells your rented rooms, for chapels the parish church, for cloisters the streets of the towns, for enclosure obedience, for grilles the fear of God".[5] This was the first congregation of women not bound by enclosure. While the post-Tridentine period saw a proliferation of congregations which in many respects fell outside the traditions of the older monastic and mendicant Orders, the church did not easily accept the position of women religious moving freely among the people outside the convent walls. "The entire history of Orders and Congregations is one of long struggle between the stability and rigour of the law and the thrust of life which, in the face of the immense and varied task facing the Church, requires them to receive religious consecration without submitting to judicial conditions unsuited to them".[6]

In the case of the Irish Dominican nuns of the seventeenth and eighteenth centuries, the law of enclosure was more honoured in the theoretical ideal than in regular practice. There were adequate excuses for divergence from the rule. The nuns of the first Galway foundation in the mid-seventeenth century were housed on a narrow city street without a garden or other suitable grounds for exercise and fresh air. Frequent egress was the norm, provided the nuns dressed modestly and acted with the accepted decorum common to ladies of their times. Under whatever disguise they took their walks or drives they were a visible and well-known presence in the town. Were they not, after all moving among their own people and were not their families living in or around Galway? While peaceful times allowed for recreational egress, political turmoil, with its forced dispersal and exile, was also a major factor in the break with the ecclesiastical laws of enclosure. For those nuns who found refuge in Spain, Belgium or other continental convents the new home might well present a far stricter application of enclosure than had been possible or even preferable in Ireland, but for the less fortunate religious the application of bitter penal laws and their return to their families spelt the end of their cloistered lives.

The Dominican women who continued to live in Ireland during the penal times had to defy what they judged to be unjust laws against their country, their church and their own communities. As "secular ladies", the nuns living in Channel Row in Dublin managed to evade the application of laws prohibiting Catholic convents. These women did not remain hidden behind walls and monastic grilles. They were indeed something of a social draw, at one period providing concerts in sacred music for members of the Establishment. With their secular parlour boarders living in close proximity to them, they had a ready ear on the latest event, scandal or political change that might promote or threaten their fragile security. They dressed modestly in the fashion of the day and this allowed them to mix with the better level of Dublin society. Through all of this period they lived their lives without the cloister and its safeguards, and they survived to form the nucleus of Cabra, the Mother House of Sion Hill and foundations world-wide, including St. Mary's, Cape Town and Holy Rosary Convent, Port Elizabeth. Despite their insertion into contemporary Dublin society these nuns preserved a Dominican tradition which has been the source of both pride and controversy in the nineteenth and twentieth centuries. They accepted recruits, paid their debts and retained their personal anonymity to their death.

It is remarkable that no contemporary record of any major scandal or public outcry by their Catholic or Protestant contemporaries, has so far been uncovered. Theirs was not an easy life either spiritually or economically. Money was always scarce and the slender resources of the convent barely met the daily needs of the nuns. As members of the Second Order they were under the direct jurisdiction of the brethren, and as far as it could be applied in the circumstances, subject to canonical visitation and the normal forces of ecclesiastical law. However the brethren also suffered from the disruptive violence of the penal system, and for them as for the nuns the full application of the Dominican *Constitutions* was not possible.

Nevertheless the concept, if not the full legal application of the law of enclosure, together with the profession of solemn vows, retained a certain sacred value for these women. They were seen as the main distinguishing marks of the real Dominican nun as distinct from the Third Order sister with simple vows. The church by its increasing control of consecrated religious, domesticated nuns in the pattern of the family structure. The church, the husband sought in its women conformity, unquestioning obedience, mildness and unstinting support and service. The nun was expected to devote herself anonymously to good works, but not to exercise political power in the Church nor to influence or formulate policy. To strike a fair balance it can be argued that while the male ecclesiastical role in respect of women was usually one of domination, however respectfully expressed, it was in a sense somewhat remote from the everyday life of the individual nun and of the community. It must also be acknowledged that within female institutions, including convents, women dominated women and the daily pressures applied were the more painful in that they were personal, immediate and often inescapable. In this, as in many other aspects of life, the nineteenth century nun shared the helplessness and frustration of her secular sisters, married and single. However in the convent as in the world there were those who overcame the limitations imposed by social convention and religious fundamentalism and found fulfilment in professional and domestic work. Few historians have acknowledged that nuns were indeed among the first professional women of modern times, and that it was within their own field of expertise that they found the fulfilment which helped them to transcend the limitations and petty restrictions of cloistered life and make a vital contribution to the religious and secular world of which they were a part.

Chapter Three

A Time to Plant:

The Irish Foundations

The community founded in Galway in 1644 was the first post-reformation Dominican convent of women to be established in Ireland. Under the jurisdiction of the Dominican Fathers it enjoyed both legal and spiritual security and the support and appreciation of the townspeople. Loyal to the Confederate cause and secure in a well defended city, the nuns put down their roots in a place where by birthright and by vocation they enjoyed a life of dedication to God and of useful interaction with the local people. The surrender of Galway to the Cromwellian forces in 1652 and the horrors of the city after the ensuing military depredations, forced many of the inhabitants of Galway, banished from their own city by the conqueror, to seek refuge abroad. The Dominican nuns went into involuntary exile and found homes in Dominican convents in Spain. There all but two of the original Galway community lived out their lives far from their home and families.

The violent upheavals of the seventeenth century experience and the pain and exile endured, created for these Dominican women a vivid and life-sustaining myth of an heroic age, of great holiness and bloodless martyrdom and of perseverance in the face of failure. This failure often included a threat of the imminent termination of a way of life that had been sustained in the face of much endurance and pain. It also conferred on the Galway nuns a firm belief in their Dominican orthodoxy. The jurisdiction and spiritual leadership of the Dominican Fathers became a pledge of the integrity and legitimacy of the nuns within the Order, even at a time when regular life was at a low ebb in Ireland and no Dominicans, men or women could claim to be living up to the rigours of the *Constitutions*. Nevertheless the status of the Galway community in the nineteenth and for much of the twentieth century, induced a sense of corporate superiority and canonised orthodoxy. This permitted criticism of the "less orthodox" status and practices of Cabra and its offshoot the Sion Hill community, which was founded in 1836. The Cabra Dominicans in 1832 sought and obtained episcopal jurisdiction. This escape from the jurisdiction of the Dominican Fathers and the Order placed the two Dublin communities, in the eyes of the Galway nuns, on an inferior level, and put in question their Dominican legitimacy and their faithfulness to the laws and customs of the Order. Was it not for the ideals of the full Dominican life, after all, that the members of the Galway community in their heroic age, had lived as political outcasts under the threat of martyrdom? The strength of the convictions of the Galway nuns and the doggedness of their claims to Dominican legitimacy had a profound influence on the history of Cabra, Sion Hill and its many missionary foundations abroad.

In 1686, during the reign of James II, two of the original members of the exiled community left Bilbao and returned to Galway at the "special command of the Master General of Ireland, Father John Browne". Juliana Nolan was appointed Prioress by the Father Provincial and her companion, Mary Lynch, Sub-Prioress. The convent attracted new recruits "noble both by descent and by virtue".[1] The nuns, never indifferent to high social status, valued those who held worldly rank and enjoyed the benefits of a fortune to support their divine call. The Galway community got its recruits mainly from the local families who had shared the life of banishment or exile common to many Irish of that time. Despite the strength and determination of the Dominicans, men and women, to promote the apostolic ideals of the Order, the forces of intolerance and military power were stronger. The Battle of the Boyne (1690) and the grip of penal law presaged yet another period of dissolution for the Galway foundation and another era of bitter exile. By 1697 the edict banishing all Regular Orders from Ireland gave the nuns until 1 May 1698, to leave their convent. The brief respite in their hometown, Galway, was over. The community of Dominican Fathers, in conformity with the law, had earlier in the year left for France. The nuns put on secular dress and at first lived secretly in the town. When this became too dangerous they were forced to go to their families and relations in the countryside.

In this form of exile the position of the Galway community was not unique. It was the common lot of religious men and women throughout Ireland. Some stayed their ground and others went to the Continent to find homes in convents there. Periods of relative tolerance interspersed with the full pressure of the penal laws made regular life difficult, indeed impossible. This is evidenced by the fact that religious women were dispersed up and down Ireland with no secure place in which to settle as a community. While this situation prevailed the Galway nuns were

St Mary's Dominican Convent, Cabra, Dublin, during the nineteenth century

given another opportunity to live community life in Ireland. In 1714 Father Hugh O'Calanan, Dominican Provincial, got permission from the Archbishop of Dublin to send a community of the Galway nuns to found a convent in the city. This opened the second heroic period in the history of the founding nuns, and it was from the Dublin foundation that, nearly 150 years later, the first women Dominicans set off to work as missionaries in South Africa.[2]

The eight Dominican women, headed by Sister Mary Bellew, came to Dublin in March 1717. After staying for a few months at Fisher's Lane, they finally settled in September in a house in Channel Row once occupied by Benedictine nuns. For a hundred years, first in Channel Row and for the last ten years in Clontarf, this community lived and worked defying penal laws, wearing civilian dress and waxing and waning in numbers. On 12 December 1819, this now virtually unknown and greatly diminished community, reduced to five members, Mother Columba Maher, Prioress, Mother Joseph Byrne, Sub-Prioress, and Sisters Teresa Dalton and Dominic Dillon, together with a novice, Sister Magdalen Butler, moved to the country property at Cabra. St Mary's Convent became the Mother House of foundations in Ireland, and missions in Southern Africa and across the world. Once again the Dominican nuns "began to receive novices as distinguished by their nobility of birth as renowned by their virtue".[3] The prioress was elected by her own community, a privilege granted to the nuns in 1721 by the General Chapter of the Order. Despite immediate uncertainties, the community hoped for a new period of growth, especially in respect of an increase of personnel to carry out its educational mission.

It was potentially a favourable time to make a new start. The legal recognition of the Catholic Church in Britain was just over the horizon, and the promise of educational opportunity was already a reality in Ireland after centuries of oppression. But the Cabra nuns had a grave problem to solve if they were to gain recognition as educators. While recruits joined the small community, the schools did not attract the prosperous middle-class pupils essential for the economic survival of the institution, and Cabra was threatening to live up to its name as "a poor and desert land". This was partly because the sisters were under the jurisdiction of the Dominican Provincial and their schools were little known either to the bishops, the diocesan clergy, or to the people of Dublin. Neither was the full Dominican observance, including the Divine Office and enclosure, seen to be reconcilable with the onerous work of education. The role of the Dominican Fathers in the life of the community, for so long the source of strength to the nuns, now for some, proved to be a grave obstacle to progress, and an embarrassment in their daily lives. Of course there were notable exceptions among the brethren, and of these Fr Edmund Cruice OP was the most noteworthy, both for his generosity and for his concern for the community. His death in 1825 deprived the nuns of a trusted friend and inaugurated a period of strained relations between the Fathers of the Order and the Cabra community. The penal laws and the dispersal of the Regular Orders had taken its toll on the Dominicans in Ireland. Regular life had fallen into decay and this did nothing to promote Dominican ideals, hitherto believed to be enshrined in the First Order. The Cabra nuns, still under the jurisdiction of the Fathers, found the attitude and example of some of their brethren difficult to bear. It was a situation where growing tension and personal animosities between the chaplain and the nuns, added to financial pressure, convinced Mother Columba Maher, at that time Sub-Prioress, that a change in jurisdiction was necessary for survival. The Prioress and Sub-Prioress in an appeal to the Sacred Congregation of Propaganda, wrote that they were contending with difficulties which threatened "the total extinction of their community". The memorial indicates that the threat was as much economic as it was spiritual:

> That these evils ... have arisen from the injudicious appointments of chaplains and the officious interference of provincials and vicars with the internal and domestic arrangements of the house ... A chaplain was a few years since, appointed who seldom except on Sundays said Mass and who by his irregular habits disedified the community. His removal was long and anxiously sought for and yet so obstinately refused, although his unfitness for office was evident to all, that your memorialists were obliged to get another priest to say Mass; and thus two chaplains at most inconvenient expense were supported by the revenue of the convent.[4]

The Prioress, Sister M Magdalen Butler, had listened to the advice to her Sub-Prioress, and agreed to appeal to Rome for the transfer of the community from the jurisdiction of the Dominican Fathers to that of the local Ordinary, at that time the Archbishop of Dublin, Dr Murray. The matter was submitted to the whole community and individual sisters were consulted. There were good reasons to support the change. The sisters hoped that they would be free then from the "interference of those who have embroiled the affairs, squandered the funds of the house" and kept the nuns "in a state of distraction and anxiety".

In 1832 the legal transfer received the blessing of Rome and the community settled into a period of growth and recognition as able teachers and educationists. But that was not the end of the story, nor was the change accepted by all. The history of Cabra and its missionary empire has been profoundly influenced by the transfer of jurisdiction, the full implications of which will be discussed later. Even within the Cabra community itself there were fundamental differences of opinion about the move, and this despite the fact that the individual sisters were consulted and had agreed to the change. In the first place it had been initiated by Mother Columba Maher, who had entered as a lay sister but because of her evident gifts and the scarcity of recruits, had been raised to the status of choir sister. In a narrow society where not only family background but also genteel education and financial status were matters of great importance, this alone could be enough to cast doubt and social disapproval on the whole matter.

Despite the poor performance of the Dominican brethren there were those who in retrospect regretted the schism and gradually came to feel that it diminished the Dominican nature of the communities involved. The substitution of Vincentian Fathers as chaplains in place of Dominicans inevitably changed the focus of the spirituality of the Cabra nuns. Both Galway and Drogheda would later claim that the unbroken link between them and the Order was proof positive of their unadulterated Dominicanism and their full and legitimate membership of the Order. In principle this was an argument difficult to refute. The doubts and uncertainties which originated in Cabra in the 1830's concerning status and legitimacy spread to Australia, New Zealand, New Orleans and to South Africa, the main focus of this study. It opened up a debate that, in an age of relatively slow communication, was remarkable for its passion, its intensity and the forthrightness and openness of its expression. Was this debate ever concluded to the satisfaction of all the protagonists? That is one of the questions that this study will attempt to investigate and answer.

For the six sisters who broke away from Cabra in October 1836, the change in jurisdiction was one of the factors that influenced their decision to make a new and independent foundation. Whether the election of Mother Columba Maher as Prioress in July of the same year was another factor in this move, is more difficult to substantiate. It is clear however that the new community, which after a short interlude settled on the beautiful property, Sion Hill, was determined to run a select school for upper-class young ladies and not for middle class girls such as those accepted in Cabra. The sisters who left Cabra at this time had been the backbone of the teaching staff and their loss was keenly felt. So also was the payment of £800 in 1838 to the young impoverished community. This was not given by Cabra as a charitable gesture, but at the command of Rome. Indeed there was little love lost between the two communities. However Cabra was recognised as the original Mother House, a fact that was acknowledged almost a century later when the debate initiated in 1832 was taken up with anxious and passionate fervour.

The *Annals* of both Cabra and Sion Hill present the story of the schism in language of charitable discretion. These *Annals*, though based on records including letters, papal briefs, personal letters, diaries and account books, were written as a celebration and not to perpetuate old quarrels. They give valuable information about the life and times of the two influential communities of Dominican women in Dublin, Ireland. They also show clearly the reserve with which the sister historians dealt with controversial matters, particularly those involving the hierarchy, whether Dominican or otherwise. A task yet to be done is the writing of a critical history of nineteenth century Cabra and Sion Hill based on the published *Annals* and other documentary sources. This would include a critical analysis of the letters, rescripts, poetry, prospectuses and other papers which the earlier writers transcribed in full in the *Annals*, but without analysis or comment. Since both Cabra and Sion Hill sent nuns to the Catholic missions in the Cape Colony, the documentary sources both printed and primary, are of great value to a better understanding of the background, education, social position and religious training of these women who came to South Africa, to Cape Town in 1863 and to Port Elizabeth in 1867. The true roots of the South African mission are in Ireland and the evidence in the case must be sought there. Cabra has account books that date back to 1717, and these reflect many of the activities, hardships and vagaries of the community over a period of 102 years. They also highlight the value of financial records as historical sources. Letters and other primary documents have also survived in the General Archives, in the holdings of Sion Hill and Cabra and in the relevant records in Rome. But up to the present day, in the *Annals* and brief histories written for public consumption, the real battles are concealed and the painful wounds neatly bandaged over.

One notable exception is the unpublished annals of the Dominican Convent, Galway. In the case of this lively and interesting record, the work of Sister Vincent Lynch should be noted. At a time of debate and controversy she virtually rewrote the annals. The new version is all in her own handwriting and includes valuable documentary material. However it is difficult to determine whether it was edited and revised by Sister Vincent or by the original writers. Neither is it clear how far this account deviates from the original which, it appears, was destroyed. In the pre-amalgamation debate of the 1920's Sister Vincent was passionately opposed to the amalgamation of Galway with Cabra and Sion Hill and their Irish filial houses and independent foundations. This infuses the whole account of the Galway interaction at that time with passion, intolerance and a strong sense of the importance and immediacy of the whole question.

The same can be said with some notable exceptions for the annals and letters, which form part of the holdings of the Regional Dominican Archives at Cape Town. Here again most of the early annals were written after the events and much of the immediacy and impact have been lost. Nevertheless they are based on day-to-day records and a close analysis of these documents reveals much of the life, struggle, achievement and adversity of the communities. It also projects diverse images of these women, strong and weak, learned and simple, strong-willed and meek. Some were easily pressurised by the law, others were determined in upholding their community rights, while most were deeply devoted to the Church and to the Order. Many of the choir sisters were well educated according to the times and some were women of refined culture. The case of the lay sisters was less happy. Despite their consecration as Dominicans they were poor and unprivileged in a society, whether secular or religious, where social status mattered and where the servant class occupied a well-defined, subservient position. But they, like their more privileged choir sisters, fit into no neat stereotype. They are all the women in the case; in most instances anonymous, and not given to self-revelation. However the records do reveal something of the real women as distinct from the stereotype. They provide evidence concerning the social, spiritual and professional interaction of the nuns with the society in which they played an essential role, and this despite the isolation imposed by enclosure. Their initial choice had been free. Some of the nuns persevered and some did not. There were those who came in good heart and became committed professional women. These found fulfilment in their life and work and endured what was difficult in their chosen vocation. There were others for whom the cloister was a refuge from the stresses of secular life. A few came and were sent away, perhaps for reasons of health, flawed moral character or perceived "lack of vocation". Of many of these nineteenth century women little is known, since discretion demanded that as far as possible personal matters, especially departures from the convent, should be kept secret. And there were the cases of the nuns who decided that their initial choice had been mistaken and a freer way of life "in the world" was a better alternative for them.

In the nineteenth century conventual world, abandonment of a religious vocation was not viewed by superiors with tolerance or equanimity. Neither secular society nor the convent provided an environment where self-realisation for women was considered to be a priority. In the convent the abnegation of self was the acceptable goal, this either accepted willingly or imposed harshly or with tender consideration, according to the character of the Prioress. The male ecclesiastical role in respect of women was usually one of domination, however respectfully expressed. But this is not the whole story. In institutions, including convents, women dominated women and the pressure applied was the more painful in that it was personal, immediate and in convents, done in the name of obedience and in accord with the social norms of the secular age. Victorian women, or more precisely ladies, had the duties of their state to perform, inside or outside the convent. And they were expected to be strong in patience and endurance. The norms of middle-class and polite society, indeed the most minor of social conventions, assumed in the cloister the sacredness of divine laws. This was especially the case in the rigid conventual environment where the dictates of ecclesiastical law were backed by the multiplicity of minor regulations made sacred by common usage and the dictates of outdated *Customaries*.

Nineteenth century women in secular society could have found soul sisters in any religious community. The Catholic church by its increasing control, domesticated consecrated women. The Church, the husband, sought in its women conformity, obedience, anonymity, mildness and unquestioning support and service. As in secular society, nuns were not supposed to exercise political power nor to influence or formulate policy. The times were not conducive to feminine freedom although the pressure of feminist protest was already being felt in the middle decades of the century, especially in the fields of female education and social reform. A paternalistic society with the power of Rome behind it did not even consider that women, and above all women consecrated to God for the service of the Church, should be given any real political power. Civil society decreed that women, including married women, should be subject to their husbands or guardians. For the latter the Church substituted the hierarchy. The position of women was that of minors without political or financial rights. How much more so was this accepted as the norm in the case of religious bound by vows, especially that of obedience. In common with their sisters in society they had to be protected and guided, and their maternal instincts had to be developed and applied to spiritual motherhood. While the working class woman usually took equal part with her husband in earning money for her large family, her middle-class counterpart had few opportunities to pursue a career in the business world or in the market-place. Nursing, in the mid-nineteenth century, was not work for a lady, unless perhaps she was a member of a religious community. The age of the woman clerk was yet in the future, and although there are notable exceptions of women achieving success in traditionally male roles, this was not common, and less so in Ireland than in England. A respectable young lady with a reasonable smattering of general knowledge and socially acceptable accomplishments could find a post as a governess, poorly paid, overworked and holding an invidious position between servants and family, and accepted by neither. With the promotion of female education the role of the teacher increased in importance, and women were asserting their right and ability to compete with men in the formal study of the arts and sciences. The education of women opened up teaching as a valued profession, and it was this profession that found its place in the Dominican missionary plan of action both at home and abroad.

Catholic Emancipation (1829) and the re-establishment of the Catholic hierarchy in Britain in 1850 opened up many opportunities in the field of missionary activity throughout the British Isles, and nowhere more radically than in Ireland. In the hands of the Irish church education became a powerful tool both catechetical and political, and the vital work was mainly entrusted to religious men and women, obedient, orthodox and committed to the cause of religious and political freedom. While the poor were getting their opportunity at free schools the more affluent were looking to private schools for the education of their sons and daughters. This was being supplied by such communities as the Dominican nuns of Cabra and its first offshoot Sion Hill. Although Cabra devoted time and personnel to the poor, the community could not have survived without the schools for young ladies, usually the main and often the only dependable source of income, apart from interest on the dowries of the choir sisters. Young ladies of good family brought prestige not only to the institution that educated them but also to the community that received them as candidates. There was apparently virtue in good breeding and, since choir postulants brought with them a dowry, family wealth was also a consideration. There were times when the nuns of both Cabra and Sion Hill and their branch houses lived in extreme poverty to the detriment of their health.[5] Money was always short, and contrary to popular belief the nuns did not receive any income from Rome or from the local church. On the contrary they paid chaplaincy fees and also contributed to the many good causes proposed to them by the hierarchy. Although the alienation of dowries was strictly controlled by ecclesiastical law, the support of benefactors and wealthy family friends often meant the difference between severe economic hardship and reasonable security. The poverty inherent in a situation where income depended on small fees and pensions derived from pupils and parlour boarders, was no stranger to some of those young women who entered the convent as lay sisters. Their state was lowly and their life in practice was one of manual labour and service on the material plane. Of those who joined the Dominican communities in Dublin, the least free were the lay sisters. They were not necessarily of humbler family than the choir nuns. One might be deficient in formal education, another be less refined in manner, but the lack of dowry perforce controlled the question. It is also true that some saw in the humble role of servant a true and appealing vocation, while for others it was a welcome escape from the world, with its insecurities and economic cares.

These women, both choir and lay sisters, their lives, their work, the aspirations which carried them forward all form the motivation for this study. The endurance of penal laws over long periods, the resurgence of the Catholic Church in nineteenth century Ireland and in the Cape of Good Hope, the dispersal of the Irish as the result of political persecution and famine during and immediately after the decade of the 1840's, created a diaspora which demanded a missionary campaign first to mainland Britain and then to the rest of the British Empire, wherever the Irish had settled. The great missionary movement of the nineteenth century called men and women from many walks of life and many Christian denominations to follow their imperial flag across the world. While the motive force was spiritual, in practice political considerations played their part. It was one of the great migrations of the modern era. The missionaries, women and men, brought with them their religion, their culture and norms, their prejudices and bigotry and their undeniable courage. If the image they presented was one of disunity and contention among Christians, they represented the attitudes of a pre-ecumenical age where tolerance in religion was weakness and numerical victory in terms of converts, a sign of God's approval. These attitudes were universal, no less typical of the Irish Dominican nuns who left Ireland for the Cape between 1863 and 1920 than of the men and women of The London Missionary Society who had preceded them to the same destination. The Dominican sisters were only one small group of missionary women among the growing body of volunteers. These included young girls setting out to marry in an alien land, brides joining their husbands on distant missions, and wives and mothers who travelled to the Cape and to other parts of the world to spread the good news. There was much in common between the nuns and their wedded missionary sisters.

The wives of missionaries who left their homes and families for a hazardous life in the frontiers of European settlement in Southern Africa had little experience to prepare them for so radical a challenge as that presented by the raw missionary situation. Women such as Mary Moffat personified female courage at its highest and most remarkable manifestation. While carrying out the difficult task of medical and pastoral care and education, especially of women, they ran households and protected their families and people during the long absences of their husbands. Journeys were long, dangerous and arduous, children at school were absent from their homes for years at a time and in the isolated missions women delivered and too often buried their own babies. The mortality rate of such women in childbirth was high enough to make the missionary vocation one of great risk and too often of short duration.

The Dominican nuns who left Ireland for the Cape, while they shared in the vocation to work in a foreign mission, did not have to face such extremes of danger. They were volunteers whose immediate task was to minister to the spiritual and educational needs of the Irish immigrants, of both the poor and middle class families. The question of the conversion of the indigenous people did not at first enter into the contract, although it was to develop later, and in practice the two independent convents at Cape Town and Port Elizabeth opened free mission schools immediately after their arrival, and private fee-paying schools a short time later. Although their economic circumstances were straitened and their educational resources limited, they formed a small community of common origin and training and they were backed by the power of an aggressive church and firmly controlled by its laws. While the missionary wives moved off into the wilderness the nuns stayed enclosed, subject to both medieval and Victorian norms and practices. They had been formed academically on a system of education which had a long tradition. In their professional work at least they were on familiar ground. In their missionary thrust they were women of their time. In the educational standards they demanded of themselves some of them were typical of the best that women of that age could hope to achieve. In their conventual life they practised the tenets of Dominican spirituality as far as they in their circumstances could do so, and aspired to the ideal of Christian perfection, the common goal proposed for all consecrated religious, men and women.

But this is not a simple narrative of good works by perfect women, nor is it the history of great success or total failure. The threads that make up the story vary in quality. Some are weak, some strong, some bright. Others are dull or even broken beyond repair. There are knots in the fabric and efforts to hide the dropped stitch and the crooked pattern. In this it proves itself to be the record of a truly human society founded, organised and developed by real women, who in many respects were controlled by men. These latter, despite their elevated position and spiritual role, acted in terms of their personalities and the dictates of church tradition and Canon Law. In one sense the story of this religious community like that of any other such body, is commonplace and follows certain conventions. A survey of annals and chronicles reveals the use of a special conventional language, the pious turn of phrase, various forms of literary canonisation of the commonplace, and a strong defence of the saintly perfection of the community. These excesses of *pietas* were not written to mislead, but from a sense of loyalty and perhaps with an eye to the Visitator who checked the annals and council records and could be expected to frown on verbal impropriety. It also reflects a certain poverty of the imagination as well as an adherence to the language of the myth which sustains the ideal of religious life against the erosions of daily mediocrity. For our Victorian ancestors, in theory at least, the nuns did not always need to be dead to be perfect, a point which could well be taken seriously by members of late twentieth century Dominican communities.

The story of these women, of whatever degree of perfection and whatever nationality, who joined the communities of Cape Town and Port Elizabeth, has many facets. It raises profound questions about conventual life, educational practice and the role and place of women in the historical church. It also involves the roles of other people, friends, pupils, professional colleagues and above all the hierarchy of the Catholic Church. This Dominican body, one of a significant number of others working in Southern Africa, became deeply imbedded in the society in which it has worked for over 130 years. It can neither claim isolated gratitude for good done nor exoneration from responsibility for the weaknesses of the society of which it was and is, an integral part. To compile the history of the life and work of the Irish Dominican women who came to the Cape Colony during the last 134 years, demands patient research and objective judgement rather than popular canonisation of the ordinary. The missionary emigration of the first Irish Dominican sisters to the Cape Colony began in the 1860's. But these women's roots were in war-torn Galway, in Channel Row and in the rival convents of Cabra and Sion Hill. Only part of the story can be told since the final destination has not yet been reached.

Chapter Four

Cabra to Cape Town

1863-1920

During the 1840's Ireland had seen not only the ravages of famine, disease and death, but also the dispersal of a great mass of its people. Despite this the two Dublin foundations, Cabra and Sion Hill flourished both in respect of their schools and in the recruitment of personnel. The exodus of the dispossessed Irish to mainland Britain, USA, New Zealand, Australia and South Africa, created a ready-made mission for the Church. The restoration of the hierarchy in Britain in 1850 and the extreme urgency of the need for pastoral care and education for the poverty- stricken Irish immigrants in Britain itself, provided a strong incentive to the Irish church to develop a home mission to save her people from the danger of proselytism, a dispossession far greater than loss of property or even of life itself. The Catholic Church in Ireland was aggressive, not only in the sphere of religion and education, but in politics as well. Having survived centuries of occupation, persecution, martyrdom, exile and imprisonment at the hands of English forces, the Irish were not prepared to allow the victims who survived the famine to be swallowed up by the very authors of their dispersal.

Although feelings ran high against Westminster, Ireland was a part of Britain and consequently many young Irishmen, mainly serving in the ranks, followed the British imperial flag wherever it was planted in newly acquired colonies. Some of the soldiers, after their discharge from the army in South Africa, settled in the Cape Colony, living in remote places where there was no Catholic presence to provide for their spiritual and sacramental needs. Many of these married and became part of their local community, often following the Reformed religion of their wives, especially when children had to baptised and brought up in some form of Christian belief. The 1820 settlements in South Africa also included Irish immigrants, many of whom were poor and illiterate. In both Cape Town and Port Elizabeth they presented a growing problem to the local church, the solution of which would be the introduction of religious educators who would teach and evangelise the families through their children. It is not surprising therefore that when Cabra and Sion Hill agreed to establish foreign missionary foundations in the Cape Colony, they should do so at the request of Irish Vicars Apostolic who were familiar with their educational work in Ireland and were personally well known to the Dominican communities in and around Dublin. And in view of the needs created by the Irish diaspora, it was logical that the first priority of the Irish hierarchy should be to educate and evangelise their own people in exile. It was indeed the pattern established on mainland Britain where the Irish mission, the main thrust of which was the education of the poor, flourished and served as an model for the colonial church.

In 1860 Cabra sent its first foreign mission to Lisbon and made its first foreign foundation in New Orleans. It was the beginning of a long commitment to the interests of missionary work which in 1863, found its next realisation in a foundation in the Cape Colony. This was the first religious community of women to be established in the Western Vicariate, and the second in South Africa. For Bishop Griffiths, an Irish Dominican and first Vicar Apostolic of the Cape of Good Hope, the founding of a community of nuns dedicated to teaching had been a hope long deferred. The new Vicariate had been established in 1837 and already in 1839 Griffiths wrote to a friend: "Had we a Lady with ten or even five thousand pounds, with a few others of moderate fortune to found a nunnery here for the education of Black and White, I have no doubt it would lead to numerous conversions among both, (and the Whites need it as much as the Blacks)". His concern was that the "boorish Dutch" would not "allow the children of colour to be educated with them in the same school ... hence these are driven to the Mahometans who are catching all the emancipated apprentices and are increasing in numbers to a great extent".[1]

Bishop Griffiths did not look immediately to Ireland and the Dominican nuns for help, although in Dublin they were already well established as educators of note. This however is not surprising since at this time the relationship between the Cabra community and the brethren of the Order in Ireland was at a very low ebb. His first choice had been a branch house of the Assumption sisters at Grahamstown, the first foundation of religious women in Southern Africa, a plan he had begun to negotiate but never finalised. In the meantime he opened his own schools and maintained them against great odds, both financial and academic. Money was very scarce and there were few suitable teachers available. By 1840 he was prepared to "institute a nunnery" from within the Colony itself, in order to preserve his Infant and Free School. This religious foundation depended on the support of an "excellent family" which subsequently was forced to leave the Colony. In his dilemma Bishop Griffiths considered the possibility of making nuns of some of the young ladies, and in what seems to have been a last resort to get "some qualified ladies from Ireland".[2] He confesses a month later: "To have a Nunnery here was always my wish", but he did not want the responsibility, though he realised that if the Nunnery were established the schools would be kept open and "myriads yet unborn" would be drawn to the Church.[3]

By January 1841 he had bought a house next door to the presbytery, "thus making preparation for the Nuns".[4] Whatever other hindrances Griffiths met with in his efforts to provide nuns to teach in his schools, reluctance to assume responsibility for the undertaking, or more specifically for the women, was the main reason for the failure of his plans. Whether the rift between the Dominican Fathers and the Cabra community in the 1830's over the question of jurisdiction had anything to do with his tardiness, is difficult to ascertain. His new Coadjutor, Bishop Thomas Grimley who arrived in Cape Town in 1861, viewed the situation seriously: "What grieved me most was the state of education. We have no respectable Male or Female Schools. I found a free Male and a free Female School ... I saw at once the necessity of raising the standard of Catholic education". He lost no time in applying for help to Mother De Ricci Maher, the Prioress of Cabra. He knew the sisters at Cabra and he was a personal friend of Sister Dympna Kinsella. He admired her efficiency as a teacher and her devotion to her pupils, the deaf children at Cabra. He also recognised in her that independence of mind and strong missionary vocation, and believed that she would be the ideal choice as foundress for the first convent in the Vicariate. He himself had been closely involved in the work of deaf education, and consequently his choice of Mother Dympna as the possible leader of the Dominican mission to Cape Town, was based on personal knowledge of her gifts and leadership ability. To support his request to Cabra he claimed that the climate at the Cape was "the finest in the world", no small incentive for a community where tuberculosis was a constant threat to life. At that time he was "residing in the new Convent. Yes in the Convent here ready for the Nuns". He had another house to go to the "moment the

Nuns come. What does Sister Dympna say to that?"[5]

Grimley did not see his new foundation as limited to teaching. Visiting the poor, helping the sick and other forms of social service were urgently needed in his Vicariate and he suggested, perhaps unwisely, the need for a broader approach to the missionary work of sisters at the Cape than would have been acceptable for enclosed nuns in Ireland. He pressed for an immediate decision on the part of the Cabra community to send missionaries to his Vicariate:

> It would be most useful if the Nuns I could get would visit the sick, I am sure the Pope would give any dispensation I would require for those who would come out here. We could have an excellent Boarding School and a flourishing Day School. Let me have a letter from you and give me some hope that I may console my poor people here who are anxious for the Nuns. Will any of your Nuns volunteer in this glorious work of God?[6]

It is significant that neither the Mother House in Ireland nor the missionary sisters themselves ever considered this latter request. They claimed to be Second Order Dominicans, bound by solemn vows and committed to enclosure. The fact that they were under episcopal jurisdiction did not mean that they were prepared to change what they perceived to be an essential element in their lives as authentic members of the Dominican Order.

What Bishop Grimley most needed was religious teachers and if possible Cabra Dominicans, so he did not labour the request for an apostolate that would demand regular egress. In an age of rapidly growing imperial expansion and missionary endeavour, he recognised that new demands were being made for personnel to staff foreign foundations. Already in 1860 the Cabra community had sent eight choir nuns and three lay sisters, together with a number of postulants, to the Dominican Convent of Bom Successo in Lisbon. During the same year they had also sent five choir nuns and two lay sisters to New Orleans.[7] He knew also that Sister Dympna Kinsella, a personal friend with whom he corresponded, was eager to work in his Vicariate. It was essential to ensure that Cape Town would be the next Cabra foundation. He pressed his request: "I expect an excellent young priest will leave Maynooth for this mission about next February [1862], he could take charge of the Nuns". Once again in his greetings to the community he had a message for Sister Dympna Kinsella whom he hoped would be appointed as the foundress of the Dominican mission to the Cape Colony. "Please remember me particularly to Sister Dympna and tell the Deaf Mutes that I do not forget them".[8]

While it is evident that Cabra community did not lack recruits, indeed they had more than they could support, nevertheless the demands that new foundations made on the financial resources of the Cabra community made it difficult to launch immediately into the Cape Town venture. The founding of a mission inevitably created problems for the Mother House. The choice of suitable sisters for the task and the financial outlay involved often clashed with the vested interests of the founding community, and not all who volunteered, especially the lynch-pins of the community and schools, could be released. In order to protect the rights and interests of all concerned an equitable method of selection had to be devised. In the Cabra archives there is no nineteenth century record of the process of selection, but an entry in the *Book of Annals* of Sion Hill Convent, in the same diocese and under the same episcopal jurisdiction, gives a well documented and detailed account of the process of consultation and selection for the projected mission to Dunedin, New Zealand.

The first step was one of consultation: "Very Rev. Mgr. Forde had a private interview with each professed Member of our Community to ascertain her views regarding the new Foundation. Finding all anxious to undertake it, he announced the Cardinal's consent". This prepared the way for the process of selection to begin. After the formal suffrages of the Council and Chapter had been carried out the following questions had to be answered:

1. Is it the opinion of the Chapter that the foundation should be undertaken?
2. How many Sisters can be spared for it?
3. What amount of money shall be allocated for the undertaking?

Once the results of voting were submitted to the Cardinal the next step had to be taken:

> The community is to be informed that while on the one hand, no Sister can be sent on the Foundation except *of her own perfectly free will and determination*, on the other, to maintain the vested right which the Community as a whole has to the services of each Sister who has been admitted a Member of it, each Sister shall have an opportunity of signifying by a secret vote to her objection to any particular Member of the Community being allowed to leave it.[9]

The objections had to be submitted in writing and solemnly presented to the presiding priest at the end of Mass. Each nun was free to sign her objections or even to hand in an empty sealed envelope. There was also an opportunity for those who wished to go on the mission to present a written justification for their choice. The list of volunteers was then submitted to the Cardinal who had it in his power to "cancel from the list those, if any" he did not wish to leave the community. When this step had been completed the Prioress and her Council, following the normal process, selected a superior for the mission. It was the privilege of the newly appointed prioress to choose, from the approved list of volunteers, sisters for the founding community. This system protected both the rights of the Mother House and at the same time ensured that the new foundress had in her community personnel of her own choice with whom she could work.

Since foreign foundations such as those of Dunedin, Cape Town and Port Elizabeth would be totally independent of the Mother House and linked to it by nothing more than mutual regard and a common spiritual ideal, the final breaking of legal and financial bonds had to formally ratified. On the instruction of Mgr Forde the process was defined:

> Each professed Sister who leaves the community for a new Foundation shall, sign a document carefully drawn up, and setting forth that she goes of her own free will, and that she is satisfied with the arrangements made, and that subject to the conditions approved by the Archbishop, and agreed upon between him and the diocesan of the new Foundation to whose authority in virtue of a *Brief* of Gregory XVI the new house is subjected, she has no further claim on the Community or its property".[10]

By January of 1862, Grimley was encouraged to hope that the Cabra nuns would soon be available for the Cape Town foundation. This was inspired by a letter from Mother Catherine de Ricci Maher, prioress of the Cabra community. He was well aware of the problems facing Cabra. It was one thing to find willing recruits, but quite another to release them from their professional or household responsibilities and provide the money to equip them for their new life. There was also the crucial question of leadership for the mission. " I am indeed most anxious to have some of your Nuns", Grimley wrote. "I am sure good Sister Dympna would not refuse to labour here for you. You can have no idea what service to Religion your Nuns would be. Many of the respectable Protestants would send their children to the Convent and no doubt many conversions would follow". The provision of convent education for "good Protestants" was not a matter of interest to Irish Catholic educationists in the 1860's, but Grimley added a little flattery to promote his cause. "I suspect if you knew the glorious prospects that lie before us in Cape Town, Mrs Maher would soon leave Cabra and offer for the Cape mission". He knew that such an eventuality was unlikely, but he had to use every argument to convince and persuade, because it was clear that the Mother House was not entirely at ease about the new South African mission. Despite this Grimley could not afford to forego, for want of trying, the possibility of a Dominican foundation in his Vicariate:

> I need not tell you that I would care [for] every one of your Nuns as I would my right eye. For the love of our good God then allow four Choir sisters and two Lay sisters to come to Cape Town. If you let them come I believe that hundreds of little infidels would attend the Schools and thus would be gained for Jesus Christ. Do not oppose then what I hope is the holy will of God that some of the Cabra Nuns should aid in the conversion of South Africa. I expect a priest from Rome in a few months, he will visit Dublin, or if any accident should prevent him, if you write to me, I will send from Cape Town one of my priests to accompany your Nuns. You perceive how very earnest I am, but really, you should be here to understand the immense blessings a Convent would confer, and then you would feel all the anxiety I do.[11]

His appeal to the people of Cape Town for funds to furnish the convent for the sisters met with a generous response, and even though no final decision had been made by the prioress and community of Cabra, he went ahead with his preparations for the arrival of the nuns. [12] By May of 1862 Grimley recorded: "I am preparing for our good nuns, they will be very happy here". But Cabra still hesitated to commit the community to the Cape Town venture.[13] The pressure of work on the Dominican nuns of Cabra was one of the reasons behind the reluctance of Mother de Ricci to finalise the matter. This was also the motivating force behind one of the two petitions which in July 1862, Dr Cullen, Archbishop of Dublin, presented to Pius IX. Papal approval of both of the petitions was to be of great importance to the Irish Dominican missionaries in South Africa. The first petition acceded to, granted to the Cabra community and its foundations, dispensation from the observance of fasts and feasts of the Dominican Order. The second ensured that sisters who went "with lawful permission to other Dioceses [would] ... be subject to the Ordinary" as they were in Dublin.[14]

Legally the ground was clear, but just when Grimley was confident that his plan would succeed he received a letter from

Mother de Ricci Maher on 3 November 1862, informing him that she was unable at that time to give him nuns for the new mission. This was less than a year before the expected arrival of the new community in Cape Town.[15] It was a bitter blow to Grimley who with characteristic forthrightness, put pen to paper to express his dismay:

> Your letter ... was enough to put me in the dismals. For God's sake do not abandon your glorious idea of establishing your sisterhood in Cape Town. Dr McMahon will tell you we have a fine Convent, and Oh, am I to be deprived of the consolation of having Sister Dympna over the little girls of Cape Town? Do not fear, there is abundance of means of supporting Nuns and great good can be done. On the 8th Inst., I received 8 Protestants into the Church. Be generous to our blessed Lady of Cape Town, recollect we have St. Mary's here too, and your Convent will flourish, you will get five postulants for every nun you give me. Do console me by helping me in this distant land. God will not be outdone in generosity. ... Four choir sisters and one lay Sister would be sufficient, we could get excellent lay sisters here ".[16]

Negotiations with Cabra were placed in the capable hands of Father McMahon and the superiors were soon persuaded to send volunteer nuns to the South African mission. It was not an easy parting for those who went or those who remained at home, since though not bound by a vow of stability, the custom of the times often made the house which received a sister, her home for life. Consequently the departure of the missionaries from Cabra in 1863, and four years later from Sion Hill, was for them the end of an era and the beginning of a venture into the unknown, and that more than simply geographical.

Emigration demanded of them not only acceptance of a new country with unfamiliar people and a strange climate, but an inner transformation which pre-supposed a willingness to abandon the security of family, friends and a well-established and familiar conventual home. Nor would certain of the sacred myths held in honour in the more sheltered world of an enclosed Irish convent, survive the harsh realities of a new and aggressive Protestant environment. While the Mother Houses remained for the immigrant sisters a memory, happy or otherwise, in Cape Town they would be on their own. For some this would be a great relief, for others a painful price to pay for the fulfilment of their missionary vocation. They were to create a unique way of viewing Dominican life, cut off as they were from the mainspring of the Order. This was a situation with strong Dominican precedent, dating back to the thirteenth century when Dominic himself sent his young preachers to distant lands far from the support of their parent foundation. For the sisters, their new mission would also be a challenge to develop fresh approaches to the problems of teaching and evangelisation. And they were to create new myths of their own heroic age, which ran its course through the last forty years of Queen Victoria's reign. The first four decades of the twentieth century were to see in both Ireland and South Africa Dominican communities moving together again in a complex dance of debate and recrimination, of approach and withdrawal, of affirmation and denial, of the opening of old wounds and the legal healing of disunity.

Without diminishing the sacrifice demanded of those nuns who volunteered for the Cape missions, it must be remembered that motives were mixed. Emigration to work on foreign missions was the modern trend, a fashionable and politically correct move in which women could fulfil a less hampered and more vital role in life. It was also a great adventure even for enclosed nuns, and a new opportunity for young sisters to assume positions of leadership and put their professional skills into practice in a new, developing educational system. For some it was an escape from difficult community situations, and for many who came during the next 75 years, a vain hope for renewed health in a more salubrious climate. Both Cabra and Sion Hill continued to send recruits, especially those who sought health but often found an early death. In addition the missions provided the Irish houses with an opportunity to secure places for aspirants who, for social, intellectual, academic or financial reasons, did not meet the prerequisites for admission as choir nuns, into Irish Dominican novitiates. More importantly it promoted the vocation of those who, like their founder Dominic Guzman, longed for an opportunity to evangelise the heathen. There were also practical reasons for the continued emigration of Irish Dominican nuns. Religious communities under diocesan jurisdiction were permitted to admit only a fixed number of sisters; those whom they could support financially. Consequently superiors were happy to send volunteers, surplus professed nuns and young aspirants, to Cape Town, Port Elizabeth, and missions further afield in Australia and New Zealand. Since the South Africa houses never had sufficient nuns to meet the constantly growing demands of the apostolate and local vocations were few, such recruits were always welcome.

However, despite the constant movement of nuns from Ireland to South Africa there is little evidence to indicate that the provision of candidates for foreign missions made any significant impact

Mother Dympna Kinsella OP (1828-1903), foundress of the Dominican foundation in Cape Town in 1863.

on the life or outlook of those who remained in Ireland. Despite this both the Cabra and the Sion Hill foundations in South Africa reflected the social attitudes, political preferences and the mutual sense of individuality that characterised their Mother Houses. Differences that distinguished and divided the two Irish communities in South Africa remained dormant for about seventy years, and for those young women who packed up their belongings and set off on the missionary adventure, the real battles ahead were spiritual, social and professional, and immediate interest in the affairs of Irish convents gradually faded from memory. Missionary women whether inside or outside the cloister had to meet new challenges, to build and staff new schools, and in the case of the Dominican nuns, bring the message of Christ to a land where Catholics were highly suspect and in the minority. They would also be forced to earn their living working mainly among Irish immigrants, many of whom were poor and illiterate.

The sisters who arrived in Cape Town in 1863 and in Port Elizabeth in 1867, while from time to time they received small financial donations from their former communities, had perforce to fend for themselves. A nun's dowry was invested and only the interest on the capital could be used during her life-time. Consequently without the assistance of the local bishop and his people there was little hope of establishing a new missionary foundation. The preparations for the arrival of the Dominican nuns in Cape Town was the result of the generosity of the Catholic community. Bishop Grimley appealed to Catholics "for the purpose of furnishing the Convent and making some necessary alterations" and the "good, poor people" contributed £205. Grimley, knowing that the Cabra community would not send out their sisters without financial resources, cautioned Father John Leonard: "Tell the good Mrs Maher of this unmistaken proof of the good will of the Cape people towards the Nuns, but ... if they have not left when you receive this do not pretend one word about the collection, as I expect Mrs Maher will give you a hand over [fares] but if she hears of this collection she may hold back. When the Nuns are gone tell her the Nuns will get on admirably here".[17]

In the event the cost to Cabra of the initial missionary contingent to the Cape was £1800, a sum which possibly included the dowries of the four choir sisters. The Mother House was well aware of its legal obligation to make a fair return to those choir sisters who moved off to new, independent foundations. The 1837 precedent had been a painful lesson. The destitute Mount Street community had asked Cabra for financial aid and had been refused. What was not donated freely was given at the command of Gregory XVI.[18] Throughout the nineteenth century, Cabra continued to contribute to the missionary expenses of recruits for the Cape Town community. Financial records confirm that between 1872 and 1905 approximately £436 was paid out for passages, £240 mainly for postulants outfits, but in 1903 this included the expenditure of £100 on clothing and travel expenses of two nuns. Gifts and books to the total value of £196 were also sent during this period. This represented a generous contribution when it is realised that Cape Town was not the only mission depending on Cabra for recruits.[19]

Perhaps it was in view of the cost to himself that persuaded Grimley to make a modest claim for sisters. In the event Cabra sent six sisters, Mother Dympna Kinsella, prioress, Sister Hyacinth Casey, sub-prioress, Sister Francis Borgia McDonnell and Sister Agnes Doran, choir sisters and Sisters Jane Carrol and Mary Connell, both lay sisters. This missionary community setting out for South Africa on the 31 July 1863, would need all the goodwill they could get. They were about to settle in a country where Catholicism was anathema, and religious intolerance characteristic of all religious denominations. The restoration of the Catholic hierarchy in Britain in 1850 had aroused fear and prejudice against Catholics, not only in the mother country but also in its colonies. The Catholic population in and around Cape Town was small, and while in England, there where outstanding Catholics, clerical and lay, promoting the image of the Church, this was not the case in the Cape Colony. The Church in the Western Vicariate also lacked financial resources and manpower to support its work of evangelisation, and the educational system was in its infancy. Adaptation to the new situation demanded of the founding community more than a simple application of their Irish conventual experience. Sister Dympna and her community no longer belonged to Cabra, an institution with strong leadership, impressive historical antecedents and as an educational institution, of considerable fashionable pretension and academic prestige. The "iron rule" imposed by Cabra on all of those who volunteered for a new mission, home or foreign, denied them re-admission to the Mother House, although in the event Sister Jane Carrol was to return to Cabra in March 1868.[20] Quite apart from the finality of their missionary choice, the six Dominican women had three major disadvantages not conducive to successful pioneering work in an aggressively Protestant country: they were Irish, they were nuns, and what was worst of all they were enclosed nuns. But these very disadvantages could be put to positive use. Part of their Irish inheritance was the capacity to evade penal laws and to treat the hostility of the

Establishment if not always with contempt, at least with amused tolerance and indifference. Their Irish penal heritage also enabled them to adapt to their own new environment in Cape Town and to set aside without scruple, many of the minor conventual restrictions imposed in the more rarefied atmosphere of Cabra.

However the need for adaptation was not one-sided. Being Catholic and Irish ensured them a certain welcome, at least from their co-religionists. But besides being a mystery to both English and Dutch Churchmen they were also an enigma to many of their own people. Their daily life was shrouded in a veil of secrecy. Their uniform medieval garb, their religious practices, their enclosure and their air of detached independence, all combined to create in the uninformed observer, at best a sense of unease and social discomfort, at worst a fear and even hatred of what could be seen as an unhealthy threat to pure, reformed religion. Young ladies such as the Dominican sisters who made foundations in the Cape Colony in 1863 and 1867 were, behind their mysterious garb and strange life-style, a contradiction to the ideal of Victorian womanhood. A woman's place was in the home. She was the loving wife, the nurturer of children and the obedient home-maker, loved by, but also subservient to her husband. These professional women fitted into neither category, and in a society where the infamous story of Maria Monk still found ready credence, the nuns had to prove themselves to be above reproach both in their professional and in their private lives.

However the full implications of the influence of religious bigotry on their lives and educational mission was only realised gradually over the first four decades of the Cape Town foundation. But the morning on which they set foot on South African soil was the beginning of the great adventure. Fervent, with the enthusiasm of youth, and an assured knowledge of the support of their Bishop, Dr Grimley, why should they doubt their acceptance by the very people they had come to evangelise? The mail steamer, the *Saxon*, docked in Cape Town harbour on the evening of the 6 September 1863, and the nuns disembarked the following day. September, the first month of Spring, is a fruitful time in the Western Cape, with nature full of new life, hope and promise. A warm welcome awaited the sisters. "On landing , they were greeted by hundreds of Irish exiles, and conducted by the Bishop to the convent prepared for them".[21] But there were those who saw the Dominican Sisters as just another contingent "of a large number of low Irish Roman Catholic Immigrants" about the admission of whom to the Colony the Cape Protestants expressed "very extensive condemnation".[22] Happily on that first day, the six sisters knew nothing of the attitude of a section of the Protestant community to their presence in Cape Town. They attended Mass in the cathedral on the evening of their arrival, and spent the next eight days preparing for their final settlement into their new home. "Though the Convent was quite ready for us", one sister wrote, "we did not altogether reside there until 15th of the same month, when we had a small room prepared as chapel, and had our Divine Lord in the Tabernacle".[23]

Their new home, which they named the Convent of Jesus, Mary and Joseph, was very different from the Irish Mother House in Dublin. In the first instance it was small and there was little ground for expansion or for recreational walks. Table Mountain towered over it, and the south-easter, blowing furiously at up to 70 kilometres per hour, rushed through Cape Town distributing debris and torn vegetation in the grounds, and spreading a film of dust on every surface in the house. In addition the town was just outside their gate. Twenty-two years earlier Griffiths had described the building to a friend:

> I believe I told you ... I bought a house next door to me and immediately adjoining these premises thus making preparation for the Nuns. ... I this day have found that the roof of it is in such a state as to require a new one and this gives me an opportunity of raising it another storey, which will accommodate all my household, and leave this house perfectly clear for the Nuns, and be amply commodious for a large community and boarders when another storey is added to part of its wide expanse.[24]

Grimley had given an enthusiastic description of the convent and garden to Mother de Ricci Maher in 1862: "The Convent is a fine commodious house, in front there is a fine garden not large but having its fig trees and Bananas. Behind the house there is a fine grapery so that for a part of the year the Nuns can have grapes from their own vines, in the rear of the Convent also is a very good garden".[25] In July 1862, Bishop Grimley, asked his good friend Father John Leonard to pass on to Mother de Ricci his most recent preparations for his new community: "If I have not time to write to the Cabra Nuns, tell them that I have got the Vine pruned and also got them a beautiful goat. The new Convent is an excellent house".[26] This was the home into which in September of 1863, the sisters settled down and began their work. Until 1871 when they opened a country house, Holy Rosary Convent, Springfield, in Wynberg, they were enclosed in a small property, stifling in summer, and very constricted after the space and country air of Cabra. Their only relief was a short annual holiday at Kalk Bay and occasional walks outside the confines of the convent, concessions made by the bishop to ensure the continued good health of the sisters.

Mother Dympna Kinsella now had to stand on her own feet, and she was not of the political stature of Mother de Ricci Maher. The latter, a member of a well-known Irish family, was one of the most powerful of religious superiors in nineteenth century Cabra. Indeed the Maher era lasted from 1836 to well into the twentieth century. It was broken only five times when the office of superior was held by other members of the community.[27] The Maher rule in some ways typified in its own conventual sphere the force and thrust of nineteenth century secular, imperial power. But the foundress of St Mary's Convent, Cape Town played a simpler role. At the age of thirty-three, supported by a small community of five nuns, the average age of whom was approximately twenty-six years, she had to establish regular life and viable schools, with only four teachers including herself, and supported by the work of the two lay sisters. There is no evidence either that she sought power or wielded authority with punitive sternness. Nevertheless she did not lack leadership qualities. Grimley, next door neighbour to the nuns and close observer of both their religious and professional lives, wrote to Cabra: "Sister M. Dympna is just suited to her position. The prudence with which she governs is admirable. I can only assure you that your Sisters are my greatest auxiliaries in promoting the interests of our dear Lord in this country. They are doing immense good".[28] Three months later he reaffirmed this judgement of his friend: "Good Mother Dympna is ruling gently but firmly, she is really in her own place".[29]

Her own place and that of her companions was not an easy one. The situation in which they found themselves demanded of the six women an inner transformation and a willingness to face the insecurity and isolation common to the many young missionary women working throughout the Colony. They represented the beginning of the great missionary dispersal which later sent the Irish Dominican women to Port Elizabeth in the Eastern Cape and to the farthest corners of the British Empire. All of these women brought to their chosen mission fields an inheritance of education and culture, of Victorian norms and values, of spiritual dedication and of religious and political intolerance, well-matched by their Protestant counterparts. They were also sustained by the myths of an heroic age, both religious and political, and were upheld by the apostolic ideals of their Dominican heritage. Their tradition, stretching back over more than six centuries, found expression in community life, contemplative prayer, shared liturgy, clearly defined written laws, medieval in origin, and a common vocation dedicated by vows to the service of God and truth. Study, a fundamental facet of Dominican life, never played the same role in the lives of the nuns as it did for the brethren. Nevertheless each mission had teachers of high calibre. These were well-versed in the arts and skilled in those feminine crafts so essential for the education of the Victorian lady. But for many of the young nuns who were selected or volunteered for the missions, their experience of religious life in Ireland had been brief. This was especially the case with the first Cape Town community. Mother Dympna was 33 years old and in religion 13 years when she arrived in South Africa, holding the two offices of Prioress and Mistress of Novices. Her Sub-Prioress, Sister Hyacinth Casey was only 20 years of age, one year professed and three in religion. Both Sister Francis Borgia McDonnell and Sister Agnes Doran were 23 years old. The former, Sister Francis Borgia had entered the convent at the age of sixteen and had seven years of conventual experience by the time she went to Cape Town. Sister Agnes was received into the Novitiate at Cabra when she was eighteen years old and was three years professed by the time she volunteered for the South African mission. The two lay sisters were somewhat older, Sister Jane Carrol being 28 years old and one year in religion, while Sister Stephana Connell was 34 years old and less that three years in religion. With the exception of Mother Dympna, this did not represent a long programme of training or an extended experience of religious life.

Many recruits for both Cabra and Sion Hill entered directly from a convent boarding school where they had lived quasi-religious lives of monastic discipline under the strict supervision of the nuns. In accordance with ecclesiastical law, these sisters, as soon as they were professed, moved directly and without a further period of probation into full community life. Some choir nuns immediately assumed leadership roles either within their own communities or, during the nineteenth century, in new missionary foundations.[30] The case of the lay sisters, which will be discussed more fully later, was different from that of choir nuns, though some of them did assume positions of responsibility in the household, especially in under-staffed missions. It must also be remembered that poverty was a real factor in the Irish communities in the nineteenth century. Sleeping accommodation was often poor and cramped, and the provision of food was not generous. For the young women who carried the seeds of the dread disease, tuberculosis, this often led to illness and an early death. The false belief which persisted far into the twentieth century, that the South African climate was ideal for those threatened by pulmonary diseases, ensured that a considerable number of candidates for the Cape missions were in delicate health before they ever reached their missionary destination. For these, life was short and the gifted, however young and inexperienced in the niceties of religious life, had perforce to serve in positions of authority. And this they did with remarkable success.

The nuns of St Mary's Cape Town, threw themselves into the work of education with exuberance, and easily won the regard and enthusiastic approval of their ecclesiastical superior. They in turn greatly appreciated the support and goodwill of Dr Grimley. He wrote to his friend Father John Leonard, just before their first Christmas in the Colony: "I am going to have Midnight Mass at the Convent. The nuns are delighted. They are giving me the greatest satisfaction. They are very happy".[31] Already by Christmas, a little over three months after their arrival in Cape Town, the nuns were in control of their schools. What had they achieved? On 28 September 1863, St Bridget's, the Poor Mission School, was opened and the school for young ladies was commenced on the 16th October the same year. In addition on the second Sunday of November they started a Sunday School for adults.[32] In both the Western Cape and in Port Elizabeth the sisters began their educational work among the poor. There were a number of reasons for this. In the first place the schools were already in existence, and though in some cases these struggling institutions were badly organised and inadequately staffed, they were the least difficult to put on a sound footing. Secondly Mother Dympna, who taught in St Bridget's during her first months in Cape Town and at the same time assisted in preparations for the opening of the Day School for Young Ladies, was following the pattern set by Cabra and its branch houses in Dublin. St Mary's, the private fee-paying school made a small beginning when it admitted its first pupils in October 1863, a little over a month after the arrival of the sisters in the Colony.[33] On the 14 April 1864 two pupils were admitted as boarders, but as they did not return after the mid-year vacation, the boarding school was closed and did not resume until October of the same year. In November 1865 a select Infant School was opened and it was on the fees provided by these small private institutions that the Dominican community lived.[34]

Gradually over the next four years the work of the sisters developed and the convent was provided with a chapel, the decoration of which was enhanced by the donation of a picture of St Mary Magdalen given by a Protestant lady.[35] Whether or not this gift reflected the donors attitude to the life of the nuns or was meant to act as an incentive to their ultimate conversion, is not recorded. While the sisters valued every adornment that would enhance their liturgical prayer, the erection of oratories and the provision of stained glass windows occupied a position of minor importance. The main preoccupation of both the bishop and the Dominican community was how to cope with the growing pressure of work. The need for more recruits was urgently felt and once again Grimley turned to Cabra. In February 1865 he begged Mother de Ricci to support him by providing another nun to assume responsibility for a school for black children. The four teaching sisters in Cape Town were already overworked, and only with the help of additional recruits from Cabra could such a new project be undertaken.

> I am most happy to inform you that your good Sisters are enjoying excellent health, and giving me all the satisfaction I could have anticipated. We are at the beginning of our work in [the] Cape. Bear in mind in this city there are 12,000 Mahometans, there are innumerable Blacks. I opened the School for black children some time ago. The Sisters were too few to conduct it. I secured the services of two young girls to teach, well one of them soon got married and left, and the other got ill, so *I* am now the Teacher of the Black school. About 12 of the children will soon be prepared for baptism. What would you say if you saw me with the blacks around me teaching *cat, dog*. Well a poor foreign missioner must do many a thing, and every thing to save souls.

Was there not in Cabra, he asked, "some Nun who has a great desire to convert the blacks ... I know that the Nuns are the best parties to communicate their knowledge to the little female blacks." He was certain that there was in Cabra "some Nun just ready for the glorious work of bringing these little ones to God".[36]

In June of the same year he again wrote to Mother de Ricci both to ask for further assistance and to acknowledge his debt to the Irish Mother House:

> It is no doubt an instinct of nature, and by Divine providence wisely arranged, that a parent takes the greatest care of the most helpless of her offspring. You are the parent of your dear Convent, and the Sisters here are the most destitute of your children. You will then look on them, I well know, and assist them. I can put my episcopal seal to the testimony of their incalculable services to Religion in this distant Colony. Now, in addition to the innumerable favours you have so generously conferred on this Mission we ask for the love of

the Holy Family that you send us a Postulant or a Nun who can teach in the first school.

It was not as though the Dominican sisters were without competition in Cape Town. According to Grimley there were a number of "most respectable Schools in this City. In order to compete and support the honour of the Convent School, first class teachers are absolutely necessary. In addition to those excellent Sisters whom you have given me, we want another".[37]

In the meantime a new project was being planned, and the bishop was looking tentatively to Cabra for a second missionary foundation in the Colony. On the first day of the new year, 1866, Grimley once again wrote to Mother de Ricci. This time he was pleading on behalf of his Vicar General, Dr McMahon who desired "nothing more in this world than a few Nuns from Cabra for his town of George". As in previous requests he could assure her that a house and garden could be purchased for a small sum, which the bishop himself was prepared to pay. "With regard to the support of the Ladies at George, I will most willingly undertake to provide for all their wants. It would be a consolation for the Sisters [in Cape Town] to have an establishment of their Order so near. The Nuns at George would do immense good".[38] By July however, he was sounding a word of caution: "With regard to the intended new House at George Town, I think it more prudent to suspend judgement until I shall have visited the locality". In October 1866 it became clear that he was in no hurry to commit himself or Cabra to this new foundation. "I shall coolly consider the case of George Convent", he wrote, "I will bide my time".[39] Whether his suspension of judgement and willingness to bide his time was, as he claimed, the result of his involvement in preparation for the arrival of the Marist Brothers in Cape Town, or because he was aware of the proposed new Dominican foundation for Port Elizabeth, it is difficult to determine. Whatever his reasons the Irish Dominicans never opened a convent in George, and it was not until 29 years later, on 6 January 1895, that six Holy Cross sisters made a foundation in that town. Between the request for new recruits from Cabra and the reply, Grimley planted twelve oak trees for Mother Dympna and her community in the convent garden.[40] It was his way of welcoming the new Dominican recruits from Cabra and of ensuring future shade for the sisters in the summer heat of Cape Town. In the event, the proliferation of classrooms and dormitories gradually invaded the shaded garden at the foot of Table Mountain, and the community, growing in number, were limited to a small space in which to recreate, walk and take the air.

The teaching expertise of the nuns and the confidence with which they expanded their work to meet the needs of the Catholic children, were both rated highly by Grimley. He hoped that gradually they would have the personnel and means to open and staff schools for "the poor heathens". In a letter to Mother de Ricci thanking her for new recruits he put forward a new request:

> What a reward will not those good Sisters have in a better world. They have in every sense, left all to follow Christ. Great work is before them. I am most anxious to gather the poor heathens into the Ark of God - the glorious Church of our dear Lord Jesus Christ. But my dear Mother de Ricci, I must have a little patience. I must begin with the children, this humanly speaking is my only chance. A school for the poor infidel is ever before my mind. Your Sisters after a little will commence the great work, will become the Apostles of South Africa.[41]

Grimley's approach to the work of religious women in the church was liberating and well ahead of his time. The Cape Town foundation was fortunate to have in its early founding years an ecclesiastical superior who respected the ability and expertise of the Dominican sisters in their evangelising role.

On 14 October 1866, four months almost to the day of Grimley's letter to Cabra, the Mail Steamer the *Norseman* anchored in Table Bay, and Father Michael Colgan safely delivered his four Dominican charges to Mother Dympna at St Mary's Convent. The party included two professed choir nuns, Sisters Aloysius Cahill and Thomas Casey, the latter blood sister to one of the foundresses, Mother Hyacinth. The choir novice, Sister Rose Manning was, like her professed companions a past pupil of Cabra. The party was completed by Sister Bernard Butler a lay sister whose arrival had been anxiously awaited, especially by Sister Stephana, who looked forward to her company and her help in the growing household work in the convent and schools.[42] The new sisters soon settled down and were put to work without delay. There was so much to be done and so few to do the work. Two of that group lived only a short time. Sister Rose was professed in 1868 and soon afterwards appointed Mistress of Novices. Even the south-easter, the "Cape Doctor" could not heal her. Her health failed rapidly and she died on 12 August 1873, less than seven years after her arrival in the Colony. This was a heavy loss for Mother Dympna since the work of formation demanded special qualities not easily available in a small community so deeply involved in teaching. Her companion, Sister Aloysius did not long outlive her, dying on 21 October of the same year. With such a depletion of Irish personnel alternative means of staffing the schools had to be considered. Ireland was very far away and Cabra had many calls on her generosity. Mother Dympna and her Council would have to look to the local Catholic families and especially among their own pupils, for suitable aspirants.

Local vocations, both choir and lay, were needed to meet the demands of the schools and the convent. A little over a year after the opening of St Mary's the first recruit, Miss Dowling, a young girl from Tipperary, Ireland, joined the community. She received the habit in March 1865 at the hands of Dr Grimley, taking the name Sister Mary Dominick. The ceremony was an occasion not only of spiritual enrichment but also of financial gain. Those of the public who wished to attend and "purchased cards of admission at the Convent were permitted to be present at the ceremony".[43] But Sister Dominick's life in religion was brief. She left the convent in September 1866 while still a novice, and returned to her family in Ireland. Mother Dympna and her community had found her unsuitable for religious life and although Dr Grimley was very disappointed at this decision, he did not interfere in the matter. She was not the only novice to leave at this time. On St Dominic's day 1866, Miss Begley, one of the pupils who had attended St Mary's School for Young Ladies since its inception, and one of the first Children of Mary, entered the novitiate. This was the beginning of hope for the young community. Local girls of good family, preferably Irish girls, would be a pledge of the effectiveness of the mission, and a guarantee of future expansion. They would provide sound members for the Dominican community, and well-trained teachers for the developing schools. But Sister Augustine Begley's stay in the convent was as short as that of Miss Dowling. When the time for profession came she "left the Convent and returned to her father's house".[44] Such arrivals and departures of aspirants from a novitiate were normal in Ireland as well as in South Africa, but in the missionary situation it was painful to lose those so urgently needed for the work at hand.

For the Dominicans during their first six years in the Colony, the situation was not entirely bleak. On the 11th April 1865 a past pupil of St Mary's, Cabra, Miss Leahy entered St Mary's Convent, Cape Town. She received the habit in October 1865 and was professed on 8 January 1867. Sister Joseph Leahy was to be one of the most impressive Dominican women of her day in the Cape Town community. During the next 23 years, both as a religious and as a teacher, Sister Joseph served as a guide and role model for many of the young women and men whom she taught in St Bridget's, and trained as teachers. Women, lay or religious, of her calibre were the soil in which the missionary ideals flourished in Southern Africa. But the colony was large, communication was slow and hazardous, and even in towns such as Cape Town and Port Elizabeth, the need for schools and trained teachers increased every year.

While Grimley valued the educational contribution made by the Dominican sisters, the constraints imposed by episcopal enclosure, from which the nuns did not wish to be dispensed, limited their potential for missionary work among the people. The only practical solution to the Vicar Apostolic's problem was the introduction of sisters of more modern congregations whose apostolic activities were not limited by enclosure. This was not an easy decision to make since both the Prioress of Cabra and Mother Dympna herself, might take exception to the intrusion of another religious body within their territory. Grimley wrote to Dr John Leonard on the 13 October 1866, the very day before the arrival of Father Colgan and four additional sisters from Cabra. "Our Convent is doing admirably. Before I die I hope to see the Sisters of Mercy or Charity in Cape Town".[45] These would be free to visit the poor and sick in their homes and provide nursing services for the Catholic community. However his first priority, which he achieved by the introduction of the Marist Brothers in 1867, was the consolidation of his schools for boys, but he did not live to welcome other congregations of sisters into his Vicariate. In November 1870, on his journey back from Ireland after his attendance at the Vatican Council, Grimley was accompanied by Sister Margaret McCabe, professed lay sister, and Sister Catherine Hanley, choir postulant, the last recruits he was to bring to Mother Dympna. His death in January 1871, shortly after his return to Cape Town, cut short his plans for the church in the Western Vicariate. However no major change in policy occurred after his death since his successor, Rev Dr John Leonard, was a friend of the Cabra Dominicans and a priest in whom Grimley had confided his hopes and plans for the Cape mission.[46] For Mother Dympna Kinsella personally and for her community, the loss of Bishop Grimley was deeply felt, but life had to go on and the schools had to be developed to meet the growing needs of the Catholic people.

On December 16, 1873 Dr Leonard, newly appointed Vicar Apostolic of the Vicariate of the Cape of Good Hope, was consecrated in the Dominican Church at Cabra, Dublin, and in August of the following year he left Cabra for the Cape Colony with four choir postulants, two blood Sisters Pius and Antoninus McLaughlin,[47] together with Sisters Patrick McDonagh and Imelda

St Dominic's Church, Springfield, Wynberg, Cape.

O'Shaughnessy. The party also included Sister Margaret McCormack a lay postulant and Sister Hyacinth Joseph McDonagh, a choir novice.[48] Two years later, in 1875, Cabra records the departure, under the care of Dr Ricards, of two more recruits, Sister Hyacinth Smyth and Sister de Paul O'Brien. In August 1881 six missionaries from Cabra, accompanied by Dr Colgan, set out for Cape Town. This party included two professed lay sisters, Sisters Michael Mallin and Anastasia Brophy, and four choir postulants, Sisters de Ricci Bean, Reginald Burke, Gabriel McCarthy and Stanislaus McCreanor.[49] In September of the following year, eight sisters were sent out from the Mother House in the company of Dr Leonard.[50] The contribution of Cabra to the community at Cape Town during the period 1871-1884 whether of trained and professed members or of postulants, was exceeded only in the years between 1898 and 1915, when 51 postulants and seven professed sisters were sent to the mission. Also during the latter period the prioress of the Cape Town community or senior nuns delegated by Council, visited Ireland five times for recruiting purposes.[51] The Mother House served as a reception, holding and despatching station for candidates for the Cape Town mission, but was not responsible for the travel expenses incurred. In 1881 Bishop Leonard reassured Mother Catherine de Ricci Maher on this count. "If the £150 - received already from Mother Borgia be insufficient to cover the passages of all the Postulants you may have ready for the Cape, I am sure Mother Borgia & the community will be ready to repay you the moment they learn how much they may be in your debt".[52] Without a doubt the Mother House was as generous as possible in assisting the Cape mission but it was not reasonable to expect it to finance the recruitment and travel of postulants.

Dr Leonard, like his predecessor, was confident that he too had the good will of the Cabra Dominicans and this was proved by the willingness of the Irish Mother House to continue to provide personnel. He looked forward to the expansion of the Dominican work in his Vicariate, and indeed even before his arrival in the Cape, a second convent had been opened. Mother Dympna had for a number of years, judged that the provision of a country house away from the heat of Cape Town in a more salubrious country environment, was a matter of great urgency. This would provide for a select boarding school as well as for a welcome holiday house for sisters working in the heat of Cape Town. Since the religious climate of the times did not favour the expansion of the work of "Roman" nuns, the purchase of the beautiful property of Springfield, in Wynberg was placed in the hands of an agent, Edmund Clear, an Irish miller who acted on behalf of Mother

Dympna.[53] The Dominican community paid £800 for the house and property in Wynberg, and there, only eight years after their arrival in Cape Town, the sisters established a new convent.[54] In September 1871 a day school for young ladies admitted its first pupils, and the boarding school opened in February 1872. Ground was cleared and a farm was established to provide fruit, vegetables, milk and eggs for the community and boarders, and as a source of revenue. Novices also spent part of their novitiate there and over the years the prioress and some members of her Council made the convent their headquarters. In the course of time Springfield became both the centre of the community effort to provide superior education for young ladies, and a constant source of funds for the building of new schools and convents, and the extension and modernisation of older buildings.

Springfield was the only foundation in the Western Vicariate for which the sisters held the title deeds. In the case of all the other institutions into which the Dominican community poured money for school and convent buildings, the deeds were held by the Church. Consequently the nuns had no security in respect of the legal ownership of their institutions. A very complicated financial partnership evolved during the late nineteenth century between the Dominican sisters and the bishops, involving the use of government subsidies for schools, interest on loans, common payment of insurance policies, and a host of other financial entanglements. The settlement of the property debate was attempted with every change of superior but it was brought to a positive conclusion only in the late twentieth century. The full story of this is still to be researched and written.

During the 1870's the main focus of attention was not however on the ownership of property but on the need for more nuns to extend the work of Catholic education and evangelisation. In 1876 a potential source of recruits was offered to the Dominican community. Leonard wrote in 1876 to Dr Ricards, Vicar Apostolic of the Eastern Vicariate, of his plans in respect of the Augsburg Sisters for the Western Vicariate:

> I have just received your lordship's letter from Queenstown, and have had a communication with Mother Dympna on the matter of the Augsburg Nuns. Mother Dympna is writing to Mother Rose by this post, and as soon as possible I will ask Mother Borgia to come into Cape Town with Sister Agnes [Doran], so that the Prioress, Sub-Prioress and 3 Discreets can take counsel together. I hope they will be able to meet on Sunday next. ... Should they decline the offer, I could not venture upon more than six for Somerset Road Schools, where I have two young female teachers at present. But of course at

least three of the *six should* be qualified to teach English ... in order to secure a Govnt. Grant of £75 for the Parochial Schools and one would be required for the pay school. The other three would be able to teach French and Drawing etc. But if the Dominican Nuns would consent to act in concert with the Augsburg Nuns for a couple of years, then it is possible that we could take 10 or 12 in all. I presume they are Cloistered nuns - at least having Episcopal enclosure.[55]

It was difficult for the Council to forego the offer of additional Dominican nuns. With an increase in personnel, Mother Dympna and her community would be able to open a new convent and take over the schools, in the new mission district of Somerset Road.

Mother Dympna, though she was Sub-prioress and not Prioress at the time, had authority in her role as foundress, to deal directly in this matter. She was well aware of the "very fair prospects for higher schools for females". However after consultation with Mother Borgia and the other sisters, it was considered against "the Spirit of their rule to have these branch houses, which necessitate the change of Sisters etc., etc., and it was resolved to take only four [Augsburg Dominicans] for a period of two years after which they may join the Dominicans for life".[56] As was common at that time, the group of Dominican convents in the Cape Peninsula was viewed as a single community under the control of one elected Prioress, each individual house having an appointed "Sister-in charge", who wielded limited power. There is no further record of the Augsburg nuns or any indication as to the reasons for the rejection of Mother Dympna's offer. When the third branch house, Sacred Heart Convent, on Somerset Road, Cape Town, was opened on 18 January, 1883, seven sisters formed the founding community. These were Sisters Francis Sherwin, Antoninus McLaughlin, Magdalen Crolly, Cecilia Crowley, Paul Cotter, with the addition of a novice Sister John Gillen and Sister Catherine Smith, a lay sister. The staffing of both the Somerset Road schools and St Anne's Mission School in Wynberg were made possible by the fact that by 1883 Mother Dympna's community had been augmented by thirteen new members, including professed choir nuns and postulants, sent out by Cabra. The manager of St Anne's applied to Langham Dale, the Superintendent General of Education, for the usual subsidy: "I have the honour to acknowledge the receipt of a communication from your office ... intimating that a grant of 30£ will be issued from 1st of Feb., to the R.C. Mission School recently opened for the instruction of the poorer classes at Wynberg &

taught by one of the Springfield Sisters".[57] Under the principalship of Sister Benignus Dowley, St Anne's had gained recognition by the Department of Education and was the third mission school to come under the control of the Dominicans in the Western Cape. Sister Benignus, a young nun, who had been professed in 1882, died in 1885 after a short illness. Her place was taken by Katie Hart, who had been educated and trained at St Bridget's, and who entered the novitiate in August 1885. Since she was at this time a young and inexperienced teacher, her work was supervised by Sister Thomas Casey, principal of Springfield.

In 1884 Leonard wrote to Cardinal McCabe in Dublin for another priest for the Vicariate: "The Dominican Nuns are now 43 in number, and are divided into three Convents - two in Cape Town, and one about nine miles from Cape Town. I have really no priest of *sufficient age* & prudence to appoint as chaplain to the nuns".[58] Over a period of ten years the number of Dominican sisters had increased by 23, and there were 13 additional priests and four extra Marist Brothers. In addition to these there were eight Poor Sisters of Nazareth to look after the old and orphans.[59] Despite the increase in religious personnel, statistics prove that during the latter half of the nineteenth century the Catholic Church carried out little active evangelisation of the Coloured people in the Western Vicariate. In 1868 there were only 50 Coloured Catholics in a total Catholic population of 3 500.[60] Almost a quarter of a century later the *Ecclesiastical Returns* of 1891-1892 indicate that in the Western Vicariate, there were only 257 Catholics of Coloured descent, 180 of whom belonged to the Filipino fishing community at Kalk Bay. In the same 12 months there were 3 269 Catholics of European descent.[61] This however does not reflect the number of Coloured pupils in Catholic schools, since at that time there was no discrimination based on religious affiliation.

It had been clear to Leonard from the outset that the education and evangelisation of the indigenous people in the Western Cape could not be remedied without the opening of more schools and the provision of additional staff, preferably nuns and brothers. He had considered introducing Loreto Sisters into the diocese to staff the Somerset Road school, and his correspondence with Mothers General indicates that he hoped for nuns who could combine teaching with social services such as house visiting, especially among the sick and the poor. Dr Colgan, discussing the possibility of a new congregation of nuns for the Vicariate, wrote to Leonard: "Cabra perhaps might make an effort to supply some sisters rather than allow another teaching order to be introduced into Cape Town. I am inclined to think this arrangement would work better than that which would bring in the Sisters of Loretto. There is scarcely room for two teaching orders in Cape Town".[62] The Sacred Heart foundation of 1883 proved that the Dominican community could staff and run additional schools both for the poorer children and for the more affluent. The Sacred Heart school for young ladies flourished and soon vied with Springfield for honours in music and later in public examinations. In April 1883 an event of considerable significance to the sisters of Sacred Heart Convent occurred. This was the appointment of Dr Colgan as parish priest of the Somerset Road district, and chaplain to the nuns. This latter role was one he exercised with vigour, conscious of his status and his authority over the sisters to whom he ministered. He was a competent school manager, and included among his managerial activities the supervision of the Dominican community, sometimes with dire results.

Not until sixteen years later did the Dominican community embark on a new foundation. After the Easter holidays of 1899 the new convent, St Agnes' Woodstock, was opened. This, like the Sacred Heart Convent, already had established "public schools ... in working order and well attended". According to their normal pattern the nuns immediately founded a private school which opened very prosperously, with an attendance during the first week of over 60 pupils. This new venture raised great hopes in the heart of the nuns as the annalist noted: "It is thought these schools will in a short time far exceed in numbers the older established houses - as Woodstock is a very rising place on account of the Salt River works".[63] One of the factors that promoted the development of this school was the appointment in 1904, of Sister Berchmans Cotter, as Sister-in-charge of St Agnes' Convent. She advocated that the two schools be united, a move that would ensure the financial viability of both institutions and allow the sisters to teach and influence a greater number of pupils. It proved to be a wise decision since it ensured that more sisters were available to teach the larger, less privileged group of children, and that grants and salaries from the Department of Education would ensure the economic survival of both school and convent.

The funding of new foundations was always a heavy burden on the community, and even where the schools buildings were available, a house for the sisters and extra classrooms had to be provided. The initial cost of St Agnes' Convent was £4 000. Half of this was paid directly by the Dominican community and the other half borrowed from Bishop Leonard and paid off within 12 years. In its day this school was to count among its pupils young boys and girls who were to serve the Church with distinction in many walks of life. One among them was Owen McCann, a man of great political insight, whose loyalty to the church was characterised by courage and devotion during the troubled times of the apartheid era in South Africa. He was the first, and so far the only cleric in Southern Africa to be raised to the rank of Cardinal. A lifelong friend of the Dominican community, he openly acknowledged his debt to his first teachers, the sisters at St Agnes' Convent, Woodstock. By the early twentieth century, while St Agnes' School was in its formative stage of development, the nuns in the Western Vicariate still depended largely on the Mother House at Cabra, for personnel. However it soon became evident that if plans for future foundations were to be realised a special recruitment drive, carried out by the Cape Town Dominicans themselves, would be necessary.

In September 1900, for the first time since her arrival as foundress of the Dominican community at Cape Town, Mother Dympna Kinsella, then 77 years old, stepped down from her position in the top ranks of the sisters. For 37 years she had served as either Prioress or Sub-prioress of the growing community.[64] She had been involved in the plans for every new Convent and school, and had a decisive voice in every major decision. And when problems threatened the life or apostolate of her sisters she was there to help them find wise and equitable solutions. Father Michael Colgan wrote of her in 1890:

> You are, then aware, My Lord, that the good Sisters of St. Dominic, who are under your Lordship's jurisdiction, were brought to the city of Cape Town some twenty-five years ago. The Superior under whom these Sisters came was a woman admirably fitted for her office, a woman of great prudence and good sense, and who thanks be to God is still amongst us. Under her fostering care the community has grown from six to over forty which it now numbers, and instead of one Convent they now have three. It is a rule of this community that a new superior be elected every three years. Owing, however, to the superior prudence and great administrative powers of the first superior - Mother Dympna - and the fact that among the other Sisters of the Community there was no one of her fitness or ability to govern, permission was granted to have her re-elected at times.[65]

In September 1900, Mother Pius McLaughlin was elected prioress and Mother Columba McAuliffe sub-prioress of the Dominican community of the Western Vicariate. It was their decision, with the "kind permission of Bishop Leonard", to send two sisters home to Ireland on a recruiting campaign for postulants. In this way it was hoped that the ageing community might be augmented by young and energetic lay and choir sisters. This visit, which once again reflects the strong links between the Dominican sisters of the Western Cape and Cabra, was not limited to recruiting. It was also agreed that the sisters should use the opportunity to visit convents and day and boarding schools in both Ireland and England. Mother Pius and her Council hoped that this would help them to bring their own institutions in the Cape Peninsula into line with the best Catholic schools in Britain. Mother Columba McAuliffe and Mother Antoninus McLaughlin were chosen for the task and in due course a record of their peregrinations was sent to Cape Town:

> They left Table Bay on board the 'Walmer Castle' on twentieth June 1902 & arrived safely in England on the 12th July. The Sisters remained in England for some weeks visiting the different Convents and Educational establishments. They then started for the 'Island of Saints' and went straight to the Mother house Cabra, where they received a welcome, never to be forgotten. After a brief rest they commenced their tour through the South of Ireland where they were most successful in the numbers who offered to give up home and country to work for God in Africa. After three months in the South, the Sisters paid a flying visit to some friends in the North, then returned to Cabra. Before their return a brief visit was paid to the Eternal city - they were privileged in seeing Our Holy Father Leo XIII and receiving his Blessing.

After visiting the churches and shrines in and around Rome they returned to Ireland to gather their volunteers together before departing for South Africa. They had been absent for nine months and returned on 21 March 1903. The fruit of their quest was the group of new postulants who in due course would make further expansion possible. It was a memorable visit for those concerned and it proved that there were Irish girls who only needed encouragement to commit themselves as missionaries in the service of God. The year 1903 also saw the celebration of the peaceful death of the foundress of the Dominican community of the Western Vicariate, Mother Dympna Kinsella, much loved and highly respected both by her own sisters and by the many men and women who had known her during her 40 years at the Cape.[66]

But her death did not presage a new era in the history of the nuns or their educational work. The forces of conservatism in the Church and in conventual life were strong, and just as Mother Dympna had held office for many years, so those who followed her had come from the same tradition and had served in positions of authority for long periods.[67] There was to be little change in the life, work, or outlook of the sisters or indeed in the society which they served. The pattern was familiar: recruits were admitted, new schools were opened, new convents established, and the well-tried system of regular life and education followed the same familiar paths. The Victorian era, which had been a time of vital educational endeavour for this Dominican community, was perpetuated in the cloisters in the dying norms and values of an age noted for its ruthless imperial expansion and the fervour of its missionary thrust. It would take a world war of unprecedented ferocity to force a complacent society into the twentieth century. For the sisters the immediate tasks prevailed. Even war and the growing demands of women for franchise and greater educational and employment opportunities, impinged little on the lives of the nuns. After all religious life did not change and the work of education had to go on.

In February 1905 the building of St Augustine's Mission School was commenced at the cost to the community of approximately £695. It admitted its first pupils on 10 April of the same year. In January 1906, a convent was opened at Rondebosch with Sister Gonzales Cronan the local superior, and with only three nuns, Sisters Alphonsus Lynch, Reginald Burke and Zita O'Reilly making up the community. Until 12 May when the Sisters took over their new residence, they lived in a cottage attached to the Public School.[68] Star of the Sea Convent, St James, built on the side of the mountain overlooking False Bay, was opened in January 1908. Sister Pius McLaughlin, at this time sub-prioress of the Dominican community, and Sister Columba McAuliffe, with two lay sister postulants went there to get the house into order for the community. On the 27 January, the first day of term, only nine pupils enrolled for the High School. The sisters immediately took over the local Catholic mission school which at the outset had about 30 children. Sister Hyacinth was appointed Sister-in-charge with a community of three additional nuns. Among those assigned to the new foundation was Sister Joseph Glynn, a past boarder of Springfield who had entered the Convent in October 1892 and was professed in 1894. She had been popular with the Springfield pupils who regretted her departure to St James.[69] Star of the Sea remained a small school but according to a contemporary report it had an excellent reputation: "Catholic children of Kalk Bay are held up to the Springfield pupils, by the Sisters as examples of diligence & proficiency in religious knowledge, piety in prayers and sacred singing. This is due to the devoted care and zeal of the pastor of

St. James. Rev. J. Duignam. He has been most kind & helpful to the Sisters since they went to his parish".[70]

The new foundation at St James was initiated at a time of economic depression and it was to Father James Duignam, the local parish priest, that the community was indebted for his advice and practical assistance. He supervised the building of the new convent and school, and promoted the work of the sisters in every possible way. This is just one of many instances when he gave support, often financial, to the Dominican sisters who regarded him as a genuine and disinterested friend. In 1920, when Sister Joseph Glynn was superior, the extension of the school premises was begun. On this occasion Father Duignam gave a personal donation of £300 towards the building.[71] This was the last convent to be established in the Western Vicariate within the first six decades following the foundation of St Mary's Convent, Cape Town. By 1908, 45 years after the arrival of Mother Dympna and her companions, and five years after the foundresses's death, the community under one prioress, consisted of six convents with their mission, public and private schools. Apart from the opening of the novitiate at Potters Bar, England in 1922, no further convents were established within the founding era.

Although the detailed history of finance and buildings soon palls, nevertheless the record of the sisters' willingness to open and staff schools and convents, to accept a lifetime of punishing debt, and to endure the poverty of their daily lives, all bear witness to their commitment to the mission proposed in 1862, to Mother Dympna Kinsella by her friend Bishop Grimley. While it was only by accepting real poverty and strict economy that the nuns had the material means to sustain their work, it was by the generosity of Cabra that they were enabled to staff each new institution with postulants, novices and professed sisters, sent regularly from the Mother House. Since the provision of personnel for each new foundation placed severe pressure on the community it was fortunate that the episcopal links with the Mother House remained strong after the early death of Bishop Grimley in 1871.

Apart from differences of opinion between the Dominican superiors and the bishops of the Western Vicariate on matters of finance and property, in general the relationships with ecclesiastical superiors remained peaceful and supportive. The sisters were well able to earn their own living, build convents and classrooms when the need arose and in addition contribute to worthy church causes. They, like the Irish Dominicans in Port Elizabeth, while they did not lack financial astuteness, accepted their position as diocesan communities, and generally tried to maintain friendly relations with the clergy who were often the managers of their Mission schools. It was also recognised that the bishops and clergy over the years had been loyal friends to the Dominicans of the Western Cape. They had served as willing chaperones for sisters travelling to Cape Town and had ensured against the isolation of the community by bringing visitors to the convents, especially St Mary's, Cape Town. These religious men and women, en route to other parts of Southern Africa, shared with the nuns, news of home and of their own experiences in other lands. Cape Town was the door of Southern Africa, and the sisters, noted for their practical hospitality, welcomed visitors from Europe and the East and set them on their way to more distant missions. For cloistered religious, there was little the Dominican nuns did not know about missions in other parts of South Africa, and there were few who passed through the welcoming doors of St Mary's Convent, who did not leave the happier because of the kindness of their hostesses and often wiser for their advice.

Chapter Five

Sion Hill to Port Elizabeth

1867-1918

In November 1867, just a little over four years after their arrival in Cape Town, the sisters gave hospitality to a group of Irish Dominicans nuns en route to the Eastern Vicariate. " Five choir sisters and the lay sister remained six days at the Convent in Cape Town. They were from the Convent of St. Catherine, Sion Hill, Dublin, on their way to Port Elizabeth with the Bishop of the Eastern District, Dr. Moran".[1] It was a happy meeting and it could have been expected that this first encounter of the Irish Dominican nuns on African soil might have created the first links of a strong bond between the two communities, and a mutual co-operation in the work of evangelisation. However during the first seventy odd years of the separate development of the Cape Town and Port Elizabeth foundations, this was not to be the case. Each community developed on its own lines, retaining to some extent at least the strengths and weaknesses, ideals and prejudices of the Irish communities from which it had originated. There were a number of factors that made any form of close interaction unlikely. It was not in the tradition of the times. A new foundation was expected to be independent, even of its mother house, although it might remain linked by the bonds of *pietas* and friendship. In the case of foreign missions distance was also a factor. During the nineteenth century, a period of slow travel in Southern Africa, there was little likelihood of social visits or regular consultation on matters of common professional or spiritual interest. And even if the two Dominican communities had wished for closer links, the laws of enclosure prohibited casual travel, and should such permission have been given by ecclesiastical superiors, the sisters would have had neither the money nor the time for regular travel between Cape Town and

Port Elizabeth. Finally while it was one thing to seek and be given hospitality in another community while travelling, it was quite another matter to move from one convent to another for holidays or other, more worldly purposes. But perhaps the most cogent reason for this lack of Dominican interaction in the Cape Colony arose, not from any ecclesiastical regulations, local conditions or personal disagreement, but had its origin in the relationship between Cabra and Sion Hill.

During the nineteenth century, these two Irish Dominican Convents which sent sisters to South Africa, were themselves independent entities with no record of mutual interaction, professional or conventual. The same held good for their South African foundations. However while these latter remained geographically isolated, there was no indication of overt animosity or criticism during the next seventy years of their history. Nevertheless because of their isolation, the Port Elizabeth and Cape Town communities, like their Irish counterparts, developed along their own lines, influenced by their immediate environment and the remembered and sometimes fading ideals and practices of their Irish Mother Houses. This was all the more likely in that many of the women sent out by both Sion Hill and Cabra were postulants, with little or no novitiate training in an Irish convent. Their Dominican heritage had to be worked out within their own community and in the apostolic milieu in which they lived. For the sisters from Sion Hill, who found such generous hospitality in Cape Town, as for the community which welcomed them, the heritage lay in a shared and at the same time divisive history of their Irish foundations, and in the history and myths of the Order itself.

The bland entry in the Sion Hill *Annals*, published in 1904, informs us that "the first foundation from Cabra was made on 24th October 1836, Feast of St. Raphael, Archangel".[2] The *Annals* of Cabra (1912) are equally non-committal in their reference to the loss of valued community members. Perhaps Cabra took its cue from Sion Hill and decided that a discreet silence was preferable to the public airing of historic disputes. Although there is no written or even implied reproach or criticism in either text, yet the story behind this departure, and the subsequent separate development of Cabra and Sion Hill and their foreign foundations, is of great importance for the understanding of the history of the two missionary communities in Cape Town and Port Elizabeth. It is also the key to certain aspects of the amalgamation debate of the 1920's and 1930's in both South Africa and Ireland, and has raised questions in the Dominican communities in Australia and New Zealand.

THE DOMINICAN CONVENT
SION HILL, BLACKROCK

Dominican Convent, Sion Hill, Dublin.

At the turn of the twentieth century when the vexed questions of status, jurisdiction and the authenticity of the Irish Dominican communities of Cabra, Sion Hill and of their offshoots was causing much painful heart searching among the sisters, Mother Ignatius O'Doherty, Prioress of Dominican Convent, Belfast, wrote to Mother Bertrand:

> The foundation of Sion Hill was a mystery to the Community in general. Some Sisters became discontented, the ex-Prioress Mother Magdalen Butler at their head. I think Mother Magdalen regretted the change in jurisdiction, and that she influenced the others. The first intimation that Mother Columba got of their movement was to see the carriages one morning drive up the lawn for the Nuns. In this business they were helped on by the V.G. of the Diocese [Very Rev Dean Meyler];[3] without some clever person like him, the Nuns could not have managed for themselves. I think the foundresses numbered five or six, the most gifted in the Community. S.M. Peter Colgan, novice, deferred her departure for a while, seeing how Cabra had been robbed of its teachers. When things settled down, she also left.[4]

This exodus was a heavy blow to the Cabra community, not only because of the loss of personnel, but also for the implied criticism of the Cabra regime and of the efforts of Mother Columba Maher to restore peace and economic prosperity to the Convent. The history of religious life records many such breaches within communities, often a source of revitalisation both for those who break away and those who remain. But whatever the long term results, the pain of loss accompanied by the immediate decline of the private school at Cabra was hard to forgive and was certainly not forgotten over the next nine decades. According to Mother Ignatius:

> Immediately after the Sisters had left Cabra for Mount St., Father Gavin O.P. walking thro' Dublin met two little girls whom he had known at the Convent. These were Mary and Nannie Gavin. Father Gavin inquired of their Uncle who was with them why the children were not at school. The Uncle replied that there was no school at Cabra, that all the Nuns who knew how to teach had gone. Fr.Gavin told him he had made a mistake in removing the children, the Uncle yielded to his advice and Father Gavin himself brought back the little ones in triumph to the Convent. They both afterwards became great stars.[5]

Mother Ignatius was herself first a pupil and later, as a Dominican nun, a teacher in Immaculata School. Her connection with Cabra from 1844 onwards ensured her a certain knowledge of the story of the Sion Hill foundation and the pain and estrangement it had caused. It is little wonder that the two convents held themselves aloof from each other for over 80 years. The depth of the rift between these communities can be gauged by the fact that the division exported so well to the Cape Colony, and influenced the relationship between the Dominicans of Cape Town and Port Elizabeth until well into the twentieth century.

The refusal of Cabra in 1837, to come to the financial assistance of Mother Magdalen Butler and her companions, then living in Mount Street, Dublin, did not improve relations between the two communities. An appeal to the Holy See to intervene in this matter ensured that the new foundation was given the sum of £800, but this was to be the last claim paid by the Mother House to the Sion Hill foundation. In the name of the Prioress and Sub-Prioress it was guaranteed that no additional claims would be made on Cabra:

> We acknowledge and declare this to be the final settlement between the said Convents, as recommended by His Grace the Most Rev. Doctor Murray, our Ecclesiastical Superior, and approved of as such by the Sacred Congregation of the Propaganda at Rome on the 17th of Sept. last. We freely then receive this sum as the last grant which we have any right or hope to claim from St. Mary's Convent at Cabra; and in pursuance thereof recognise the two aforesaid Convents to be wholly distinct and separate, having no connection with or dependence upon each other.

The members of the new community also forfeited "any and every claim or right which we ourselves or any member of this community of St. Catherine's might have had of returning to, or residing in the said Convent of St. Mary's at Cabra".[6]

The final conditions set down in this agreement; the relinquishing of all claims on the Mother House by a new foundation, served as a legal model in the case of missionary sisters such as those who left Sion Hill to found Holy Rosary Convent, Sion Hill in Port Elizabeth. So also did the financial arrangement between Cabra and Mount Street community (1838) create a precedent for initial funding of later foundations. The final request to their ecclesiastical superior to give approval for the Dominican mission to Port Elizabeth makes the position clear:

> May it please Your Eminence to grant permission to the undernamed Nuns of St. Catherine's, Sion Hill, Blackrock to establish a Convent of their order in Port Elizabeth in the Apostolic Vicariate of Grahamstown, South Eastern Africa

under the jurisdiction of the Rt. Rev. Dr. Moran V.A. and Bishop of Dardania. The Srs. having freely offered themselves for the undertaking and We knowing of no disqualification to prevent their being good and helpful religious, await now the final decision of your Eminence. The Community decided on alienating for the mission £700.

This document which includes the names of the volunteer sisters, was given under the signature of Sister Clare Elliott, prioress of the founding community of Sion Hill.[7] The sum of £700, £100 less than that handed over to Mother Magdalen Butler and her impoverished sisters in 1838, did not however express the full extent of the investment in the Port Elizabeth foundation. Nor did it express the spirit of the Irish Dominican Mother Houses. These, especially in the nineteenth century, gave occasional financial contributions and also equipped the sisters before sending them to the missions. In addition, the later recruiting and reception of aspirants and their despatch to South Africa was costly in time, effort and quite often in money as well, and no evidence has as yet come to light that these services were grudged.

In the setting up of a foreign foundation Sion Hill was faced with two options. Two bishops had applied for nuns, Dr Allemany OP of San Francisco and Dr Moran of the Eastern Vicariate of the Cape Colony. Since the American plan would have involved the merging of the Sion Hill nuns with those of the Californian Dominicans, Dr Allemany proposed that some delay would be necessary so that he could consult the sisters of his own diocese. When the choice of destinations was put to the Sion Hill Chapter the decision to go to South Africa was "almost unanimous". Why did they make this choice? According to the *Annals*: "One reason that the Sisters voted to undertake the S.E. African Mission instead of that of San Francisco was, that Cabra had a flourishing establishment in Cape Town, and the former Bishop, Dr. Griffiths, had left the field of his zealous labours ready for religious and educational work of our nuns".[8] In fact Bishop Griffiths had not personally extended his educational work to the Eastern Districts of the Cape Colony, but the 1860's was a time of educational development in South Africa, and Dr Moran needed the services of reliable and committed teachers for his schools. The Sion Hill community knew nothing of the conditions or circumstances under which their sisters would live and work in South Africa, but for all of them the "first Mission, and to so distant a land, appeared a great and novel undertaking", as indeed it was. For the modern Dominican sister for whom mobility is a characteristic of life, the concept of leaving an enclosed and much loved community, and a homeland all the more precious for having endured centuries of occupation and persecution, is difficult to conceive. For those remaining in the relative security of the Mother House the parting was poignant: "It would be impossible to describe the desolation caused in our Community by this first separation. From our top windows we watched the vessel 'Lady Eglinton' steering out from Kingston, and we envied the kind Sisters in St. Mary's [Kingstown] giving our dear ones hospitality and seeing the last of them".[9]

The six sisters who set off on 5 October 1867 on the first leg of their journey, were as a group older and more experienced in religious life than those who had gone to Cape Town in 1863. Mother Rose Whitty was seventeen years in religion and had served as Novice Mistress in Sion Hill. Her sub-prioress, Mother Thomas Kelly was twenty-one years in the Convent and had also held the office of Novice Mistress. Sister Aloysius Cowley and Sister Hyacinth Potter had already given twenty-one years and nine years respectively as teachers in the school, while Sister Baptist Taaffe had held the responsible position of Mistress of Schools. The sixth member of the founding party was the lay sister, Sister Michael Morton who had been six years in religion at the time of departure from Ireland. They, like the missionaries from Cabra, were volunteers. They too realised that they had made a final choice and that their home at St Catherine's was closed to them for ever. The sisters also knew that unlike their clerical counterparts, the Irish priests who served the Eastern Vicariate, they would have no opportunity of returning to Ireland, even for a visit. But despite the fact that this was voluntary exile, the missionary sisters were the envy of their community, some of whom were to join them in the years that followed.

The adaptation from convent seclusion to life on board ship, was the subject of interest in the letters of the sisters, and a further proof of their sense of adventure and social adaptability. Mother Rose reported that they were quickly "accustomed to eating in the presence of the passengers", but they found it difficult to concentrate on letter-writing because there was so much chattering going on around them. This was certainly not part of their convent experience. "Some time ago I had a gentleman translating French to me while I was writing to my mother", reported Mother Rose to her former prioress. No doubt this was the more exasperating, since like the ideal Victorian lady, she herself was fluent in both spoken and written French.[10] On the 9 October the sisters transferred to the *Celt* "a most beautiful steamer all freshly painted in a very pretty pea green ". It was a more comfortable ship than the *Lady Eglinton*, but on their first day aboard they felt that it lacked the welcome of their previous vessel. The captain had not yet "deigned to address" them. This situation was soon remedied however and within twenty-four hours Mother Thomas Kelly reported: "All around us [are] seeking our comfort and convenience - particularly the Captain and Stewardess - nothing could exceed the kindness of the former. He has a true Irish heart and is a sincere Catholic". The sisters also learnt that their strange dress, their obvious Catholicity, their silent air of detachment and their exclusiveness as a group, did not win much favour with the Protestant passengers on board.[11]

Whatever may have been the coldness of some of their fellow passengers the nuns had in their Bishop, Dr Moran a very attentive cicerone and friend. "Do not for a moment ... think we are neglected, as Dr. Moran is after us morning, noon and night attending to all our wants. His kindness is beyond description". Nor was he as their ecclesiastical superior, slow to correct a too exuberant enjoyment of life at sea. Mother Rose was instructed in her duties as prioress. "As we entered the Ladies' saloon he took me aside by the arm. ... After this he called me into my cabin and in plain language told me to look after the sisters' health, and then cautioned me about our manner and conversation saying that it must be quite different from what it was in the other vessel as we are now surrounded by a different class of people all English Protestants, a silent reserved people". The prejudice that the Bishop and the sisters experienced was to be expected in the climate of the 1860's, and no doubt the "stiff cold Protestants" who stared at them "unmercifully" and laughed at them occasionally, were also keenly aware of the mutual prejudice of the Catholic party in their regard. However Bishop Moran knew well how easy it would be to create a false image of nuns, already the focus of suspicion, and in many cases, of irrational fear. He promised to tell Mother Rose herself if he found anything "reprehensible" in the conduct of the sisters. However, in the event and apart from recurrent sea sickness during the early part of the voyage, the nuns met his exacting standards of behaviour and the bishop found nothing indiscreet or unbecoming in their conduct.[12] Nevertheless it is clear from the onboard correspondence, that past conventual experience and withdrawal from the world had done nothing to repress the nuns' capacity for enjoyment. As one sister protested to Mother Thomas Kelly, "for mercy's sake laugh no more, you do nothing but pray and laugh". The Bishop arranged that the nuns could have all their meals alone in the ladies' saloon, including even the postulants he was bringing for another mission. Nor were the comforts laid on for the travellers by their Sion Hill and St Mary's communities meagre. As Mother Thomas wrote to her former prioress: " Oh! never can I forget your anxiety to have every thing for us". This was written on the sisters' last day in the British Isles. Mother Clare was assured that everything they could have wanted she had liberally supplied.[13]

The nuns spent five days in St Mary's, Cape Town, where besides the pleasure of shared Dominican interests and the familiarity and comfort of a convent environment, they were advised on various aspects of life on the missions. On the question of lay sisters " dear Mother Dympna told us *one* would never do, that we would feel much inconvenience if we had not soon a second to help Sr. M. Michael, but the servants out here are !!! but as yet we have no work for a second". Mother Thomas, while later assuring Mother Augustine of their loyalty to Sion Hill and the unbreakable bond between the Holy Rosary community and the Mother House, also paid tribute to their Dominican hostesses in Cape Town: "Now good-bye again and may God be ever with you all, we are ever with you in spirit, nothing can ever separate us from the loved ones in Sion - the nearest and dearest we ever met after them are the holy fervent Cape Town Sisters. I cannot tell you how we clung to them and no wonder, for their kindness and affection exceeded everything!" At the end of their visit to the Cape Town Dominicans, the sisters sailed round the Cape to Port Elizabeth, landing on 23 November 1867. They were assured of a warm welcome from their compatriots and the Port Elizabeth society at large for whom, in the early days of their mission, the nuns were a novelty:

> We have had visitors of all creeds and classes - the poor Irish Catholics distinguish themselves by crying with joy at seeing us - one old woman asked at the hall door to see 'the holy women who live here'. M.M. Rose said she'd decline going to her, not being a holy woman. They kneel down to get our blessing, brought a baby to be blessed by the nuns. No end of scenes of this kind if only I had the time to relate them with effect. ... Some fine ladies are lamenting that the Nuns cannot go out and mix among them. They would give such a tone to society! God help us! Sr. M. Baptist has told you of the report of one of us being an Earl's daughter - it was old Dr. Murphy told us this - he says he will not deny it and if asked which it is, he will say 'the tall lady'. So here I am, called by vicious Sisters and Superiors 'the Earl's daughter' ".[14]

Mother Thomas had a keen eye for the social scene and clearly enjoyed the snobbish pretensions of the limited society of Port

Foundresses of Holy Rosary Convent, Port Elizabeth. Mother Rose Whitty is seated second from the right.

Elizabeth, and the rumour that the convent might shelter a lady of blue blood did nothing to lessen the social attraction of the cloistered Dominicans.

Living as they did in the centre of a small town, a port through which many travellers passed, the Port Elizabeth Dominicans, like their sisters in Cape Town, saw and entertained many visitors, most of whom were en route to or returning from distant missions. These included men and women, lay and religious from many countries who, by their visits, their tales of missionary experience or their family or business sagas, kept the sisters in touch with the reality of life in the Colony and increased their awareness of the growth of the missionary church abroad. It also developed that culture of unstinting hospitality which up to the present day, has been a characteristic of the Irish Dominican communities in Southern Africa.

While walls might close them in, and this by their own choice, the nuns missed nothing of the passing scene and, like their Port Elizabeth neighbours, they would greet each newcomer with enthusiasm, and a welcome that was at once practical and genuine. There is little record of the reactions of the local Irish community in Port Elizabeth to the arrival of the Dominican missionaries, but the letters of the nuns to Sion Hill, express an exuberance and joy in life despite the inevitable loneliness and the very straitened circumstances in which the six sisters found themselves. Although the sisters were always short of money, life was never dull. "That reminds me", wrote Sister Baptist Taaffe in November 1868, " that there was great excitement here by a merry-go-round being got up. Rich and poor amused themselves by the novelty. We could not help laughing at the nonsense. I think after some time as they succeeded so well with that they will introduce the other varieties of the Donnybrook". It is not clear whether or not Sister Baptist feared that she might scandalise the lay sisters of Sion Hill by these tales, for she sounds a pious word of caution. "Carnival - there is vice enough without it".[15]

The original house in Port Elizabeth where the sisters first made their home did not shield them from the cheerful distractions of town life right outside their gate, and it is evident that they enjoyed the simple milieu in which they found themselves. According to Sister Baptist, their convent was small and inconvenient:

> This is a great house for draughts. There are two or three doors on every room. Our cottage is considered grand because it has chimneys in it. Very few houses have the convenience

of fire-places - they cook their food in the yard as people used to do at Donnybrook Fair. The want of water is felt very much here. Few houses have pumps or tanks - people buy brackish water in barrels and are glad to get it.[16]

In May 1868, the Vicar General, Dr Murphy, wrote a letter to the superior of Sion Hill apologising for the simplicity of the accommodation which the Vicar Apostolic had provided for her sisters:

I was rejoiced to learn from [your letter] that your children here were not disheartened at our poverty and littleness. Rosary Convent is indeed very diminutive when contrasted with St. Catherine's, Sion Hill. Yet the good Nuns tell me they are quite satisfied. After a little we may be able to enlarge it and make things more comfortable for them.[17]

His relief was understandable since in July 1867 he himself had bought the house for use as a convent and without question it was unsuitable for community life.[18] It was fortunate that the nuns during their first few years on the mission were too involved in the business of running the schools to have time to dwell on the inconveniences of their temporary home. As Sister Baptist wrote :

I have not much news. We meet once a day at late recreation and even then our conversation is much on the schools. Indeed our chief amusement is getting up a dinner or tea party where we can speak. It is no easy task considering we have choice only of the kitchen or reception room, places liable to be invaded at all times. Mother Prioress manages to send our youngsters [boarders] for a walk to the Park by themselves, that is our safest place.[19]

During these founding years of adaptation to the new social and professional environment, and to the spiritual isolation inevitable in the missionary situation, the sisters had little time or opportunity to keep in constant contact with the Cape Town foundation. Their Dominican spirit could only be strengthened by their own efforts and sustained by a liturgy as correct and full as they, with their limited personnel and liturgical expertise, could achieve. On the 4 August 1868 after their first Retreat "as poor missionaries - on a far off desolate, degraded shore", they celebrated St Dominic's feast. For Mother Thomas Kelly this was the first time in 22 years that she had commemorated this day outside her Mother House. Writing to Sion Hill she paid tribute to the liturgical efforts of the Port Elizabeth community: "M.M.

Dominic would have been enchanted had she heard the singing at Mass on Our Holy Father's Day. It was the first time, and we had four children from the Free School to join. They have exquisite voices, but nothing like our own three, who are so much improved that you would not know them. Sr. Baptist never gave out her voice at home as she does here. Sr. Hyacinth is more than you could expect and Sr. Aloysius at vocal and instrumental - an adept". The sisters tried to enhance the celebrations with as much solemnity as possible, and Father Murphy could inform his housekeeper that "they are in full dress on the Hill today". Sister Michael reigned in the kitchen in her white habit, the admiration of the sisters who came to visit her there. This was evidently not her normal clothing for household work.[20]

The second major celebration of the year 1868 was the first Foundation Day, held on the 23 November. Sisters Baptist and Aloysius gave gifts to each member of the community, Mother Dympna receiving a "valuable set of *Jones' Lessons*" and Mother Thomas " a beautiful set of *Quadrilles*". But there was sadness as well and the sub-prioress in a moment of loneliness and depression, wrote to Mother Dominic, her friend and confidant at Sion Hill: "You know my dear Mother, how I cling to old times and old people. How different all classes here are from those at home - you could not *wish* for *nastier* people - no fear of becoming too fond of them - and all the better. God alone must be the Missioner's motto". In her happier moments Mother Thomas would have condemned this as an unfair and prejudiced judgement of the local Port Elizabeth people, Catholic, Protestant and Jewish, who had entrusted the education of their children to the nuns. These parents gave the sisters moral support and showed their appreciation and goodwill in many practical ways.[21] However there was considerable justification for Mother Thomas's expression of disillusionment. Religious bigotry, a common factor involving all religious groups, found frequent public expression in a general condemnation of the life style and educational work of nuns.

For the Dominican nuns their first twelve months in the Colony had been lonely, and it was difficult to take an objective view of opinions and criticisms which were political rather than personal. The sisters had accepted their cramped cottage with a good grace and had thrown themselves into the work of founding and sustaining schools. But though the missionary honeymoon was over and real life had begun to press more heavily on the community, the story of the first year was not without its victories. While Mother Thomas and her colleagues had a right to moments of weariness and depression, they had laid the foundations for an educational mission the evident value of which would become clear only in future decades. The next three years were to see the firm establishment of their mission, the provision of adequate housing for the community and the development of the schools under their charge. For this they needed vocations, educated young women willing to commit themselves to the life of a Dominican missionary nun, not an easy choice in the new world of more rapid travel, burgeoning commerce and the hope of better opportunities for women. With new buildings and a growing community, domestic work also increased, and this in turn demanded the admission of more lay aspirants.

Since the Cape Colony was not so likely to provide sufficient candidates to meet the needs of the schools, the Bishop and the Prioress, Mother Rose Whitty, looked to Ireland both for volunteers, and also for help in the recruitment of personnel. Within ten years of their arrival the community consisted of the six foundresses and nine new recruits. These latter included two professed nuns, Sr Margaret Mary Alacoque Rooney, choir sister and Sr Monica Moore, lay sister and one postulant, Sr Agnes Keon, sent by the Mother House, Sion Hill, in 1870.[22] Two years later a choir postulant, Sr Josephine Hodgens, and a lay postulant entered the novitiate in Port Elizabeth.[23] In 1874 the daughter of a medical doctor, an immigrant, joined the community.[24] This young lady, Louisa Housley, (Sister Dominic) was very acceptable as a choir candidate, and since she was a doctor's daughter, she was highly rated on the social scale. Miss Housley, twenty-two years of age and London born, was the first South African to enter the novitiate of Holy Rosary Convent. In 1875 four postulants, Julietta Whelan, Minna Behan, Ann Kilkinger, and Maria O'Connor, a lay candidate, joined the community from Sion Hill.[25] This gradual increase in community membership eased the burden within the convent and it also made possible the continuation of the work of adult instruction, begun in 1867.

But the business of schools, which was to preoccupy so much of the sisters' time and dominate their conversation even at recreation, took priority over all other concerns. The 20 January 1868 saw the opening of St Mary's Day School with the admission of six pupils. It was not a promising start but for the next four years Mother Rose and her sisters bolstered their income by giving private tuition to young ladies. In 1868 two thirds of their fees came from private pupils, and the following year there were ten girls on St Mary's roll and 21 private students. In 1871 four boarders were admitted bringing the total enrolment up to 18 pupils. Between 1870 and 1902, when the boarding school was transferred to St Dominic's Priory, the enrolment of boarders exceeded 30 only three times, the fluctuations in numbers coinciding with the periods of economic recession in the Colony. St Mary's day school also grew slowly and it was not until 1900 that its numbers exceeded 100 pupils.[26] When it is realised that this total included children from kindergarten to secondary level it becomes evident that the maintenance of such an institution placed a heavy burden on the small community.

The shortage of pupils did not reflect any deficiency in the education provided by the sisters either in this, or in the free schools which came under the control of Holy Rosary Convent . The Catholic population in Port Elizabeth was small, and many families were too poor to pay the modest fees of the private school. This is clear from the 1868 enrolment of St Joseph's Free School. In its first year 205 pupils attended, compared with the six who were admitted to St Mary's Private School. However there were young ladies whose parents sought for their daughters the refinements of female education, French, music, literature, fine needlework, dancing and elegance of manner. For the Dominican nuns the foundation of true refinement was in the development of the spiritual life of their charges, though good social status with a sound financial backing was an added bonus. Neither was there was any doubt in the minds of Mother Rose and her community as to the importance of religious practice and instruction for the pupils in their private and mission schools. Nor did they, within the limitations of their resources, deny to the poorer children the refinements of singing, instrumental music, needlework and drama. It gradually became evident that the schools were gaining public approval. In 1869 Langham Dale, Superintendent General of Education, made his first official visit. He was no stranger to the educational work of Mother Dympna Kinsella and her community in Cape Town. He noted in St Joseph's Free School, Port Elizabeth, which had opened in February of the previous year, a promise of the same competence in school organisation and sound teaching as he had seen in Dominican schools in Cape Town. He found Sister Hyacinth Potter in charge of St Joseph's, with 269 pupils on the roll. In the circumstances she needed all her managerial and teaching skills to maintain the interest of her pupils and the sanity of her staff. Dale's visit passed without mishap and although his official duties did not include the inspection of private schools, he visited St Mary's and gave the sisters the benefit of his knowledge of the educational situation in the Colony and assured them of his goodwill in their regard.[27]

Three months later, on the 26 September 1869, the sisters had a visit from Dr Allard, the Vicar Apostolic of Natal. He was en route to Rome for the Vatican Council and he celebrated Mass for the nuns and the following day "examined the Schools". This interest in the educational work of the nuns, and the examination of schools by clerical visitors, was more in the nature of a social visit rather than an academic exercise. It also provided the clerics with a yardstick by which to measure the standard of their own schools, of which they themselves were the managers and in which they often taught at elementary level, a wide range of subjects. Clerical managers of mission schools, whether Vicars Apostolic or their delegates, were aware that it was not fitting for ladies, and more specifically nuns, to deal directly with government officials. Consequently they usually corresponded with the Superintendent General of Education on behalf of the sister principals. This however did not stop the nuns, when circumstances demanded it, from making direct appeal to the Department of Education. This they did even when there was a good relationship between school manager and the principal. The Vicars Apostolic also interested themselves in the building plans for convents and schools run by religious, and often provided short-term loans for building projects.

The small beginning made in Port Elizabeth, followed the same pattern as that of Sion Hill in its founding years. The community began a long and expensive process of building. The first priority was a dormitory for boarders. This was commenced on 14 September 1869, with financial help from Dr. Moran. The fact that boarders had been accepted increased not only the pressure on the limited space available to the community, but made it imperative to extend the original convent property.[28] By January of 1871, once the schools had been firmly established, Mother Rose Whitty, on the advice of Mgr Murphy their ecclesiastical superior, bought "Mr. Holland's house, incurring a debt of £1650". The nuns took possession of the property on 1 March and by August, with the construction of a boundary wall, paid for by Dr Ricards their new Bishop, their enclosure and privacy were ensured.[29] In January 1872 a piece of ground adjoining the Convent property was bought, and by May of the same year the debt on the Holland property had been cleared by the community, an amazing financial feat in view of the economic constraints under which the nuns lived and worked.[30]

By July of 1871 the classrooms were undergoing alterations at the expense of Dr Ricards, whose financial support, while part of his obligation to the newly established community, was very generous, considering the many calls on his purse. Indeed such contributions were possible only because Ricards, a popular public speaker, raised funds by his sermons and lectures, and used the proceeds to finance his projects and to assist new religious foundations. In 1873 he helped the sisters to clear the debt on St Joseph's with a contribution of £312.11.7, a not inconsiderable sum at that period.[31] Debt incurred for the provision of adequate accommodation in both the mission and private schools was not the only financial burden the community was to accept. In May of 1872, through the agency of Dr Ricards, Mother Rose and her community purchased a new house in the North End of Port Elizabeth, at the cost of £2560.[32] This new property, Star of the Sea, served both as a branch convent and a holiday house for the nuns. During the year 1874 Mother Rose paid off three instalments on the debt and in April 1874, made the final payment. Star of the Sea High School had a short life-span. It was closed in 1876 because there were too few sisters to staff two convents. St Bridget's Mission School was continued by two secular teachers superintended by one of the priests. This school was already flourishing, with an enrolment of 105 pupils when the Dominican community withdrew from the North End. The property was put up for sale, but since there was no immediate offer, it was rented to tenants. It was not until almost five years later, in August of 1881, that the entire property was sold for £2500, at a loss of £60 on the original purchase price.[33]

The disposal of this property, and handing over to secular teachers the responsibility for the two additional schools, enabled the sisters to concentrate on the educational work they had begun in 1868. St Mary's, though a small school, had a good record. Like its sister schools in the Western Vicariate it adapted to the demands of a developing education system. This gradually placed opportunities for higher education within the reach of girls and imposed a multiplicity of examinations which have dominated the educational policy of South Africa until the present time. St Mary's, later named Holy Rosary Convent School, flourished in the present century and made a name for itself in the Eastern Province. It continues its work in Port Elizabeth today as a co-educational school under the name of Trinity High School, still under the aegis of the Congregation of Dominican Sisters, Cabra, but run by a lay principal and assisted by lay teachers.

St Joseph's Free School, which served the local Coloured and African children, made excellent progress under the Dominican nuns. At the outset the sisters were limited to English as the medium of instruction and this often made communication and teaching difficult. Sister Hyacinth a humorous observer of life and human idiosyncrasies, loved her pupils, and though she admitted that she found it strange to hear them chattering together in their own languages, found them eager pupils and soon reasonably adept at English.[34] Sister Baptist Taaffe also noted the speech peculiarities of the mission school pupils: "The children here have such a funny way of speaking, they will always say she instead of her - she wants she bottle - you did not give she clothes. They always call sweets lolley pops and lackers [lekkers], and when children are naughty they grumble in Dutch or Kaffir language".[35] This mixture of languages did not make teaching or learning easy but despite the problems of communication St Joseph's continued to grow rapidly within the official system of education in the Cape Colony. During the first eight years of its existence the school flourished and became a small but steady source of income for the community. The numbers on the roll ranged between 205 in 1868 to 296 in 1874. Between 1875 and 1890 the enrolment declined to below 200 with the exception of 1879 when it rose to 230. During the period 1890 to 1904 the number of pupils dwindled from 85 to 7, clearly a sign to the Education Department that the school was no longer serving that sector of the community for which it had been founded. At the end of 1904 the Government grant was withdrawn and the school was closed.[36] The mid-1890's which saw the decline of St Joseph's, witnessed new Dominican ventures in other parts of Port Elizabeth. The Superintendent General of Education, Dr Muir asked Mother Rose to accept responsibility for the supervision of the North and South End Catholic Schools. The community of Holy Rosary Convent assumed this task from 1 July 1895. According to convent records the two schools were to be considered as branches of the Convent school system and were to be visited regularly by the sisters.[37]

This was a pattern common to Catholic mission schools throughout the Colony. As Dr Muir and his predecessor, Langham Dale, became aware of the teaching ability and management skills of religious communities, they handed over struggling Catholic mission schools to nuns and brothers. Since these institutions were often under the management of priests representing the local bishop, the transfer of responsibility was easily effected. Mother Rose Whitty and Mother Thomas Kelly lost no time in checking the new institutions placed under the care of their community. On the 9 May 1895 they visited St Dominic's, Sherlock Street, Port Elizabeth, one of the schools they had been asked to supervise. The money to finance the building of this school had been donated by the people of St Augustine's parish. There were 61 pupils on the roll and it was run effectively by two teachers, blood sisters, the Misses Mary and Marcella Kennedy.

Mother Rose and her companion found that the organisation of the school and the standard of teaching were "very satisfactory". There is no record at the outset, that nuns were assigned to teach at St Dominic's, perhaps because the Misses Kennedy were so competent at their task. Mother Rose and her companion were less satisfied with the standard of work at the South End school, which was providing subsidised education for European children. It had 69 pupils on the roll and the teaching and organisation were judged to be "very unsatisfactory". On the 1 July 1895 this school was dedicated to the Sacred Heart and placed under the supervision of Sr. Paul Comley. Alice Comley, from Somerset East in the Cape Colony, had entered the novitiate at Holy Rosary Convent in 1883 and was professed in 1885, at the age of twenty-four.[38] She had been teaching for ten years before she entered the convent, so did not lack professional experience. She was the first of a number of Dominicans in Port Elizabeth to teach in this school which continued to serve the local community until well into the twentieth century. She was also one of those nuns dispensed from the rigours of enclosure in order to carry out her professional work. She and those who later taught under the same conditions, travelled daily to "out-schools", in towns and in country districts. This type of regular egress was monitored by superiors lest apostolic need be made a pretext for more worldly interests. Under Dominican control, Sacred Heart Primary School attracted considerable support. However during its first two decades enrolment seldom exceeded 200. Like St Bridget's in Cape Town, it provided a Catholic education for young boys and girl, mainly the children of Irish immigrants, who could not afford private education in institutions such as Holy Rosary Convent School. Sacred Heart Primary continued to serve the community for many years and when it closed its doors, the grants were transferred to St Joseph's, Kabega Park, a private school, opened in 1959. As a state-aided primary school under the auspices of the Cabra Dominicans, this institution, now run by lay staff, still serves the people of Port Elizabeth.

In 1898 the sisters of Holy Rosary Convent opened St Monica's Coloured Primary School at Nelson Street, South End.[39] For over two decades it developed slowly, for seventeen years with an enrolment of less than 100 pupils. For 75 years this school benefitted generations of Coloured boys and girls. In 1938 the founding of Maris Stella Convent at South End ensured more direct apostolic and social interaction between the sisters and the local community. But only 35 years after the opening of this convent, South End was declared by the government to be a group area for Whites only. This application of the Group Areas

Act of 1950 forced the Dominicans to close St Monica's in 1973 and to transfer St Thomas' High School to Gelvandale, a Coloured township outside Port Elizabeth. The following year the sisters withdrew from Maris Stella Convent. Holy Rosary Convent built new premises for St Thomas' High School and it flourished under a Dominican principal. While it did not escape the disruptive consequences of school boycotts and police interference during the 1970's, it survived the last years of the apartheid regime. In 1979 the Congregation of Dominican Sisters, Cabra, handed the school over to the Cape Department of Education. An authentic picture of the work done at South End Dominican schools and the experiences of those who lived there through the worst years of the apartheid era, deserves a fuller canvas than this study can provide.

Mother Rose made another foundation eleven years after the community's withdrawal from Star of the Sea, North End. The decision to open a convent and schools at Uitenhage was made during the 1880's, a time of economic hardship in the colony: "This year [1885] was one of great poverty and depression in business of every kind - in consequence our schools are much decreased".[40] Two years later, in 1887, Mater Admirabilis Convent was opened in Uitenhage. It was a branch house, not an independent convent. The contemporary record makes its position clear: "The convent is not separate from Holy Rosary Convent, Mother Prioress being Superior". Six sisters were appointed to serve in the new community, two of whom were from among the original foundresses of Holy Rosary Convent. Sister Hyacinth Potter, a woman noted for her gentle spirit, was appointed Sister-in-charge. She was assisted in household matters by Sister Michael Morton, the first lay sister of the Holy Rosary community. Four additional choir sisters completed the community; Sister Augustine Keon, 37 years old and professed 15 years, Sister Reginald Gordon, 29 years old and professed nine years, Sister Raymund Dowling aged 33 and nine years professed and the youngest member of the new community, Sister Joseph Scallan, a South African, 23 years old and four years professed.

The community settled in a rented house in Cuyler Street and two years later the Dominicans bought a property in Baird Street for which they paid £600, a sum Dr Ricards had instructed them to borrow. Since at that time money was very scarce, it was not until December 1897 that a decision was taken to build the convent on the new site. It was an ideal place for the sisters, since in 1895 the building of a parish church and presbytery on part of the convent property had been set in hand. The donation of land for the parochial project carried with it certain conditions:

> The Sisters assembled in Chapter unanimously agreed to give
> over to our Bishop a portion of the Convent Ground, 140 ft
> by 58 ft., measured along the hedge of Seven Oaks, for the
> erection of a new Church on the following conditions:
> 1st. That the public entrance to the grounds be outside the
> Convent grounds.
> 2nd. That a choir be built for the nuns at the chancel end of
> the Church, having a grill with a lock and key, which shall
> separate it from the Church.
> 3rd. That an entrance into the Choir opens into the nun's
> Convent or garden.
> 4th. That if at any future time alterations be made to the
> Church, the above conditions be adhered to. This donation
> had already been consented to by the Council of Holy Rosary
> Convent".[41]

This insistence on the rights of the sisters to enclosure within
the church building is remarkable in that it bears no logical
relationship with the practice of egress in vogue at that time.
The nuns were constantly on the road, travelling to and from
Port Elizabeth, going daily to teach in schools outside the convent,
and spending their holidays in non-conventual holiday houses.
In addition the Prioress and her *socia* visited the Uitenhage
convent regularly to hold Chapter and to inspect the educational
work being done by the nuns. It is evident that when it came to
their rights to enclosed space in which to participate privately in
public liturgy, it was quite another question. In May 1896 two
members of the Uitenhage community had to go to Port Elizabeth
to write LLA examinations. What would the rest of the Mater
Admirabilis community do in these circumstances? To the sisters
the logic was clear: "As there was but one Priest in Uitenhage,
the rest of the Community went with them, in order that they
might not be obliged to attend the Parish Church for the Sunday
Mass".[42]

During the first twelve years of the Uitenhage foundation the
nuns had little privacy. They lived above the schools and were
seldom free from the presence of children and their parents. In
February 1898 the new convent building was blessed by the
bishop, Dr McSherry and in April of the same year the nuns took
out a second bond, thereby increasing their debt to £1000. "This
sum and the £750 lent without interest by Rosary Convent,
together with our own savings was sufficient to pay the expenses
of the new Convent".[43] On the 10 September 1898 the sisters
took possession of the house, which was completed before the
parish church.[44] In May of 1899 the church was blessed. The

Dominican Sisters were present at the Solemn High Mass "within their enclosure which became from that day of obligation".[45]

The founding of Mater Admirabilis Convent extended the work of the Dominican community beyond the confines of Port Elizabeth. Holy Rosary Convent had its own urgent need for expansion and the provision of a healthier and more spacious environment for boarders. The only solution open to the community was to borrow money and accept the responsibility for fresh debts. The annalist recorded:

> Purchased 2 houses at the corner of Bird Street and Trinder Reserve. The amount given is £5600, this together with auctioneers dues, transfer fees etc. will amount to nearly £6000. £5600 has to be borrowed at 5%. The property is valuable and when the homes can be pulled down and the ground enclosed, will prove an immense boon to the future community.[46]

Despite this heavy financial burden a new venture was undertaken the following year. "Purchased an estate of 30 acres of ground about 7 miles from Port Elizabeth - this will be called St. Dominic's Priory, Emerald Hill, and will be the site for a new Convent and Boarding School when the means allow of the necessary building and furniture. The estate cost £2000, which was borrowed from the Guardian Assurance Co. at 6%".[47]

At the time of purchase Mother Catherine Behan, was prioress and Mother Dominic Housley sub-prioress.[48] Already the former, although only 40 years old, was feeling the burden of office, as well as responsibility for the growing debt on Holy Rosary Convent. Consequently it was Mother Dominic, accompanied by Mother Rose Whitty, then 69 years of age, who with Bishop McSherry took possession of the Emerald Hill property on 25 April, 1900. "They inspected the home and the grounds remaining the greater part of the day". It is not without interest that just six days after the Dominicans took formal possession of the estate at Emerald Hill, four postulants received the habit and commenced their novitiate at Holy Rosary Convent. Among these was Rita Wilmot, a South African and daughter of John Wilmot, a Papal Count, a Parliamentarian, scholar and author of note and a man of considerable influence in the Catholic community of the Eastern Vicariate and in the local church.[49] Sister Thecla Wilmot was to become one of the outstanding teachers in Holy Rosary Convent. She was a woman noted for her intellectual honesty and unremitting work in the cause of education. After the amalgamation of the Port Elizabeth Congregation with the

Cabra Dominicans she served with competence as a member of Council and as Regional Directress of Studies.

At the end of May 1900 Mother Catherine Behan wrote to the bishop asking permission to resign from her position as prioress. Mother Dominic Housley was elected in her place in June 1900, with Mother Rose Whitty as sub-prioress. Mother Dominic pressed on with her plans, and on 21 December 1900 six choir nuns and three lay sisters moved into their new home, St Dominic's Priory, the branch house at Emerald Hill. Included in this group was the prioress, Mother Dominic, Sister Bridget Neville, 37 years old, and Sister Xaveria Higgins, seven years younger and professed in 1895. Two nuns at the beginning of their teaching career, completed the professional staff. These were Sister Anthony Melia, in her 24th year and only three months professed, and Sister Imelda Best, a South African from Cradock who was professed in 1898 at the age of twenty-four. On 24 January, 1901, the new boarding school at St Dominic's Priory admitted its first 20 boarders, while Holy Rosary Convent provided for the day scholars. To ensure the smooth running of the new convent and school, Mother Dominic remained at Emerald Hill, returning once a week to the Mother House, where the sub-prioress acted as Sister-in-charge.[50]

As in Cape Town, the Dominican communities in Port Elizabeth were highly centralised, and nothing could be organised or decided without the presence and supervision of the reigning prioress or her delegate. This was an approach that was to have a lasting influence on the two communities and persisted even when the individual convents had their own superiors and when in theory, more liberal practices prevailed. However, at the turn of the century the Port Elizabeth community was small and in terms of available personnel, could ill afford the luxury of independent houses and a multiplicity of superiors. Statistics show that at that time the Port Elizabeth Dominicans were suffering from a crippling lack of personnel. In June 1901 there were only 31 sisters, a very small group to deal with the work involved in running three convents and six schools. Recruitment in the colony was slow, and the stream of volunteers from Ireland was drying up. Between 1899 and September 1915, Sion Hill sent one professed choir nun, six choir postulants and two lay postulants to the Port Elizabeth community. Between 1898 and 1920, the community was augmented by 44 recruits, 30 choir and 14 lay postulants. Of these, nine left before profession, three lay and six choir candidates. Of the remaining 35, at least 17 were sent out by Sion Hill, some came directly from Ireland and

Germany, and others from immigrant Cape families, both Irish and German. The first fifteen years of the twentieth century was a period during which the Dominican nuns of Port Elizabeth saw their institutions threatened with closure. Between 1911 and 1914 four choir postulants, the potential teachers of the future, were received into the novitiate, and two of them left, one after only three months of postulancy and the second in her novitiate year. The aging superiors, who had paid off virtually all the major debts incurred at the turn of the century, could do little themselves to ensure the future survival of the community. They had provided at great personal cost, the structures, conventual, apostolic and educational for a future generation. But where were the young women who would bring promise of a new Spring, the future leaders of a more liberal and enlightened age? When hope was at its lowest ebb, Sion Hill was preparing what was to be its last significant contribution to the independent Dominican mission founded in 1867. The year 1915 was to be a good year and the beginning of the revival of the Dominicans in Port Elizabeth. However the rescue was effected not by the young and liberal but by a conservative veteran of forty-eight years.[51]

On 23 October 1915 Mother de Ricci Harkin, a teacher and former Novice Mistress at St Catherine's Convent, Sion Hill, arrived at Holy Rosary Convent with two choir nuns, and four choir and two lay, postulants. However it was not simply the new recruits that changed the fortunes of the community, but the woman, Mother de Ricci herself who had been the inspiration behind this rescue party. A native of Derry, in the North of Ireland, born in 1867, the year Holy Rosary Convent was founded, she displayed many of the authoritarian characteristics of her early politico-religious environment. Small of stature and delicate of build, elegant in dress and fastidious in her habits, she was in spirit an absolute ruler, strong, imperious and indefatigable in the realisation of her goals.[52] On 25 November 1916 at her Silver Jubilee celebration, her role as benefactor was given due recognition: "On this occasion Mother de Ricci was appointed a Mother of Council by the Bishop, as a recognition, on the part of the Community of the great services rendered by the Jubilarian to Holy Rosary Convent in bringing with her such a numerous band of Workers for Our Mission at a time when help was so sorely needed".[53] The sisters took the first available opportunity to confirm their confidence in her. She was elected prioress of the Dominican community of Port Elizabeth in December 1918, and again in 1921, an office well suited to her inclination towards reform, the promotion of strict monastic observance, and the perfection of an attitude of humble obedience in her subjects. Not accustomed to personal involvement in household tasks, she could exact the most meticulous service of others, an ability she also applied to ensure the efficient running of schools. In many respects she was for the sisters, the woman of the hour, and they accepted either with gratitude or at least with patient endurance, the tensions she created in the pursuit of her goals. The results seemed to justify the pressures imposed on them, and for many of the sisters, during the years that followed, she was seen as the saviour of the Dominican mission in Port Elizabeth. This was the moment when the community could feel that its future both as a religious body and as dedicated teachers was assured. It was also an earnest penny of the validity and future progress of the work begun in 1867. After almost 50 years they had only three foundations, managed and run by a relatively small number of nuns. Now in a community with strong and determined leadership, there was a hope of spiritual revitalisation and professional and academic development. It was in a sense a new experience of that quest for spiritual perfection, expressed in every aspect of life, and echoing the memories of the novitiate, the age of spiritual innocence when simple obedience was the answer to every problem.

Chapter Six

Dominican Missionary Women:

The Quest for Perfection

The apostolic obligation of teaching, accepted by the Irish Dominican nuns of Cabra and Sion Hill at a time when the education of Catholic children was a matter of great urgency in Ireland, provided a healthy outlet for the energies, gifts and apostolic aspirations of the sisters involved. The nuns enjoyed corporate confidence as members of a stable community dedicated to education. In this they were more fortunate than other single women, governesses or teachers outside the cloister, who often led lives of isolation and insecurity. Religious discipline was stringent enough, but if gentler attitudes prevailed, the women living within the enclosure with the same community for a lifetime, could find professional satisfaction, peace, security and cultural and spiritual growth. During the nineteenth century, although apostolic opportunities may have been curtailed both by social conventions restricting female activities, and by the limitations imposed by formal enclosure, the nuns met the urgent educational needs of the day with confidence. Within the community the creative Prioress could make the limits of a narrow conventual environment into a world of opportunity. A loving and sensible lay sister would be remembered with gratitude by women whom she had tended and comforted in the lonely childhood exile of a boarding school, even though social contact between the lay sisters and the pupils was not encouraged. A committed and gifted teacher could raise the standard of education for her pupils to heights far above the level of the day. A devoted missionary, even if she had no opportunity to travel to distant continents could and did find her Cuman Tartars within the confines of the convent property or at the gate. And some at least of these sisters would be the inspiration to the modern girls to follow the same vocation. Even the gates could be and were opened, and where charity pressed the road was open too.

The sisters who volunteered for missionary service in the Cape Colony chose the open road, and voluntarily settled in a distant country far from family, and the familiar world of childhood and adolescence. This choice had a profound influence on the ways in which the sisters adapted to their life and work in a world essentially Protestant and conservative. The foundresses of missionary institutions such as Mother Dympna Kinsella and Mother Rose Whitty, were as children, convent educated and later formed in religious life within the rigid conventual and social discipline of Cabra and Sion Hill. They and their companions, were profoundly influenced both by their convent education and by their spiritual training and life experience as members of Irish Dominican communities. However, in the Cape Colony they were in a new and alien environment, where some at least of their Irish conventual and educational ideas would have to be modified to meet the demands of the missionary situation. Although the humble cult of conventual anonymity has deprived us of most of the personal records of the missionary foundations, sufficient evidence has survived to make it possible to study the life and work of these women in the Cape Colony. Whatever else their convent training had done for them it had not deprived them of the spirit of adventure. In this they were women of their times, educated, middle-class, professional, and carrying with them not only their spiritual values and experience in the field of education, but also an old and proven heritage of Irish missionary zeal. These are the women in the case: the leaders, the professionals, the domestic workers. Some came directly from the Irish convents as fully fledged choir nuns or lay sisters. Others, young girls fresh from school, travelled as postulants to an unknown life and destination inspired by missionary ideals. In addition there were the daughters of Irish immigrants already settled in the Cape Colony. These were educated by the sisters in Cape Town and Port Elizabeth, and when their schooling was complete, they threw in their lot with their Dominican teachers. The new generation of Dominicans, those working in Port Elizabeth and Cape Town during the nineteenth century, were the pledge of a missionary thrust that had its spiritual origin in the first foundation made by St Dominic at Prouille in 1206. Those who came from the Irish convents did not develop a totally new way of life or view their work as distinct and fundamentally different from that of the communities which they had left. The candidates who offered themselves in the Cape Colony had been taught and trained as teachers by the sisters, consequently convent discipline was familiar to them. However for those who came to the Cape Colony as postulants or novices the change was great and the process of adaptation not an easy one. "The country was new, the climate was trying, ... labour was not easy to get, and money was not to spare."[1]

Whatever pre-conceived idea they may have had of the missionary life ahead of them, these Dominican missionary women still carried with them the baggage of the past. They were the products of a convent culture, medieval in origin, and this to some extent at least was reflected in the laws, customs and practices which governed their daily lives. Their national heritage, while it was in essence Celtic and Catholic, was profoundly influenced by the norms and standards of the power and restraining force of Roman authority and law. But the Establishment also played a role, and this not least in the spheres of religion, politics and education. The family life of Irish Catholics was generally permeated by a religious spirit which took for granted the superiority of a vocation to the priesthood and the religious life, and recognised that the dedication of a son or daughter to the exclusive service of God, was for the family concerned, an honour and a privilege. For some of those who joined the South African mission between 1863 and the present, the most immediate influence on their choice was a convent education and the example of individual nuns who had taught them. There was also that inner flame, that passion to follow Christ, which defies historical analysis. It drew these young women into a lifelong commitment which even they found both difficult to explain and impossible to resist.

Whether they liked it or not, these Dominicans were also women of the Victorian age, a period noteworthy for aggressive imperialism, in education and religion no less than in politics and economic expansionism. It was also an era of growing feminist protest, expressed initially in the struggle for women's rights to fair educational opportunity. While the conventions of ecclesiastical law and monastic custom did not allow for public participation in political debate, the sisters both in Ireland and in the Cape Colony played a leading role in the development of female education. This was achieved not through public protest or debate but in the classroom, among both the affluent and the poor. The second main expression of late nineteenth century feminist protest, the battle for the enfranchisement of women, found little echo in the life or records of Dominican communities of women. Since these nuns were committed to a life of vowed obedience, were cloistered and seldom saw a newspaper, they could have had little knowledge of the on-going suffragette battles for the enfranchisement of women. While the nuns were familiar with legal voting procedures, decision making within the convent was not normally open to universal vote, and indeed even the prioress and her council were subject to their ecclesiastical superior in many matters. Despite their involvement in educational affairs, nineteenth century nuns were not expected to involve themselves in secular politics or in public protest.

Even in an age where submission in a woman was seen as a sign of good breeding and gentle feminine virtue, the aspirants who applied to the Dominican convents for admission needed radical training to fit them for the rigours of convent life. One of the aims of an effective novitiate regime was to break the worldly ties that bound the novice to her former life. She had to be led into the path of submissive obedience and the pursuit of perfection. The model novice, happily rare, could scarcely be called human, as the following idealised portrait indicates:

> She penetrates herself thoroughly by meditation with the great truths of religion.
> She never commits a fully deliberate venial sin.
> She conceals nothing and wishes nothing concealed from her Superior.
> She is not annoyed when others make known her faults to superiors, and gladly receives undeserved penances.
> She always speaks of things becoming the lips of a Religious.
> Her exterior is so modest that scarcely any defects can be distinguished in it.
> She encourages no natural affection for any one. She opposes self-love in all things, mortifying it with the Superior's leave.
> She gives way to no voluntary listlessness in prayer, reading, or other spiritual exercises.
> She avoids the least infringement of the least rule, thinking nothing little that conduces to perfection.
> She desires often to speak with her Mistress, and to be guided by her in rooting out faults, in acquiring virtues, and in perfecting daily more and more interior and exterior acts.
> Resigned in all things she has no particular preference for any office, occupation or place.
> She is always bright and happy; never gloomy or morose.
> She practises great custody of the senses, always being on her guard against giving too much liberty to her eyes, ears, tongue, etc.
> She 'obeys promptly and devoutly, as to God and not to man, willingly, simply ... and with perseverance'. Ven. Humbert, Master General. 'It is the Key of Obedience that opens the door of Paradise'. St. Catherine of Sienna.

> She never condemns the words or acts of others, always
> putting a favourable construction on what they say or do. 'In
> the book of holy Charity I have learned and studied more
> than in any other; in that volume we learn all things'. Words
> of St. Dominic".[2]

This leaflet given to a young sister in 1889 has the inscription,
"May this be your portrait my dear child". It is a daunting picture
of the ideal novice but one that would have been familiar to the
Dominican sisters in Ireland and in the Cape Colony, not only in
the Victorian era but also until well beyond the mid-twentieth
century. The pursuit of personal perfection in conformity with
the laws, customs and norms of the Dominican community, was
the first aim of novitiate training both in the Victorian and
Edwardian periods and far into the 1950's. While there is no
written record of the feelings and attitudes of the Irish Dominican
at the Cape during the nineteenth century, ample oral evidence
exists for the period 1925 to 1997:

> Religious laws or the application thereof were used as a means
> of control. Conformity was of extreme importance. Very
> valuable sisters were lost because they did not conform in
> little ways. People with originality either had to conform or
> go. It didn't pay to be original. One was punished for
> originality. If you didn't fit into the preconceived idea of
> religious life, you could not survive. This approach was a
> threat to one's integrity. There was a fear motive at the back
> of it all.[3]

Despite the fact that this judgement is supported by numerous
witnesses, Sister Thérèse herself like many of the idealistic
aspirants long before and after her time, did survive without losing
either her creativity, originality or joy in life.

The tyranny of institutionalism and the domination by petty
regulations was not unique to convents. It was common to other
conservative institutions such as training centres for nurses,
army barracks and in naval colleges or on board naval training
vessels. In all of these bodies where effectiveness and efficiency
were seen to demand instant and complete obedience and
conformity to even the most petty of regulations, despotism,
benevolent or otherwise, often prevailed. And despite the idealism
of the young sisters and the good intentions of superiors, a
totalitarian approach both to the temporalities and to the spiritual
aspects of life, was often canonised by usage and convention.
Medieval laws combined with Victorian social expectations of
proper female conduct could well have been seen as appropriate
by the nineteenth century South African missionaries in the Cape

Colony. However the survival and application of these rules fifty or sixty years later certainly suggests a high level of monastic isolation and conservatism, which in the case of the Congregation of Dominican Sisters, Cabra, has its roots in the protracted struggle for recognition of status, and the need to achieve the perfection of observance in every aspect of Dominican life. According to a past pupil of Sion Hill, Sister Vincent Drew, who as an aspirant from Ireland entered the novitiate at Holy Rosary Convent, Port Elizabeth in 1925, the divergence between life in the real world and in the convent was clearly evident: " In customs as well as in reading we continued to live out a Victorian heritage. It was maintained almost as if it were a religious virtue. Religious decorum, such as was practised at that time was really the perpetuation of dead social norms".[4]

This was especially the case in a milieu where both the role of women and proper feminine virtues, were narrowly defined and closely monitored, usually by men, lay or clerical. For many of the girls who entered the communities of Cabra or Sion Hill in the nineteenth century, the novitiate regime, though probably painful, would have come as no surprise. In spiritual exercises, discipline, isolation from worldly influences, the public confession and correction of faults, silence and the development of responsibility for 'charges', there was little to distinguish school life from the convent regime. Even during school vacations when pupils might expect to be free from conventual restraints, they were hedged round by regulations and admonitions: "Vacation is given as a recompense for past applications, and as a preparation for future assiduity. It is not a time that will be unclaimed by God, or which may be unfruitful in merit". The relevant school rules clearly lay down the proper approach to both the spiritual and the social obligations of a Cabra pupil during vacation:

> Therefore the pupils will prepare for it diligently, resolve to adopt proper means of persevering in fervour, and agree upon some prayers for the same end, and promise one another, a mutual remembrance before God during the time of vacation. They will make their prayers and Meditations, and approach the Sacraments as they were accustomed to do in St. Mary's. ... The pupils will make it a study on all occasions to yield to the good will of parents - to be self-denying, ever ready to serve and to oblige, polite to all - minutely attentive to the wants of others. They will contribute gaily and sweetly to the gratification of their Brothers and Sisters, in a word strive to promote the happiness of all around them.[5]

This was a form of admonition, formulated in monastic terms, that was familiar to the novice. Social graces and polite consideration for others were valued highly. And for a gently bred young lady, subdued cheerfulness and a smile rather than audible laughter, indicated a happy aspirant, and won the approval of both the Mistress and her companions in the novitiate.

The rules of etiquette played an important part in the preparation of young ladies for their role as home makers and mothers. Nor were these social skills less important for those who were destined to move from the classroom to the cloister. Indeed without a sound understanding and practical experience of the social norms and customs of the day, and an informed acceptance of the proper position of women in society and in the church, it would not have been easy to find acceptance or to persevere in religious life. In superior convent schools as in secular institutions of the same standard, instruction in the right conduct for a lady in all circumstances, was a daily event. In Sion Hill the Assistant Mistress read aloud for ten minutes each day "selected portions or passages from Modern books on etiquette for the young lady Boarders". Even the choice of texts was laid down: *Modern etiquette in private and public: Christian politeness, manners and tone of good society,* with its companion volume, *Society small talk,* or *What to say and when to say it,* were recommended for this purpose.[6]

While small talk had no place in the cloister, polite and attentive silence during recreational gatherings was as much a sign of good breeding in the convent as it was in the drawing room. For boarders the rule of silence governed their lives from morning until night and from night until morning. This was common in most boarding schools but in the convent schools it was linked with religious observance, and all residents, children as well as nuns, were controlled by it. Not only was silence strictly imposed at appropriate times and in special places but in certain cases conversation was forbidden with one or other category of person . In Sion Hill boarders were "forbidden to speak *to day-pupils* when they happen to meet them".[7] The choir nuns, in terms of their constitutions, were also subject to the same kind of regulation. They were not permitted to hold conversation with novices or lay sisters except on special feast days, nor indeed with each other except at fixed times of formal recreation. Silence was seen to be "one of the most important points of religious observance". The Constitutions approved for the Dominican community at Port Elizabeth in 1888, note the ordination of the General Chapter of the Order held at Rome in 1608:

> We ordain that the most holy law of Silence, so strongly recommended by our Fathers, and whose observation offers so many spiritual advantages in Religion, be kept with great care and diligence. Superiors who neglect to punish very severely transgressors of silence, should themselves be punished very severely.

Three years later, in 1611, the Chapter held at Paris confirmed this:

> We ordain that the most salutary Constitution which commands the observance of Silence, in certain places and at certain times, be observed with much care and diligence. We charge for the day of Judgement of Jesus Christ the conscience of Superiors if they do not punish, with the greatest severity, the daring violators of the holy law of Silence.[8]

For the novices as well as professed sisters silence was one of the essential elements in conventual life. Novices were "not to speak in forbidden times or places without permission".[9] In addition it was argued that the "complete and constant *isolation* of the Simple and Professed, is, in the hands of Superiors, one of the most powerful means for the maintenance or reform of observances in the Convent". Whether or not it promoted reform is a moot question. It certainly ensured that there was little real, creative communication within a community where the regulations were rigidly applied. This was especially the case among novices and young professed sisters, not only in the nineteenth century but also until the changes brought about by Vatican Council II. The following expresses the opinion of a significant number of sisters in the Region of South Africa:

> We lived like institutionalised hermits, cut off from each other by silence. Conversations were only permitted at recreation times and exclusive conversation was never acceptable. Our cells were sacred, private and places of silence. Only the superior could come in there. We were cut off emotionally by silence and by other rules and regulations from the support of our peers.[10]

What is not in doubt was the value of hallowed silence to a prioress wishing to eliminate criticism, positive as well as negative. However the superior could deviate from rules pertaining to social isolation "in order not to render the yoke of Religious Life too heavy for the young Sisters".[11] The mistress of novices was expected to teach her charges "to show reserve in their words, ... and when obliged to speak, always and everywhere to say what is useful".[12] There was always a danger that a strict application of the law of silence would prevent discussion on what was useful, or even essential for the good of the community and the individual. This was realised by some of the nuns in South Africa in the 1950's, a time at once characterised by a spirit of close conformity to the law and an urgent official pursuit of perfection. It was also the decade during which a number of sisters who had been through the Kerdiffstown novitiate and had taken up their work in South Africa, began to question seriously the value and sense of certain regulations under which they were obliged to live. Among these was the fanatical enforcement of silence. In St Mary's Convent, Cape Town a number of discussions took place, all officially infringements of silence. Members of this informal discussion group accepted that monastic silence was important for prayer and study, both essential elements in Dominican life. They also agreed that no regulation inside or outside the convent could control gossip or criticism, and that greater openness and a more flexible approach to the law of silence, would to some extent, obviate the need for secret, and sometimes seditious conversation. These sisters came to an agreement that they would speak in private to anyone who needed their help, and this at any time, including the hours of profound silence. They also decided to watch their words especially during recreation and devised a signal which said, "Stop! Change the topic. We are on dangerous ground". The basis for this decision was the law of charity which is above all other regulations. It was not speaking that mattered so much as what was said and where, and above all for whom. Nor did it seem to matter then how the love of Christ was expressed as long as our voices were available to those in need.[13]

However in the Irish Dominican novitiates between 1850 and 1960, it was also a matter of great concern that the speech of the novices should reflect not only the spiritual ideals to which they aspired, but also the intonation and accent befitting young ladies destined to teach in the select schools. In the novice as well as in the pupil of Dominican schools, good diction and a pleasing accent could indicate a superior family position in society or disguise a deficient social background. This was recognised by the nuns, the success of whose schools depended on the ladylike qualities of their pupils. According to the 1914 school rules of Immaculata, Cabra:

> Pupils are required to take great pains to correct any defect in manner or accent, and to make earnest, persevering efforts to acquire a ladylike easy manner, and a refined pleasing

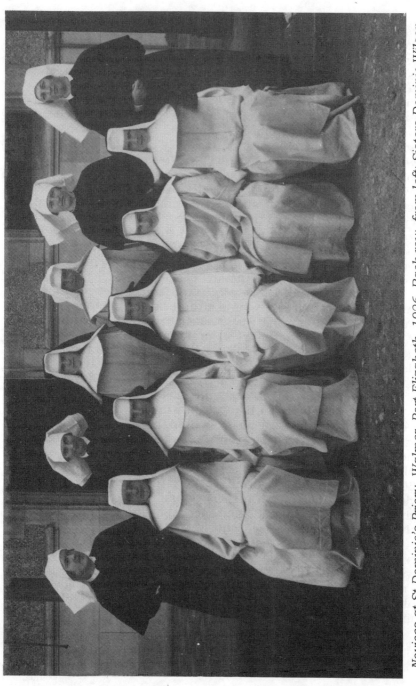

Novices at St Dominic's Priory, Walmer, Port Elizabeth, 1926. Back row, from left: Sisters Dominic Wilson, Lucy Maher, Elizabeth Oldham, Monica Carr, Evangelist Raleigh, Vincent Drew. Front row, from left: Sisters Alphonsus Cummins, Emily O'Keeffe, Margaret Mary Hogan, Bernard Mackesy, Benvenuta Ivers.

accent. To secure a marked improvement in accent, manner and bearing requires constant persevering effort, and no one should be so wanting in Common sense as to allow human respect or shyness to prevent her from doing all possible to improve in these essential points.[14]

According to the same rules what was appropriate in the speech of young men could not be condoned in the case of young women. Pupils were to remember that it was "contrary to all etiquette and ladylike demeanour to make use of vulgarisms, slang or certain phrases, which used by their brothers, would be harmless and inoffensive, but when spoken by young Ladies would betray a great want of self respect and refinement".[15] However the novitiate was not a simple extension of the typical Dominican school with its socially privileged pupils and its familiar rules, enforced by favourite nuns. What applied in the schools as regulations for the guidance of young ladies, became in the novitiate rigid laws, and aspirants soon realised the value of verbal discretion both in public and even in private conversation. But for the novice it was not simply *what* was said that mattered but *how* she enunciated her words. Accent revealed the social status and regional origins of the speaker, and this was especially the case for the sister assigned to read in the refectory during mealtimes. Here the novice exposed her own eccentricities in accent and pronunciation, and where the standard was less than acceptable, verbal correction was swift and often painful. Fortunately many of the young aspirants were accustomed to the stringent demands of their teachers, and they also accepted in this as in many other matters of discipline, that they were being trained in humility and perfect obedience, even when the testing methods of the novitiate sometimes included the use of unjust accusation and unkind reprimand.

Instructions on all aspects of daily life familiar to the Victorian schoolgirl, were applied with equal rigour not only in the pre-amalgamation novitiates, but also in Kerdiffstown during the mid-twentieth century. This Irish novitiate common to the whole Congregation, which opened in 1941, was to be the binding force of the new young recruits who flocked in during the post-war years. It did indeed train these girls, the majority for the Irish convents but also a significant number of volunteers for the mission in South Africa. While in theory the ideal of a full Dominican life was presented to the aspirants, in practice the reality was very different. In the new age of enfranchised women many of the outmoded regulations and other mechanisms of social control, that had served novice mistresses in Ireland and

South Africa in the past, were applied without discrimination. The young Congregation of Irish Dominican Sisters, uniting the convents in Ireland (1928) and South Africa (1938) that had their roots in Cabra, Dublin, was achieved with much pain and mutual sacrifice. Nevertheless, like its missionary foundations across the world it too continued to carry too much of the impedimenta of the past. It united communities with strong individualistic concepts as to their own correct interpretation of what was and what was not Dominican life, and what was appropriate for the training of novices. It also brought together a body of remarkable Dominicans, strong, self-confident women of vision and intellectual ability, and authoritarian men. These worked together with enthusiasm and zeal to form from the scattered foundations of the past, a *perfect* Congregation of Dominican Sisters. Although it was a difficult goal to achieve, the pursuit by the Congregation was relentless. This was evident from the purist approach to Canon Law and above all in the scrupulous application of the minutiae of often outdated Dominican customs governing liturgy and everyday life. It was difficult for the novice to separate the essential from the trivial when often petty regulations jostled for greater attention, often obscuring for young neophytes, the fundamental elements of religious life.

This approach took cognisance neither of the rising tide of change in the role and mission of women in the church, already evident in the 1920's, nor of the need to apply more modern principles of the social sciences to the formation of aspirants. It was not until the late 1950's that the whole question of training programmes for novices was given serious attention and even then the forces of a long conservative tradition were difficult to break. In the nineteenth century there had been some correlation between contemporary social norms and novitiate regulations, and the aspirant, striving for religious perfection could adapt to a more rigid code of the cloister. But for the modern girl of the mid-twentieth century, although also a product of a conservative society, reversion to Victorian norms of conduct and the petty tyrannies of the novitiate, were at best accepted as a test of vocation, at worst as an insuperable obstacle to a genuine call to Dominican life.

Novitiate experience varied. Much depended both on the suitability of the mistress of novices and her assistants and on the personality, life experience and background of the candidate. Those involved in formation were not themselves free. They had to satisfy superiors that proper discipline was being imposed, that candidates were making spiritual progress, that the *Constitutions* were being taught and applied, and that the novices were learning to conform in all things to the obligations, to which by religious profession, they would commit themselves to God's service for life. Aspirants represented all personality types, each with her own preconceived ideas as to what to expect in the convent and what would be demanded of her in return. All were certain it would be a difficult and trying experience, and indeed it was. During this time of formation some accepted the discipline without question but this was not always the case. For the majority of those sisters who have shared their views on the novitiate for the period under review, between 1938 and the late 1950's, most confessed that they had maintained a low profile and endured a regime which they experienced as narrowly repressive and in some cases, personally destructive. Aspirants were treated as children not as adults. They had no real contact with community sisters or with the reality of normal conventual life. The law was the thing and strict adherence to the letter of the law left little opportunity for the normal celebration of youth. In this Dominican novitiate for women there was no free access to books, and even spiritual reading was strictly controlled. Consequently there was little intellectual challenge and no facilities for private study. Only youthful exuberance, a sense of humour, prayer and a strong confidence in their own vocation, made certain aspects of novitiate life endurable, even happy, for most of the novices. Some emerged from their novitiate years in urgent need of healing. Others abandoned the life and returned to the world. What is remarkable however is that so many survived the experience and found in the post-Vatican years, freedom from a neurotic concentration on personal perfection, fresh inspiration in their religious dedication, and spiritual fulfilment in the apostolic opportunities opened to them.

To do justice to historical truth it must be conceded that in Kerdiffstown in particular, the facilities were poor and often the numbers were too large for effective personal communication and formation. This resulted in the application of control mechanisms to the detriment of the spiritual training and the individual guidance of novices. Constant surveillance and limited opportunities for legitimate self-expression led to tensions and fears of dismissal for minor infractions of the rules. It was not a healthy environment in which to develop that freedom of spirit characteristic of Dominican life. Criticism of the regime was frowned on in all novitiates, but this was not conducive to openness demanded by tradition of the perfect novice. If the discipline of the novitiate put iron in the soul of the aspirant, perhaps it could be argued that it also provided an essential buttress to the spirit of those women about to face the storms of the modern world. However it was an argument that could not be justified in the circumstances. For the modern woman the imposition of silence regarding matters of grave importance, often put them in conflict with principles of intellectual integrity, inculcated in the best Dominican schools both in South Africa and Ireland. It is not surprising therefore that for many of the young professed sisters, normal community life, study and teaching confirmed for them what one novice mistress claimed, "that whatever else it was, the novitiate was not a model of Dominican life as it is truly lived". That this was not always the case is confirmed by records, written and oral, of earlier novitiates of both South Africa and Ireland prior to 1941. Those young women who completed their novitiate in either Potter's Bar or Tamnaharrie had a different experience. The training in Potter's Bar may have been less rigorous, but youthful exuberance was given an outlet, and aspirants did not experience the tensions and pressures, inevitable in a large, tightly controlled group.[16]

However, even in pre-amalgamation days there is no record of a perfect novitiate. One of the main criticisms of earlier formation programmes was that the novices were constantly in a school environment. The ideal of isolation from the world during the novice's canonical year, a matter of law from 1917 onwards, was often overtaken by the urgent needs of the classroom. In the South African foundations postulants continued their training as pupil teachers and novices participated, to some extent, in the active apostolate in the schools. As late as 1917 when the education of sisters was becoming a matter of urgency for the Cape Town Dominicans, the Provincial proposed "that the Education Department be approached on the subject of making the Noviceship a Pupil Teacher's Training Centre, with a Method Mistress in receipt of Government Salary".[17] In 1918, at the very time of the strict application of the laws regarding canonical novitiate were being enforced by the church, the Council proposed that "Novices [were] to complete their course of Pupil Teacher training before profession". While this curtailed the time given to instruction in liturgy, prayer and study of the Constitutions, it also created an awareness for both the Mistress and her subjects of the active, apostolic vocation for which the young aspirants were being prepared. According to the revised Code of Canon Law (1917), the canonical year of novitiate was for training in the spiritual life and not a time when novices should be involved in active apostolic work. That the withdrawal of postulants and novices from active involvement in the work of the schools caused staffing problems, is clear from the records, not only of Cape Town but also of Port Elizabeth, the Irish convents and in the

Dominican foundations of New Zealand and Australia. For aspirants who had some teaching experience during their novitiate years, the link between novitiate discipline and the school rules which they themselves applied in the classroom, placed novitiate regulations in perspective. At the very least the novices could see in practice the value of good order in their chosen field of apostolic work and accept the restrictions of their own lives as a necessary preparation for their future role as religious teachers.

For many of the sisters who entered in the nineteenth and early twentieth centuries the religious training in the novitiate was adequate enough to ensure admission to reception or profession. In some cases at least the novice mistress was seen as a loving guide. Mother Francis Gunn who served for a time in that difficult office at Tamnaharrie, the pre-amalgamation novitiate set up by the Irish Dominicans of Port Elizabeth, is remembered with affection:

> She was very gentle and approachable, very understanding and kind. I was a postulant in Tamnaharrie in 1933 and we all loved her. We did our novitiate in Holy Rosary Convent in Port Elizabeth. It was a big change but I was very happy and had no regrets about becoming a Dominican. We were kind of lay sisters but we never thought about the distinction. We accepted it as a part of religious life. I didn't think that the discipline was too strict. It was what I expected. My only disappointment was that I was not able to do active missionary work.[18]

On the question of religious training received by the novices of that pre-amalgamation period, opinions differed widely. Generally it was accepted that the spiritual training was "nothing special". However the novices were part of a larger community and were made secure in the spirit that prevailed in the convent:

> We had togetherness in prayer and we celebrated the big feasts. It brought us peace, and of course we had each other. Discipline was very strict but we did not question that. Now [1991] you have to think for yourself. The individual has to be reliable and responsible in a way we did not know then. No one said we should develop ourselves and grow, as they do today. We learned not to speak. That is one reason why I found the Western Cape very different in little ways and in spirit. The sisters were more ready for personal confrontation. This would have been impossible when I was young.[19]

One sister looking back to the novitiate at Holy Rosary Convent in the early 1940's recalled how her very strict, but fair and just

Novice Mistress defended her novices when they came under attack by members of the community. Her training in the theory of religious life, apart from the normal study of the Constitutions, concentrated mainly on the Divine Office and writing on religious topics. The constraints of the novitiate and the survival of the individual under such difficult circumstances, were in her opinion proof enough of a true Dominican vocation.

> I never, never thought of leaving the novitiate. I wanted to be a Dominican and look at us now [1991]. The changes are tremendous, a sort of emancipation. Some things have gone haywire but we are no longer encaged. While we must be sure that our opinions are sound we can be grateful for renewal in religious life. Life is marvellous, very different from our young days. Now, women are getting their rights, and about time. This is life as it should be and we can now make our contribution *our* way.[20]

For Sister Lucia McDermot who entered the Cabra novitiate in 1929, life was very peaceful and quiet. Her novice mistress, Mother Jordan Hardy was a "gentle, holy and quiet nun. She never harangued us and we all looked up to her. Some considered her to be too lenient. She did not correct us often". Like most of her contemporaries in Ireland and South Africa, Sister Lucia never saw a newspaper in the novitiate, but had to limit her reading to spiritual books which they could freely choose. "Each novice had a personal copy of *The Everyday life of a Religious*, a commonplace book, not at all inspiring". The small volume, *Catechism of the vows* had to be studied as it was the basic text for the canonical examination for novices before profession. It served at least as a useful source of information, while the *Imitation of Christ* "was very depressing. Daily reading and constant repetition dulled the impact". It was certainly not a programme to stimulate the mind or to encourage the young sisters to pursue intellectual studies, even in the sacred sphere.[21]

However the fundamental task of the novice mistress was "not merely to enlighten [the novices'] intelligence". Indeed this was of less importance than the formation of character and development in the will of all virtues. Ideally such a programme demanded constant vigilance on the part of the mistress whose task it was "to watch over the dispositions and natural inclinations of the Novices".

> [She is to] take opportunity when occasion arises, *or even make opportunity if desirable*, to moderate in each irreligious propensities, especially such as forwardness and obstinacy

in their own opinions, vanity in their conduct, a certain air of brusqueness or offhandedness, curiosity, egotism, love of ease, etc., and she shall endeavour to bring out of them frequent acts of true humility and self-renunciation.[22]

This placed a heavy responsibility on the mistress, while at the same time it gave her great power over the lives of the aspirants. For the novices as for those in charge of their training in religious life, the novitiate year could be a time of stress and painful adjustment. The standard of conduct demanded of them was daunting and often bore little relation to gospel values. Where the strictures of the law were ameliorated by the wisdom, kindness and good humour of the mistress of novices, most young girls, secure in their vocation, moved with confidence to full membership of the community. However, as has already been noted, this was not always the outcome of novitiate training. Some novice mistresses applied the regulations with scrupulous attention to petty detail. Where conformity was king and individuals had to fit neatly into the accepted pattern of perfection, the casualties were the more creative and less pliable. These found many of the practices trivial and the penances unjust. It was in the formation of these latter aspirants that the system found its justification:

> The novices must learn how to take corrections and reprimands; not to excuse themselves, unless it be necessary for higher spiritual motives; to always keep guard over their affections, so as not to become attached to any creature; that they should always be amiable and courteous towards everybody, and not insist on their own opinions.[23]

Constitutions and customaries nowhere demanded that the Novice Mistress should be chosen for rigidity or severity of temper. Indeed this was a office most difficult to fill, especially so in first missionary communities where experienced sisters were scarce and training in formation informal. The ideal novice mistress like the ideal novice was impossible to find, but Directories attempted to formulate the qualities necessary for the task as well as the duties to be performed:

> The Mistress of Novices should be prudent and mature, and capable of instructing the Novices in those things which they will have to practice when professed. She must be well instructed, of exemplary life, given to prayer and works of mortification, prudent and charitable, uniting affability with gravity; have a zeal for God tempered with meekness, removed from all passion, especially from anger and impatience; one

in short, who is fitted to give them an example of every virtue
and who will seek rather to be loved than to be feared by
them.[24]

It should be remembered that often enough in the Dominican
novitiates in both nineteenth century Ireland and the Cape
Colony, novice mistresses were appointed who were neither
mature nor experienced. Some had been professed for only a
year or two, and were not much older than their charges, though
this was not always the case. Others by temperament were
unsuited for so onerous and powerful a position within the
community. There were also those who in the early decades of
the twentieth century, were too old to deal with the needs and
problems of young girls. They had been in positions of authority
for a lifetime and often perpetuated outmoded social norms and
petty regulations to the detriment of individual aspirants, and to
the development of religious life in the twentieth century.

This was to be the pattern for the future in both Cape Town
and Port Elizabeth: young women applied for admission to the
convent, some persevered and others left, either of their own
account or requested to do so by the Prioress or by the bishop.
For girls just out of school it could be a lonely life, especially in
the early founding years when a shortage of personnel and
limitations of space made the establishment of an adequate
novitiate difficult to achieve. The teaching nuns were overworked
and it was seldom possible to provide the novices with a Mistress
who could give more than a small fraction of her time to their
instruction. Indeed the novices, isolated in community, often had
to adapt to a situation where there was no one in whom to confide
or with whom to discuss the life in the novitiate, or to recall
happy memories of home and family. For the school girls there
were good friends with whom to share news, complaints and
gossip about the daily mishaps and inevitable confrontations
with authority. For the novice the official situation was somewhat
different. Particular friendships were banned both in the schools
and in the convents, and this well into the second half of the
twentieth century. Pupils could and did ignore this regulation
but the novice did not enjoy the same freedom. In the novitiate
and later in full community life, there was no incentive to share
family histories or personal confidences unconnected with
professional work. Indeed novices were forbidden to discuss
personal or family matters, prohibitions that went far to isolate
them from each other and from their identity as members of their
own families. For those candidates whose families lived in the
Cape Colony, visits from parents and brothers and sisters were

still a possibility, but such visits were infrequent and brief, and the nuns were never permitted to discuss their life or any internal business of the community. Those novices were fortunate who in their school days had been trained at either Cabra or Sion Hill in the elements of restrained social interaction. The school rules prohibiting special friendships put into perspective the more rigid novitiate regulations.

In Cabra the pupils were "forbidden to form exclusive parties or particular friendships" because they were "the cause of disunion, unhappiness and dissatisfaction and ... in every way contrary to the Spirit of union and charity".[25] In conversation the pupils were to "avoid with the utmost care every fault contrary to charity", and they were to treat each other with the utmost kindness avoiding too much familiarity: "Pupils are required to be at all times most reserved regarding the affairs of their companions, making no inquiries concerning them, their families, pursuits, etc. Such curiosity betrays a littleness of mind and renders one unworthy of being ranked amongst the pupils of St. Mary's". It could have been an embarrassment to the nuns running an exclusive school, since not all who could afford a private education had the social rank that many parents would expect of the daily companions of their own children. This interpretation is supported by the fact that pupils on vacation were requested "not to correspond with their companions. When school days are over they should avoid unnecessary letter-writing as a cause of waste of time and money". The nuns believed that "refinement and self respect should prevent any pupil intruding letters or visits without the sanction of her own parents and the approval of the Parents or Guardians of her friends".[26] These regulations, though they do not appear in any specific text of the constitutions, were still being applied in the novitiate of the Congregation of the Irish Dominican Sisters from 1938 until Vatican II reforms changed the whole approach to religious formation.

Despite the inherent snobbery revealed in many of the minor, convent school regulations, the nuns took a serious view of their role as educators. The original prospectus of Cabra published in 1835, condemned the contemporary approach to fashionable, female education. The position of the Dominican teachers, and their goal as educators, was made clear:

> The Nuns solely intent on being usefully employed in promoting the temporal and eternal welfare of their pupils, will not in any manner sanction the imprudence of parents, who attach undue importance to what is called a fashionable education, waste time and money in having their children

taught, to the exclusion of useful and necessary knowledge, accomplishments for which they have neither taste, capacity nor use. No fashion is recognised in this Establishment but such as becomes the children in their respective stations in life, at the same time no effort shall be left untried to make them acquainted with the nature and fitness of things, that should circumstances permit them fairly to rise in society, they will naturally fill them with propriety, ease and dignity.[27]

It was not the nuns' intention however to educate them in such a way that they would grow "restless and unhappy in their proper sphere, or prematurely urge them to change their positions in society at the risk of incurring ruinous expense, and involving their families in endless miseries".[28]

This was the social, educational and spiritual background of many of the sisters who joined the convents of Cabra and Sion Hill and came to South Africa between 1863 and 1920. They had a strict upbringing and a sound education according to the accepted standards of the day. Above all the nuns had ensured that they were well versed in Christian doctrine and had what was virtually monastic training in religious practice and discipline. This solid background in what was a secure and happy school environment, made entry into the convent to some extent, a natural process and a continuation of a familiar life style. However there was one essential difference. These young women, caught up in that indefinable desire to give themselves wholly to God, were now potential members of a specific Dominican community and had to be formed in virtues and social practice appropriate to their calling. Those who had absorbed lessons in the graces appropriate to a young lady in the world, could as teachers impart these skills to their pupils, but the cloister had its own norms, social and spiritual. To accept the restraints of monastic living, and at the same time keep alive the bright flame of love that had inspired the request for admission into the convent, was not a task for the faint-hearted.

Not all the candidates for the missions were former Dominican pupils though most were the products of convent education. However the Irish Dominican tradition was strong enough to ensure that the best aspects of the Irish novitiate training were transplanted successfully on African soil. There it was, in many respects, an exotic growth and over the early decades of development, adapted to the alien environment. Those who were trained in the novitiates in the Cape Colony were not subjected to some of the more rigid applications of the minutiae of the law, and they never experienced the full restraint of monastic enclosure. Nevertheless they could not easily escape the petty tyranny of trivial and narrow social norms. Many of these had little to do with spiritual perfection but were useful tools that promoted the smooth running of the community. The need to control the least daily activity in the convent was not a nineteenth century phenomenon. The new Customary drawn up by Gijlswijk and promulgated in 1924 for the Provinces of Cape Town and Port Elizabeth, expresses a narrowness of vision and a need to regulate the most insignificant of the daily activities of the sisters. In the post-war world of the 1920's the role of women in society was changing, but this had little effect on convents where the superiors had been in office for thirty or more years, and where Victorian and Edwardian values and constraints persisted without change.

Despite the conservative nature of religious life, the postulants who joined found what they had expected: a group of like-minded women dedicated to community life, prayer, obedience, voluntary poverty, chastity and apostolic work. The superior spoke with the voice of God and who could gainsay that? The little rules and regulations were sent to try the new aspirants, and if they were petty, so were the school regulations, and they had survived those. The new recruits were young and idealistic, and above all they believed that they had a special vocation for Dominican life. In the truest sense of the word, they were in love. Even those who found the reality of religious life painful could not easily reject the call, and when the novitiate came to an end and the sister began her career as a teacher, there was a healthy outlet for the energy and creativity of youth, and a remedy against the frustrations of an over-regulated life.

The goal of the novitiate, profession and full acceptance as member of the community, was not achieved by the sole efforts of the novice. The final approval of a candidate was a matter for the community represented by the prioress, the novice mistress and the discreets. These members of the Council, had studied her character, attitudes, spiritual progress and her ability to participate in the life and work of the community, and voted according to their insight in her regard. This was not always an easy decision since there was no formal training of the Dominican superiors or novice mistresses either in Ireland or in the Cape Colony. In most instances the prioress and the novice mistress had to build on their own life experience, and this could make the task of formation and discernment the more difficult, indeed often haphazard. However the *Constitutions* clearly laid down the laws of the Church in respect of choice, admission, testing and training of those who applied and were admitted into the convent, and at no time in the history of the two Dominican communities in the Cape Colony is there any evidence that these laws were either unfamiliar or ignored. The libraries of St Mary's, Cape Town and Holy Rosary Convent, Port Elizabeth had much the same literary resources as those of the Mother Houses in Ireland, and commentaries on religious life, the vows, prayer and meditation and the quest for perfection were equally available to superiors and sisters alike. A diligent mistress could present a novice for reception of the religious habit or for profession who was word perfect in her knowledge of the obligations of the religious state, but no one would expect her to have the experience or perfection of practice which is the work of a lifetime. The perfect novice was the ideal, and one seldom realised:

> She passes from the Noviceship to the Community so well formed, that is with such a hatred for all sins and imperfections, with such a love of virtue and perfection, that she will live as religiously, perfectly, and prudently alone as she would under the eyes of the most revered Superior. Begin then generously; a good beginning is half the work. 'If you begin', says St. Bernard, 'begin perfectly; for if you perfectly begin you will quickly arrive at the summit of perfection. On the other hand, if you do not begin well you may never afterwards acquire the true spirit of your holy state'.[29]

To reach this enviable state the novice mistress had to instruct her charges in "the daily actions, the daily duties, the daily defects, the daily prayers, the daily difficulties, the daily helps and hindrances, the daily perfections and imperfections of the ordinary life of a religious".[30] It is clear that the standard set was high and that it required of those appointed to the office of novice mistress a mature level of spiritual and psychological insight. It also demanded endurance and a sense of humour in the neophytes who were the object of such intensive programmes of formation. In practice, in Ireland as well as in South Africa, postulants and even novices had to assist in teaching in the schools and the care of children. Where foundations were young and superiors often no more than a year or two out of the novitiate themselves, the niceties of ecclesiastical law and the urgency of acquiring perfection rapidly, gave way before the pressing demands of school and the apostolate.

The apostolic aspect of Christian life had been stressed in the Irish Dominican schools for young ladies. This is clear from the vacation regulations of Immaculata, Cabra:

It is particularly recommended to the children during vacation
and after they leave school to assist their parochial clergy in
teaching the Catechism. Thus, they will prove their grateful
sense of the mercies of God towards themselves - thus, they
will co-operate with their Divine Saviour in the great function
of the salvation of souls.

This was certainly a Dominican approach and one that fitted
into the accepted social role and duty of all young Christian ladies,
Catholic or Protestant, in the home or in the cloister.[31] The novices
had the advantage of a training in doctrine and spirituality which
was apostolic in focus. Generally the age for admission, fifteen
years, ensured that in the nineteenth century, responsibility came
to the young and formation was often, though not always, in the
hands of those barely out of their teens. It was fortunate for the
missionary foundations that in many instances they received
from Ireland some sisters who were already professed and fairly
well established in religious life. These became the leaders among
those professional women dedicated to the apostolate of teaching,
who carried the work of the Irish Dominican nuns from the more
sheltered environment of Cabra and Sion Hill to the Cape Colony.

Chapter Seven

The Professionals

The term professional, while seldom applied to women in the nineteenth century, was especially appropriate for vowed religious, men and women. Nuns and brothers together with priests who were members of religious orders or congregations, made public profession of the vows of obedience, poverty and chastity. Profession was a solemn declaration of the individual's intention to undertake a firm commitment and make public witness to a life totally dedicated to the service of God. This was the fundamental aim of the novitiate training and the foundation on which fruitful apostolic work could be built. While it is possible, to some extent at least, to measure the academic achievements and professional expertise among the Dominican teachers of Cape Town and Port Elizabeth, the same cannot be said in the spiritual sphere since there is no yardstick for measuring the spiritual. Nevertheless the primary dedication, a radical choice of God, and a solemn commitment to the spread of His kingdom, influenced all the specific work done by each individual sister and by the communities of which they formed a part.

For the Dominican nuns of Cape Town and Port Elizabeth, as for their female contemporaries in society, the perceived role of women did not include professional involvement in public life. In this as in many other ways, the Irish Dominicans at the Cape Colony differed little from their dedicated sisters in the world. They had one advantage however, they were members of an Order renowned and respected for its intellectual life and apostolic service. Although as women the church denied them the right to preach, the special Dominican charism, they carried out the apostolic work of the Order through the ministry of teaching. In this sphere they did not confine themselves to formal education in the classroom. Immediately on their arrival in the Cape Colony they provided for the spiritual care of adults, and also for those outside the school system who were in need of practical skills. They saw their work of teaching not only as an honourable profession, as well as a means of economic survival, but also as the realisation of a common apostolic vocation. The gifts and expertise of each sister contributed to the success of the mission, and the qualifications of the individual enhanced the work of the whole group. Although the education of youth was their main apostolic thrust, and success in this field was essential for the future of their mission, the nuns were not encouraged to seek personal recognition either for their own individual achievements in the classroom, or among the adults whom they instructed. Nor were they permitted to discuss their academic and professional qualifications, either privately among themselves, or in the parlour. Indeed within the anonymity of the cloister they would not have considered themselves to be professionals, despite the fact that they recognised the value and dignity of their educational work. The conventions of the society in which they had been reared and the refinements of which they regarded as sacrosanct, influenced the way in which they viewed their own lifestyle and work :

> The early Victorian image of woman, her status, her wifely duties in the home, and her maternal role, derived largely from her economic dependence, the rigidity of social conventions limiting her field of activity, and the poverty of her formal education and intellectual development. This image was not peculiar to Britain or British overseas possessions, but it did survive with amazing persistency in colonial environments among the upper and middle classes, who were determined to maintain the conventional standards of their homeland.[1]

This generalisation did not apply without qualification to the choir nuns who came as teachers to Cape Town and Port Elizabeth during the nineteenth century. Just as there were many lay women "whose attainments lifted them above the commonplace", and who by vocation gave their services to the pastoral ministry in the distant and often hazardous mission fields, so too it was with the Dominican nuns. That they were not given due recognition by their male counterparts, in no way negates the powerful role many of them played in the evangelisation of their people. Indeed it is difficult to imagine how the Catholic Church could have found a firm footing in Southern Africa over the past century and a half, without the unremitting work of professional women religious.

The nuns sent out by Cabra and Sion Hill together with those who joined the communities in the Colony, were for their times, well educated. They included in their ranks linguists, musicians of note, experts in the art of lace making and fine needlework, teachers with a strong professional sense of vocation, and educators of the deaf. Among them also were formidable leaders and competent administrators of their own economic affairs. They were not, like some of their less fortunate middle class sisters in society, viewed as mere playthings in the home, sweetly helpless and frivolous. Neither were they drudges sharing the harsh lot of poor women who, working side by side with their husbands, tried to earn the minimum necessary for the survival of their large families. However, while in the cloister as in the home sweetness in a woman was much approved, though perhaps not quite so common as might be expected, frivolity in a nun would not have been tolerated. And while hard work and great material deprivation were often the lot of the sisters, their social status and professional role were clearly defined, both in the church and in society at large. This was perhaps some compensation for the cloistered life of obedience, poverty, and chastity which they had chosen. Conventual life was strict, sometimes unduly so. Discipline had to be maintained, and the success of the schools, their source of livelihood, depended on the expertise, integrity and hard work of the teaching nuns, the professionals. Women who had accepted the responsibility of living a vowed life, of seeking the perfection of charity, and of spreading the Kingdom of God, could not be incompetent, worldly or extravagant. Furthermore the nuns were expected to accept the consequences of their vocation, including voluntary poverty. Indeed the most powerful force for control, obedience and conformity among religious and clergy, was in the nineteenth century, as it is today, their personal economic dependence, a state that did not change whatever the financial status of the community.

Mother Dympna Kinsella and Mother Rose Whitty were well aware that without suitable buildings, convents to house the nuns and classrooms to accommodate pupils, there would be no opportunity to develop their educational mission. Indeed the prolific establishment of schools and the erection of pleasing buildings were in the best tradition of both the founding communities in Ireland and of their offshoots in South Africa, the United States of America, Australia and New Zealand. That the elegance and space did not normally extend to the cells and dormitories of the nuns, was usually accepted as one of the consequences of the vow of poverty. Both Mother Dympna and Mother Rose with their communities, experienced in their Cape missions the poverty inevitable in new, virtually penniless foundations. Although the world of finance was traditionally a male preserve, the two foundresses and their successors in office, together with their discreets, had to develop business skills in order to survive. While clerical advice was readily available and often generously given, it was not always disinterested, and money borrowed, even from a kindly bishop, had to be repaid with interest. At the outset buildings were poor and inadequate, school equipment was minimal and basic, and ready cash was scarce. During the founding years the community in Port Elizabeth depended on their ecclesiastical superior for temporary financial aid. This placed them in a perpetual state of debt to the local church and the bulk of their income from professional work was used to build new classrooms or convents, and to settle old debts, a task they performed with remarkable speed and proficiency. Often when interest on loans and debts was paid there was little to spare for anything other than the most basic necessities. Both the Cape Town and the Port Elizabeth nuns knew what it was to be hungry and cold, not only in the early founding years, but well into the twentieth century.

Despite the shortage of capital the Port Elizabeth community held the deeds of the land on which they built their convents and schools. This placed them in a strong position to negotiate in respect of their own property, and to have secure ownership of their own buildings. Such was not the case in the Western Vicariate, where with the exception of the Springfield property purchased by the nuns in 1871, the deeds of all the land on which, over the years the Dominican sisters had erected new buildings, were held by the reigning Bishop. This was a state of affairs that threatened both the economic security of the community, and at times the mutual relationship between Bishop and Dominican superiors. For Mother Dympna "debt was a thing she never saw her community contract, nor did she ever appeal to the public for funds to carry on: the building and purchase of suitable schools was always done by the labours and at the cost of the community".[2] On November 26, 1863, a little over two months after the arrival of the first Dominican community, Bishop Grimley made a financial arrangement with Mother Dympna which he recorded in his diary: "Had today an interview with the Lady Superior of our new Convent respecting the government salary for schools: she agreed not to ask any of the government money, but I would keep the school in repair and procure the necessary School furniture".[3] This initial agreement could not be sustained once the number of schools increased. It soon became evident that the Dominican community could no longer supply sisters to fill every professional post. Consequently the bishop, as manager of the state-aided schools, was placed under a legal obligation to pay the lay teachers out of the government grant. Father J. J. O'Reilly summed up the economic usefulness of nuns and brothers in the Catholic school system in his evidence to the Education Commission of 1891: "We could not possibly support these teachers were it not that, for the most part, they belong to Societies which are bound by a vow of voluntary poverty, such as the Marist Brothers and the Dominican Sisterhood. It stands to reason that no ordinary lay teacher can live on £66 a year in this Colony".[4] Nor indeed could an ordinary sister. The nuns accepted a life of personal and corporate poverty while new foundations were made, additional classrooms were built, chaplaincy fees were paid and contributions were handed over to support every church charity and each clerical celebration or parish project. While it could be argued that such an approach could scarcely be classed as businesslike, it must be understood that as a body of professional women and as missionaries, the provision of the best possible educational facilities for the people they served was a matter of priority for the nuns. In addition it was sound diplomacy that they, as members of diocesan congregations, should maintain a good relationship with their ecclesiastical superiors.

The bulk of the income that ensured the survival of the Irish Dominican communities in the Cape Colony, came directly from school fees and later, from government grants and teachers' salaries. This did not exclude fund-raising efforts, both for charity or for some special building project. But as professionals the nuns earned their living by teaching in both government-aided and private schools. In 1888 *The Wynberg Times*, out of goodwill, made an appeal for support of a fund-raising effort, St Dominic's Bazaar:

> The cause of education nowhere receives more generous support than it does for our Roman Catholic friends, and the success they achieve, while gratifying in itself, is but a fitting accompaniment of the energy and self-denial characteristic of all their efforts to spread the advantages of learning. They are always extending their generous sphere of usefulness ... and never wearying in well-doing.

For these reasons it was appropriate that the public should support the nuns in their fund-raising efforts to "enlarge and improve St. Dominic's School". Since the money was needed not for the work of the sisters but for building a parish hall, Father O'Reilly hastened to correct the error:

> I thank you heartily for the kindly notice of our Bazaar which appears in your last issue. However as there are one or two errors concerning third parties, I will ask your permission to

make an explanation. The Bazaar is not in aid of the
Dominican Sisterhood, who, since their arrival in the colony
just twenty-five years ago, never sought other support than
that which they earned by their own teaching.[5]

In 1885 Bishop Leonard was to boast that the Dominican
institutions in his Vicariate cost him on an average only £10 per
year.[6] In respect of economic independence, the founding
prioresses and their successors in office followed the tradition of
the Irish communities from which they originated. Although from
time to time they were the recipients of legacies and donations,
and more especially of services and support from loyal
benefactors, private and professional laymen and women, the
schools have remained their only stable source of livelihood in
Southern Africa for about 135 years. The Irish Dominicans also
provided employment for the many teachers, some of whom had
been educated and trained by the sisters.[7] During the nineteenth
century finance for the provision of qualified staff, buildings,
books and equipment for the schools, as well as the personal
needs of the community, had to be met out of the earnings of the
professional nuns. All schools had to exact fees, a common
practice throughout the Colony. Even the poorest of the pupils
in the mission schools were expected to contribute something.
In 1868, St Bridget's, classified as a mission school, charged
between one penny and sixpence per week. As soon as the school
received grants, the fees were reduced, but because of the larger
number of pupils, the poor mission schools helped to contribute
to the upkeep of the communities as a whole. It was not until
1920 that schools funded by the Government no longer charged
fees. This however did not apply to private academies.[8] In 1864
St Mary's School in Cape Town, which accepted boys as well as
girls, took in fees amounting to £34.1.4, not a large sum on which
to initiate and support a new mission. In respect of school fees
as in other matters, economic and professional, the South African
communities followed the tradition of their Irish Mother Houses,
but in an alien environment without the security and backing of
family, friends and benefactors.

As the school enrolment grew and the work of the sisters
became known, development was possible. It was a slow process
and demanded untiring work and constant improvements in the
teaching qualifications of the nuns, both those from Cabra and
Sion Hill and the candidates who joined the communities in Cape
Town and Port Elizabeth. The last decade of the nineteenth
century was the beginning of a period during which the
importance of formal academic and professional qualifications
for teachers, women as well as men, were being stressed. But

the level of examinations in these areas was often elementary both in the theory of education and in academic subjects. It was fortunate that in the Cape Colony some basic provision was being made, not least in Dominican institutions, for the apprenticeship, training and examination of pupil teachers. Although these were children, boys and girls beginning their training, during the 1860's and early 1870's, at little more than Std IV level, nevertheless the three years of apprenticeship which included normal school subjects, practical teaching under supervision and theory of education, provided a sound introduction to a professional career. This was specially valuable for girls who had few professional opportunities outside the teaching profession.

From 1875 onwards the development of the public examination system, including the certification of teachers, challenged all groups engaged in formal education. The two cities of Port Elizabeth and Cape Town, where every academic success or failure became a matter of public comment and often of acrimonious debate, were socially parochial in outlook. The press, starved for news in a narrowly conservative colonial society, ensured that schools and educational matters in general were laid open to public scrutiny. The publication of examination results, the comment on social events in schools and the lively debates on religious issues, kept the lifestyle and work of the nuns before the public eye. The convent schools in particular aroused interest, curiosity, sometimes fear and frequently not a little envy. In these circumstances it would have been strange if the nuns, however reluctant they were as individuals to attract publicity, could have hidden all of their individual successes or failures behind the veil of anonymity within the cloister.

When in 1864 Langham Dale made his first visit to St Bridget's Mission School, he found Mother Dympna Kinsella teaching a group of 80 girls. The total enrolment was 121 pupils and it was clear to him that she needed a separate class for infants.[9] It was not until two years later that she was allotted one pupil teacher, but by that time she herself, with the help of new recruits from Cabra, had already initiated the Irish system of pupil teacher training in St Bridget's Mission School. This was to be the beginning of a process that lasted for almost 60 years and supplied qualified recruits not only to the Dominican community and schools in the Western Cape, but also to other educational institutions and to groups of families in isolated rural areas across Southern Africa. Among those who were trained as teachers in St Bridget's was Winifred Coughlan (Sister Dominic Francis), the first recruit from the Cape Peninsula to persevere in the Dominican community. She entered the convent in 1871, at the age of sixteen, after completing one year of pupil teachership under the supervision of that great Dominican woman, Sister Joseph Leahy, principal of St Bridget's Mission School. The Annals record that "two of the pupils were received into the novitiate, Miss McAuliffe from the High School, and Winifred Coughlan *from the Public School, Lay Sister*". The annalist made no mention of St Bridget's and the reference to lay sister status was heavily scored out by another hand and pen. It was certainly not meant for the eyes of posterity. In 1873 Sister Dominic Coughlan completed her apprenticeship as pupil teacher and made her profession as a choir sister in 1875. She entered the novitiate, was received and professed during the superiorship of Mother Dympna Kinsella, who overcame her own reluctance and that of the community, to accept as a choir sister, a girl from a mission school. Winifred Coughlan was one the children of the "labouring classes", who according to government regulations, were to be given a plain education. Fortunately the Dominican teachers in St Brigid's, St Anne's and St Patrick's mission schools gave their pupils all the educational advantages available at that time, and they "competed successfully with Springfield and St Mary's for leading places in the university [school] examinations".[10]

Notwithstanding the personal excellence or academic merit of such candidates, the acceptance of working class girls into the professional body of the community was a socially daring, indeed dangerous practice, and one to be put into effect only with the greatest discretion. Would the parents of young ladies take exception to their daughters being taught by working class teachers? Was it possible that such women could have the necessary refinement of accent and manner to deal with young ladies socially more sophisticated than they were? It is clear that while it was seen as wise to conceal the origins of certain choir nuns, Mother Dympna and her successors in office could in special circumstances, place the urgent needs of the mission above the demands of social pressure and the petty constraints of middle class snobbery. That such candidates were accepted, was also a strong vote of confidence in the education and training given at the Dominican mission schools. There was however a more serious consequence of this practice. Was it not, after all a deviation from the more rigid selection criteria applied in the Irish Mother Houses, and did it not perhaps have an adverse effect on the quality of the personnel in the missionary communities? This departure from accepted norms was indeed noted by Cabra and Sion Hill, the main sources of vocations for the Cape between 1863 and 1920, and it may have been one of the reasons why they sent to South Africa choir postulants, some of whom they would have hesitated to admit into their own communities. It may also have given rise to the assumption, that survived well into the second half of the present century, that the integrity of Dominican life, social acceptability and educational standards were lower in the Cape foundations than in the Irish convents, and in the eyes of the Dominicans in Port Elizabeth, higher in the Eastern Cape than in the West.

The missionary communities *were* different: more tolerant in the religious sphere, more adaptable socially, less bound by the protecting and imprisoning walls of enclosure, and in the vanguard of the evolving educational system of the Colony. The nuns were, in the Cape as in Australia and New Zealand, a scarce commodity, loved by the Catholic, often Irish people whom they had come to serve, and appreciated by those Protestants, Jews and Moslems who valued the education and social training they offered to their children. To add salt to their experience of living in a Protestant society, the sisters were also envied, feared and hated by some as representatives of the "Roman danger", a growing threat to Protestant orthodoxy. Nevertheless the acceptance of working-class girls as choir sisters was not a policy that found favour with some of those nuns in Cape Town and Port Elizabeth. For these the social norms of Cabra and Sion Hill remained sacrosanct. It was fortunate therefore that despite opposition, a number of the local vocations together with aspirants sent out from Ireland, brought a more egalitarian spirit into the communities, and also that many of the Irish candidates sent by Cabra and Sion Hill, did their novitiate in South Africa.

The application of a more open policy of selection of postulants depended largely on the preference of the ruling Prioress and her Council. However at times social status took precedence over personal worth and academic ability. As a consequence potentially excellent local candidates were turned away, to the benefit of other more far-seeing Congregations. One of those admitted to choir status was Katie Hart (Sister Aloysius), another of Sister Joseph Leahy's successful protégés. She was born of Irish parents, poor immigrants who could not afford the luxury of a private education for their daughter. She was reared in Cape Town, educated by the Dominican sisters, and trained as a teacher at St Bridget's. She was a simple girl but very intelligent and well-read and as a student gave Sister Joseph Leahy great satisfaction. Her parents strongly opposed her entrance into the convent, but not long after she had completed her apprenticeship and passed the Third Class Teachers' Certificate, she applied for admission.[11] In the eyes of Mother Dympna, prioress at the time, and her discreets, the young aspirant's warm-hearted disposition and great aptitude for teaching stood her in good stead. She was accepted as a choir postulant, and at the age of nineteen entered the convent and was professed in 1887. Her teaching career, in St Anne's and Somerset Road, was brief, as was her life. Like many of her Irish colleagues she fell victim to tuberculosis and died at the age of thirty-one. Her early death was a great loss to the community as she was among the more promising teachers trained by Sister Joseph.[12]

Sister Joseph Leahy was born in Tipperary, Ireland in March 1845. She was one of many pupils of St Mary's Cabra, who at the end of their schooldays applied for admission as candidates for the foreign missions, a tribute to the teaching and example of their Dominican mentors. She was the first postulant from Ireland to offer herself as a candidate for St Mary's, Cape Town. On April 11, 1865, at the age of twenty she was accepted into the novitiate. She came under the direct influence of Mother Dympna Kinsella who at that time filled the two offices of prioress and mistress of novices. She was admitted to profession in January 1867, after 18 months of training in the novitiate, and immediately began her career as principal of St Bridget's Mission School. There is no local record that she had any previous teaching experience or that she had served as a monitor at Cabra, although this is possible. It was a common practice for young ladies to assist in classroom supervision and teaching as a preparation for work in schools, or to earn their living as governesses in private families.[13] Whatever her experience in Cabra, Sister Joseph soon earned the respect and appreciation not only of Mother Dympna and the boys and girls she taught and trained as pupil teachers, but also of Langham Dale and his inspectors.

> Sister Joseph, who was principal of the biggest Catholic mission school in the Western Cape, and the one responsible for the training of so many Catholic [as well as Protestant and Jewish] teachers, emerges from the obscurity of the past as a vital and dynamic personality. ... In her there were none of the characteristics attributed, often unjustly to the typical Victorian lady. Grimley spoke of her in the early days of her long principalship as 'the indefatigable Sister Mary Joseph' and was full of admiration for the excellence of her teaching. Her correspondence as principal and director of pupil teachers was crisp, businesslike and formal. She knew her rights and those of her pupils, and was aware of the regulations which limited her power, and at times curbed her enthusiasm.[14]

She used her opportunities to develop a course of studies, including the methodology of teaching and classroom practice which would be of greatest benefit to the poorest as well as to the more affluent of her pupils. Her enthusiasm and her portrayal of the greatness of a religious vocation, encouraged girls to enter convents in different parts of the Colony.

Sister Joseph's public career is more open to scrutiny than her hidden participation in the daily round of prayer and other duties in the convent. The veil of anonymity and silence on personal matters behind which the private life of the sisters was hidden, and the pious platitudes used by the hagiographer singing the praises of deceased nuns, make the work of historical reconstruction almost impossible. However, in respect of those nuns who worked in government service in the schools, official records provide a richness of evidence as to their attitudes, interpersonal relationships, management skills, and teaching ability. The virtue and religious excellence of such teachers as Sister Joseph cannot be measured by educational statistics or government reports alone, and even less so by the platitudes of pious, conventional obituaries. Nonetheless this is often all the evidence available and in the case of Sister Joseph it indicates a woman of exceptional commitment, able to combine public service with monastic life to the advantage of both.

> In respect of her aspirant teachers she permitted of no negligence in the classrooms or during study hours. The lazy had to make way for the diligent, but when a student had achieved success, Sister Joseph ensured for her a good position in a local school. Indeed in her approach to teaching as a profession, and to woman's role and duty in that sphere, she represents the best type of professional Victorian womanhood - confident, efficient, unobtrusive and hard-working.[15]

She died in 1890, only forty-five years old, but her death did not bring to an end an exceptionally rich era in Catholic teacher training in the Western Cape. The pupil teacher method flourished for another thirty years. The fruits of her work long outlived her and some of the teachers whom she had trained were still serving in South African schools in 1939, at the outbreak of World War II. She was one of the Dominican women who made a strong impact on education in the Cape Colony. Her work in the training of teachers was recognised and appreciated even by those who could only deprecate the dangerous presence of Roman nuns in the schools. Since the sisters accepted pupils irrespective of religion, this meant that over the years the Dominican schools produced teachers for Jewish, Protestant and Catholic schools as well as governesses who carried their skills to the farms and small dorps of the Transvaal and the Orange Free State, and even as far afield as Natal.

From the time of their arrival in the Cape Colony, all the Irish Dominican convents and filial houses provided schools for young ladies in addition to their mission schools, and all the communities promoted the training of their own sisters and of pupil teachers. Even with the available records, reports and official commissions, the educational level attained by the nuns is difficult to determine with any certainty. By 1861 there was " no defined classification of teachers, nor any system of examination" in the Cape, and "competent teachers were in short supply". In order to compensate for this lack, Dale followed the British precedent in this as in many other educational dilemmas. The *Educational Report* of 1863 noted that recognition would be given to practising teachers under certain conditions:

> Authority is granted to the Superintendent-General of Education to issue Certificates to teachers in aided and other schools, in cases which he may, after due inquiry, deem the teachers to be qualified, and the schools which they conduct to be suited, for the training of young persons as teachers.[16]

Since both private and Government-aided Mission schools under Dominican control were soon participating in the training programme, it is clear that the nuns were officially recognised as competent and qualified teachers. Bishop Leonard accepted the training given to the nuns in their own institutes, as sufficient for school teaching. Had not the whole life of the sisters as convent pupils and later as nuns, been an adequate preparation for their work in the classroom?

> While still pupils at the school, young girls carried out monitorial duties and gave lessons to younger children under the supervision of the nuns. Later, as novices, they could be sent to observe good teachers and work under their guidance. Leonard when asked whether he required certificates of qualification from the religious employed in the Catholic schools, replied without hesitation: 'They have no one to get a certificate from except the superior of their own community. The inspector of schools does not find any fault with their teaching'.[17]

In 1883 Donald Ross, a school inspector newly arrived from Scotland, submitted a report to Parliament on the actual level of education in the Colony, as distinct from that proposed by principals in highly pretentious syllabuses. He maintained that in "by far the largest number of schools it would be an absolute waste of time to examine the pupils in detail, so very elementary were their attainments and so inferior was the quality of the instruction imparted". He realised that the new system at the Cape had "grown out of many elements" and there had been no time to "apply rigid or uniform terms or definitions to all its parts". It was not a situation that gave much support to those who lacked teaching qualifications and experience, and Ross found across the vast extent of the country there was a "large proportion of uncertificated or nearly illiterate teachers employed", and even in Cape Town many of the mission schools were characterised by a "very small attendance and a very large roll". In such institutions either "it was Monday, when the scholars had not arrived for the week, or it was Friday when they had ceased to come, or it was a Malay holiday, or the washing day". Effective reform of such a system demanded a consistent educational policy which would ensure that the teacher, who had achieved a clearly defined level of professional and academic proficiency, would be granted formal recognition by the Department of Education. [18]

The comparatively high standard of private schools, Dutch Reformed, Anglican and Catholic, taught for the most part by teachers with no formal qualifications, was recognised:

> But it is both remarkable and highly significant that even in towns where a first-class school exists, with high or with moderate fees, the bulk of education of those who can afford to pay high or moderate fees, is received outside the public school system. There is probably no other country where private schools, unaided by the state and altogether unendowed, have risen so rapidly, or upon the whole succeed so well against the natural competition of the Government Schools, which are liberally supported out of the public funds. [19]

It is not surprising that Catholic girls of reasonably prosperous families attended the convent schools in both Port Elizabeth and Cape Town. If they wanted a "superior education" they had no alternative, since the Church forbade their parents, under pain of excommunication, to send their children to any other than Catholic private, mission or public schools. But what is of interest is that Protestant and Jewish families also chose the convent schools for their daughters. They were aware that these academies in both Port Elizabeth and Cape Town, as well as those in other parts of the Colony, were noted for their high moral tone, sound training in social graces and an excellent academic education. That they also gave priority to religious instruction and practice, in no way discouraged parents of different religious persuasions, though it did alarm their church elders.

Two decades after the arrival of Mother Dympna Kinsella in Cape Town, and within 17 years of Dominican work begun by Mother Rose Whitty and her community in Port Elizabeth, Donald Ross was attesting the value of the education being provided by church schools:

> No public provision has yet been made for a most important section of the girls of the Metropolis [Cape Town] - those of the higher, the upper middle and the lower middle class. These have been left to Church schools, like the Good Hope Seminary in connection with the Dutch Reformed Church, or St Cyprian's, under the patronage of the Church of England, or the convents at Wynberg and Cape Town, ... whilst the boys who desire a practical and useful commercial education wisely seek it from the Marist Brothers or in some private institution, rather than the South African College School, whose energy is cramped and whose utility is crushed out in the groove of an obsolete or unreal curriculum.[20]

Ross acknowledged that there were "a large number of schools of good size, which may be accepted as doing sound work, giving satisfaction to the parents, and to a large extent meeting a felt want, such as the convents at King William's Town, Port Elizabeth, [Holy Rosary Convent], Panmure, and Cape Town".[21] Why did the Catholic Church encourage the establishment of such schools? In the first place many of the missionary foundresses, themselves the product of private education, simply followed the pattern of their mother houses. This was certainly the case for those from Cabra and Sion Hill. Secondly, for the Irish Dominicans in particular, these schools were their main source of livelihood, and without them it would have been economically impossible to support the poor mission schools. Donald Ross, considering the 100 private schools, catering for approximately 4000 pupils "of the superior class", found other and equally valid reasons for their exclusivity:

> These keep aloof from the public system, either because the regulations of the system itself would seem to exclude them, or their patrons prefer greater freedom of choice in the curriculum, or more amenity of manners and morals than they can imagine can be had in public schools, or because their course of study is manifestly more modern and more in harmony with the needs of the age, or because religious scruples and convictions urge exclusion.[22]

Religious scruples and convictions certainly played a decisive role in the decision of the Catholic Church and the nuns to run both private and mission schools. It is also clear that the nuns valued the freedom which gave them the right to plan and carry out courses of study appropriate to the children whom they taught. This did not mean that the poorer pupils of mission schools were deprived of instruction in fields outside the narrow curriculum set by the educational authorities. In institutions run by the nuns, whether private or Government aided, there was often little or no distinction in the teaching, curriculum or the ambition of the sisters to achieve success in public examinations. The nuns who both studied and taught music, entered pupils from all of their schools for Royal College of Music examinations, and with remarkable success. The first Dominican music teacher in the Western Cape was Sister Agnes Doran, one of the six founders of the Cape Town mission from Cabra. She combined a great gift for teaching instrumental music with a beautiful voice and the lessons in singing, piano, violin and harp which she initiated, first at St Mary's and later at Springfield Convent, Wynberg, did much to attract pupils, including "even Dutch girls [who] were to be found within our Convent walls". This was all the more remarkable in that among the Dutch in South Africa "there was much bigotry" at that time. The fact that Sister Agnes, with her youth, exuberance and joyful nature, was the first mistress of boarders at Springfield did much to make the convent school regime attractive to the pupils of all nationalities and religious affiliations.[23]

Another musician of note was Sister Francis de Sales Sherwin, a past pupil of the high-class day school opened in 1834 by the Cabra Community at 34, Ushers Quay, Dublin.[24] There she was taught by Mother Borgia McDonnell, who later volunteered for the Cape Town mission. After completing her schooling, Miss Sherwin went to Italy and entered the Convent of the Presentation Sisters in Turin. Although she loved the sisters, she found the life too difficult. She left the novitiate and returned to Cabra. There she was encouraged to apply for admission to the Dominicans in Cape Town, where she commenced her postulancy in 1872. Mother Berchmans Cotter, who knew Sister Francis personally, spoke highly of her:

> She was a gifted musician. Forty years ago (written in 1925) C.Town music had not the hold in Cape Town it has today. Sister Francis had a great deal to do then in drawing public attention to the way in which the piano and harp were being taught at St. Mary's, and pupils crowded to her. Today you can hear her name mentioned lovingly by those pupils of long ago, and here and there you will find a grand ... harp

purchased through her. Sr. M. Francis had a very beautiful
voice. It was a joy to hear her sing in the choir.

She also entertained the sisters by singing Italian hymns at
recreation, with a voice "so sweet, so clear, so thrilling that it
drew one away from the earth".[25]

Sister Francis was the first sister-in-charge of Sacred Heart
Convent which was founded in 1883. In order to support Dr
Colgan, the parish priest, in his plans to build a church she
used another skill common to many of the nuns both in the
nineteenth and in the twentieth centuries. She "used her brains
and her fingers to help in the great work. She had very deft fingers
and her Fancy-work was admired and purchased generously in
the great cause".[26] Needlework was one of the subjects taught in
all of the Dominican schools and those girls who remained at
school long enough, learned the art of fine embroidery and
lacemaking. These skills were often a source of revenue for the
community, and a valuable accomplishment for young ladies, as
well as for those who could earn their living by dressmaking.
Irish lace made by the sisters and the more advanced girls,
including pupils of the Deaf School, found ready purchasers
amongst visitors attending regular exhibitions and sales of work.
Singing, elocution, drama and dancing also played their part in
the curriculum and public or semi-private productions, reported
lavishly in the press, attracted public notice and approval.

As the academic demands imposed by the examination system
increased, the Dominican sisters were often at a loss to provide
for the needs of the small minority of secondary pupils, girls who
aimed for and achieved first matriculation and finally a bachelor's
degree. The nineteenth century Irish Dominicans in South Africa,
unlike their counterparts in Cabra and Sion Hill, could not depend
on the expertise of masters for academic subjects. These were in
short supply in the Colony, and even such as available were not
Catholics and consequently would have been unacceptable in a
convent school. It was only in the 1890's, when the matriculation
examination became the goal in the most advanced girls' schools,
that the help of Dr Kolbe was accepted by Springfield. The cost of
this one cleric, a good friend and mentor of the community, was
as much as the Dominican finances could sustain. However his
services to the school were highly appreciated. The pupils reported
in *Silver Leaves*, their school magazine:

> The great event for us of the last term was that Dr. Kolbe
> again took up his lectures. His lessons, twice a week during
> the past year were only given to the highest class and were of
> course too advanced for us; now he again gives a general

lecture which all the High School standards attend. We offer our heartfelt congratulations to Dr. Kolbe on the success of his pupils at the Intermediate Examination in Arts, held in June last. We celebrated the event in our usual fashion, by a whole holiday and great rejoicing. We take special pride always in the success of all Dr. Kolbe's pupils for he is the only Professor lecturing at this Convent, on Science, Mathematics and Literature, and whatever success we have had so far, at those examinations, has been due, directly or indirectly, to him. Meantime we all in the other standards, are highly pleased to have the usual Wednesday lectures resumed. Dr. Kolbe began by giving lectures on Cape Geological formations. This series, besides the interest taken in it by us, gave great pleasure to those of our teachers [the nuns] who had studied the geology of other countries.[27]

Kolbe, a brilliant teacher, added greatly to the expertise of the sisters with whom he shared his enthusiastic interest in both literature and the sciences. He was always available to the Dominicans and over the years contributed greatly to their academic development and professional expertise. He set up science museums in both St Mary's and Springfield and introduced both teachers and pupils to the mysteries of chemistry, physics and the natural sciences.[28] Kolbe's educational work for the schools was not limited to the Western Province. He travelled around the country and assisted where he could, in rural areas as well as in the towns. In June 1909 he visited Port Elizabeth and gave lectures on teaching to the Dominican community there. This however was not the only time that the Holy Rosary community received outside help in their professional work. In August 1895 Miss Fox spent a fortnight at Holy Rosary Convent helping the nuns to "reorganise" their private school, and three years later the prioress, Mother Magdalen Slattery and her Council invited Miss Moloney BA and Miss Emery LLM from England to assist the sisters in their professional work.[29] They spent two months in Port Elizabeth helping the community, and then moved on to Grahamstown.[30]

The provision of a sound education both for themselves as teachers and for their pupils was a matter of extreme urgency for the Dominican teachers. Most of the choir nuns who came as postulants from Cabra and Sion Hill during the early decades of the South African foundations, had little in the way of formal academic or professional qualifications. To meet the demands of the developing educational system the founding superiors saw the need to promote the academic and professional interests of the nuns as well as that of their pupils. In the Cape Colony it was not until the 1890's that there was any consistent secondary education, although in some private schools, including those run by nuns, certain subjects were taught at high level while others were elementary. When in 1873 the University of the Cape of Good Hope was constituted, it accepted in principle that women could graduate at any level. This new academic goal for women, together with the school examination system, introduced a more competitive spirit into the schools and gradually raised academic standards. The institution of the Elementary Teacher's Examination (T3) provided an opportunity for both teachers and their pupils to gain professional certification. This latter examination was often the first step towards matriculation, and for a small minority of women, to a degree in the Arts or Sciences. In 1874 there were 74 female matriculants in the Cape and eleven years later, in 1890/91 there were 142. The standard of the T3 was not high, but for many colonial candidates it was the highest they could achieve, for others quite beyond their reach. However Donald Ross was impressed by the work of certain candidates:

> "Some of the papers were distinctly superior. I was much struck with the difference in form and matter between the best from the higher seminaries of the Western Province and the best from the [Dominican] convents. The former while more careless in style and form, indicated greater thoughtfulness and greater individuality. The latter in form and appearance were the finest I have ever seen, but their weakness was in individuality of thinking. If the excellence in the one set could be conjoined with that of form in the other, we should have a very pleasing result indeed".[31]

For many candidates from less fortunate institutions, the teaching and preparation in the schools gave them competence neither in creativity nor in form and style. The most elementary knowledge of academic subjects and of teaching methodology was lacking in the teachers. For those who had spent a short time in school even the term kindergarten was foreign and esoteric. One student had "merely a faint recollection of once hearing something about the Kindergarten system", while another stated that " Kindergarten was greatly defeated and his army fled and he was killed". A third confessed: "I have seen Kindergarten written above a door in some house in Cape Town, but *unfortunately* that is all". Knowledge of elementary physics was equally bizarre. One student claims: "Electricity and Lightning are of the same nature, the only difference being that lightning is often several miles in length while electricity is only a few inches". Another candidate is certain that electricity "is the orbit described by the sun around the earth, but in reality the earth around the sun". The explanation of the law of gravity, clearly mistaught to a group of candidates, indicates the level of ignorance among some of the teachers: "If the earth was to have no gravity and if we climbed to the top of a hill and jumped a little above the top, we would stick fast in the air, and thus there would be an end to our existence". And again "if we let a thing fall it would not fall to the ground but stick just in the place where it fell out of our hand".[32]

That many of the younger Dominican sisters and some of their pupils entered for and passed the T3 examination with distinction, does not necessarily imply that they had more than a fairly elementary knowledge of academic subjects, and a basic familiarity with teaching methodology and the principles of school management. What it did reveal however was a growing sensitivity of the Dominican superiors to the professional status of the teacher, especially the female teacher, and the need to provide opportunities for the nuns to qualify academically, professionally and in the special subjects for which their private schools were noted: music, drama, art and needlework. Between 1892 and 1900 sixteen sisters in the Western Cape entered for and passed public examinations. Two passed the School Elementary, eleven the 3rd Class Teachers Certificate, (T3), and one, Sister Bertrand Dowley the First Class Teacher's Certificate. In addition seven members of the community achieved what was at that time the high academic goal of matriculation, Sister Bertrand over 45 years of age at this time, getting the highest distinction in all subjects in the examination. In 1896 Sisters Berchmans Cotter and Augustine Barry passed their needlework examination with distinction.

The Port Elizabeth community took a somewhat different course in pursuit of higher academic qualifications. In 1895 seven sisters entered for the "government examinations", of whom six passed.[33] During the same year three of these, Sisters Reginald Gordon, Xavier Gordon and Vincent O'Donoghue, together with Sisters Peter Murphy and Joseph Scallan, registered for the LLA Diploma Course given by St Andrew's University, Scotland, and completed it successfully. From about 1915 onwards Dutch and commercial subjects were added, and in each of these subjects some of the sisters were qualified. However it was not until the twentieth century that the nuns attended secular training colleges and universities. Both Mother Rose Whitty and Mother Dympna Kinsella knew only too well that "if the schools are to be raised, it can only be through the teachers. What the teacher is the school shall become".[34] This belief they held in common with the more committed educators throughout the colony.

The formal training of teachers in the Western Cape was the result of a Dutch Reformed initiative. The Rev Stegman successfully established the Normal College in Cape Town in 1878 because he believed "that by training teachers and by their acquiring a certificate from the Government, giving them a standing, we should give to the whole status of teachers generally a very different complexion from what it has been hitherto".[35] However the Normal college, a Dutch Reformed institution, was seen as a threat to the faith and morals of Catholics, and Leonard and his successors did not encourage Catholics to attend. In the late nineteenth century the Dominicans, as women and enclosed nuns, would not have been permitted to attend any training centre outside their cloister. They took a realistic stand on their own and their pupils' need for formal qualifications. However since in general their own standard of education far surpassed the level of the colonial school examinations, they first passed the 2nd or 3rd Class Teachers Examination and then concentrated on achieving the higher goal of matriculation.

In terms of the times, and even without the benefit of formal certification, the sisters were well equipped academically and by professional experience, to train pupil teachers. These young boys and girls, apprentices with only a basic elementary education, were only children. It was no small achievement to prepare them for a professional career and at the same time give proper attention to the general work of teaching in the school. From 1875 onwards the sisters presented pupils from both their mission and private schools for the Third Class Teachers' Certificate, a practice which benefitted both the pupil teachers and the institutions responsible for their training. A number of local aspirants, who later joined the Cape Town community, had already passed this examination before they entered and some had already matriculated. This policy gradually led to an increase in the number of certificated teachers supplied by Dominican schools. Donald Ross could well say in 1883: "The Catholics have ample means for training candidates up to any standard the Government may fix; but I am not aware that the Church of England has at present any effective machinery for preparing teachers for its mission schools". At that time the "larger part of the Examination for Middle Class teachers [was] left to the University and made to coincide with that of Matriculation". Ross expressed "grave objections" to this because the majority of the candidates were female and could not be expected "to undergo the Matriculation Examination". Nor was the University "subject to the direct control of Government", and partly for this reason, Ross considered the course for matriculation to be "most unsuitable for teachers". However candidates had to be prepared for teaching and the lure of academic study was to win the day, both inside and outside the cloister.

Between 1871 and 1892 the Dominican community of Cape Town admitted 12 local girls, eight of whom were choir sisters and teachers. The academic education, and the theory and methodology of teaching and practical classroom experience of most of these aspirants had been provided in the mission and private convent schools. Once they had completed their novitiate these young sisters were a valuable asset to their religious community and its educational mission. During the last three decades of the nineteenth century, these young Dominicans, qualified both by education and their experience of life in the colony, formed approximately 20% of the professional staff of the Dominican schools in the Western Vicariate.[36] Within the period 1867-1938, of the 115 sisters who were professed as members of the Port Elizabeth community 95 were of Irish origin, 12 were South African born, five were Bavarian, and one each was from Russian Poland, Scotland and New Zealand. Among these were some of the best Dominican teachers in the Eastern Province, most of them educated either through private study or at the Colleges of Uitenhage, Grahamstown or King William's Town. The academic and professional proficiency of the founding community, can be judged only by the results of their work as teachers. It is clear however that their claim to be professionally competent was never questioned either by the Department of Education, by the public at large, or by the parents of their pupils. Mother Rose Whitty was a woman of culture, well versed in English literature with a sound proficiency in both spoken and written French. Indeed it appears that the sisters of her community preferred to read spiritual treatises in the original French rather than in an English translation. Among the five founding members of Holy Rosary Convent, Mother Thomas Kelly, Sister Baptist Taaffe and Sister Hyacinth Potter reveal in their correspondence keen powers of observation, a discerning interest in people, with their idiosyncrasies and foibles, and the ability to express their ideas with confidence and in excellent English.[37]

Not all the Dominican teachers were Irish born, nor were national prejudices as strong as they were to become during the first three decades of the twentieth century. In December 1854 Ann Kilkinger, was born in Augsburg, Bavaria. In October 1875 she and three other postulants came out from Europe with Dr Ricards, to join the Dominican community in Port Elizabeth. She received the Dominican habit in 1876 and was professed in Holy Rosary Convent in October 1877. A much appreciated member of the community she soon proved herself to be an excellent scholar, a good teacher of German and French and a competent mistress of novices.[38] She was the kind of recruit that Mother Rose needed to ensure the development of St Mary's School, but a little over six years after her profession she died, just four months before her thirtieth birthday.[39]

In the Cape Colony in general as in the two Irish foundations of Cape Town and Port Elizabeth, there were never sufficient qualified and competent teachers to meet the demands of a developing education system. This is evident from an 1892 entry in the *Education Manual.* On the recommendation of a Deputy-Inspector, acting teachers could be granted Certificates of Competency without any formal examination. The conditions under which this concession would be made, were laid down by the Department of Education :

> I. They must (a) be 30 years of age; and (b) have been acting teachers of schools in connection with this Department for at least five years; and (c) produce satisfactory testimony of good character.

> II. The deputy-Inspectors must report (a) that they are efficient teachers and their schools are in every respect satisfactory; and (b) that not less than 15 per cent of the scholars presented in the last examination passed in the third or some higher standard.[40]

Some at least of the older and more experienced nuns who had continued their education on a part-time basis, were granted this concession. The public and mission schools which fell under the control of the Dominican nuns, catered for very poor children, and because of the missionary potential of these institutions, superiors were encouraged to assign some of their best teachers to this work. However the majority of the sisters were assigned to the private schools, especially since the employment of lay teachers would have placed an insuperable burden on the limited financial resources of the community. In 1904 when Mother Berchmans Cotter was made local superior of St Agnes' Convent, Woodstock, she united the private and mission schools into one establishment. Both she and Sister Augustine Barry used all their professional skills to upgrade the educational standard of the pupils, many of whom were from very poor families. Later in the same year the Department of Education gave due recognition to the excellence of the work and academic standards of two of the sisters teaching there: "The school flourished & the numbers were over 400. Both Srs. Mary Augustine & Berchmans held [a] Cape Matric Certificate & 1st Class needlework. Mr. Noakes was so content with the work that he got the Dept. to confer Second Class Teachers' Certificate on both".[41]

Mary Linda Barry, born in Cape Town in 1862, was a Dominican pupil. She began her education in St Mary's Convent School, and when Springfield was founded, was among the first boarders there. She was fifteen years old when, in 1877, she was admitted into the novitiate and her study for the matriculation examination was done after she had entered the convent. She was a strong-minded woman, fearless in the face of authority and prepared to challenge even her religious superiors if she felt that right procedures were not being followed. She was also a dedicated teacher, and for the times in which she lived, she was well qualified professionally. Mother Berchmans Cotter had been a pupil both of the Sacred Heart nuns at Roscrea, Ireland and of the Dominicans at Cabra. There in 1884 she entered the novitiate as a postulant for the Cape mission. In this choice she was following the example of her sister Margaret, (Sister Paul Cotter) who in 1882, as a professed nun, had preceded her to Cape Town. Sister Berchmans, like Sister Augustine Barry, also improved her academic qualifications, acquiring her Cape Matriculation Certificate at a time when this was a rare achievement for a woman.[42]

In 1892, at the end of his period of office as Superintendent of Education in the Cape Colony, Dale noted that among the teachers in the Colony there were those "who by choice, fitness, and training have entered the profession, while others, not a few, have been pressed into service by force of circumstances". He looked forward to the day "when entrance into the teaching profession will be effectually barred against unqualified intruders as in the professions of law and medicine". This might well sum up the situation in most voluntary missionary bodies in the second half of the nineteenth century. Necessity knew no law and in the case of religious sisters, as with the wives and daughters of missionaries, the general education and training received either in school or from governesses and tutors, was claimed to be a fair substitute for formal academic certification and professional training. For the older sisters their school studies had stood them in good stead but the educational system was developing and the academic demands increased year by year. During the first 38 years of the twentieth century, not all the sisters achieved success in public examinations, and not everyone who taught was a registered teacher. Nevertheless the superiors were ever conscious of the force of public opinion, and the need for sisters to acquire recognised certification not only academic, but also in the professional sphere.

Chapter Eight

The Professionals: Deaf Education

Of the Irish Dominican volunteers who came to South Africa during the last four decades of the nineteenth century, most of the choir sisters had the academic support of their convent school education in either Cabra or Sion Hill. While some came to the mission as postulants, others were well experienced both in the teaching of academic subjects and in the accepted refinements essential to the education of young ladies. This however was not the only professional field in which the Dominican women had expertise. Although Mother Dympna Kinsella had proved herself to be an efficient teacher in St Bridget's Mission School in Cape Town, in Cabra she had gained experience in the relatively new field of deaf education. At the outset she had no opportunity to put her expertise into practice in Cape Town, but her interest in individual deaf children and in the plight of those whom a rural society hid away from public view on distant farms, never wavered. She was aware that in a situation where the provision of even the most elementary schooling put pressure on the colonial system, still in its infancy, special education of a largely hidden minority, could hope to gain little or no support or sympathy from the government authorities.

While from the sixteenth century onwards there had been both theoretical debate and limited application of accepted theories to the education of the deaf children of the rich, the majority of such handicapped people, often regarded as mentally deficient, lived in an isolated world. The early work in deaf education although it benefitted only a small elite, prepared the way for formal schooling of deaf children, the poor and most neglected sector of the potential school population. The earliest attempts to place deaf education on a formal basis in organised schools date back to the eighteenth century when Abbé Charles-Michael de l'Epée founded an institution for deaf children in France. In time he passed on to his pupil and friend the Abbé Sicard both his own love and commitment to deaf education, and the methodology he used. Sicard refined and adapted these methods, and it is from this source that in 1846 the first Catholic school for the deaf was founded in Great Britain, at St Mary's Dominican Convent, Dublin. The Irish institution provided the inspiration, and Mother Dympna was the moving force behind provision of the first special school for the deaf in Southern Africa. This opened at St Mary's Convent, Cape Town in 1874, and for many decades to come it was to remain a very small and insecure foundation.

It had been her skill as a teacher and her ability in the Deaf Institute that had first brought Mother Dympna Kinsella to the notice of Grimley, who himself had been deeply involved in Catholic deaf education in Dublin. *The Nation* in 1859 reported a meeting chaired by "the Lord Bishop of Elphin", where the Very Rev Canon Grimley and the Rev John Burke represented the "Dublin Catholic Institution for the Deaf and Dumb" then only twelve years in existence. The working Committee of the deaf institution at Cabra included the names of "learned and respected ecclesiastics", among whom was Dr Grimley. The school for girls was run with considerable success by " the holy Dominican nuns of Cabra, who educate the Mute girls, and the Christian Brothers … who educate the boys".[1] One of these "holy Dominican nuns" was Sister Dympna who planned to introduce deaf education into the Cape Colony when the time was right, that is when economic resources and suitable staff would guarantee some measure of efficiency and success. Although she could not immediately on her arrival in Cape Town, give her time and resources to formal deaf education, her interest in their welfare never faltered. Deaf boys and girls in the Colony were often hidden away, a source of embarrassment and shame to their parents. Living in isolation and without formal education, they had virtually no means of learning to communicate or to gain any knowledge of God or the truths of religion. They could neither hope to find employment nor to live with any ease among people with whom they could not communicate. The potential that education could unleash in the deaf was familiar to both Mother Dympna and to Grimley himself. This was a specialisation that the Dominican nuns of Cabra were to bring to South Africa, through the agency not only of Mother Dympna, but also through the work of teachers who were themselves deaf, and had been educated and trained by the sisters at Cabra.

Although from 1863 onwards Mother Dympna had shown an interest in the welfare of individual deaf boys and girls who came to her notice in Cape Town, it was not until 1874 that her plans for a formal school, the first South African institution specifically for the deaf, could be realised. This move was made possible by the work of a young deaf teacher, Bridget Lynne who volunteered to come to Cape Town to join Mother Dympna, a well remembered and much loved teacher. She travelled under the protection of Dr John Leonard and arrived in September 1873.[2] She had been one of the better pupils at the Cabra Institute for the Deaf and Dumb, and after completing the normal six years of schooling had entered the pupil teachers' training course. A few of her deaf contemporaries entered the convent and as Dominican sisters, carried their expertise to other missionary countries. However Bridget Lynne, who at the age of twenty-four, volunteered for the South African mission, was not a religious sister, but a lay woman. She was to fulfil her vocation among the neglected deaf children of South Africa, and her story is part of the history of the mission to the deaf of Cabra and of the Dominican community at Cape Town.

In 1857, Cahirciveen Union, Co Kerry, recommended that Bridget Lynne, an eight year old orphan be admitted into the Deaf Institute at Cabra.[3] She spent 16 years there, first as a pupil, later as a pupil teacher and finally as a member of staff. She had been taught by Mother Dympna, and when the request came from the Cape community to Cabra for a teacher of the deaf, Bridget came to a woman whom she could trust to guide and support her in her difficult task. Her arrival at last made possible the opening of a Dominican school for the deaf, and she was to work virtually single-handed until her death only 13 years later. According to the local Cape Town press:

> The Mother Prioress of St. Mary's Convent and some of the ladies who are associated with her in carrying out the work of education in Cape Town, have had considerable experience in connection with schools for deaf mutes in England and elsewhere, but in consequence of other claims made upon them, they were unable to devote so much of their time as would be required to work such an undertaking efficiently, and the services of a special teacher were secured for that purpose. The lady [Bridget Lynne], who is herself a deaf mute, entered upon her duties early in the present year, and it was for the purpose of estimating the progress which her pupils have made since that time, that the examination on Saturday was held.[4]

This was a public examination, that is the pupils were tested before about 20 lay visitors together with Bishop Leonard and the local clergy. The children answered questions on grammar, geography and arithmetic, and as in all such Victorian occasions, there was music. This was provided by the "young ladies of the

Convent School singing the well-known and beautiful hymn 'My God, how wonderful Thou art', the deaf mutes accompanying the words with appropriate movements of the hands and head". For those who were convinced that the deaf were ineducable, this public exhibition of proficiency in communication by signs and writing, was a revelation:

> Yet a visit to the school for the deaf mutes ... would certainly remove any difficulty not only as to the facts that the deaf and dumb can be educated, but that it can be accomplished with facility, certainty and even comparative rapidity. It was with something akin to wonder that we saw children who we were assured 12 months ago were absolutely ignorant of spelling or writing, now exhibiting a considerable amount of skill and proficiency in such elementary subjects as orthography, arithmetic, English grammar, sacred history, and writing.[5]

This was no small victory for Bridget Lynne who only about six months earlier, in March of 1874, had welcomed the first two pupils to St Joseph Deaf and Dumb School, with four more to join them in the same year; a humble beginning of a very difficult venture.[6] For the next thirteen years she and Mother Dympna co-operated to lay the foundations of deaf education in South Africa. It was a happy partnership since both were keenly aware of the needs of the deaf pupils. Mother Dympna, as foundress constantly held office in the community either as Prioress or Sub-Prioress, and consequently had many other urgent calls on her time. Nevertheless she knew that she could safely entrust the day to day teaching of the children to Bridget's care. The latter had personal experience of the methods of instructing the deaf both as a pupil and as a teacher at Cabra, and her immediate success at the first public examination of her school proved her competence in the writing method of teaching the deaf.

The *Eleventh Annual Report* issued in 1857, reflects the approved methodology used by the Deaf Institute at Cabra. This was in the very year that Bridget Lynne was admitted as a pupil. Three means of instruction were used: "signs, natural and methodical, dactylology, and the analysis of written language". According to Father Bourke the first method could be a refined instrument of communication:

> Signs form a language common to all deaf mutes, by means of which they are enabled to communicate their ideas to each other. Before instruction this language, for ought that we can discover, serves for no other purpose than for making known their wants and desires, their pleasures and pains. As the

work of education advances it becomes more rich and varied
and soon displays all the expressions of ancient pantomime,
enabling the deaf mute by a slight movement of the body and
features, to describe a scene, an action, a character, as
faithfully as the master strokes of a skilful pencil.[7]

Methodical sign language developed by Abbé de L'Epée used
specific signs for words, but he did not conceive of the deaf being
able to use the written word as a means of communication. His
friend and successor in the development of deaf education, Sicard,
promoted the written word as the main means of education and
communication for the deaf. This latter was the method in which
Bridget Lynne and her contemporaries were trained and in the
use of which Mother Dympna was familiar. It was seen as superior
to signs since it is "the language of the civilised world" while
"signs are peculiar to the deaf and may be compared to a
barbarous language, without books or literature, which serves
only to impede the enlightenment of those confined to it". Not
that the Institute at Cabra either condemned or prohibited signs,
"on the contrary it [had] adopted a regular system of them,
including dactylology", that is the spelling of words by using the
manual alphabet, a skill in which all the teachers of the deaf had
to be proficient. But for Cabra as for the School for the Deaf in
Cape Town, this was not the principal method used:

> Of the five modes of instruction ... that may be used in the
> education of the deaf and dumb, our institution attaches itself
> almost exclusively to that of writing, considering this the one
> best calculated to develope (*sic*) their reason and to be of
> service to them in after life. ... The deaf mute sees that his
> education is conducted in writing - that the chalk or pen
> must be forever in the fingers - that every question of any
> importance must be put in writing, and a written answer
> required, no credit being given to him for knowledge which
> he is not able to express in writing - that this is the language
> that entertains him in his library, the language of educated
> men; while signs create an invidious distinction, and mark
> him out as belonging to the caste of deaf mutes.[8]

Although the use of the oral method was gaining ground
elsewhere, writing remained the medium of instruction in the
deaf institution in Cape Town for about 45 years. This was
inevitable where the lay teachers were deaf and the sisters who
shared the work with them, while they learned the sign language,
had no opportunity to gain formal training in the use of the oral
method.[9]

By the turn of the twentieth century the battle of signs versus speech was rousing keen interest among those involved in the education of the deaf. While it is not possible to enter into a detailed analysis of this heated debate, it is interesting to note the resolution of the World Congress of the Deaf held at St Louis, Missouri in 1904:

> Resolved, that the method, which withholds from the congenitally and quasi congenitally deaf the use of the language of signs outside the schoolroom, robs the children of their birthright, that those champions of the oral method, who have been carrying on a warfare, both overt and covert, against the use of the language of signs by the adult deaf, are not friends of the deaf, and that in our opinion, it is the duty of every teacher of the deaf, no matter what method he or she uses, to have a working command of the sign language.[10]

For the experts in deaf education at St Louis, one significant point could not be ignored. Since the "best educated deaf in the world, as a class [were] in America, and the American deaf sign almost to a man", the value of this mode of communication could hardly be in doubt:

> Too many make speech itself as an end. This is a mistake. Speech is not in itself English; it is only one way of expressing that language, and we are little concerned to enquire by what means the pupil expresses himself in English so long as he does so express himself, whether in speech or writing or finger spelling. It is not the mere fact that he can make certain sounds or write certain letters or form the alphabet on his hands that should signify. It is the actual language that he uses, whatever be the means, and the thoughts that are enshrined in the language, that should be our criterion when judging of his education.[11]

For both Mother Dympna and Bridget Lynne the written word, combined with signs and the use of the finger alphabet, were familiar methods of communication and teaching. The pressing task of the deaf teachers who worked in the Cape Town foundation was not to invent new methods but in the early years to apply and where possible, perfect the old. At the same time they had to ensure that their pupils were not only competent in the use of English but were properly instructed in the truths and practices of religion. The special school in Cape Town applied no religious test in the admission of children. Since at the outset it was the only institution of its kind in South Africa, it opened its doors to those who applied whatever their religion, and Protestant parents had little choice but to send their deaf children to the nuns. This was seen as a threat to deaf pupils whose parents were not Catholics, and it aroused the anger of the Dutch Reformed Church. The Rev C Rabie of Malmsbury objected to the presence of one of his flock in so dangerous an environment:

> "Bij een der bezoeken aan de hulpkerken had ik ds. W. Murray met mij medegenomen. Ik verhaalde hem toen dat er een eenige zoon van de heer Theunis Smit, Kleinklipfontein, was, die doofstom was. De ouders die welgesteld waren wilden die jongen of naar de inrichting voor de Doofstoom bij de Roomsen zenden of zoo niet dan zou de moeder met hom naar Holland Gaan waar hij onderricht kon ontvangen".[12]

The Dutch community had its quota of neglected deaf children and adults, and Rabie could confirm that there were in his own Dutch Reformed congregation at least a dozen deaf members, old and young. Ds. Murray saw that the only remedy for the situation was to open a deaf school for their own children at Worcester, a happy solution, and another important step towards the implementation of special education in the Cape Colony. In the meantime since these deaf children were isolated from their own community and their own church, Bridget Lynne and Mother Dympna saw it as their duty to instruct them in the faith, and with parental permission, prepare them for reception into the Catholic Church. Often parents without any deep religious convictions, were happy to see their children become part of a church that had provided so well for their education and welfare.

By 1893, of the 37 deaf children who had been admitted to the school, 12 pupils of Protestant parentage became Catholics, and three whose parents were Catholics, were prepared for the reception of the sacraments, while three others were under instruction.[13] In mission and private schools it was not the normal practice of the Dominican nuns to influence Protestant or Jewish children to become Catholics, although if parents were agreeable, children were accepted into the church. This however was a rare occurrence since most pupils came from families which practised some form of religion. With the deaf children the situation was different. They came to the Dominican School for the Deaf with no knowledge of God since their own pastors lacked the expertise to communicate with them, and consequently could not provide them with any form of religious instruction. Bridget Lynne, and the deaf teachers and Dominican sisters who after her death carried on her work with the deaf pupils, had no alternative but to instruct them in the Catholic faith, but only with the approval of their parents. However the school did not constitute a real threat to any of the local Christian churches since the enrolment was very low and the number of converts negligible. Within the first twenty years of deaf education in South Africa, the combined intake of deaf pupils of the two schools for the deaf at Cape Town and Worcester, together with the small institution founded by the King William's Town Dominicans in 1889, never exceeded 58 in any one year. This is evidence enough that the religious instruction and admission into the Catholic Church of isolated pupils, made no significant inroads on the Dutch Reformed congregations. It also indicates that public education in awareness of the needs of these handicapped children was a matter of urgency. For Bridget Lynne and her lay deaf colleagues, as for the Dominican nuns involved in the school, the work of evangelisation was of more importance than the growing competence of their pupils in communicating through writing, in accurate and grammatical English, though the latter skill was promoted with enthusiasm and remarkable success.

Financial constraints presented a greater threat to the school than did religious bigotry, though the latter also hindered the recruitment of pupils, essential for the survival of the institution. For the first eight years of its existence the school for the deaf was a private institution, and the small and irregular fees paid by the pupils, were the only source of income. The financial burden of supporting the work fell on the Dominican community until June 1881, when, through the intervention of Dr Leonard and Mother Dympna, the school was given a government grant. "Accept my very sincere thanks for your goodness [on] behalf of our Poor Deaf Mutes" wrote Mother Dympna to Langham Dale, "the Grant will indeed be welcome and shall I trust be well employed for the advantage of these afflicted beings".[14] The grant provided an allowance of £15 per annum for six of "the more indigent scholars", and a further £50. This covered other expenses, including part of the lay teacher's salary.[15] In 1882 Father J J O' Reilly as manager of the school, could assure Dale that although there was a " rather large excess of Expenditure over Receipts ... caused by the erection of more suitable classrooms and the purchase of school requisites", this would not be a financial burden on the management. "The Sisters have taken upon themselves the entire support of the school".[16] Despite the grant and the provision of £15 *per annum* for some of the more indigent pupils, for many years the school was hindered by a lack of funds and adequate space for building and development.

In most cases the children came from poor families who could ill afford to pay regular boarding and school fees. Carl, a German immigrant, was fed at the convent and the nuns paid for his lodgings in town. Two other pupils, Gert and Joanna Van Wyk from Durban were partly supported by the grant, while the parents of Edward Goodwin, Willie Lee, Benjamin and George Godfrey and Willie Burmeister could afford to pay only a small fraction of the prescribed fee. "Miss Hugo, the daughter of wealthy parents has always paid her own expenses".[17] Since there was no boarding accommodation for the boys, the majority of the pupils, these had to be housed in cheap lodgings, while the girls lodged in Nazareth House. Despite repeated resolutions of superiors, it was not until 1918 that "a house at the top of the Convent Garden was rented as a home for the Deaf". Though this was not an ideal solution, it was the best the community could afford at that time:

> For all the years the Deaf were only day pupils and had to be boarded out where a place could be got for them. This was a great loss to the upbringing of the children. The position of the house made it very desirable, though the house itself is an old ramshackle and costs us a great deal to keep it in order. Yet it is a great blessing to the children to be with their teachers all the time, and the work progresses much more quickly.[18]

The provision of a suitable boarding school for the Coloured pupils, St Dominic's School for the Deaf, did not come about until 1937, when on the eve of amalgamation, the new building at Wittebome was ready for occupation. During the 50 years between the death of Bridget Lynne and this important development, the deaf institution in Cape Town went through many vicissitudes and not a little conflict. It is not always possible to trace from available records, the movements of staff or the early attempts to prepare the nuns professionally for this special branch of education. However it is clear that teachers who were themselves deaf, considered that they were best qualified to teach deaf children, and this to the exclusion of the Dominican nuns who from time to time were assigned to work with them in the school. It was not an easy situation for either the deaf teachers, who saw their livelihood threatened by unqualified outsiders who had the power of the Dominican community behind them, or for the Dominican nuns who, whatever their feelings, had no choice but to do the work assigned to them by their superiors.

Complete records concerning the tenure of the deaf teachers and the Dominican nuns who were on the staff of the school during its first 40 years are not available. However there is sufficient evidence to prove that the school faced many difficulties during its founding years. While sisters did not put their complaints into writing or appeal to educational authorities against the rulings of their superiors, the same restraint was not practised by the deaf teachers. In 1896 Annie Marsh came to St Mary's Convent, Cape Town as an "Assistant teacher of the deaf and dumb".[19] She was well known in Cabra having received part of her education there. In 1883 in response to a threat by her parents to sue the Cabra community for their daughter's wages, Mother Catherine de Ricci Maher, the Prioress at that time, wrote:

> When a properly trained teacher we would give her a salary, small in the beginning and rising according to her progress as a teacher ... We found her very backward in her education. She had not even got the usual period of six years at school and the employment in which she had been engaged had left her no time to improve herself. ... Great pains were taken with her education from 1875 to 1878 and meantime we supported and clothed her. In the case of other Deafmutes, we are paid for them for the usual period of six years, then if they wish to become pupil teachers they remain still at school, and until they are trained teachers and of use to us we receive a certain sum for their maintenance.[20]

Annie Marsh had been teaching in a deaf school in England and applied for the post of assistant teacher in Cape Town. Mother Dympna was aware of her academic and professional record and knew that she was not a woman to be trifled with, nor was she a young girl without experience in deaf education. She claimed that she had been teaching since 1872, though it is difficult to reconcile this with her Cabra record. However it was common in many schools for senior pupils to act as assistants in the classroom, and it is partly to this early experience that she may have been referring. By 1900 the School for the Deaf at Cape Town was at a low ebb and there was serious question of closing it altogether. Annie Marsh was the only teacher on the books, a normal situation in small deaf institutions at that time. Singlehanded she had acted as "Head Teacher and with so much success that a good [inspector's] report was the immediate result". The manager of the school, Father J J O'Reilly asked the Superintendent General of Education, Dr Muir, to appoint her as Head Teacher as from 1 October 1900. Miss Marsh had "promised to look out for a suitable assistant during the holidays".[21]

By October 1902 Annie Marsh made application to be allowed to "train one or two of the pupils as pupil-teachers for the future". She claimed that this had been the strategy suggested to her by her teachers at the Deaf Mute School, Cabra, Dublin. Her letter accompanied an application for a teaching post, made by Alice

Collins, a deaf girl from the "Oral School for the Deaf and Dumb in Dundee, Scotland". She was to turn 15 years old in less than a month and had been a pupil of the Dominican school in Cape Town for three and a half years. Her application, supported by her head mistress, was approved, and she was eligible for an allowance of £15 per annum.[22] Almost immediately her newly granted pupil teachership was threatened. At the end of December Annie Marsh was given one term's notice by "Rev. Mother of St. Mary's Convent, Cape Town", the superior of the Dominicans in the Western Cape. Her complaint at this summary termination of her services was, in her opinion, justified. Mother Pius McLaughlin had "turned her out for no reason", and this in the opinion of Miss Marsh, was a poor reward for the excellent work she had done:

> I am sorry to have to leave the deaf-mute School at Tuin Plein, Cape Town, because I have had my long experience in teaching the deaf-mutes for about 30 years. I have been in St. Mary's for 7 years. When I leave School, I shall start a school of my own account in the Cape. I feel much to think that I had made a sacrifice in leaving England to come to the deaf-mutes in St. Mary's as I had charge of nearly 40 deaf-mutes there; now I am turned out for no reason as the new Mother said in the notice that she has no complaints to make on my part. I would like to remember (*sic*) you that the deaf-mute school in Tuin Plein was threatened with being closed in 1900 because of failure, and I was left alone to do the work from October 1900, to December 1900, and in December 1900 I was handed a paper by Rev. J. J. O'Reilly appointing me as the Head Teacher because of the success, and ever since, I kept getting increase of pupils so I saved the School from being closed. I have done my best to get everything into order, and I feel sorry to part with the pupils who show every good sign of learning fast. Poor deaf-mutes will miss many good opportunities, such as Night-School etc.[23]

Her notice was rescinded and she continued to work in the school for a few more years. In 1904 she went to Victoria West "on an educational Mission to look after some Deaf-Mutes in the Hugo family and to bring down a young Deaf-Mute child, then on to Pretoria to bring here a deaf-mute boy named David Purcell".[24] It is clear that the Head Mistress did not limit her activities to the schoolroom nor to the supervision of pupil teachers. Her task was also to recruit and accompany deaf children from their homes to the school when necessary, and for the task of training pupil teachers she got assistance both from the nuns and from Dr Kolbe.

In the development of deaf education, both the sisters and the lay teachers were supported by Dr Frederick Charles Kolbe, a convert, priest and educationist of note in the Colony. Among his wide range of interests in education was the progress of the deaf, both teachers and pupils. Early in May 1888 while on an overseas trip, Kolbe visited England and spent some time at the institution for the deaf at Boston Spa. There he met Father Dawson and "learnt a good deal about Deaf-Mutes". Later in the same month he visited Cabra and St Gabriel's School for deaf girls, run by the Dominican sisters.[25] To ensure that he could be of use to the deaf teachers and that he could administer to the pastoral needs of the children he learned the sign language. He became a good friend to the struggling school, and for the pupils a much loved teacher. With an elegance typical of the written communication of the deaf in those days, the pupils congratulated their clerical friend on the anniversary of his ordination to the priesthood:

> Words are inadequate to express the gratitude and affection which we entertain for you, dear Father, for your great zeal in having instructed us and received us into the Catholic Church, and also for all you have done for our spiritual welfare. We cannot tell you how happy we are and how highly we prize the inestimable blessings we enjoy.[26]

In 1899 he was prepared to assist the Department of Education in the drawing up of a special syllabus for a teachers' qualifying course for deaf candidates, since he believed that they could not compete with ordinary candidates.[27] Prior to this period both Sister Berchmans Cotter and Sister Alberta Bean had held in turn the position of principal of the School for Deaf Mutes in Cape Town. Sister Berchmans, who was professed in 1886, probably took over the school during the last illness of Bridget Lynne. It is not clear when Sister Alberta succeeded her in the work they both loved. In 1908 Hannah Farrell a deaf teacher from Ireland, who had come to Cape Town two years previously to teach in the Dominican school for the deaf, appealed against her dismissal from the school. In a written dialogue with a representative of Dr Muir, the Superintendent General of Education, she claimed that she could see no reason for this unfair treatment she had received at the hands of the Mother Superior:

> "I got a *months notice* on *26 November* but I did not get a full notice as the Rev Mother was trying to put me on the boat one day that gave me a great shock so I refused to go as I did not expect to go so soon".

" Does the Rev. Mother wish you to go to Ireland?"

"Yes, but I won't as I have little money to go with".

It is clear from her evidence that she had clashed with Sister Telchilde Kolbe, Dr Kolbe's sister and the new Principal of the school, whom she claimed did not know how to teach the deaf:

> Did you know I left the Institute since Xmas [1907]? The school has been in disorder all the year because we have a nun in charge of the D & D, even she does not know to talk in signs. I worked hard with the children in the school and sometimes got troubled when the nun ... went out of the school and left the children alone playing. She does not understand the D & D.

She could appeal to her experience in Cabra to prove that her complaint was not against nuns in general but against one individual in particular:

> I always got on splendidly with Sr Mary Hyacinth Skeehan when she was in charge of the D & D. She was the best mistress of classes in Cabra Convent. She taught the D & D for eighteen years and understands the D & D as if she were a deafmute herself. We all can hardly get on with Sister Mary Telchilde this year as she does not understand the D & D. I taught her signs & helped [her] to teach the D & D for her. No nuns except Sister Mary Hyacinth and Sr. M. Berchmans [Cotter] could hardly work with the children.

She had come to Cape Town in 1906 with the expectation of employment for a fixed number of years, with free board and lodgings and a good salary. On no .point was she satisfied. She did not get the full salary, she did not like or respect her Principal, and she could not accept the constraints placed upon her in her social life. She was reminded that "the managers of the school [would] tell the story from their side too", but she was adamant as to the justice of her case and certain that all criticism of her conduct was the result of malicious gossip:

> I heard they were spreading false reports to the friends of the children saying that I am naughty and disobedient & that I encouraged the children to be so but the friends of these children did not believe in these as they know what sort I am. How could I be? ... I do not agree with my head teacher that came to us lately. I got short notice because I came home one night late after coming from Wynberg seeing about a deafmute pupil as I was always anxious & earnest about the children. The nuns there wished me to follow the rules of the convent

but sometimes I did not mind as I am not a nun but I always
worked all day in the school.

Her complaints in clear and remarkably correct English, prove
both that the young teacher was less than diplomatic in her
approach to what could have been judged a legitimate complaint,
and excellent in communicating through the written word.
Although she must have realised that she was not likely to regain
her post, nevertheless she rallied her friends, deaf teachers and
pupils, past and present, who wrote to the Department of
Education criticising the administration and teaching of the nuns.
Florrie Marshall, a past pupil of the school, was one who reported
that two deaf boys were selling rosettes when they should have
been in school, and that Sister Telchilde "sometimes did not teach
children because all the children don't understand her". Hannah
Farrell was unfortunate in her choice of champion. The
Department of Education noted that she and Florrie Marshall
were staying at the same address in Mowbray. This in itself
suggested to the authorities that the latter was a prejudiced
witness.

Miss Farrell, though not conciliatory in respect of the staffing
situation, had a clear view of the needs of the pupils: "The children
in the town are badly off, even looked after. It would be preferable
that if they get up an Institute in the Country - like Rondebosch
or Wynberg. Or any country else, as the Institute in the town is
badly situated". But even as she pleaded for support and proved,
in theory at least that her cause was just, she knew that her
chances were slim. "I have heard that they have got an assistant
named Sr. Mary Lelia [O'Connor] who has taken my place, she is
quite ignorant of anything about the D & D, the present two
teachers do not suit these poor children. The two nuns know
little about the D & D only lately".[28] Her final shot was aimed at
the manager of the school: "Fr. O'Reilly may tell you the different
story because the Rev. Mother has to tell what he has to say to
Dr. Muir, but he never saw with his own eyes how the school has
been going on".[29]

Sister Lelia, the newly appointed teacher, was one of a large
party of Postulants who came from Ireland in 1903. She was
professed in 1906 and the following year went to St Agnes'
Convent to study for her Teacher's Certificate. When in 1908 she
passed this examination, she was assigned to St Mary's, Cape
Town to work in the Deaf School. Hannah Farrell may indeed
have been correct in her judgement of the readiness of Sister
Lelia for her task, but practice and study soon gave her the
competence she needed. She spent the rest of her short working
life teaching the deaf, children most dear to her heart. She died

of tuberculosis in 1919 and so did not live to see the great changes that were to take place in the institute in which she had found a happy outlet for her apostolic vocation.[30] All available records indicate that from the outset the progress of the pupils was remarkable. Their ability to communicate by means of written English, was exceptional, and this was at a time when facilities were poor, staffing was less than adequate and the provision of teaching aids depended on the ingenuity and skills of individual teachers. Despite the proficiency of the pupils in written English, it was becoming more and more evident that the Cape Town Institute for the Deaf was lagging behind her two rivals in South Africa. As early as the 1880's both the deaf institution at Worcester and at the Dominican school at King William's Town were using the oral method:

> The old method of teaching the deaf-mute to translate or interpret the movements of the fingers is pursued in Cape Town; but the German or Heinecke's method of treatment, by which the pupils are taught to watch and interpret the lip movements, is coming to be regarded as the more successful. The lip-teaching method is practised at Worcester.[31]

In was not until 1922, when Mother Berchmans Cotter was superior and first Provincial of the Dominicans in the Western Cape, that Sister Alocoque Broderick was sent to King William's Town to study the "labial system". She spent a number of months with the Dominican community there and studied the theory and practice of the oral method of instruction. On her return to Cape Town at the end of the year she immediately began to teach the children the use of lip-reading and speech, and soon won the approval of the inspector.[32] This was an important step in the development of deaf education in the Cape Peninsula, and Sister Alacoque's contribution was officially recognised. When in 1929 a National Council for the Deaf was formed, she was a member of the Executive Committee. Her work was never easy since the school urgently needed adequate premises for classrooms and boarding facilities, as well as additional qualified staff. In 1927 the Grimley Institute for the Deaf had a staff of only two Sisters and one secular teacher. These had to cope with 45 pupils, each one of whom needed personal attention. In addition the lease on the boarding house had expired and "matters concerning the future housing of white boarders [was] still in abeyance". The small number of Coloured children were either day pupils or, as in the nineteenth century, were boarded out with private families in Cape Town. By 1928 the situation had become urgent. The "Deaf and Dumb School, Grimley Institute, was removed from Mr Kerchoff's house, the children being boarded in the convent. The girls occupied the open-air cells and the boys two rooms on the ground floor. Certain temporary partitions were put up so as to separate, at least to a certain extent, the convent from the children's premises".[33] This could not have been more than a temporary arrangement, and in 1931, Sisters Alacoque and Ceslaus Coyle accompanied their pupils to Rondebosch where they were to stay until the new school was built. This latter was to be erected on the site of Mr Kerchoff's house, which had been purchased from him, and demolished in 1931.[34] The staff and pupils returned to the newly built school in April 1932 and the formal opening took place in March of 1933.

The next step, and one of great concern to Mother Teresa Coleman, the Prioress General of the Dominican Congregation in the Western Cape, and also to Sister Alacoque Broderick and all those involved in deaf education, was the provision of adequate, qualified staff for the Coloured deaf children. The early 1930's was a time of growing concern of the Catholic Church for the development of educational facilities for the indigenous people of South Africa, and Mother Teresa was anxious to give the support of her Congregation to this cause. It was fortunate that the urgent need for additional teachers coincided with the influx of young sisters from the novitiate at Potter's Bar. This was the beginning of a new era, when for the first time in the history of the Dominicans in the Western Cape, there was the possibility of providing the two deaf schools with an adequate number of bright, enthusiastic, well-qualified teachers, who were to devote the whole of their professional life to the deaf in Southern Africa. Although the sisters who became teachers of the deaf had no personal say in this choice of specialisation, nevertheless they developed a vocation within a vocation and became a competent and highly committed professional body.

Most of the young women, some of them very young, who entered this field, had little or no secondary education and first had to pass the hurdle of matriculation. For this examination they were taught privately by Sister Ignatius Curtin, at St Michael's, Rondebosch. This was not an experience for the faint-hearted since Sister Ignatius was a woman of formidable scholarship with little patience for halting progress in Latin or literature. The next stage for the young temporary professed sisters was a two year Primary Teacher's Certificate. For this they attended Mowbray College of Education, a permission reluctantly given by the hierarchy, since the prevailing Protestant atmosphere was judged to be detrimental to the spiritual life of the nuns. The sisters did not specialise at a South African university because in the 1940's, no suitable programme was available. Manchester University offered a part-time correspondence course of studies for a Diploma in Deaf Education, and this was followed by those who had qualified for a primary teachers' certificate. The outbreak of war in Europe in 1939 made the choice of an overseas university hazardous. Postal services were erratic and enemy action at sea could mean the loss of those precious assignments on which a sister's academic success depended. To protect their work, duplicated copies had to be made one of which was kept safely in South Africa.[35] Practical experience in teaching the deaf was gained initially at the Grimley Institute in Cape Town and from 1937 onwards, also at St Dominic's, Wittebome. Practical examinations for the Manchester diploma, in which the Dominican candidates did remarkably well, were conducted by a South African panel of examiners, including Inspectors of Special Education and experts in the methodology of deaf education.

Among the Dominican teachers of the deaf and their lay colleagues there developed a strong system of mutual support and instruction. Those who were qualified and experienced assisted those on the way. An excellent tutor in the methodology of deaf teaching was Miss Janice Breitweiser who joined the staff of St Dominic's, Wittebome in 1937. She held a BSc, and a Masters in Deaf Education, and during the two years that she spent in South Africa she instructed the sisters in the practical application of the current methodology of deaf teaching. Another source of support and encouragement was Sister Germaine Lawrence, who, after she herself had qualified, shared her study material and expertise with those following the Manchester diploma course. She was always available to give support and encouragement to the staff in Cape Town and Wittebome, and this was especially fortunate for those studying and teaching in St Dominic's where she succeeded Sister Alacoque as principal in 1940.[36] In 1945 two qualified teachers, Sisters Benedicta Gillen and Cosmas McKeever, came directly from St Gabriel's School for the Deaf, Cabra, where they had gained a diploma in deaf education. They brought new expertise to the staff of the two deaf schools, and helped their colleagues, especially those who were still in training.

Sisters Amata Tuohy, Mannes Daly and Damian McDonald arrived in Cape Town from Potter's Bar in January 1934. Sister Amata was immediately assigned to St Mary's Convent to begin studying for matriculation and to gain teaching experience in the Grimley Institute, while her two companions went directly to Rondebosch to complete their matriculation course. She together with Sisters Basil McCarthy, Damian McDonald, Alexius

McGonigle, Mannes Daly, Finbar Conway and Gilbert Dowd, were among the forerunners of professional teachers who were to develop deaf education not only in the Cape, but also in the Transvaal and in Swaziland. For these, as for many of their Dominican colleagues, it was to be the beginning of a lifetime of ongoing study, practical training, excellent service and total commitment to the cause of deaf education.

The opening of St Dominic's School for the Deaf at Wittebome in 1937, built at the cost of £10665, was to Sister Alacoque the fulfilment of her dreams. It was also a victory for those who had negotiated for the transfer of the Coloured Deaf from Cape Town to Wittebome. Among these was Dr Abdurahman, who championed Catholic rights and helped to bring the matter of the transfer to a successful conclusion.[37] Work for the formal education of the deaf, begun in Cape Town in 1874, was by the late 1930's about to enter a new and creative phase. By this time Sister Alacoque was within three years of retirement, but in spite of the short period of official service ahead of her, she was appointed the first principal of the new St Dominic's School for the Deaf. Of the twelve initial members of the new community four were assigned to teach the deaf, Sisters Alacoque, Damian Mc Donald, Cyril Brick and Sister Alexius Mc Gonigle, a qualified Domestic Science teacher. Sister Emily Garry took over the cooking and catering single-handed, while Sister Colmcille Nagle, on a visit from Holy Trinity Convent, Matroosfontein, helped to plan and lay out the grounds. In 1939 Sister Finbar Conway filled the eleventh post in the school and later moved to the Grimley where she taught for six years before returning to Wittebome. Among the sisters assigned to the deaf were those who would continue to study part-time for a Diploma in Deaf Education.[38] In 1938, the year in which the school was granted full salaries for teachers, Sister Amata Tuohy, joined the staff as the tenth teacher on the payroll. On the roll were 125 pupils with space for another 75 boarders. In the same year the situation in the Grimley school was less prosperous. There was a decrease in the number of pupils and "only one teacher was necessary".[39] The assignment of teaching staff to the two schools depended on the immediate needs of each institution and on the availability of teaching posts. Many of the young Dominican teachers of the deaf moved from one school to the other as circumstances demanded. In 1949 Sister Germaine who had served as principal of St Dominic's on the retirement of Sister Alacoque in 1940, was transferred in the same position to the Grimley School. In Wittebome Sister Amata, who had been vice-principal for nine years, assumed responsibility for St Dominic's with Sister Michael

Morgan as her next in command. In 1950 the latter attended Stellenbosch University in preparation for her bi-lingual examination in Afrikaans. She surprised all her colleagues and delighted the inspector by achieving her goal in only six months. She was later to serve as Principal in the Grimley school. The work of the sisters assigned to the deaf schools was not confined to school hours nor was it limited to academic work. Where most of the pupils were boarders, boys as well as girls, there was a need for constant supervision and ongoing informal education. Teachers who spent their days in the classroom, also devoted their evenings and nights and often holidays as well, to the care of their charges.

In September 1980, after over 100 years in Cape Town, the Grimley School, which at this time provided for the educational needs of the European deaf children, was transferred to its present beautiful setting in Hout Bay. This not only ensured that the school could develop in more spacious surroundings and with modern facilities, but also that the children were living in a healthy and visually stimulating environment. It has had the good fortune to have intelligent and committed leadership, most noteworthy in recent decades that of Sister Macrina Donoghue, who as principal has promoted the oral method, developing in the pupils of the Grimley School a remarkable facility for communication through speech. In this as in other aspects of the education of the deaf she has been supported by a lay staff and by a strong team of Dominican teachers, Sisters Paulinus Conroy, Cynthia Thompson and Francis Krige. In the academic field the senior pupils today follow the usual secondary syllabuses leading to matriculation and the possibility of tertiary education. Over the years the need for technical courses became a matter of urgency, and consequently in the 1970's technical drawing was introduced as a class subject and the secondary pupils wrote the National Examinations for Stds VI, VIII, IX and X. In the mid-1980's, the pupils were given the choice between an academic and a technical course of studies. In order to give those following the latter syllabus greater experience, they wrote the N1, N2 and N3 examinations in engineering drawing. The boys and girls who chose the technical stream and passed engineering drawing, engineering mathematics, engineering science and logic systems, by adding English and Afrikaans to their course of studies, could obtain a full National Senior Certificate.[40] The vision of the staff and their determination to develop the full potential of the pupils, reflect the spirit of Sister Dympna Kinsella, Bridget Lynne and those Dominican sisters and lay teachers who, in a simpler and less sophisticated age, opened the doors in Cape Town to the least among the children of the Colony the "deaf and dumb".

African children had been admitted to St Dominic's School at Wittebome, but early in the 1950's it was clear that this ran counter to the new racist legislation of the Nationalist government. Although the process was relatively slow, the exigencies of apartheid laws forced the Cabra Dominicans in the Region of South Africa to found a new school specifically for African deaf children. These formed the most neglected minority among the rural African boys and girls of school-going age, the majority of whom had little hope of any formal education. In April 1962, St Dominic's School for the Deaf was opened at Hammanskraal. The foundresses of this convent and school were Mother Alexius McGonigle, the first Prioress, together with Sisters Michael Morgan, Gilbert Dowd, Fabian McWeeny and Ceslaus Melvin, all from the community of St Dominic's Convent, Wittebome. The new school served Sotho and Tswana boys and girls and instruction was in the mother tongue. All the teachers, including the nuns, had to become proficient in one or both of these languages. English was also taught to the older pupils in order to prepare them for future employment. Like St Dominic's Wittebome, the new school at Hammanskraal provided instruction and practical training in typing, sewing and cooking for girls, and carpentry, welding and shoe repairing for boys. Practical gardening was also taught. At the outset many of the pupils were too old to benefit from speech training but all gained spiritually and socially from the care and commitment of the staff. Here many of the Dominican teachers of the deaf served for longer or shorter periods. And it was here that Sister Finbar Conway, besides assisting teachers preparing for their Deaf Diploma, also carried on an active apostolate among the adult deaf, especially the young men working at Babelegi, an industrial complex situated a short distance from the Deaf School. Here also Sister Ronan Drury, a volunteer from the Institute at Cabra, added to her daily teaching in the classroom the task of preparing teachers for their Deaf Diploma examinations.[41] The principalship of the school is now in lay hands, and Sister Siobhan Murphy, who held the office of principal for a number of years, is presently one of the Vice-Principals. She works for the school drawing up curricula and planning for and promoting every aspect of deaf education. One of her goals was the provision of secondary and technical education for deaf boys and girls. This bore fruit in 1994 when St Paul's, formerly a minor seminary, was ready for the use of deaf pupils who wanted to continue their education at secondary or technical levels.

In 1976, after protracted negotiations, the Dominican sisters opened the first school for the deaf in Swaziland, at Siteki, near the Mozambique border. In a meeting between representatives of the Swazi Government and the Dominican Congregation, including the founding members of St Margaret's Convent, Swaziland, Sisters Madeleine Corcoran and Gilbert Dowd, the responsibilities of both parties were clearly defined. The relevant government departments were entirely responsible for the building and future extension of the school, and for all salaries and subsidies necessary for the day-to-day running of the institution. Pupils were to be taught through the medium of English and Seswati. Proficiency in English would ensure that pupils reaching secondary level would be able to cope with public examinations. The Cabra Congregation accepted the invitation of the Swazi government, on condition that the financial conditions were honoured, and that the sisters were provided with a furnished house. Their task would be the training of teachers of the deaf, lay or religious, who were studying on a part-time basis. It was agreed that the Dominican nuns would remain in the school until the local teachers were ready to take full responsibility for the institution. When Sister Madeleine Corcoran took office as principal in October 1976, Mr Mncube and Miss Rose Dlamini were already studying at the College for Deaf Education at Accra in Ghana. On the completion of his studies Mr Mncube was made principal and Sisters Gilbert and Ancilla Griffiths remained on the staff as teachers. He was later succeeded in that office by Rose Dlamini [now Mrs Rose Nxumalo]. Sister Gilbert Dowd ran a two-year inservice training course for the teachers working in the School of the Deaf. These later gained their Diploma in Deaf Teaching at the Education Centre for the Deaf in Limbe, Malawi. In 1979 Sisters Gilbert and Ancilla resigned their teaching posts. The latter was made Advisor to the Deaf, a post she held for one year. Sister Gilbert was appointed to help in the training of teachers for the deaf and in this position she worked until her retirement in October 1995.

The Cabra Dominicans in Siteki did not limit their work to deaf education, but extended their expertise to the schools and adults in the surrounding rural areas. Sister Mairéad McGlade was assigned to St Margaret's community in October 1976. She taught in Lubombo High School and in 1981 she joined Sisters Eileen McCarthy and Ann Maher in a programme for teacher upgrading. Sister Mairéad also promoted needlework skills among the women. When St Margaret's community took up residence at Manzini, neither the work for the promotion of education in general nor the apostolate among the deaf, came to an end. Sister Gilbert as a member of the Board of the School for the Deaf,

Siteki, is always available for consultation, and frequently visits the campus to share with her colleagues there, her long experience, expertise and interest in the education of the deaf.

Her main work lies in the pastoral care of the adult deaf. This she carries out in conjunction with Father John Turner, his brother Brian Turner, both past pupils of St Vincent's School for the Deaf, Melrose and Debbie Eaton, a past pupil of St Dominic's School for the Deaf, Wittebome. These form a team the aim of which is the pastoral care of hearing impaired people in Southern Africa. Sister Gilbert works together with this group, organising resident and non-resident meetings and retreats for the adult deaf of Swaziland. Her work in the local parish has promoted liturgical involvement of the deaf in one of the weekly Masses, and on every third Sunday which is now established as Deaf Sunday. Every week the deaf parishioners sit together during Mass and one of their number interprets the readings and prayers. On Deaf Sunday all the lay functions at the service: the collections, the offertory procession, and serving at the altar, are carried out by members of the deaf community. Not only has this incorporated the deaf members more fully into the life of the parish but it has increased public awareness of the needs and rights of the deaf in the church and in society as a whole.[42]

The full history of Dominican education of the deaf in Southern Africa still remains to be thoroughly researched and written. It involves the unique stories of individual women, religious and lay who in the nineteenth century, laid the first simple foundations on which in a later era, committed teachers of the deaf, with the best qualifications available worldwide, developed primary and secondary schools of a high standard. The Dominican women who introduced and continued to promote this field of special education in Southern Africa, have a wealth of historical resources. Much of the documentation is contemporary and unclassified, consequently it is not yet easily available for research purposes. However the problem of properly classified resources is presently in the process of solution and it reveals the elements of a history that is complex in respect of the debate and the application of theories on the question of appropriate methodologies best suited in this special field of education. But even more interesting is the unravelling of the complex interactions of the Dominican women who over the last 124 years founded, sustained and developed the schools for the deaf in Southern Africa. It involves the personal history of a number of professional Dominican women who worked in schools for the deaf either for a lifetime or for shorter periods, and also of those who supported the professional work of the sisters and lay staff in the many offices of household management.

Chapter Nine

Dominican Missionary Women:

The Lay sisters

Of those young women of the Irish Dominican foundations in Southern Africa who freely made the radical choice to witness as vowed Dominican religious to the Kingdom, the least privileged in human and social terms, though not necessarily the least influential, were the lay sisters, the "hewers of wood and the drawers of water". For the working class woman brought up in a nineteenth century industrial environment or coming from a farming community, a life of unremitting and often thankless service was familiar. Those who worked as servants had few recognised rights, and no comforts or privileges. In most working situations protest against injustices ensured instant dismissal. Within the conventual system this section of society was represented by the lay sisters. These young women chose religious dedication, rather than marriage, or a lifetime of menial employment in the secular world. While the inability to pay a dowry may have been one of the official reason for refusal to admit a young woman into the ranks of choir sister, more often the lay aspirant came from a poorer family where the need to become a wage-earner left little opportunity for anything more than most basic primary education.

This is especially the case in post-famine Ireland and among the poorer Irish immigrants in the Cape Colony. Without a reasonable education a young girl could not contribute to the professional work of the community, nor could she be expected to read prayers in Latin or mix with the more socially elevated members of the community. Snobbery played its role in the interpretation and practical application of minor regulations controlling the duties, social interaction, and official forms of prayer seen to be appropriate for the lay sisters. It is clear from the records that the norms of the times had a greater influence in this matter than the laws of the Gospel. Despite the potential harshness of the life of the lay sister, many freely chose that way of life and persevered in it. The choice of such a vocation and perseverance in it are not, from the worldly point of view, easy to understand. Nor are the limitations it imposed on the lay sisters, easy to forgive. What then were the main criteria used to support and justify the vocation and role of the lay sister in the Dominican community?

In Dominican tradition as in that of most other religious Orders of medieval origin, the acceptance of lay members was the norm rather than the exception. But even if that had not been the case there was a ready justification, that of need. Where enclosure was strictly imposed, in theory if not always in practice, the difficulty of obtaining servants who would not become a disruptive presence, was acute. The manual work had to be done both in the contemplative convent and in those that combined contemplation and an active apostolic ministry. In the social context of the nineteenth century, there was a distinct gap between the tasks expected of the educated young lady who offered herself as a choir sister, and those occupations properly allocated to servants. When Mother Josepha O' Halloran was sent from Siena Convent, Drogheda to be Prioress of Galway, her first effort towards the restoration of regular life was to dismiss the servants who had "access to all the rooms and in consequence there was no exclusion of seculars from rooms on the ground floor". The newcomers found that the "great obstacle to regularity was the absence of lay-sisters". This quest for the perfection of religious life and the assiduous observance of the Rule and Constitutions, especially in respect of enclosure, was therefore another legitimate reason for the admission of lay sisters into the community. Mother Josepha implemented this plan without delay and in 1885 put into effect the " first important domestic arrangement ... the introduction of lay sisters: Mary Cole prioress of her group of Tertiaries in Westmeath, and Ellen Gorman, a native of the same district entered".[1]

According to the 1843 *Constitutions* of Cabra, the community was "allowed to receive some few lay-sisters into the monastery" when it should "appear expedient, in a moderate number, to assist the other sisters".[2] This was not foreign to Dominican tradition. The division of labour in a preaching or teaching community ensured that neither the daily needs of the community nor the public apostolic mission were neglected. In the case of missionary foundations, both Cabra and Sion Hill followed this principle, and the Mother Houses always included lay sisters in missionary groups sent abroad. However, those who applied for admission as lay sisters seldom realised fully the implications of the choice they had made. There were those young women, a minority, who irrespective of their education or social status, accepted the vocation of lay sisters in a religious community. Whatever the social or economic milieu from which they came, lay aspirants, like their contemporaries, the choir postulants, desired to consecrate their lives to God. That the lay sisters offered their services for the temporal good of the community, did not in any essential way lessen the spiritual or apostolic value of their vocation. They made a free choice and so did the community, and as in the case of the choir sisters, the *Constitutions* determined their acceptance or rejection, and clearly laid down the laws and customs that would govern their lives. In the matter of choice the law was realistic in their regard: "Let such subjects only be admitted to the class of lay-sisters, as shall be found, by their humility, penitential spirit, good sense, and bodily strength, to afford just grounds that they will render service, as well to the spiritual as to the temporal interests of the community".[3] In Ireland of the post-famine period the bodily strength of the candidates was often in doubt. Many of the young women admitted to both lay and choir status developed tuberculosis, and virtually every group of volunteers who came to Cape Town and Port Elizabeth in the nineteenth and early twentieth centuries, included those sent out for reasons of health.

Whatever the health of the individual, in practical terms the lay sister's position in her community was often little more than that of a servant. Despite this the vocation was regarded in theory at least as of special significance and this is reflected in the relevant constitutions:

> Let these sisters, during the time of their probation, be ... impressed with the deepest conviction, that the accomplishment of the divine will, which is the soul of perfection, consists in the faithful discharge of their duties, however humble and laborious. Let them, in a spirit of entire and loving conformity with the divine will, seek, in the midst of their labours, to draw consolation from the reflection, that their poor and humble condition brings them to the closest imitation of the life and sufferings of our divine Lord and Master.[4]

This in religious terms, was a noble and exalted ideal which must have inspired many of the young women who offered themselves for this onerous vocation of service. It was fortunate for religious superiors therefore, that the role and status of the servant clearly defined in secular society, translated so well into the conventual system. In practice, and in line with the customs of the Order, the lay sisters could be admitted "to take the Habit and to commence their noviceship immediately after a year, or two, of trial as Seculars", that is as servants.[5] This in fact was the common practice, though the period of service before admission was not of uniform duration for all candidates. Cunnigunda Fischer (1879-1965) who entered the novitiate at Holy Rosary Convent, Port Elizabeth in July 1917, had "acted as a secular servant for 3 months prior to her admission, during which time she gave general satisfaction". Sister Anne Fischer took her vows in 1920 and made her final profession three years later. A German by birth, she served for about 48 years as a domestic sister in the predominantly Irish community in Port Elizabeth, witness enough to her charity and long-suffering. Although in principle the division of the community into two classes had been abolished in South Africa in 1922, she with most of her contemporaries who had begun their religious life as lay sisters, continued to play a domestic role in the community. Many also followed the old custom of social segregation. They seldom attended community recreations but kept their own company except on special days of celebration. Indeed pressure of work did not permit them to enjoy fixed periods of leisure, a situation often shared by the choir sisters. Sister Anne is remembered still as a prayerful, gentle, quiet lady who worked hard to the end of her life. She was one of many of the old class of lay sisters, German, Irish and South African, who gave much more than a lifetime of labour to the community. They gave love, loyalty, spiritual support and an example of dedication that encouraged those with whom they lived out their Dominican vocation.

In December 1870 Dr Grimley, en route to Cape Town writing to Dr Leonard of the stormy voyage, paid special tribute to the lay sister who was one of the party: "Now with regard to my nuns etc. I have to tell you that Sr. Margaret [McCabe] was the best man among the whole of us. Srs. Agnes and Monica were very sick for some time".[6] Sister Margaret made her profession as a lay sister in Cabra in September 1870 and left almost immediately afterwards for her mission in South Africa.[7] According to Mother Berchmans Cotter she was a fine nun and a splendid laundress, who worked both in St Mary's Cape Town and later in St Agnes' Convent, Woodstock She entertained the nuns with her "wonderfully correct knowledge she had of the

Royal Family. Often I went to her for information on Royalty for I was sadly deficient on this special point".[8] Her expertise in this field could only have been achieved by reading and study, proof enough that her interests and abilities were not limited to the domestic scene.

Mother Berchmans Cotter, one of the strong missionary women sent from Cabra to Cape Town in the mid 1880's, observed with sympathy and humour her friends of a lifetime, the Dominican lay sisters and choir nuns who formed part of the various communities in the Cape Peninsula. In the Necrology which she commenced in 1925, she wrote at length on the lives of the lay sisters she had known and whom she clearly loved and appreciated.[9]

While obituaries as historical sources must be treated with caution, it is clear from Mother Berchmans' testimony that she knew personally, those about whom she wrote at length. As a superior she had observed them and their work, and as a friend had shared interests and ideas with them. Where the life span of a sister ended before Mother Berchmans Cotter had entered the community, she based the obituary notice only on information available in written convent records or on the oral evidence of those who had lived with the sister concerned. It is fortunate therefore that she knew and held long conversations with Sister Stephana Connell, a lay sister and one of the foundresses of the Dominican mission in the Western Vicariate. Sister Stephana was already 34 years of age when she came to Cape Town. She was professed in Cabra in January 1863, and left for South Africa about eight months later. She was the oldest of the group and outlived all but Mother Francis Borgia McDonnell who survived to celebrate the Golden Jubilee of the Cape Town foundation in 1913. Mother Berchmans knew Sister Stephana personally over a period of thirty years and in that time had "never heard her complain once". She worked in St Mary's, Cape Town during the difficult years following the foundation of the mission, and when the Wynberg property was purchased in 1871 she was assigned to the Convent of the Holy Rosary, Springfield. Her task there was to set up a farm on land that was, at the outset, a wilderness. It was a heavy task for a woman, but one which gave scope for her creativity and love of nature. Happily she had as assistant labourers two young men who worked beside her for years, creating and maintaining the small productive farm which contributed to the support of the community and the boarding school.

> Under her dear work-worn hands the farmyard sprung up -
> cows, pigs, fowls. Then a bakery where she made the bread
> for nuns and boarders. The cemetery likewise was laid out,
> and of course the garden was cultivated. ... And dear Sr.
> Stephana was the beginning and end of it all. She was an
> ideally loveable character. I thank God in having known her.
> I can see her now, bent down in the garden outside, weeding
> and planting, see her raise her bent body up and look at you
> happily from her bright blue Irish eyes, her dear hands rough
> and worn from the work, her skin browned from the sun.

This is certainly not the picture of a disgruntled, browbeaten
servant but rather that of a mature, serene and creative woman
who loved her work and valued the life which gave her such
opportunities to serve others. It also says much about the
chronicler, Mother Berchmans Cotter who confessed in her
declining years: "How glad I was, when I was superior at St. Agnes'
and she was sent there for a little change. It was a joy to have her
holy presence in the Convent. She would work there too. There
was a strip of garden, later turned into a playground, and a fowl
run, and these she looked after. My great comfort was to get her
to come and sit with me - tell me of the early days of our
Congregation in this dear country". Sister Stephana died in 1913,
the year of her Golden Jubilee, and left behind her "a record not
easily surpassed". She falls into that category of women, also to
be found among the strong missionary wives, widows and
daughters living in the remote mission stations of Southern Africa,
who put their hands to many unfamiliar tasks in the cause of
evangelisation.[10]

Another remarkable character and a contemporary of Sister
Stephana, was Sister Bridget Burke, a "quasi Lay Sister" who
was one of a party of sisters who, in 1874, came out to South
Africa with Dr Leonard.[11] It is difficult to determine the canonical
status of Sister Bridget with any certainty. Mother Berchmans
never mentions the title lay sister in her obituaries because in
1925, when the necrology was begun, the division of the
community into two classes had just been abolished, and the
term 'lay sister' was no longer acceptable. Sister Bridget's main
work fell within the normal occupation of a lay sister although in
many respects she was an individualist and created her own
opportunities to use her gifts. As with Sister Stephana she spent
many years in Springfield, where she supervised the boarders'
dining-room and their needlework and mending. In due course
she was made sacristan, a position which gave her some influence
among the priests. With them as with the members of her
community she was outspoken and not at all backward in saying

anything she considered to be appropriate, whether to priest or nun or pupil, whose speech, actions or attitude did not meet with her approval. According to Mother Berchmanns she would "lay down the law so strongly and pull us up if she saw us tripping". Sister Bridget did not limit her interests to domestic chores or the office of sacristan. In and around the Springfield estate there were many Coloured children, poor, unschooled and without religious instruction. These she gathered together in a building in the farmyard, thus forming the nucleus of a small school under the patronage of St Augustine. Today the beautiful school, St Augustine's at Wittebome, stands as a witness to a woman who did not allow any obstacles, social or conventual, to stand in the way of the Dominican vocation which she had come so far to fulfil. Sister Bridget extended her catechetical skills not only to children but throughout her religious life, both at Wynberg and at St Agnes' Convent, she instructed adults in the Faith. In the latter convent she is also recorded as having, for a short time, run a private infant class.[12]

Mother Berchmans admired the hard work and humility of the lay sisters and saw them, not as servants, but as good nuns and earnest domestic workers. Of Sister Patrick Rice, South African born, a Dominican pupil and one of her own contemporaries, she wrote:

> Sister Patrick Rice came to us as a domestic Postulant in 1885. She made her vows on 9th Jan. 1888. She was a wonderfully holy soul with unlimited faith. The boarders had discovered this great gift of hers, and in their school difficulties they would come to her. Locks that could not be turned by the girls, would turn under Sr. Patrick's holy hand, when she made the sign of the Cross on them. Punishments that were expected without doubt, failed to come when Sr. Patrick prayed. Once she was baking bread in an oven out in the open and not too near the Convent the bell rang for a duty. Was she to go and answer the call of the bell or stay and look after the bread? She knew if she left the bread it would be burned and useless on her return, she asked Our Lady to mind the oven! When she returned the bread was beautifully baked.

She spent only ten years in the convent, dying in 1895, but for Mother Berchmans her memory remained green, and she is one of the community around whom life-sustaining legends grow.[13] Of Sister Patrick, Mother Bertrand Dowley wrote that she "always showed an earnestness in her duties which were trying in those days for one so young". No doubt in such circumstances she needed all those little miracles of life to sustain her.[14]

Mother Berchmans also celebrated the short religious life of another of her contemporaries, Sister Anne Kearney, who arrived in Cape Town "in a party of priests and nuns with Dr Leonard in 1884". Besides being a "good and holy nun", she was a hard worker. She was a competent laundress, working first in St Mary's Cape Town for a number of years, and later in Springfield. With her Irish sense of humour she brought laughter with her wherever she went and was remembered as a nun who loved the community.[15] There are many more records of the lives and influence of lay sisters, not all of whom were able to sustain the pace or endure the pressure of life as domestic workers. The lay sister who was judged to be unsuitable for religious life, or who herself decided to leave the convent, was usually found a position either as a priest's housekeeper, or as a servant in a safe family, or in another convent. The records give no indication of the future plans of Mary Woods, a simple lay novice who left Holy Rosary Convent on 12 December 1916.[16] However the case of Mary Moser, also a lay novice reflects the normal practice. She "was taken by Mother Prioress to Uitenhage Convent as a domestic servant to replace Sister Walburga who returned ... to Holy Rosary Convent that evening".[17] An Irish girl, Mary Dullaghan, who entered the Convent in June 1899, and received the habit in December of the same year, left Holy Rosary Convent in September of 1900. She went to Cape Town where the Dominican nuns agreed to receive her and for six months give her work as a servant.[18] Such an arrangement was often made to provide protected employment for these young women while they earned their passage back to Ireland. Life in both Cape Town and Port Elizabeth, was considered to be spiritually hazardous for unattached and unprotected Catholic girls. Consequently both the nuns themselves and the bishops saw repatriation as the ideal solution in cases of choir or lay sisters who, either before or after religious profession, left the convent.

In the Dominican convents in Cape Town and Port Elizabeth, domestic work was no stranger to all members of a community. With so few lay sisters to meet the demands of household work in growing institutions, all members of the community had to contribute to the good order and cleanliness of the schools and convent. However the isolated community life of the lay sisters was firmly controlled in all its facets, and it took a strong character to rise above the limitations imposed by ecclesiastical law, and the constant supervision by superiors of every aspect of social interaction and domestic work. Despite this, during the nineteenth century there is little record in Annals or Council

Books of adverse comment or open rebellion on the part of lay sisters. However, since in the convent they represented the voiceless minority, the absence of written evidence cannot be taken as proof that lay sisters accepted their lot without protest. A small group of strong-minded women, lay or choir nuns, could and at times did exert a powerful influence, positive or negative on the community.

It is clear that in the Cape Colony some at least of the lay aspirants did not enter on their Dominican life in ignorance of conditions of work, or of the social divisions in the convent. Neither did the communities which received them act without responsibility in their regard. In many instances where young women were employed as servants by a convent, and later requested admission as lay sisters, they were well prepared for the life they had chosen. The superiors for their part were reasonably certain that by temperament, physical strength and religious spirit the aspirant would be an asset to the community. In some cases the young women were impoverished Irish or German immigrants who were directed by a priest or bishop to the safety and protection of the cloister. If the nineteenth century South African records truly reflect the attitudes of the choir sisters to these women who served them in the domestic sphere, then it is beyond question that in general they were loved and cherished for their holiness and dedication, their hard work, and for the care they had for the sick and for the general welfare of the community. But in a very real sense they were minors with no legal voice in the affairs of the convent. According to the Dominican *Constitutions* they had no vote in the election of the prioress, no voice in the community chapter when it met for general consultation on matters of policy, and no right to consort socially with the choir sisters with whom they shared a common Dominican vocation. The relevant *Constitution* adjures them "whilst employed in the kitchen or in other menial works, to nourish a spirit of fervour and cheerfulness", inspired by such models as Martha and St Catherine of Siena, neither of whom had lived in strict enclosure in the guise of servants.[19]

Within their own class the lay sisters were all equal and could "claim no privilege of precedence", so jealously guarded among the ranks of the choir nuns. They were to promote among themselves "union, peace, and charity" and they were to "assist and console one another in God's service". At the same time the prioress and the choir nuns "were to treat this humble and precious class with the utmost charity and tenderness". The lay sister was not to be given work beyond her strength and ability, nor was she to be permitted to idle her time "murmuring at the work assigned to her, or culpably allowing the goods of the Monastery to be wasted". Should such a fault be discovered she was to be "speedily admonished", and if she should continue in this fault she was to be punished.[20] In the correction of faults as in most other constitutional regulations, the lay sisters were subject to the same laws as the choir nuns. They followed the same liturgical calendar, though they did not say the choral office. In Cape Town, as in Cabra, the Little Office of the Blessed Virgin was said chorally by the choir sisters, while in Port Elizabeth from 1888 onwards, the Latin "Great Office" was celebrated.[21] The lay sisters said a daily office of *Paters* and *Aves* and also recited the suffrages for the dead. In principle, they were subject to the same fasts and other penitential exercises common to all members of the Dominican Order subject to the dispensations granted in the nineteenth century, to Cabra and her foundations at home and abroad. However their black scapular distinguished them from the choir sisters, and there were other minor differences which stressed the lowly position they held in the community. This was expressed not only in work, daily prayer and social isolation, but also in the sacred occasions such as clothing and profession: "Their Reception to the Habit, as well as their Profession ... [was] like that of the Choir sisters; except that at the Reception Ceremony the *Veni Creator* ... [was] recited instead of being sung."[22]

Although the Lay Sister was "called to religion for manual labour", which mainly involved household work and in a subordinate role, household management, she was not permitted to hold office as procuratrix, even "with the consent of the bishop". Neither could she change from lay to choir status "even during the time of probation before Profession". In the rare circumstance of a lay sister being permitted to become a choir nun, she would have a voice in the elections only after twelve years dating from her change in status. The wish to change status was not regarded by superiors as a sign of virtue:

> In a Lay-Sister the thought of becoming a Choir-Sister is often a very dangerous temptation, it often arises from ambition, it fosters emulations, gives offence to others, and causes in themselves a dislike and disregard for their present condition. The devil often tempts souls representing to them the good they *cannot* do, that they may neglect the good they *can* do; and he often makes them seek what they are not able to obtain in order to make them discontented with what they have. Therefore, it may be said, that if changes of this kind were easily allowed, they would prove pernicious and very injurious both to the Convent and to the Sisters.[23]

The conventual records of the Irish Dominican community in the Cape Colony reveal no evidence that after profession, such a change was requested by a lay sister. However absence of written evidence cannot be taken as proof that the lay sisters were either satisfied or unhappy with their status, or with their social position and work within the community. Devine was clear as to the proper treatment of lay sisters in view of their role.

> It is well known that these Sisters deserve great consideration, and in dealing with them great kindness and charity should be used. Their duties are numerous, arduous, and sometimes very difficult. They often receive different commands and requests from different Sisters, and they have to bear many trials and mortifications. [The choir sisters] should remember that it is the poor Lay-Sisters who have to do the heavy work of the Convent, in the kitchen, the refectory, the corridors, the dairy, the clothes room, etc., and that on them devolves so much, all those duties in connection with the cleanliness, the tidiness, the brightness, and the poverty of the Convent, and all should endeavour to make their lives happy and peaceful according to the true spirit of holy charity.[24]

Despite the constant plea for such kindness and consideration it is clear that as an uneducated member of a professional, teaching community, the position of the lay sister was seen as inferior. A choir nun had to be "guilty of very grave faults" before she could be demoted to the "state of Lay Sister".[25] The vows were the same for all members of the community, whatever their status, since all were religious in the fullest sense. However this was small consolation to the lay sisters, especially those with the intelligence, the basic education and the potential to be teachers. What these lacked was further formal education, a dowry, and in some instances, social status. There is no record in the two South African congregations of the demotion of choir nuns to lay sister status. However the existence of such a regulation and the terms in which it is stated, stress the lowly condition of the lay sister in the eyes of ecclesiastical law as expressed in the *Constitutions*. It would do violence to history to judge that in terms of such laws and the social norms of the times, the lay sisters in the Cape Colony during the late nineteenth century were spineless servants, without the opportunity or will to live their religious life in harmony and peace. Surviving records, some of which have already been noted, argue otherwise. Although the lay sisters who served their Irish Dominican communities so well in the nineteenth century have left virtually no personal record of their thoughts or feelings, there is evidence enough to indicate that they were women familiar with the pressures of the cloistered life and the long hours of work. They, like the choir nuns, had among their ranks individualists who wielded an influence within the whole community, either for peace or for disruption according to their temperament. There were also those who rose above the written limitations of the law and found in their communities and in the poor an opportunity for the exercise of their apostolic zeal.

The hungry who came to the kitchen door for alms often found in the lay sisters a source of spiritual strength, good counsel, informal religious instruction, or perhaps a timely reprimand and a ready ear to listen to their complaints. Within the cloister there were few influences to compare with the efficient and cheerful service of a good cook, the gracious welcome of a portress, or the loving sympathy of a motherly lay sister to a small boarder lonely, fearful and far from home. There was also the problem of numbers. Apart from the restrictions imposed by the *Constitutions* and the limited economic ability of a community to support them, the admission of a large number of lay sisters into one community might lead to the development of pressure groups. Such groups could disturb the peace and hence hinder the apostolic mission of the community.

In the mid-1920's the admission of lay sisters as a distinct body, living under the maternal guidance and authority of a mistress and distinguished by dress, occupation, forms of prayer and social status, was found to be inappropriate for Southern Africa. This was not necessarily or even likely, the result of altruistic reflection on the part of the choir nuns on the sad lot of their humble sisters. Nor were the lay sisters prepared to accept without complaint, perceived injustices. In times of weak government in a convent, disaffection could and did arise, and if this was brought to the notice of the episcopal authorities, official action was taken. Father James Kelly, a good and loyal friend of the Dominican community in the Western Cape reported to his bishop in February 1912:

> The result of my visit to Woodstock yesterday was to make my acquaintance with what are supposed to be injustices or hardships in the conventual life: some of them against or outside the rule, and some of them supported by a rule that is said to be in some respects not suited to the time and place. I have made a few notes and for the first time I have seen the book of rules. I shall make known to you My Lord, what was said, ... In the meantime I may say the headings are:

1. Treatment of lay-sisters & their discontent.
2. Treatment of the sick.
3. The Council. Its work nil.
I have often heard the same complaints before, but one is slow to take notice of complaints against authority. Consequently I have simply listened.[26]

This period was one of decline in the official administration of the community in the Western Cape, as Sister Augustine Barry wrote to the bishop:

At the end of this term we shall be having our elections, and there is a matter I would put before you, not in a private way; for you are at liberty to use the contents of this letter, as far as your prudence dictates. My object is not to complain, but to rectify matters, for are we, older Sisters not bound to hand down to posterity, our Constitutions intact? And in what I am going to say, I *know* I am voicing the feelings of the majority of the community (in all the houses) at least those of the older members. Now to proceed to business. We shall be asked to vote for discreets, to form members of a Council. For years there has been *no Council.* ... In Mother Dympna's time every three months, the members met at one of the convents, but now the office of discreet is a farce. [27]

Such a situation, which aroused feelings of insecurity, gave ample opportunity for discontent and complaint from choir nuns as well as from lay sisters.

In November 1918, in many respects the dawn of a new era in the life of the two Irish Dominican communities in South Africa, the old order still prevailed for the lay sisters. Father C O'Rourke, Vicar General of Oudtshoorn, made visitation of the Cape Town convents. His report on the situation and role of the lay sisters prepared the way for the abolition of the class distinction during the 1920's. In his report on the visitation of Springfield Convent he wrote: "The Rule provides for what are known as Lay sisters in the community, and, the distinction amongst the Novices as well as amongst the Professed Sisters gives grounds for real or apparent unkindness by times". The visitator noted not only the lack of kindness but also the results of perceived social inequality:

Consequent on having assigned to them the more menial duties in the Community, there is a decided line drawn between the Lay sisters and Choir sisters in Community life that is very undesirable. This engenders a Spirit of Superiority in the one Class and a feeling of inferiority in the other. At best, there is a temptation of those spirits that does not make for religious perfection.[28]

He suggested that it might be necessary to "submit the Constitutions and the Rules of the Dominican Sisters in the Peninsula to a close examination on the matter of lay sisters, in terms of Canon 489 of the 1917 Code". Would it perhaps be found "that the distinction into Lay and choir sisters should disappear altogether; and this the more readily if the privilege of substituting the Little Office of B.V.M. for the Canonical Office be continued"? The visitator was aware that some immediate steps would have to be taken and his advice was clear:

> In any event, while the distinction is maintained, great care should be taken to fully make known to the Novice, destined to fill the place of Lay Sister in the Community, after Profession, what her duties are to be and the marks of inferiority she will have to submit to. Notwithstanding this instruction there will always, especially to a poor girl faced with the alternative of going back into a pitiless world, unprovided for in every way, remain the danger of choosing the lesser of two evils and making profession rather out of moral fear than from a desire of attaining perfection as a Lay Sister. The Complainants [lay sisters], however, seek to make themselves happy but would very emphatically dissuade others from joining the Order while this distinction lasts.[29]

It was a problem that was to be taken up by Mgr Gijlswijk, who by 1924, in law if not always in practice, put an end to the distinction between lay and choir sisters. It was not a solution that had the approval of all the sisters, and the old attitudes towards those responsible for the domestic work in the community, died hard. In 1962 Sister Philomena Mulcachy, a prayerful old lady of great charm, confessed that what she found hardest to understand during her religious life was the change of status of the lay sisters: "It doesn't seem right somehow, they being the same as us because they aren't really. You know Sister, they can come to recreation with us and even wear the white scapular. Why did they change this?" And this was almost forty years after the legal change had come about. Perhaps it was all the more difficult to understand since at that time all the communities of the Congregation of Irish Dominican Sisters, with the exception of those in South Africa, still retained the distinction between lay and choir sisters, with virtually no amelioration of their conditions of life or of their social isolation within the community.[30]

The process of change did not even begin in the Congregation of Irish Dominican Sisters in Ireland for another thirty years, eight years after the first ever Congress of Superiors General, for women religious held in Rome in 1952. Among the many changes this Congress proposed was the "abolition of class distinctions" in communities, but it laid down three conditions:

a) That the change insure absolute equality of rights and obligations;

b) that the superiors be fully empowered to appoint any religious to any office, due regard being given to the individual capacities of each one and the needs of the community;

c) that all the religious, irrespective of the class to which they may have previously belonged, contribute their share of effort in providing for the common needs of the community. Saving these principles, the abolition of the distinction between classes will be approved by Rome, but the S. Congregation will never use pressure in order to bring this about in any particular institute.[31]

Such a change would have to be put to the vote and approved by a General Chapter. However in the General Chapter of 1954, the Dominican Congregation in Ireland was unprepared to take so radical a step as the introduction of a single class of sisters, and indeed there had not been enough time to consider the implications of such a move. In a resolution to be submitted to Rome for approval, it made no more than a grudging sartorial concession to the lay sisters, which left them in every respect except in dress, in the same situation as before: "We declare that the advisability of uniformity in habit for Choir and Lay sisters was discussed. It was decided by unanimous decision that the Holy See should be petitioned for an Indult granting permission for Lay sisters to wear the white scapular".[32] The Sacred Congregation of Religious had given permission for this change on a trial basis, for a period of five years,[33] and the General Chapter of 1960 confirmed that this had been "extended for an indefinite period". As well as providing for uniformity of dress this Chapter discussed the feasibility of introducing the Little Office of Our Lady "in the vernacular as an alternative to the Office of Paters and Aves for our lay sisters", and it was agreed to begin preparation for the Office in September 1960.[34] This was a clear indication that in 1960 the Cabra Dominicans in Ireland had no immediate intention of eliminating the class distinction between lay and choir sisters.

It is clear that such changes were little more than cosmetic and did not meet the aspirations, or improve conditions of life which fostered discontent among the lay sisters in Ireland. Whether or not the representatives of the Region of South Africa played any significant role in these decisions is not clear. However it is clear that the capitulars of the Regional Chapters of January 1954 and 1960, were not asked to express any opinion on the question of the lay sisters in Ireland. At General Chapters the voting power of the Region of South Africa was very weak, since out of a total of 34 capitular sisters, only four were from South Africa and of these one, Mother Catherine Dixon, was by a life-long tradition and attitude of mind an *Irish* rather than a South African Dominican.[35] The capitular sisters meeting at Springfield in the Cape in January 1954 had their own solution to the problem of domestic work:

> We declare that the problem of Domestic work in our Convents was discussed. As it was felt that seculars are too unreliable and wasteful to be entrusted entirely with the running of a kitchen, and as there is no likelihood of our receiving from Eire Sisters for this type of work only, it was proposed that all young Sisters be trained in the running of a house. The experiment in this matter will be carried out this year in Springfield, where a full-time secular teacher will be employed to relieve, in turn, each of three young Sisters, to enable them to get this training.[36]

Whatever the practical outcome of this specific plan, all sisters in the ranks shared in the domestic work, and in cooking during the school vacations. For the rest of the year the kitchens and households were organised and managed in the Western Cape by those sisters assigned to specific duties including the supervision and training of lay domestics whom the convents employed to meet the growing needs of the community. A number of the sisters followed appropriate courses at the Technical College, and were, like the majority of the nuns, highly skilled in embroidery, dress-making and crafts.

As the decisions of the 1954 and 1960 General Chapters indicate, the tradition of lay sisters was too strong in Ireland to allow of rapid change.[37] These decisions reflect the persistence of fundamental conservatism in those who had worked so hard in the 1930's and 1940's, and with such apparent success, to build an authentic Dominican community. They were devoted to and protective of the Congregation that they had created, and this with justification. The delegates who participated in the 1954 and 1960 Chapters included among their numbers such formidable leaders as Mother Reginald Lyons and Mother Alberta Grant. These and others Dominican women of like stature, had co-operated with Dr Finbar Ryan OP to produce the 1947 book of *Constitutions* which was accepted as a model of its kind. However it did not reflect the changes in society and in the Church, evident even during the 1940's, the decade of its preparation and publication. It was the crowning achievement in the battle for full Dominican legitimacy, not the beginning of a new, creative age in the life of the Congregation. It did not testify to the fact that the age of the socially marginalised servant, readily available and poorly paid, was over, and this as much in the cloister as in the secular world. It was difficult for those aging superiors, who had held high office in the Congregation for 32 years, to keep pace with the social, economic and ideological changes brought about by World War II. Nor did they take cognisance of the demand for greater freedom of expression and a more egalitarian approach to life, even religious life. This was especially the case in respect of the lay sisters.

The post-amalgamation Constitutions 231-235 of 1947, while the tone was moderate the reality behind the law was harsh. "Apart from the minor duties which may be allotted to the Choir sisters, the main material works of the Community are entrusted to the Lay sisters". No one questioned "the great importance of the works entrusted to them: by their labours promoting the smooth and efficient working of the Community, enabling the Choir sisters to be free for their work in the Schools, and securing economy and avoidance of waste".[38] They were reminded of their duty "as members of an apostolic Order to preach, if not by word, at least by example, all virtues, especially charity and patience".[39] In practice the lay sisters remained socially isolated within their own community, and often bore a heavy burden of unremitting manual labour. But while work of one kind or another was the common lot of all the sisters, social isolation was painful and bred memories not easily healed. Even in the important question of rank within the community, the professed lay sisters were placed below the most junior choir postulants, uninitiated girls fresh from the world.[40] The change, when it came in 1967, at the first post-Vatican II General Chapter of the Congregation, was complete and like the proposed revision of the *Constitutions*, not equally acceptable to all: "We declare that there is but one category of Sisters in our Congregation. This is to be fully implemented in all our Houses on the 4th August 1967 - the Feast of our Holy Father Saint Dominic".[41]

Many of the choir sisters who were trained in Kerdiffstown in the 1940's and 1950's, as well as those who had done their novitiate at an earlier date, had felt deeply the situation in which the lay novices found themselves, but were powerless at that time to take any action in their defence. Even today many sisters, who have spent their lives working in the field of education, express strong regret at the treatment meted out to lay sisters and the effect it had on their lives:

> As the lay sisters grew older they came to realise what they had missed. A lot of the lay sister candidates came from better homes than the choir sisters. They would have been well able to study and to teach but they never got the opportunity. Even though they had no secondary education when they entered, they had the ability to study.[42]

Lay sisters in Ireland who personally experienced this change in status, with the possibilities of social integration and apostolic opportunity, and other members of the community who came to a better understanding of what the life of a lay sister had entailed, must realise that the full history of these sisters in Ireland and indeed in South Africa, waits to be told.

From 1920 until 1938, when the two Irish Dominican communities of Cape Town and in Port Elizabeth amalgamated with the newly formed Congregation in Ireland, those who entered for South Africa found themselves in communities comprised of one class of sister only. Whatever their education or family background, or the financial status of their parents, the nuns shared a common novitiate which provided training in Dominican life, liturgy and work. After 1938, the amalgamation agreement between the Congregation of Irish Dominican Sisters and the Dominican foundations in the Eastern and Western Cape, ensured that no lay sisters would be introduced into the South African communities. Nevertheless it was recognised that sound household administration in competent hands remained the practical foundation of economic and domestic stability. In each group of aspirants some candidates were chosen to serve in the domestic sphere while others, having completed their secondary education, were trained and assigned to teach in the schools. The rationale behind the discernment process was never clearly defined, and there is no written record justifying the application of fixed criteria or sound principles in the assignment of sisters to either household or professional work. In a group of young women, such as those who entered at Potter's Bar in England for the Western Cape in the 1930's, or Tamnaharrie in Ireland for the houses in the Eastern Cape, it would have been difficult to choose between candidates. Many of them had no more than a sound elementary education at a rural Irish school. Others had higher academic qualifications, but most were faced with the possibility and need for further study if they were to be prepared for the teaching profession. There was often little to differentiate one from the other in terms of family background, domestic experience in household management or intellectual ability and the vocation for teaching. The tradition which linked domestic work with the status of lay sister persisted, more in the Eastern Cape than in the West, but there was no legal base for separate classes within the communities. In practice the attitude of the sisters involved in domestic work, and their complete involvement in all aspects of Dominican life, had a far greater influence on the development of a united community spirit than any written law.

While tacitly accepted divisions based on work orientation were not meant to indicate social status, the role of the teacher was often given greater respect than that of the sister involved in household management. This however was not always the case. Those who had joined the South African communities before 1924, themselves tended to cling to the old ways and in some respects passed on to those who entered in more liberal times, their concepts of the appropriate role of the domestic worker. The same approach was evident in some superiors, who for too long had held positions of authority. For these the change was acknowledged but never fully implemented. This was part of the anomaly of the new Gijlswijk *Constitution*. While in theory legislating for a single class of sisters within the community, it did not create the means for implementing unity. On the question of precedence, jealously defended in a hierarchical society the new position was clear:

> The Professed Sisters always precede the Novices and the latter the Postulants. Among the Professed the order of precedence is according to seniority in profession: among the Novices and Postulants according to that of reception and admission respectively. *The Sisters, under either temporary or perpetual vows, formerly called Lay-Sisters, shall on the publication of these Constitutions each according to the date of her profession rank immediately after the Professed Novices.*[43]

This did not express the ideal of equality proposed in the change in lay sister status, but in the 1920's such a principle found little support either in the theory of religious obedience or in the practice of humility appropriate to a consecrated religious. Nevertheless the Apostolic Delegate, reflecting the mind of the Church in this matter, was sincere in his attempts to bring about an equitable change in the lives of the former lay sisters. He urged them to "be content with the work and place assigned to them by obedience". It was the intention with which the work was done in obedience that counted, and "not each one's desire that must determine our occupation".

> The Sisters should therefore be content with the work and place assigned to them by obedience, and try to render themselves useful to the Congregation; for by their labours, chiefly domestic they can greatly contribute to its welfare. Indeed the domestic Sisters, aiding by their labours the Sisters chiefly engaged in teaching, contribute to the salvation of souls, and have an equal share with the teaching Sisters in merits and good works of the Congregation and of the whole Dominican Order.[44].

Although the 1924 *Constitutions* effected little change in the role and status of those who were already lay sisters, it paved the way for the changes that were to come in the 1930's and later. Many of the young sisters of the 1930's, with experience and some training, were remarkable for their professional approach to all aspects of household management. Indeed in some cases they chose the kitchen and household rather than the classroom. In the Western Cape the choice was often based on the aptitude of a sister for cooking, sewing or other domestic skills. Some of the young nuns with excellent potential as teachers, themselves chose to specialise in domestic duties. In the 1930's such a choice was a gift to the superiors since every convent needed reliable personnel to deal with the complexities of catering, the care of the household, including boarding school facilities, and the supervision and training of servants. Some of those who were experienced in household work both in practice and in theory, found greater fulfilment in the convent than in secular employment. The work of the boarder's mistress was greatly facilitated by trustworthy support staff, nuns such as Sister Clement Gleeson, who with gentle patience gave many years to the care of the linen room, and shared in the supervision of junior boarders. Sister Barbara Power, among others, followed in the footsteps of Sister Stephana O'Connell. As a sturdy worker and organiser she ran the farmyard at Springfield Convent, Wynberg. There were also those who for one reason or another, never recorded, were assigned, with little or no choice, to domestic duties. This led to frustration and sometimes bitterness, even though the work of such sisters was valuable, if seldom praised. There were also those who, whatever the circumstances, threw their whole life and energy into the work assigned to them and became pillars of the community.

While in theory the status, work and social isolation of the lay sisters was potentially painful and oppressive, in practice many of the young nuns who committed themselves to this vocation were women of vivid and arresting personality, and in the missionary context made a vital contribution to the development of the temporal and spiritual work of the Dominicans in South Africa. One group however, the German lay sisters, deserve special mention. Their life was not easy, they were foreigners and their presence was not always given the full support of superiors, though their capacity for hard work was acknowledged and appreciated. These entered the community of Holy Rosary Convent between 1905 and 1915 and served for many years. Marie Morscher (Sister Walburga), a Bavarian, entered Holy Rosary Convent in March 1906. She was thirty-one years old at the time and she, like the other German sisters who joined that community during the next fifteen years, found herself, culturally at least, in an alien environment. While religious life was strange enough for all new recruits, it was especially so for a minority in a community where all that was Irish was held in high regard. Sister Walburga had to learn a new language and adapt to new ways of living, but she chose Holy Rosary Convent and was accepted as a lay postulant. She was a hardworking woman with little time for pettiness, and her acquired English was used with effect on the offender. Many of the stories that surround her life belong to her declining years and do little justice to her kindness, forthrightness, love of animals and a strong and evident spirit of prayer.

Josepha Reck, Sister Carmel, a native of Wurtemberg, was another of the German candidates who helped to introduce a more cosmopolitan note into the Irish Dominican community. She with her German contemporaries, all individualists, portrayed in their lives devotion to duty, a capacity for hard work, loving kindness without weakness or sentimentality, and a directness of speech not always appreciated by some of their Irish sisters. She too made a deliberate choice of the Irish community. She had left the Dominican Convent at King William's Town because she and her novice mistress could not see eye to eye. She then applied to the Irish Dominican community in Port Elizabeth. There she entered in July 1915, at the age of twenty four, and made her final profession in 1921.[45] This was the beginning of a religious life that lasted for 66 years. Her decision was not an easy one. She was a German immigrant in a British colony at a time when Germany was the enemy in the war then waging in Europe. From the outset she was a strong-willed woman, quick-minded and forthright in speech. She knew what she wanted and could persevere in her choice once she was convinced it was the right one. Assigned to St Dominic's Priory in 1919, she helped to look after the boarders, and her kindness was remembered and acknowledged 62 years later, when she died in 1981. Her love and devotion extended to animals, including wild cats that lived in the bush behind the convent. These she fed and cared for, to the displeasure of some of the sisters. She had a true full voice and in her younger days sometimes could be persuaded to sing for the community at recreation. She is one of the lay sisters who, though she received the white scapular, and lived for over half a century in a community where there was no longer any legal class distinction, never really changed her approach to the life to which she had adapted in the early years of her religious training.

One of Sister Carmel's contemporaries, Sister Martha Müller, also made her first assay into religious life in King William's Town. After refusing to have a badly infected arm amputated she left the convent and came to Port Elizabeth. There, at the request of Bishop McSherry, she was accepted into the novitiate at Holy Rosary Convent. This movement of candidates between the King Dominicans and those in Port Elizabeth was a two-way process, and does not indicate either mutual competition or criticism. If a young woman was strong, reasonably biddable and with signs of a vocation to religious life, then she would be an asset to any convent that accepted her. Some of the German sisters could not thrive in an Irish community and so could apply to their German sisters, while for others the Irish environment was more acceptable. Vivid memories of her European past accompanied Sister Martha Müller into the cloister, and if the admonition to "forget all things" had been given to her on 14 April 1915, when she knocked on the door of Holy Rosary Convent, she might have turned away, sad. She had many rich treasures both to hold in memory and to share. Born in Russian Poland she served in the houses of kings and of the nobility in Austria, and she knew and condemned the weakness or wickedness of some, while upholding the nobility of character and sanctity of others. One of her greatest heroes was Frans Josef of Austria upon whom she conferred her personal testimony of private canonisation, and to whom she prayed. She was a good cook, having been trained in Europe by a French chef, though indeed courtly food found no place in the convents where she exercised her domestic skills. Her manner was not conciliatory, nor her choice of words always monastic in tone, the result of a language, the niceties of which were foreign to her to the day of her death. She was not one of those who lived without regret or bitterness of soul. If she felt anger she expressed it, nor did she hide her pain or disapproval. However her kindness of heart was proof enough of her goodness to those whom she might have offended, and her satisfaction with the food she prepared for the community was exceeded only by her determination that all would be eaten and enjoyed. She with her German contemporaries added salt to life and their forthrightness was a happy contrast in a monastic environment where perfection was often equated with passive submission and silent endurance. Their outstanding characteristic was humanness, expressed equally in their interaction with God and with their sisters. "This was a healthy antidote to that concept of dedicated life which over emphasised the spiritual to the detriment of wholeness."[46] These were the women who never quite escaped the old ideal and pattern of the proper role of a lay sister, whatever the title or dress.

The tradition that linked domestic work with a separate class, died hard, more in some areas and in specific convents than in others. Nevertheless the new generation of aspirants, who entered for Port Elizabeth and Cape Town between 1924 and 1938, and whose main work was in the domestic sphere, gradually evolved their own roles and status. Some developed special expertise in household management and others in book-keeping. The domestic chores were no longer the sole responsibility of any specific group within a convent and where servants were employed the heavy work could be shared more equitably. Some of the sisters, especially those who had spent most of their lives in the Port Elizabeth convents, freely volunteered to share their memories. Among these was Sister Gerard Crawford,[47] a serene woman, who shortly before her death, told the story of her life as a domestic sister:

> There were no lay sisters in 1929. We were all in the one category and we all had the same spiritual training but we [domestic sisters] said Paters and Aves, not like the teaching nuns, who recited the Little Office of Our Lady. When the Divine Office came we all said it. All sisters had a household charge but domestic sisters did the laundry, scrubbed cells and did the heavier work. At the Priory during the Summer holidays we restuffed the coir mattress. But we were together and we laughed a lot. We were never asked what we could do, what we were best at, but we were just given work. Even though the domestic work was hard I never really wanted to teach. I was not really discontented. I never had any enemies. They are all so kind to us.

With the early death of their father the Crawford children were sent to relations in and around Newry, Northern Ireland. There the Dominican community, and the fact that Christine's aunts were Tertiaries, ensured that she and her sister Josephine were familiar with the Order and its ideals. Christine Crawford left school when she was twelve years old and in Standard V. She was sent on a four-day visit to her aunt near Tamnaharrie and stayed for nine years cooking and housekeeping for her unmarried uncles. The Novitiate of the Port Elizabeth community at Tamnaharrie, where she attended daily Mass, was a strong incentive to herself and her sister Josephine to offer themselves for the South African mission. The postulants could be seen walking or recreating in the grounds and praying in the chapel, and this inspired them to apply for admission. Josephine entered in 1929, a month before her sister. Christine told her uncles that they had better get married without delay as she intended entering the Dominican novitiate. She was twenty-one when she entered, a gentle young woman with the skills of a housekeeper far beyond her age. "Josephine had worked as an assistant cook in Captain Hall's domain and she entered straight from the job".[48]

Among those who entered in the early 1930's with both experience and training were Sisters Oliver Fearon and Finbar Lawlor.[49] The former from the parish of Kileevy, South Armagh was the youngest of nine children. After completing Std VI in the local National School she went to work in a hotel in Warrenpoint. At the same time she took a three year course in domestic science and dress-making. She too had the advantage of proximity to Tamnaharrie. She entered the Novitiate in 1933 at the age of twenty-three and her choice was clear:

> I always wanted to be a nun and I had heard about the Dominicans. I was advised by a Jesuit to apply to them. It was an honour to belong to the Order with its prayers and customs. While at Tamnaharrie and for a further two years we were not allowed to say the Little Office of Our Lady. We felt that we were not fairly treated but we were warned that if we voted for amalgamation with Ireland we would all be lay sisters again. Sister Gabriel left of her own free will because she protested against having to wear the black scapular. There were no more lay sisters after our group.

Despite the threat of return to lay sister status, the five domestic sisters voted unanimously for amalgamation with the Irish Congregation. They "knew that ultimately the Order would have to obey the Church". There was no vocational training for these sisters in the Eastern Cape and they saw their role as a humble one. "The educated sisters had to be on top. The domestic sisters had to work very hard; cooking, cleaning, laundry. They gave very devoted and loyal service. We did not worry much about the difference between us and the teaching sisters. We were too busy to bother about things like that, and anyway we were taught that one job was as important as another".[50]

Sister Finbar Lawlor (1913-1997) also entered in 1933. She spent six months in Tamnaharrie and completed her Novitiate in Holy Rosary Convent, Port Elizabeth. Because her mother had died when she was only two years old, she was brought up partly by aunts and partly in her father's house. She studied home economics with the Irish Sisters of Charity at the Stanhope School in Dublin and at the age of seventeen she left school and was invited by Mother de Ricci Harkin to enter the Novitiate at Tamnaharrie. She had no regrets about the choice she had made:

> I was very happy there. I loved the Novitiate and I had no hesitations about my vocation. I helped in the laundry and did some housework. We were kind of lay sisters but I never thought of the distinction, but accepted it as part of religious life. Mother de Ricci never told us that we would be lay sisters so we did not really understand what this would mean in our lives. The worst distinction was not being allowed to say the Little Office. That was very hard. Giljswijk made a big fuss and Sister Francis [Gunn] said to Mother de Ricci that the lay novices would have to learn the Office. Sister Bernard [Mackesy] taught us Latin.[51]

In the opinion of the domestic sisters there were other aspects of life in the Dominican Province of Port Elizabeth that demanded review and reform. Recreation was still separate and the domestic sisters were not included in some of the spiritual opportunities available to the other sisters. They "felt this intensely". This exclusion may have been the result of pressure of work or on the grounds of relevance to their specific vocation, but it had sad results. "A representative of the Legion of Mary came to Holy Rosary Convent to give a talk on Our Lady, but we, the domestic sisters, were told that we could not go to hear it. We were very shocked at not being allowed to attend and one of our group, Sister Brigid, was so insulted at being excluded that she left the convent because of this". Another problem that faced some of the sisters at this period, and it was common to all those involved entirely in domestic work, was the lack of active missionary work among the people. While the teaching nuns had apostolic contact with the pupils and their parents, and regularly gave religious instruction to adults, the domestic sisters had very limited opportunities in this regard. Sister Finbar found this one of the great disappointments of her early years in religious life: "I didn't think the discipline in the convent was too strict. It was what I expected. But I was very disappointed not to be able to do active missionary work. It was not what we expected when we entered. We believed that we would have more time for prayer and active missionary work". When she was assigned to St Dominic's Priory in 1959, she and Sister Henry Costello (1917-1993), that indefatigable and much loved missionary, visited the people of Salisbury Park in their homes and "had tea with them".[52] This is one indication of the gradual changes that were taking place in religious life and practice in the decade prior to Vatican Council II, the first tentative stage in the implementation of the 1952 *Roman Instructions* to Major Superiors. In the 1950's however the strict rules of enclosure still applied in the Cabra Congregation, though clearly less rigidly in South Africa than in Ireland. It must also be remembered that many of the Sisters engaged in household work had an active apostolate among those women and men employed for domestic work in the schools and convent, and in the maintenance of playing fields and gardens. In their own sphere, the sisters, who in practice if not in theory, were responsible for the smooth running of each conventual household, also had political power. In the 1930's they too had a vote, if not a voice, in the process of debate that was to determine whether or not the South African province to which they belonged, would amalgamate with Cabra, Ireland. The question of their status as Dominicans they would never have held in doubt, and their keen interest in the outcome of negotiations between Cabra and her South African foundations was of equal interest to all the nuns, irrespective of their real or legal status in the community.

Chapter Ten

The Debate: Crisis of Identity

The vexed question of the status of Dominican women, the first religious group to be founded directly by Dominic Guzman himself, has never found a satisfactory solution. According to Simon Tugwell:

> Dominic had long taken an interest in the *needs* of women religious, and at Prouille, Toulouse and most recently Madrid he had been involved in the setting up of monasteries for them, but this is the first time we hear of such monasteries actually belonging to the Order of Preachers, though this was no doubt the idea in Madrid too. *Prouille had naturally not been founded as a monastery of the order, because the order did not exist then.*[1]

This is no more than an interesting variation on a theme that has been reiterated by male Dominican historians down through centuries. It suggests that the Dominican Order was created for clerics and merely by law, and not by the prayers, inspiration and ideals of those who laid the first foundations. In the vanguard were the women, some of the Second Order, with solemn vows and strict papal enclosure, and later, others of the Third Order who followed a more active form of apostolic life. These nuns and sisters have not only formed the majority of those who followed Dominic, but for the almost seven centuries of the Order's existence have had a profound apostolic influence in the Church. However, despite the fact that women played an early and positive role in the development of the Order, there is a reluctance to acknowledge the provenance of the first foundation of Dominican women, and its close links with the Order. The difficult position of the nuns in relation to the clerical brethren is echoed by Hinnebusch who entitles the first chapter of his history of the Dominican Order, "Prelude to the foundation of the Order".[2] This history covers the period of Dominic's early preaching against the heretics, and the founding of the monastery of Prouille, which served as a spiritual support for his apostolic work. But how can a prelude be detached from a total harmonious composition?

The work of the first brethren, as that of the first nuns, could not be regarded as a "short independent" work bearing no connection with the ultimate legal formalisation of the Order. In music a prelude, by definition, is among other things "a movement preceding a fugue or forming the first part of a suite". In the fugue, "a polyphonic composition is one in which a short melodic theme, the subject, is introduced by one part or voice, and successively taken up by the others and developed by their interweaving".[3] Did the nuns not indeed introduce the "subject" that was later taken up by the brethren? Had not the women who responded to Dominic's call, a "voice" in the total composition of the Order? This is surely the way to view the role and status of the first Dominican women of the Order and of their sisters down the centuries, rather than to relegate them historically to a kind of limbo outside the legal bounds and full membership of the Dominican Order.

The negative attitude displayed not only by historians but by many of the brethren, in respect of the nuns and sisters of the Order, has led to a fundamental error in the approach to the history of Dominican women. Despite much evidence to the contrary, historians continue to interpret the history of these women as though Dominic gave his contemporary followers the final blueprint of the Order on which all future generations, men and women, were to base their lives. Dominic founded an order, not a club. He *founded* an order. He did not complete it. Dominican women, who formed the first formal religious community to accept his leadership and to rally to his cause, did not remain static through the ages. The nuns helped to develop what Dominic had already initiated in the distaff branch, over ten years prior to 1217. In that year Honorius III issued a second bull *Gratiarum omniun*, the final "confirmation of the Order".[4] Dominican women, in common with their clerical counterparts, developed the Order, not in terms of medieval social and religious norms, but in the changing times, each with its unique problems and apostolic needs, limited though the nuns were by restrictive ecclesiastical laws. While the Order, in its male branch could well appeal to the forces of past usage and tradition as grounds for the claim to full legal membership, it is difficult to accept the tenacity with which these attitudes were maintained and have persisted, and that far into the twentieth century.

According to the *Basic Constitution* the Dominican men form a clerical order since " the ministry of the Word and of the Sacraments is a priestly office". Nevertheless "the co-operator brothers, exercising in a special way the priestly aptitude common to all Christians share in the mission of the Fathers "in many ways". Since the "total commission of the Preacher to the proclamation of the gospel by word and work is fulfilled in the fact that by solemn profession he is entirely and perpetually identified with the life and mission of Christ". From this it is clear that ordination and solemn profession are the prerequisites for full Dominican membership, from which, by definition, even the co-operators brothers are excluded.[5] But lest the brethren be accused of exclusivity, especially by that great cloud of witnesses, the thousands upon thousands of women of the Order who, over the centuries, have proclaimed the gospel by word and work, the *Basic Constitution* concludes with a saving statement: "The Dominican family comprises clerical and co-operator brothers, nuns, sisters, members of secular institutes and fraternities of priests and lay-folk".[6] Here the brethren appear to make a distinction between Order and family and it is clear that though it may be claimed that all Dominicans are equal, the clerical brethren still subscribe to the outdated notion that some Dominicans are more equal than others. That the superior status of the clerical arm of the Order was confirmed by the *Constitutions*, is not in question. Nor can it be claimed that Dominican women are without blame for their excessive dependence on their intellectually and spiritually superior clerical brethren. Strong Dominican women in home foundations and on distant missions, must accept responsibility for the adulation and humble and uncritical admiration which they gave to the ordained men of the Order. In this way they perpetuate or create anew, a false image of the role and function of the brethren in their lives, as Dominican women. While this approach to the status of lesser, female Dominicans world-wide has a firm historical foundation, it reflects neither the spirit of St Dominic, nor an awareness of the changing attitudes to women in the secular world, or the growing power of women even within the Church today.

The history of the status debate, a long and painful battle by the women of the Order for recognition as true Dominicans, is a theme that dominated the history of many communities of women in the late nineteenth and early twentieth centuries. Although this debate was not unique to Cabra and its offspring, a brief introductory discussion will focus, though not exclusively, on Cabra, Sion Hill, and their missionary foundations in South Africa, New Zealand, Australia, and New Orleans. Over the centuries Dominican women had sought to establish their authenticity as Dominicans through the male branch of the Order, the "real Dominicans". In fact their real authenticity comes directly from Dominic himself, and to deny this is to put in question both the very foundations made by him, and his vision of the work of the nuns. It also reflects a profound misunderstanding of Dominic's approach to his work. Tugwell's reflections on the innovative approach of the founder to the formation of the Order are significant: "If he ended up as the father of an entirely new kind of religious order, the Order of Preachers, ... it was not because he deliberately set himself to fashion something new in the church, but because, step by step, he yielded himself faithfully and with the utmost generosity to the mysterious dictates of providence". In this he did not always find men of equal imagination among his followers, great and illustrious though many of them were. It is reasonable to contend that the living people of our past, men and women, were enmeshed in the net of contemporary custom and practice and were unable to accept women, consecrated though they were to the service of the Church, as worthy of full membership of their Order. Certainly if Tugwell's perception is to be accepted, the very founding of this body of preachers was the result of Dominic's ability to take risks and by his actions to defy the narrow conservatism of the church in his day.

> If we want to meet him, we must not look for him alone; his story constantly turns into the story of other people. It was his essential greatness to be part of something greater than himself. In concrete terms, this meant that almost all the fundamental choices that shaped his life were made by people other than himself. This did not signify that he was weak or unsure of himself; on the contrary, he could make, and if need be change, decisions of the most radical kind, without ever betraying the basic convictions which animated him.[7]

Tugwell asserts that Dominic's "adaptability came from strength". Radical adaptability takes great insight, courage, and detachment, and it certainly was not a characteristic of some of the men and women Dominicans, who entered into the status and jurisdiction debate at the turn of the twentieth century. Nor was it the first time that women had to fight for their rights within the Order, and as in the more distant past, the questions being raised were fundamental to those women involved. They reflected the assault that was being made by some of the brethren, against the very essence of their religious dedication and identity. Were the Cabra nuns and their missionary offspring truly Dominican? Did they conform to the essential criteria for legal and spiritual membership of the Order? Were they a product of a schism, claiming under false pretences, to a membership to which they had no valid right? Many of these questions arose as a result of the anomalous position of women religious in the church and the blurring of distinctions between Second and Third Order communities.

The Constitution *Circa pastoralis* (1566), of Pius V which imposed enclosure on all women religious of simple as well as solemn vows, made claims of superior status based on solemn profession difficult to sustain. Fortunately spiritual and apostolic needs demanded the circumvention of such laws in practice and this was the case in Dominican communities as well as in those more modern congregations, founded to meet the social needs of the people. But while for the Dominican women who traced their origins back to seventeenth century Galway, a greater part of their history provides evidence that strict enclosure was the ideal rather than the practice, nevertheless the claim to Second Order status was a jealously guarded treasure and an earnest penny of authenticity and Dominican integrity. Their efforts to gain recognition from Rome and from the First Order of their traditional position as nuns, bound by solemn vows and following the authentic Dominican Constitutions, was one modern example of the kind of battle that commenced shortly after the death of Dominic Guzman their founder and continued sporadically through the following centuries. The links that bound sisters and nuns to the First Order varied from place to place and from age to age. As early as 1235, just two years after the canonisation of St Dominic and only 14 years after his death, the General Chapter of the Order decreed that the brethren would be released from the care of the nuns of Dominic's first foundation, the convent at Prouille. An appeal by the nuns to Pope Gregory IX was successful. He revoked the decision of the Chapter. This however was not the end of the struggle to cut free from the burden of responsibility for Dominican women, if indeed there were any such. In respect of the nuns at Prouille, Hinnebusch writes: "The feminine community experienced the painful vicissitudes of the Dominican nuns".[8]

The *Book of Annals* of Sion Hill Convent, the Mother House of the Dominicans of Port Elizabeth, was compiled at the turn of the twentieth century and published in 1904, the period in which the jurisdiction and status debate was at its height. Although it deals with the matter briefly and with discretion, nonetheless the experience which the communities underwent made a deep impression on those involved, and had consequences that had a lasting effect on the development of the Congregation in later decades. This vexed question, which put into doubt the status of Cabra, her Irish foundations and the independent missions in

New Orleans, South Africa, Australia and New Zealand, had its origin in the 1832 transfer of jurisdiction from the Order to local episcopal authority. From 1860 onwards, it had linked communities across the world in an anxious and often angry debate. They, like many of the groups of female Dominicans before them, were trying to determine their legal and spiritual position as members of the Order.

After recounting the founding of Prouille by Dominic Guzman in 1206, and of San Sisto in Rome 1219, which were directly under the jurisdiction of the Order, the Dominican author of the Sion Hill *Annals* summed up the jurisdiction debate as it was discussed both in her community, and by letter across the world. Her summary is well worth reading. At the outset the nuns fell under the direct control of Dominic and after his death that of the Master General. Finally as the number of Dominican convents for women increased, they were placed under the ordinary jurisdiction of the Provincial. The date of this transfer is difficult to fix. According to the sister annalist: "We may conjecture, with some reason, that it was after the conflict which arose between the Brothers and Sisters of the Order in the course of the thirteenth century. *This conflict was famous in the early times of the Order*". The subsequent decision of the brothers to seek release from this burden did not find the Prouille nuns without resources to fight their decision. The nuns "could not understand" the position taken by their brethren, "and wished ...to remain subject to the Order". The main argument was that some of them "had made profession in the hands of St. Dominic". While Jordan of Saxony, the Master General, accepted the ruling of Gregory IX, and Prouille, "by special privilege", remained under the direct jurisdiction of the brethren, this did not apply to many of the convents of religious women who found legal identity in the church under the Dominican banner.

The contentious question of jurisdiction did not find any permanent solution, and for the Irish Dominican nuns and their missionary offspring it remained a major issue.

> In our days [early 1900's] opinions still differ, and feelings run high on this debatable point. *The Fathers, who, in the early times of the Order, were the originators of the contest, sometimes use hard words, and cast a great slur on those Convents of ours which, by the authority of the Apostolic See, as well as owing to the necessities of local circumstances, have been withdrawn from the jurisdiction of the Order and placed under the jurisdiction of the Ordinary of the Diocese.* The Fathers have created the precedent - it seems a contradiction that when carried into effect by lawful authority

they should be so opposed to it, and go so far as *to stigmatise
as not genuine Dominicans* those who accept a rule in
accordance with the decision of a General Chapter.[9]

This is the crux of the matter. It was not simply the question of
government, but rather the refusal by some of the brethren to
acknowledge as part of the Order, three Irish Dominican women
of the much reduced Cabra community who in 1832 had chosen
to accept episcopal jurisdiction for themselves and for their future
foundations.

That this was a common practice, and recognised as such by
both the Master General of the Order and by the Church, made
no difference to the male protagonists in the debate. Nor was it
noted that many Dominican communities of women in missionary
situations, including those in the Cape Colony, were for almost
the first sixty years of their existence without the benefit of the
spiritual ministration of their own brethren. Just as Cabra came
under the strong influence of the Vincentians, so did the two
South African congregations depend on the Jesuits for retreats
and in the Eastern Vicariate as special confessors. It is evident
from all available records that the South African communities
remained faithful to the Dominican ideal and promoted the
apostolic work of the Order, and that they like their Irish
counterparts, longed for the fullness of the life they had chosen.
This is clear from the fact that in 1938, they freely sacrificed
their independence and joined the Irish Congregation, a body
that regarded them with tolerant superiority. Despite evidence
to the contrary it was generally believed that those cut off from
direct ties with the brethren, or placed as Cabra was, under the
spiritual care of the Vincentians or other clerics outside the Order,
could not be true Dominicans. This debate disturbed the
communities concerned and in some cases created a debilitating
sense of insecurity and a temporary loss of identity. On the
positive side it forced the sisters to look closely and critically at
what constituted acceptable criteria for membership of the Order,
and to put the ideals into practice. It also made clearer to both
Cabra and Sion Hill the need for mutual reconciliation, both
among themselves and with their disaffected brethren. However
the process with its complex legal issues was exacerbated by the
emotional conflict which found expression in busy tongues. The
fact that there was truth on both sides and stubborn adhesion
to fixed opinions in the debate did nothing to bring about a rapid
and happy solution.

The Cabra nuns, like those of Galway and Drogheda had been
under the direct jurisdiction of the Order, not a satisfactory

situation in the eyes of some of the sisters. The brethren were few, and by 1831, so soon after the Catholic Emancipation Act of 1829, their role as chaplains and ecclesiastical superiors became both an economic burden and an embarrassment to the nuns. According to the Prioress of Cabra the nuns could no longer sustain the jurisdiction of the Fathers and consequently appealed to the Cardinals of Propaganda to take action:

> [The nuns] have had to contend and are still contending with difficulties ... which threaten the total extinction of their community. That the evils ... have arisen from the injudicious appointments of chaplains and the officious interference of provincials and vicars with the internal and domestic arrangements of the house. ... A chaplain was, a few years since appointed, who seldom except on Sundays said Mass and who by his irregular habits disedifyed the community. His removal ... was long and anxiously sought for, and yet so obstinately refused, although his unfitness for office was evident to all, and your *memorialists* were obliged to get another priest to say Mass; and thus two chaplains at a most inconvenient expense were supported by the revenue of the convent.

As if this were not enough, the nuns were being "threatened with penalties" if they did not adhere "to those measures by which the funds of the community have already been dissipated". They were also denounced by their provincial "in the severest language as resisting authority if they presume to remonstrate on the impropriety of those changes and arrangements by the adoption of which the house in the course of a few years became indebted in the sum of £600", a very large sum to a poor community. The memorialists begged, "as an only means of preserving their little community, to be placed under the immediate jurisdiction of the archbishop and thereby to be freed from the interference of those who have embroiled the affairs, squandered the funds of the house and kept your memorialists in a state of distraction and anxiety".[10]

The above extracts are only a small sample of the petitions and documents supporting the urgent requests made to Rome. On 22 April 1831, less than two months after the first appeal to Propaganda the three surviving choir members of the Community, Sisters M F M Butler, Anne C Maher and Teresa Catherine Dalton, sent another memorial:

> We the undersigned professed nuns of the Order of St. Dominick living in community in the convent of St. Mary of Cabra, near Dublin, consulting as we firmly believe the good of religion and of our establishment, most humbly implore

His Holiness to commit us to the care of the most Rev. Doctor Murray and his successors. Our funds are reduced almost to nothing and our numbers to three choir sisters by the bad government of provincials and the injudicious interference of other friars. If His holiness knew but the half of the evils we have suffered from those who should have been our protectors, we are certain that he would look on us with pity and save us from utter destruction by granting our petition.[11]

The nuns did not spare their brethren and every weakness and fault was laid before the critical eye of Roman authority, a tribunal with a long memory. Dr Cullen, later Cardinal, in a letter dated 20 December 1831 to his cousin Mother Columba Maher, one of the above memorialists, while excusing the delay in his answer on the matter of transfer of jurisdiction, wrote: "I was so fully persuaded of the piety and virtue of the Irish nuns that I could not doubt even for a moment, but that you and your Sisters would await the decision of the Pope with the greatest indifference, and the most perfect resignation to the will of God". This reply, while reflecting the correct response of religious, particularly nuns, to the trials of life, misread the anxiety and tension among the sisters and the desire to have the conflict settled once and for all.

It was a vain hope. The transfer to episcopal jurisdiction, was granted the following year without loss to the Cabra nuns of their privileges and status as Dominicans. In addition the Archbishop of Dublin later obtained for the sisters dispensations from the Divine Office and the substitution of the Little Office of the Blessed Virgin Mary. While these changes were seen as necessary for sisters involved in teaching, they were a source of regret even to some of those who had accepted them as inevitable. However the actual change in jurisdiction and the dispensations granted by the Holy See were less important than the breach of confidence within the Cabra community itself and between the brethren and the nuns.

Now began the circulation of certain reports, which, however silly in themselves, nevertheless afflicted the honest heart of Mother Columba [Maher]. It was maintained by some that because the community had been transferred from the care of the Brothers of their Order to the control of the Bishop of their Diocese, they thereby lost the privileges and Indulgences of the Order - in fact they ceased to belong to it.[12]

In 1862 a further dispensation was granted by the Holy See at the request of the ecclesiastical superior of the Cabra and Sion Hill communities. The postulation reads as follows:

> Most Holy Father, the Archbishop of Dublin, with the most profound respect, represents to your holiness that there are in the aforesaid Diocese some Houses of Dominican Nuns, under the jurisdiction of the Ordinary. They labour with great success in the education of the poor, of the Deaf and Dumb ... As their occupations are thus continuous, the supplicant begs that they may be dispensed from the observance of the fasts and feasts belonging to the Dominican Order. The said nuns also beg, that when with lawful permission, they go to the other Dioceses, they may be subject to the Ordinary, as they are in Dublin.

This petition was granted at an audience with Pope Pius IX in July 1862, a significant date in a decade that saw the dispersal of Irish Dominican nuns to New Orleans, South Africa and to the furthest corners of the British Empire. It ensured that these missionaries brought with them the seeds of doubt and dissension sown by the quarrels and divisions between the Dominican nuns and the brethren in Ireland.[13] Some of the brethren, who resented the criticism and perceived disloyalty of the Cabra nuns, and the rejection of their services, which in the past had contributed to their own livelihood, did not hesitate to disown them as members of the Order. As a result the infamy of the Mother House and its missionary offspring was spread abroad. This raised grave doubts both among the sisters themselves and the people they had come to serve. Even in the Cape Colony the Dominican sisters did not escape from the uncertainty arising out of the doubt cast on their authenticity and their membership of the Order. However they were fortunate in that their bishops were not only Irish but were close and appreciative friends of the Cabra and Sion Hill communities and had no doubt as to the fact that their nuns were true Dominicans as well as religious of high reputation as educators.

The question of the identity and status of Dominicans, who had originated from Cabra, arose within seven years of the first South African foundation, that of Cape Town. In June 1870 Père Jandel, the Master General, wrote to the prioress of the Irish Dominican community at New Orleans:

> I have not received the Book of Constitutions referred in your letter ... Its perusal is not, however, necessary to enable me to reply without hesitation to the question you put to me. When, as in your case, the Sisters of our Order, are under the jurisdiction of Bishops, it is not necessary that I should be informed of the Foundations which may from time to time take place and there are in the world a large number of Dominican Convents whose establishment is quite canonical,

with which nevertheless I am in no wise concerned. I have indeed told M L'Estrade that I have no knowledge of your community, but these words do not signify that I consider your affiliation doubtful, irregular or null: I have formed no opinion on the question. I could not possibly have done so, being quite ignorant of your affairs. Now that you tell me that your convent is a Foundation from that of Cabra in Ireland, I have every reason to believe your institution is regular.[14]

This was the first salvo in the resumption of a long, bitter and acrimonious battle which spread from Ireland to Rome, to Australia, to New Zealand and to South Africa. The Cape Town and Port Elizabeth sisters while well aware of the accusations made against them by their own brethren, had little direct contact with the Fathers and so were spared the pain of personal animosity. Assumpta O' Hanlon OP in her book *Dominican pioneers in New South Wales*, published in 1949, gives an excellent analysis of the debate, together with complete copies of relevant correspondence from the files of Cardinal Moran. While some of her conclusions could be challenged her summing up of a most complicated and emotional issue, is masterly.

The upsurge of hostility against Cabra and its offspring gained new momentum in the last decade of the nineteenth century. Father V M Sutherland OP writing in 1893 to Mother Catherine de Ricci Maher, Prioress of Cabra, in connection with the slurs being cast on the Dominican nuns by one of the brethren, expressed his indignation and recommended that she write to the Vicar-Provincial, Fr Conway, "and relate to him the circumstances *in extenso*". He also advised her to ask the latter to inform the whole province of the circumstances surrounding the transfer of 1832. He could not, however ignore the seriousness of the situation:

> I may not disguise from you the fact that there is anything but an agreeable impression among most of our fathers in your regard arising I believe from false notions as they have regarding the circumstances of yr. transfer, but if it can be shown that your relations to the order is the same as that of our nuns in Stone and a hundred other places, who are immediately subject, as you are, to the Diocesan, and if this knowledge permeates through the Province the present attitude of the Fathers must and will at once cease.[15]

The following year he wrote: "You are Dominicans, you are members of the Order of St. Dominic, as no one reading the Decrees which you have furnished me with can doubt. The Church addresses you by the title and no one therefore must dare to regard you in another light".[16] But the Dominican brethren did dare and this brought increased anxiety to the sisters. In 1901 Mother Ignatius O'Doherty, then Prioress of Dominican Convent, Belfast, an independent house founded from Cabra, wrote to Mother Imelda Kavanagh, Prioress of the Mother House:

> There still exists in members of our community an uneasiness and a want of secure feeling as to their status. This uneasiness is caused by the repeated assertion of priests and others that we are not Dominicans of the Second Order, in a word these poor Sisters feel that they are regarded as frauds, and that they have made profession under false pretences. I don't think I told you before that one of the first Retreats after the Foundation of the Convent here in 1870, was given by a Dominican Father now deceased. It was before my time, but when I came to Belfast, facts in connection with that retreat were very vividly before all minds, and I was assured that this good Retreatant had declared to the Sisters that the transfer of jurisdiction in Cabra, from the Order to the Ordinary of the Diocese had not been canonically obtained - that it had been got through the intervention of an insane Friar.

This was not the only reason for the unhappiness of the nuns in Belfast. Sister Ignatius also noted three additional statements made by brethren of the order:

> In my own time, a young girl who had been educated here, expressed a strong desire to join the Community. One of the Dominican Fathers used all his influence with her friends to prevent the accomplishment of her desire, as he had done at an earlier date in endeavouring to withdraw her from the school. At another time a Dominican Father giving a retreat or mission where the friends of one of our sisters resided, was requested by them when passing through Belfast, to call to the Dominican Convent in Belfast. They insisted that their friend was a member of the Community. 'No', rejoined the Father 'these Nuns are not Dominicans, they do not belong to the Order'.

What the sisters needed, according to Sister Ignatius, was "a declaration from Rome that they are nuns of the Second Order of St Dominic, ... that their Vows are solemn, that their rule is Dominican and approved by Rome, and that they are bound to enclosure in the manner and form prescribed by the Ordinary of the Diocese".[17] The problems of status, the solemn nature of the vows, and episcopal jurisdiction, could be solved, but was the Rule truly Dominican? And if the Rule by which the nuns lived was adapted and approved by a local Ordinary and not by the Order could it be called Dominican? Six years earlier in reply to a request to settle the question for the Dominican community in New Orleans, Louis J Hickey OP had written:

> The canonical position of these pious ladies seems clear enough. They are a 'Congregation' under Episcopal jurisdiction ... I have great sympathy for them and the other Communities similarly situated, but it would take an abler canonist than I claim to be, to make out for them the right to call themselves, or to be, Sisters of the Second Order of St Dominic. ... What does seem a bar, and an effectual one, is to change the Rule and Constitutions. This the Cabra Sisters did, as the book I have states, for they seek approbation for their Rules, etc., and Dr Murray gravely gives it. Do you think the Rule of our Order needed Episcopal or any approbation in the 19th Century? And as a fact, often our Generals have visited Ireland since, but never did one of them put foot inside the walls of Cabra.

He advised that the sisters seeking recognition by the Order should "put themselves into communication with the Sisters of Drogheda, or Belem near Lisbon and get from them, and begin to practice, the true Rules of the Order".[18] It is clear that the 1832 transfer of jurisdiction and the severe criticism of the brethren by the Cabra community had bitten deep, and the memory of rejection by the sisters had been kept alive in the Order. It is indeed true to say that in the case of Cabra and her offshoots in Ireland, New Orleans, Australia, New Zealand and even South Africa "bitterness had obscured the main issue; and charges were being made which had nothing to do with what was fundamentally a legal question".[19]

The manuscript for the first printed version of the Dominican Constitutions for the Cabra community was submitted for approval to Dr Murray in 1843. This was "an exact translation of a very old Italian work printed for the Second Order, and bearing the approval of a Master-General of the 15th Century". They had inserted regulations about schools, and "some other advice for the guidance of the Sisters". Mother Columba Maher wrote to Murray that the sisters had been "deprived of the comfort and advantage which almost every religious community in existence possesses, namely, that of having their Rule and Constitutions printed". She assured him of the authenticity of the text:

> Your Grace will readily perceive, that no departures from our original Rule, as understood and enforced from time immemorial amongst us, has been permitted; no duties or

obligations introduced; no exercises or practices prescribed; no additions made, but what have been sanctioned by our Constitutions themselves, or by our long and duly established observances. No pains have been spared to render this reading of our Rule strictly conformable to the original; the mistakes which had crept into our manuscript copies have been carefully corrected; quaint and occasionally inconvenient expressions have been altered; and wherever the occasion required it, the wording has been made to harmonize with your Grace's authority and jurisdiction over us, as well as our subjection and obedience to you as our ecclesiastical superior.

She also reassured Dr Murray that she had submitted the Rule and Constitutions to the "entire Community assembled in chapter" which was "approved and adopted" by the sisters, and awaited the seal of episcopal recognition.[20] This is the printed version of the Constitution which was accepted by Sion Hill in 1858 and was brought to the Cape Colony by the foundresses of the Dominican missions in both Cape Town and Port Elizabeth. It is evident that while this book of *Constitutions* deviated little from that used in the Dominican Convents of Galway and Drogheda, it carried the seal of Cabra, not a recommendation in the eyes of Sion Hill. The substitution of the Little Office of the Virgin Mary for that of the Divine Office, while it reflected the *status quo* in both convents, was to Sion Hill and to her South African foundation not the Dominican ideal, and this especially in view of the rumours already circulating in clerical circles in Ireland and in Rome, concerning Cabra and her foundations.

On September 7, 1888 Mother Rose Whitty wrote to Mother Clare, Sub-Prioress of the Sion Hill community:

> The Bishop has at last granted our petitions in allowing us to translate the French Constitutions and get dispensations from the General for the parts we cannot observe. His Lordship held out for a long time saying Sion was to take the initiative. In answer I told him I had frequently written to you, imploring, entreating of you to take some steps. We have also, if the majority of the Sisters wish it, permission to say the Divine Office. The K[ing William's Town] and Grahamstown nuns say it so we are the only religious in this Bishop's Vicariate who do not use the Breviary.

The choice made by Mother Rose of the French version of Dominican Constitutions was an excellent one. Sister Thomas, of Sienna Convent, Drogheda, a Second Order foundation, wrote to Cabra in 1901, at the height of the status controversy: "Père

Potton's French Edition of 1878 is of course the most perfect of all as it includes all legislation, observances and customs to our own times".[21] The translation from the French of Père Potton's version of the Dominican Constitution for Second Order nuns, was made by Mother Rose herself. In this task she was assisted neither by a Dominican Father nor by the sisters of Sion Hill. In his introduction to the new Constitutions Bishop Ricards made clear the reasons for this change:

> In assisting the Reverend Mother Prioress and the senior sisters of Holy Rosary Convent, Port Elizabeth, in the preparation of Constitutions, as near as their school duties will permit, to the approved Constitutions of the Dominican 2nd Order of women, compiled from the best authorities by the Rev. Father Br. Marie, Ambroise Potton, I have had in view the peace of soul of the community. ... This peace of soul has been disturbed in the Dominican nuns of this Convent by certain priests of the Order, who assured them that they were not, as being under the jurisdiction of Vicars Apostolic, and guided by mutilated Constitutions, real children of St. Dominic.[22]

Nor did Ricards hesitate to approach the Master General on every point that he considered to be anachronistic or impracticable, and to secure his approval for all minor modifications of the text. Ricards realised that "Any customs and laws strongly tinged with the rude simplicity of Medieval times might excite a prejudice in the minds of those who, although they would rather die than sacrifice a sound principle, yet feel that a certain deference must be paid to the tastes and habits of the age we live in". In the matter of public penance the Bishop desired that "some penance be substituted for the discipline, and absolutely ... [forbade] the use of the discipline in the presence of the community". He wanted to be certain that all public acts "according to present usage and habit" which were "calculated to lessen self-respect and to degrade should be avoided".[23] He did not approve an expurgated version of Potton's *Constitution*, the full text was given, but he made it clear what was and what was not acceptable for religious women and for the image of the church, in the late 1880's. In this Ricards was "guided by a long experience of colonial life", and he, with the agreement of the Prioress and her Council, made changes where the ancient regulations might "seriously impede our Educational work in South Africa".[24] The Bishop was wise in his decision to bring the *Constitutions* of the sisters into line with contemporary standards, if not in text at least in statements making clear essential modification of usage. Dr Ricard was well aware of the fact that the times were not propitious for Catholics, and the local Church could ill afford a scandal concerning nuns and their life-style.

The celebration of the bicentenary of the Revocation of the Edict of Nantes in 1885 had aroused religious animosities in South Africa, especially among Protestants of French ancestry, who viewed the growing influence of the Catholic Church with suspicion. Despite the re-issue of a book written by William Stone, *A Refutation of the Fabulous history of the arch-imposter Maria Monk*, (1836), the old story, over seventy years in print, began to do the rounds in the Colony. This anti-Catholic campaign was ably supported by the writings of an ex-priest, Charles Chuiniquy: *Fifty years in the Church of Rome* and *Priest, woman and the confessional*. Such propaganda was given local support by the anti-Catholic publications of C F J Muller, *Rome and her doctrines* in 1888 and *Romish assertions refuted*, in 1889. In addition the local press together with regular anti-Catholic reports in that bulwark of Dutch Reformed orthodoxy, *De Kerkbode*, kept the debate alive. Among those who fell within the ambit of Protestant disapproval were the nuns. These were involved, very successfully, in educational work throughout the Colony. Had they limited their services to children of their own faith they would have constituted no more than a minor hazard to the Calvinist community. But this was not the case. That convent schools were as popular with Protestant parents as with Catholics, exacerbated the situation, and this led to a lively and heated debate not about education, but on the illegality of enclosing women, even Catholic women, under lock and key, and it was suggested, often in chains. In these circumstances medieval laws for nuns, with their harsh penances and restrictions on personal freedom, would have provided sensational material for public debate, to the discredit of the Church.

Whatever the claims of authentic Dominicanism or the need for perfect conformity to the ancient Rules of the Order, the modifications of the *Constitutions*, in practice if not in text, proved Dr Ricard right. In 1890 Hammond, a self-styled Doctor, travelled through the Colony vilifying the Catholic Church and especially the nuns. One of the results of this was that the Dutch Reformed Church presented about nineteen petitions to Parliament "praying for an enquiry into and examination of the working of our convents".[25] The Rev W Smith Foggitt, wrote in the *Cape Times:*

> Not as a religious institution do we attack the nunnery, but because it is an unnatural and anti-social establishment which threatens the liberty of Romanist and Protestants alike.

> Exempt as it is from the operation of the law, what is to hinder
> that a Protestant child, drawn within its fair and fascinating
> professions, may consent to immure herself in one of these
> places, that, afterwards she may be held herself against her
> will.

This kind of attack, made against the Sisters of Nazareth in
Cape Town, who took care of orphans, did not appeal for
government rights of inspection, but rather for proof that the
inmates of such institutions had free access to the civil
authorities. The whole debate, which involved the redoubtable
Dr Frederick Charles Kolbe, led to stronger support of the
charitable work of the Nazareth Sisters, from Protestants as well
as Catholics.[26] It also gave rise to a world-wide investigation to
the total discredit of Dr Hammond.[27]

With the help of police and detective services of Scotland Yard,
and other eminent bodies in Europe, Canada, the USA and
Australia, Vicars Apostolic of missionary territories and Bishops,
especially Irish bishops across the world, set in motion a
formidable investigation of the claims of Dr Hammond. In the
meantime nuns throughout the Colony continued their
educational or nursing missions, unperturbed. Letters flew from
one continent to the other proving the falsity of Hammond's claims
and newspapers and journals continued the debate, but this had
little or no impact on the lives of the Dominican sisters. They did
not read newspapers, and though they would have been well
informed as to the progress of the investigation, their interest
was in other things. Were not members of the Port Elizabeth
community with their new *Constitution* and the newly won
privilege of saying the Divine Office, making happy progress
towards the perfection of the Christian life, in the authentic
Dominican way? It is significant that for Mother Rose and her
community it was not the Irish Mother Houses that initiated the
movement towards what was perceived to be a more Dominican
way of life, but the missionary sisters themselves. They had
appealed for help but Sion Hill had been tardy in its response,
though it is clear that this latter community was moving in the
same direction as Holy Rosary Convent, Port Elizabeth. Indeed
Mother Rose and her sisters did not need to turn to Ireland for
the necessary impetus to return to an old and venerable
Dominican tradition, the daily recitation of the Divine Office. Had
they not an excellent example at hand in the German Dominicans
of King William's Town, and an ecclesiastical superior who
doubted neither their status nor their true Dominican spirit?

In 1896 the settlement of the status debate was placed in the hands of Cardinal Moran by Mother Catherine de Ricci Maher of Cabra. His high office in the Church, his ability to deal directly with the Supreme Pontiff, and his understanding of Roman politics, made him an ideal ally in the circumstances. He had remained a staunch friend of the Dublin Dominicans, and as the ecclesiastical superior of the Dominican sisters in New South Wales and a friend of the communities in Adelaide, he was anxious to put an end to the rumours and accusations still circulating among the brethren. It was not a matter of settling a simple case of scandal-mongering. The ongoing debate placed in doubt the validity of the vows taken by the nuns. While it is difficult to trace the reasons for the growth and bitterness of the opposition to the sisters during the last decade of the nineteenth century, there can be no doubt as to the seriousness of the situation. Mother de Ricci made clear to the Cardinal that the "old vexed question of Jurisdiction" was causing "grave troubles" in some of the houses. "Before the transfer", she wrote, "we were regarded as belonging to the Order, and true Dominicans. Since the transfer, although we in no way departed from our former mode of life, we were regarded as having no right to the name. ... Now doubts are cast on our position by our own nuns in different countries, as statements of externs reached the ears even of our own Sisters".[28] Her analysis of the situation was corroborated in 1901 by Mother Ignatius O'Doherty, who also appealed to the Cardinal for help:

> God only knows the destruction done by reports that we are imposters - that we have deceived young girls - that we are not true Dominicans. You may say there is no foundation for any such opinion, but yet the harm is being done. For God's sake, Your Eminence, do all you can to help us. I speak from bitter experience. [We] know not what to believe from the reports spread abroad as to our condition, and to some, I fear, there may be danger in the delay of a definite answer to their doubts and difficulties. ... Kindly excuse, my Lord Cardinal, the earnestness of my pleading, but I feel that if we lose this chance, all is gone.[29]

In 1902 further letters were exchanged between Cabra, Sion Hill and St Mary's Dominican Convent, Belfast and Cardinal Moran. The Prioress of Cabra assuring him of the present attitude of the sisters to their Dublin brethren: "One thing I should like Your Eminence to know - that is, that our Dominican Friars here have *never* by any means given us the very slightest cause for uneasiness, but have always been most kind - we prefer them to any others for retreats, etc. - a proof that they have been good and friendly with us".[30]

Cardinal Moran placed the whole matter of the status of the Dominican nuns before the Sacred Congregation of Propaganda Fide, outlining the history of the change in jurisdiction, and of the "calumny" spread abroad " in Australia, in Ireland and in Rome itself". He requested a definitive statement as to the status of the Dominican sisters in Australia and "of the Community of Cabra in the diocese of Dublin in Ireland from which the aforesaid Australian communities spring". The request was presented to the Master General, who noted that this group also included sisters in New Orleans and South Africa. He advised against submission for examination by Propaganda:

> Should a Consultor of the Sacred Congregation be commissioned to examine on the one hand the Constitutions of the Dominican Sisters of Cabra approved on April 22, 1843, by the Apostolic Visitor, the Archbishop of Dublin, Monsignor D. Murray, of venerable memory, and on the other hand the request made by His Eminence, the Cardinal Archbishop of Sydney, for a decision on this matter, I have no doubt whatever but that his answer would be in the negative, not only as regards membership of the Second Order but even perhaps of the Third Order - if we take into account the conditions prescribed by the Sacred Congregation of Bishops and Regulars on June 28th, 1901, paragraph 2, No. 16, page 8. As I have said above, the solution offers little difficulty, but to put it into effect would be laborious and would lead us far afield without compensation of practical results. Furthermore, I venture to say that it would be hurtful to the Sisters themselves, creating disturbance among them, confusion and distress.[31]

He proposed that the "useless" matter be shelved and that it would be better "to try instead to reinvigorate these souls and encourage them in the holy purpose of their vocation, a vocation indeed that has borne much and splendid fruit wherever a house of these Religious has been established". The Master General, while engaged in canonical visitation of the Order in Ireland in 1897, had gained for himself personal knowledge of the work and influence of the Dominican sisters although they did not fall directly under his jurisdiction:

> I was able to see for myself, to my own unspeakable satisfaction, the immense good that is being done by these Sisters. The testimonies of the Bishops of other countries do but confirm the impression I brought away from Ireland, so

that not only shall I have no difficulty in acknowledging them to be members of the great Guzman family but I shall be happy to declare them, according to their express wish, to be daughters of St Dominic and to grant them without delay the necessary documents which will enable them as far as possible to share in the graces and privileges of the Order of Preachers.[32]

In the interim, while awaiting this reply, Cardinal Moran had visited the Dominican sisters in Ireland, and no doubt gained first-hand knowledge of the debate. On his visit to Rome in 1903 he decided to put the case before the Holy Father himself. In a long audience with Pope Pius X he explained the dilemma of the sisters and with such persuasiveness that the Supreme Pontiff issued an Apostolic Brief restoring to Cabra and its foundations all their rights as members of the Dominican Order. According to Moran the Brief "being a decree and Apostolic Letter direct from the Holy Father sets aside all obstacles and cancels everything that could lead to doubt as to the true position of your convent and all its branches. I wish you to bear in mind", the Cardinal wrote to the sisters in Ireland, "that it was the inspiration of the Pope himself to issue the Decree in the form of a Brief or Pontifical Letter. When I broached the subject to His Holiness he expressly mentioned that this would be the most effective and decisive manner for settling the matter and removing the difficulties".[33] The Apostolic letter is clear:

We concede and grant that the Dominican Sisters of the Monastery of St Mary's, Cabra, and other houses founded in different places by the daughters of the aforesaid Monastery, who have already been admitted to the habit and profession, or who in future shall be duly admitted, be partakers of all the Privileges, Indulgences and Spiritual Favours which the Nuns of the Second Order enjoy, and this participation, We do, by our Apostolic Authority, renew as far as renewal may be necessary. It is our Will, too, that the said Sisters faithfully observe the Rule and Constitutions as at present in force among them, and that they obediently submit to the Jurisdiction of the Ordinaries of the respective places. These presents remain in force for all future time. Given at Rome under the ring of the Fisherman on the 15th day of September, in the first year of Our Pontificate.[34]

The Holy Father had spoken, the Dominican sisters rejoiced, and technically the debate was closed. However, in the church as in civil society wounds are not healed or doubts laid to rest, solely by the application of law, however exalted the legislator.

The old questions remained. Were the sisters real Dominicans? And if so into what category did they fall, Second or Third Order? Were they in their community life of contemplation, liturgical prayer, penance and apostolic work, fulfilling the ancient and traditional laws, customs and ideals of the Order founded by Dominic Guzman in the early thirteenth century? What essential elements were missing in their lives, elements, in theory at least, common to the lives of the Fathers? And in what ways however minor, were they failing to fulfil perfectly the Dominican vocation which they had chosen? These questions revealed the profound sense of uncertainty which was to characterise the Irish Dominican communities for the next 25 years. It set them on a course of reform, of interaction by letter and in meetings both at home and abroad, of a strong movement towards union, and of a growing dependence on the advice and judgement of the Dominican brethren. These latter while eager to assist their sisters, were not slow to spell out for them the weakness of their position and the tenuous nature of their understanding of the essence and practice of the Dominican charism.

In this situation members of the Galway community also played the mentor's role, though they themselves resisted all invitations to become part of a union. To accept would, they believed, force them to relinquish what they perceived to be their privileged position as nuns of the Second Order, with solemn vows and under the direct jurisdiction of the Dominican Provincial. The desire for the higher status survived the years of struggle for union, the creation of a stable congregation of Dominican women, and the gracious acceptance by amalgamation of the South African communities in 1938. A petition to the General Chapter of 1960, which proposed that the question of solemn vows be revisited, clearly indicates that for some of the sisters, at least, the yearning for the highest form of Dominican life persisted. Wisely no decision was made by this body, which in the event was to be the bridging Chapter linking a dying age to a totally new and vibrant era for religious life in the church and in the Congregation. It was also the beginning of a period of intensive interaction within the Congregation, reminiscent of the efforts of Irish and colonial Dominican sisters during the 25 years following the 1903 Apostolic Letter of Pius X.

Chapter Eleven

The Union

Between 1903 and 1919 the efforts of the Irish sisters to consolidate their position as Dominican nuns of the Second Order, had little impact on the communities in Cape Town and Port Elizabeth. For the Dominicans of the Western Cape this was a period of growth and relative prosperity, but for Holy Rosary Convent and its satellite houses in the Eastern Cape it was, until 1915 and the arrival of Mother de Ricci Harkin with a group of sisters, a time of decline and indeed possible closure. Mother de Ricci brought to the Port Elizabeth community, over which in December 23, 1918, she was elected superior, the spirit of extreme conformity and loyalty to Dominican ideals and practices, outmoded though many of the customs were. In the educational sphere she ensured that the teaching sisters were adequately prepared for their apostolate in the schools, while meticulous care of the household imposed hard and unremitting work on all, work which left little or no opportunity for idleness.[1] The Dominican ideals learnt in Sion Hill on matters Dominican had always had an impact on the community of Port Elizabeth and with the arrival of Mother de Ricci this influential bond was made more immediate. Since the sisters already claimed to be members of the Second Order and said the Divine Office, they could anticipate a stronger bond, spiritual if not legal, with their Irish Mother House.

There is little evidence that the sisters of the Western Cape questioned the authenticity of their Dominican life, or of their legal membership of the Order. They were aware of the debate that had caused such heart-searching in Ireland, but it did not strike home until 1922 when Bernard Jordan Gijlswijk, the newly appointed Apostolic Visitor to the Dominican sisters in Southern Africa, cast grave doubts on their right to call themselves Dominicans. That in 1913 the superiors were concerned about such minor points of discipline as "uniformity with regard to shoes, and handkerchiefs, and visiting days", does not argue any anguish as to identity or status.[2] They were in touch with their Mother House, Cabra, not only by letter but personally. In 1914, Mother Pius McLaughlin, Prioress of the communities in the Western Cape, together with two of her Councillors, Sister Columba McAuliffe and Sister Berchmans Cotter, were given hospitality by Cabra while they were on a recruiting visit to Ireland.[3] In 1913 it was not the question of status or Dominican authenticity that claimed the attention of the Cape Town superiors, but rather the wisdom or otherwise of setting up their own training school for postulants either in Ireland or in England and to ensure a supply of good, useful subjects for the mission.[4] Although the visit to Ireland did ensure that the community was adequately supplied with new recruits, there was no talk on the part of Cabra of union with her South African foundation. Nor did the mission in the Western Cape hope for further recruits from the Mother House. The plan proposed in 1913 was not realised until the opening of the Novitiate at Potter's Bar, England in 1922. This house became the first and last independent training ground outside the Western Cape, for a large number of young women who entered specifically for the Cape Town mission.

Personal contact with the sisters in Cabra and Sion Hill, and attendance at meetings such as the Education Conference held at Bloemfontein in January 1913, helped to bring the sisters into the wider world of Dominican politics, as well as into the problematic arena of government control in respect of teachers' qualifications and their appointment in government-aided schools. By 1917 the forces of change to promote regular life and a measure of uniformity, were clearly at work in the Irish Dominican communities of the Western Cape. At the Council Meeting held at Cape Town on January 6, 1917, the regulations concerning silence in the refectory were laid down, and a "uniform diet [was] as far as possible to be kept in all houses".[5] Three months later the same Council reflected the intervention of Cabra and the willingness of the superiors to conform to the practices proposed by Ireland. The Council decreed that "the changes in the ceremonial of the Office and Grace be adopted according to the regulations received from Cabra". This also included a change in the horarium according to the Irish model.[6] In addition Cabra agreed "to receive and educate girls who desired to offer themselves as postulants for the South African mission". These would be examined by the Irish superiors, and if found to be suitable, would be sent for schooling to Santa Sabina Convent at Sutton, the only branch house under the control of Cabra. For this service the Prioress of Cape Town would pay a fee of

"£30 a year each for those who would not be able to defray their own expenses".[7]

The need for suitably educated recruits was to remain a high priority for the South African communities since the dangers of attendance at secular colleges and universities was believed to be a moral threat to the young sisters. A second matter of concern for the Irish Dominicans, as it was for religious communities throughout the Catholic world, was the urgent need to bring Constitutions into line with the *New Revised Code of Canon Law* promulgated in 1917 and in force in the following year. For the first time the laws governing consecrated women had been clearly defined and a degree of uniformity was imposed, and where possible centralisation and amalgamation were strongly advocated. Temporary profession was to delay final canonical commitment of a candidate for three years, and the laws controlling the novitiate were to be strictly enforced. Rome looked to the Mother Houses to promote the reunion between themselves and their independent foundations, at home and abroad and the Master General of the Order was strongly in support of such amalgamations. It was a new and often puzzling age, a time when the ecclesiastical legislation had to be interpreted and put into practice by women who under the old regime, had been in and out of office for a lifetime. Neither the South African sisters, nor their Irish counterparts were qualified to deal with the intricacies of Canon Law. Those in positions of responsibility were mainly the oldest members of aging communities. They were not accustomed to the pressures imposed by implementation of ecclesiastical regulations that often rendered their missionary work more difficult and their conventual life more complex.

The changes implied a complete revision of the Constitutions, the submission of the interim revised texts to Rome for approval, and after a suitable period of trial, further revision and re-submission. This was a process more easily achieved in Ireland where the help of Dominican canon lawyers would be available. In the circumstances a Cabra initiative in 1919 was welcomed and debated, with due caution, by the sisters of Cape Town and Port Elizabeth The main points of the letter sent by the prioress of St Mary's Convent, Cabra, to Mother Berchmans Cotter in Cape Town, are summed up in the Council minutes of November 8, 1919:

> A letter was read from the Mother Prioress of St. Mary's Convent, Cabra, requesting the Mother Prioress, her Council and the community to consider the advisability or otherwise of Cabra and all its foundations, home and foreign

amalgamating with Sion Hill, Blackrock, and its branches, home and foreign. The celebration of the Second Centenary of the Cabra foundation had raised the question and a great desire for union on the part of various communities in Ireland had given hope that the movement would lead to good results. Amalgamation would lead to many changes in government, in customs, etc. hence there was need ... for much prayer, careful consideration, broad mindedness, and generosity. We, decided to place the information on the subject (which was but meagre yet) before the community, to pray, and to reply to Cabra that we would fall in with all reasonable changes when we had time to give them consideration.[8]

A similar letter, in which the reasons for the initiation of the amalgamation debate were given, was sent to Sion Hill, which in turn passed it on to the Prioress of Holy Rosary Convent, Port Elizabeth:

In conformity with the desires of the Holy See we are now about to look into and arrange the Constitutions so as to bring them into harmony with the new Code of Canon Law. This is a serious and most responsible undertaking, in which the most sacred interests are involved, for the present and future of all those communities observing our Constitutions. ... A further project has been proposed for our consideration, namely - "amalgamation", or Centralisation, as being in accordance with the spirit of the Church and the spirit of the Dominican Order. If our communities at home and abroad entertain this idea, it is well to know that it has been impressed on us by most reliable an authority that now is the most fitting time for the step.

Mother de Ricci Harkin, only four years in South Africa and less than a year in office as superior of the three convents in the Eastern Vicariate, was well informed on matters of Dominican politics in Ireland. She was also aware of the conservative attitude of Dr McSherry, the local ecclesiastical superior to whom she put the amalgamation proposal. Her reply to Sion Hill was characteristic:

Your letter, enclosing the Cabra copy, reached its destination last Thursday, the 6th. I read the two with mingled feelings of thanksgiving, wonder & doubt: thanksgiving that 'Amalgamation' was really coming, wonder that Cabra had moved, and as to how Cabra would bend and blend, and finally doubt of our Bishop's consenting to H.R.C. and its branches 'joining up'. We had our annual visitation yesterday. I read your letter to the Bishop and then gave him Cabra's to read to and for himself. When he had done so, he calmly remarked that he 'had anticipated a move towards amalgamation, but that he was decided not to approve of it for us' - (ostensibly) because of the inconveniences, etc. cropping up for Convents *Juris Pontificii',* but, in reality, I suppose, because if we remain *Juris diocesani,* he is more or less (chiefly more) our supreme ruler. Now, though disappointed at the Bishop's refusal to consent, I do not believe that if 'amalgamation' is in accordance with the Spirit of the Church & of the Order, an Ordinary has power to prevent a branch from uniting with the parent stem. Will you ascertain the law on this point, please? There is no priest here to whom I can refer - . The few seculars we have do not care to be bothered with the affairs of nuns, and the Regulars of the Vicariate are far away from P.E.

She took a legal approach to the matter. "Not having the Bishop's consent to the proposed amalgamation I cannot, of course, question the Communities of our three convents on the subject; nevertheless, I believe I can take the gauge of the *general mind* & say that all, with perhaps two exceptions, would favour the scheme. Should His Lordship come round to the proposed union, I shall *at once* confer with the Sisters, and communicate the results to you".[9]

In 1921 Mother de Ricci was "longing to hear of the Easter happenings in the Amalgamation movement" in Ireland, but the situation had not changed in the Eastern Vicariate.

Our Bishop is still of the opinion he expressed in November last. I wish he could be approached from some influential quarter and shown how our not joining up must end in our extinction. He should have no difficulty in seeing this. He told me himself that in 1910 he was downright anxious about the existence of H.R.C., and its branches. Now when we are better in numbers both in Convents and in Schools he forgets that the old order must return, if we sever all connection with Sion Hill.[10]

The Cabra Council sought the views of the sisters on the question of union and also asked for suggestions as to any changes "necessary" in the Constitutions.[11] Permission for meetings of representatives of Cabra, Sion Hill and their branch and independent houses in Ireland, was at first refused and finally grudgingly acceded to by the Archbishop of Dublin. The agenda for the meeting was ambitious and showed little awareness of the complexity of the process into which the communities were entering. Every aspect of Dominican observance was to be considered, including the procedure as to the form of application to be used for the formation of a congregation, financial arrangements and the title and status of the new religious body.[12] The first meeting which took place in January 1920, lasted for three days and involved 24 sisters, representatives from the Dominican Convents of Cabra and its branch houses Sutton, Kingstown, Wicklow; Belfast and her branch foundation at Portstewart, and Sion Hill, together with Eccles Street, Muckross Park and St Stephen's Green. There were two camps and the mutual ability to compromise, even on minor matters, was not easy to achieve. Two days after the final meeting on January 11, Mother Gonzales, Prioress of St Stephen's Green, was writing to Father Louis Nolan OP, one of the Irish Dominican brethren in Rome, who was to play a leading role in the amalgamation process, both in Ireland and in South Africa. After reading and discussion of the new draft constitution drawn up by the Prioress of Cabra and Mother Bertrand on the Kentucky model, the discussion turned to one of the main areas of contention, the Divine Office. Sion Hill, like Holy Rosary Convent, Port Elizabeth had this official prayer of the church, and was not prepared to sacrifice it.

> The Divine Office was strongly opposed - not even the singing of Compline on Sundays or feasts - not to mention Novitiate - would be accepted. Votes were taken against the wish of the Prioress and of course we [Sion Hill supporters] were out-numbered, we were only 7 against 17. The Little Office of B.V.M. according to Dominican Rite was not settled though we maintained that we should use the Dominican Rite if we are to be recognised as Dominicans. This [was] also left to the decision of Rome which means you. Use of woollen sheets [was] also left for the decision of the General Chapter by desire of Cabra which objects to their use. Cabra absolutely refused to have "Retreat by Dominican Father" inserted in Constitutions or Customary.

The questions of the formula of the vows and the public reading of the Constitutions in the refectory, were raised, as also the matter of abstinence on Wednesdays, and the opposition of Cabra was noted. It was also recorded, not without a sense of humble superiority, that Cabra was unfamiliar with the practice of the Venia, a penitential prostration familiar to all good Dominicans. Neither side was above scoring points, but in the matter of final decisions Cabra had the advantage in numbers if not in the finer points of authentic Dominican practice. There was no opposition to the notion of amalgamation. Indeed it was seen to be "most desirable", but the early realisation of this union was another matter altogether. "We thought ", wrote Mother Gonzales, "that as we are not united on so many points - it would be better to delay forming a Congregation till our differences are removed after the General Chapter when perhaps the General may come over, and when you may also be here".[13]

Problems relating to "Colonial Houses" were also raised and it was recognised that a special appendix to the constitutions would be necessary to accommodate the needs of such missionary institutions. In 1920 this aspect of the debate was not seen to be of high priority, but Cabra and Sion Hill still envisaged amalgamation with their foreign missionary foundations, and the two South African congregations were kept well informed of each halting step on the road to union. The Dominican communities in Ireland realised the doubtful advantage to themselves of uniting with the communities of Cape Town and Port Elizabeth. However since the post-war years saw an upsurge of missionary zeal, there could be distinct advantages in a Dominican Congregation incorporating communities already well established in South Africa, a country with great missionary potential. Such a move would be consonant with the mind of the Church and a true expression of the authentic Dominican charism. These considerations escaped neither the attention of the delegates assembled at Cabra, nor that of the superiors six thousand miles away in South Africa. These latter awaited, though not with bated breath, the outcome of the meetings on which their future might depend.[14]

All of these women, hewn from the same rock, were determined, whatever their differences, to protect their Dominican heritage. The variations in practice, though stressed in the heat of debate, were of minor importance in terms of the common apostolic ideals which sustained them. However the next eight years were to see the anxious pursuit of conformity and uniformity in the minutiae of conventual life, the Dominican way. It was an exercise in corporate scrupulosity contending with individual common sense, and advisors were not wanting. The need for reassurance gave to communities such as that of Galway and Drogheda, the "real Dominicans", the opportunity for detached participation in the fascinating debate as to the perfect way to live the life which had been proposed to the women of the Order nearly eight hundred years earlier. The letters of Mother Vincent Lynch of Galway, written between 1920 and 1928, are full of detailed information about the daily life of her community. It would do violence to history to accept Mother Vincent's instructions on Dominican customs as an indication of the ignorance of Dominican law and practice or indeed a sign of decadence in Cabra, Sion Hill and their foundations. In point of fact all evidence indicates that Mother Vincent was simply ensuring that no pearl was lost, and she herself was surprised at how many customs they all had in common. She was a strong-minded woman who wielded a ready pen, both to assist her less fortunate sisters living outside the jurisdiction of the Order, and to defend the position which she took for the protection of her own community. She also enjoyed the debate for its own sake while she herself stood strongly against the inclusion, during her lifetime, of the Galway community into the projected new congregation.[15]

However in this crisis facing the Dominican sisters in Ireland, Mother Vincent did not stand alone. In both the Irish communities and in the two congregations in South Africa, there were women of insight, determination and political acumen. Some saw amalgamation as the ideal way to ensure unassailable membership of the Dominican Order and a practical solution to need for the recruitment, spiritual training and education of personnel. Others, while longing for the perfection of Dominican life, saw little benefit in a union either among themselves or with Ireland. For many sisters in the ranks the debate was academic and these accepted the fact that the final decision did not rest with them but with their superiors, themselves subject to episcopal authority. Unlike Mother Vincent, the Provincials of the missionary foundations in South Africa, in theory at least, welcomed the possibility of union at some future date. They also knew that a union such as that proposed by Cabra could only be attained by mutual willingness to lay aside stubborn adherence to customs and traditions which were not of the essence of Dominican life. That for the Irish communities this was not an easy or rapid process, is evident from the mass of correspondence that has survived. One important step forward was taken at the second amalgamation meeting held at Cabra in July 1920. After a discussion on status, agreement was reached. "The majority expressed the belief that they were ... Second Order; but said that if it be necessary in order to form such a Congregation as the Holy See required that they merge into ... Third Order, they were willing to do so".[16]

In Cape Town Mother Berchmans and her Council received the minutes of the amalgamation meeting of January 1920. They followed the debate, took cognisance of points of difference, and held their peace.[17] Well informed of the process taking place in Ireland, they noted in March 1921 that the amalgamation movement was at a "stand-still". This was mainly the result of disagreement on the question of the Divine Office. Sion Hill and its branch houses supported its adoption, while Cabra and its branches opposed such a move. Both parties needed time to consider their options and this was provided by the political upheaval in Ireland. Meetings were discontinued because of the disturbed state of the country.[18] By September 1921 the Cabra sisters, who in the interim had been trained in the chanting and rubrics of the Divine Office, withdrew their objection to its adoption should such a move be necessary.[19] It was an important step forward proving that Cabra could "bend", even if the process of blending would take longer and cost more.

In the meantime the South African sisters used every means to increase their knowledge and practice of Dominican customs. Mother Berchmans Cotter in her letters to Mother Imelda and Mother Gonzales, who were on a recruitment drive in Germany, Holland, England and Ireland, and also during her own visits to Dominican houses in the Eastern Cape, comments on the customs and practices of the various Dominican congregations, both at home in South Africa and abroad. In this search for authentic Dominicanism they were assisted by an English Dominican, Father Shapcote OP. After preaching the annual retreat in January 1921, he met the Council members in session and "gave advice on points concerning Dominican custom, but he recommended that no change be made in our customs unless sanctioned by Cabra". In June 1921 he informed the sisters that Rome was sending an Apostolic Visitor to hold visitation of the Dominican sisters throughout Southern Africa. Father Bernard Jordan Gijlswijk OP, whose missionary experience had been in Curacao in the Caribbean, brought with him to Southern Africa full confidence in the authority invested in him by Rome, and a certain knowledge that he knew all the answers, canonical, spiritual and social, in respect of the Dominican women he was sent to visitate.

Gijlswijk's first formal visitation of the convents and subsequent meetings with the Council were to be a source both of support and of discouragement to the community at Cape Town. He had come from Rome well versed in the ramifications of the status debate that had been officially settled by the Apostolic Letter of Pope Pius X in 1903. Although he was clearly aware of the provenance of the communities from Cabra and Sion Hill, nevertheless he had no hesitation in informing the Council and senior sisters in Cape Town that whatever else they might claim to be, they were not Dominicans. He advised them to request the Master General of the Order to regularise their position. Mother Berchmans and her council wrote to Father Louis Theissling OP in January 1922:

For the past sixty years, we have laboured in the Cape Peninsula Division of the Western Vicariate of the Province of the Cape of Good Hope as Dominican Sisters. We are at present 104 in number, and are distributed among six convents where we carry on the work of teaching in three classes of schools, viz. High schools, Government-aided schools for poor white children, and mission schools for Coloured children. Our Sisters came originally from Cabra, near Dublin, Ireland. Now we are separated from Cabra financially and administratively and are under the jurisdiction of the Vicar Apostolic of the Western district of the Cape Province. In the course of time we have received from Cabra professed Sisters and postulants and at present they help us by recruiting postulants.

She proceeded to give details of the Apostolic Letter of 1903 and then came to the crux of the matter, paraphrasing the opinion of Gijlswijk:

Although the first Convent at Cape Town was founded by the Sisters of Cabra, the Sisters are in doubt whether they are still partakers of the Privileges, Indulgences, and Spiritual favours, as actually the Sisters at the Cape of Good Hope are separated from the Convent of Cabra from the beginning of the foundation at the Cape.

The rest of the draft letter was clearly dictated by Gijlswijk. "If this is the case they do not partake any privileges whatever, as they are not enrolled in either the Third Order of the Soldiery of Jesus Christ or the Third Order of Penance". Mother Berchmans, the kindest and most charitable of women, ends with the plea: "These are the reasons why we humbly pray you, Most Reverend Father General to arrange this matter according to your judgement".[20] Since Gijlswijk was en route to Rome he promised to give his support to their petition.

Early in January 1922, Gijlswijk convened the Council and subjected Mother Berchmans and her Council to six days of intensive meetings. It was a bleak and traumatic week for the sisters involved. He covered every aspect of their daily life, in the cloister and in the schools, stressing the new demands of Canon Law, and laying down draconian regulations which he proposed as essential in the faithful pursuit of the Dominican ideal. The question of dispensation had no place in his plans, and this first serious interaction with the sisters left its mark. Mother Berchmans wrote to Mother Imelda in September of the same year:

> I am sure Fr. Jordan will do his best for us here in C.T. We
> left a mark on him, no doubt. But he knows and understands
> it was not our fault. I am hopeful his visit to us will yet do real
> good and that the bitter suffering some of us went through in
> those awful weeks in Jan. will yet reap some fruit for the
> community.[21]

The fact that many of these regulations were merely a variation
on common monastic practice and as such were familiar to the
sisters, did little to alleviate the pain experienced by those
involved. No doubt Mother de Ricci, a formidable woman and
one not easily pressurised, was better able to deal with the
intransigence of the Apostolic Visitor. Gijlswijk was also a man
of sincerity and one capable of learning from experience. Whatever
the reasons, the meetings he held in Holy Rosary Convent, Port
Elizabeth seem to have been more diplomatic. On the question
of amalgamation "the Consensus of opinion was in favour of a
Dublin Congregation to be composed of Sion Hill & other Home
Houses". On the possibility of amalgamation with the community
"in the Western District, C.P. the chief divergence ... [would] be
the recitation of the Divine Office and the wearing of woollen
garments".

The problems arising from union with Ireland or Cape Town
was not the most urgent concern for Mother de Ricci. "Before the
close of the Council Meeting the Visitor was informed of the
general satisfaction the Sisters had in their existing Constitution
... A request was made to have it brought into accord with the
New Code & also that a Ceremonial be supplied.[22] While the
Minutes of the Council Meetings with Gijlswijk in Port Elizabeth
are brief and non-committal, the battle lines were already drawn
up and Mother de Ricci was preparing to defend the position of
her community against forced amalgamation either with the
Dominicans of the Western Cape or with those of King William's
Town, Oakford or Newcastle. The ideal union, to her mind would
be with Sion Hill, and if Cabra and her foundations were to form
part of the new congregation, as seemed inevitable, this would
have to be accepted. "It would never do to go aloft before the
crystallization of the Dominican developments for which you have
prayed & striven during so many years. Our Visitor Apostolic
seemed to be of the opinion that Rome would *soon* legislate or
regulate for all Dominican nuns". On the question of the German
Dominicans her prejudices were strong:

> I understand that two sisters from Cape Town OSD's are on
> their way to Germany, Holland and Ireland. Mother
> Berchmans will make a mistake if she imports foreigners.

The King William's Town communities - those in which
Germans predominate have royal rows at times. Germans
'contend' without really knowing they are doing so - we see
this in our seven Lay sisters.[23]

It took one dominating woman to recognise the trait in others,
and it is clear that in the political climate of the early 1920's, the
memories of the Great War were fresh and anti-German
propaganda played as successful a role inside the convent as it
did in society at large. Mother de Ricci, a just woman, realised
that in the matter of Dominican practice the German communities
led the way in Southern Africa. "Mother Berchmans returns here
next week from King William's Town. The Dominicans there are
of Augsburg descent sisters ... very observant of Dominican Rules
and Customs. They are mainly German sisters - choir (working
and teaching classes) and Lay sisters. Latterly they are reinforced
from Ireland".[24]

The position taken by Mother de Ricci in respect of German
candidates was to a lesser degree shared by the new Provincial
of the Western Cape, Mother Berchmans Cotter. On her return
from the Dominican Convent at Cradock, where she had left one
of the sisters for a period of recuperation, she visited the
Assumption Convent at Grahamstown and wrote of her findings
there to the two sisters on a recruiting drive in Europe:

We had a long talk with M Baptist and the present Superior.
They were talking of the Germans, they have three of them in
their Community and both urge us not to take these people
with ours, they say they are just impossible. They say that
they influence the young against authority, and they simply
go their own way. Of course if we took a small number of the
better class and divided them in the Community it might not
be bad, but it is well for us to know the experience of others,
and these mean very well towards us. Mother de Ricci too,
would not like to have Germans, so I know you will be very
careful. Belgians, Hollanders, French yes, but a very small
modicum of the Germans. They want to push forward and
have power, that is the idea. When they are in a Community
of their own nation they are admirable and under their own
German Superiors, but there is always a danger in their spirit.

This was clearly a summing up of the information that Mother
Berchmans had gathered on her travels in the Eastern Vicariate,
but she was also aware of the feelings among her own sisters in
the Western Cape. "I put this before you for thought and
consideration. You know that in our Community there is a certain
amount of antipathy to the Germans, though I do not have it".[25]

Indeed Mother Berchmans, for reasons of economy, considered the possibility of opening a novitiate house in Germany, a plan which made sense in a time of recession when the German mark was at a low ebb. She and her Council gave this idea serious consideration: "Yesterday the Council was in favour of a house in Germany and I think too, it would be better there. Living is more simple, an occasional good German subject might be got, our money is much more value there than elsewhere. ... Irish girls would go more readily to Germany than to England".[26]

At home in South Africa Mother Rose Niland offered three domestic postulants to Mother Berchmans. She was assured that while these would not be " fit for field work ", they would be able for household tasks and needlework. The candidates were welcomed by Mother Berchmans as "the beginning of a German element" which they could "keep in moderation".[27] The decision to admit these postulants, based as it was on the word of Mother Veronica and corroborated by Mother Rose, did nothing to promote a greater understanding either of the German communities or of future interaction between the Cabra and Newcastle Dominicans. Mother Berchmans decided to take the three recruits into St Mary's, Cape Town so that she would be able to see how the "German element" would work.[28] Immediately after their arrival early in July 1922, the Mother Provincial acted as procuratrix in order to ensure that their introduction to the household tasks would be facilitated.[29] Studying the three girls Mother Berchmans concluded that they had a "fair groundwork" and she attributed this to a number of factors. She wrote to the sisters recruiting in Europe and Ireland: "Of course the solid German nature with its spirit of Faith and Piety and the subjection of German women all tend towards the spirit of Novitiate", she wrote. Already the girls were finding their "lives hard and their surroundings so very different from Newcastle" where Mother Berchmans believed, there must have been "a very fine spirit".[30] As time passed it became clear that the three postulants were not settled. One had an incurable heart disease and all three were "disappointed with the life. 'Rules not strong enough, no Penances, too much concerts'". One of the postulants was advised by Father Glynn to write to the Zambezi Mission and to hand in her letter sealed. Mother Provincial promised that she "would have something to say to him" when she was well enough to confront him.[31] Father Glynn was not the only target of Mother Berchmans' reproach. She felt strongly that she had been misinformed by Mother Rose Niland as to the suitability of the German postulants. At this time while her sisters were negotiating the purchase of a house for a novitiate in England, Mother Rose offered her St Paul's, a convent in Holland. The offer was attractive. It was a country at peace, and "with the political outlook in England ... so black that there is much talk here of a revolution". But Mother Berchmans was not one to be trapped in the same net a second time.

> But what Mother Rose's price would be and her arrangements for payment I know not, and she has taken me in once, so I'm not too anxious to have any transactions with her. I am going to write to her at all events re her treatment of me in the matter of the 3 Postulants. I really don't know what we are going to do re the girl Elise. It was a cruel and unworthy act not to tell us of the girl's state and they knew it all. I don't think it would be wise to have many Germans in our Community, their attitude of mind is so very different from ours.[32]

Since Mother Rose was not German this was a rather unfair indictment. Her father was Irish and her mother was a Smit of Huguenot origin. However it is a clear indication that the Irish communities were well informed as to the perceived character of German candidates, and were reluctant to admit them in numbers into their novitiates.

The German question was in 1922, a minor problem in the face of the upheaval that Gijlswijk was to bring into the lives of the two communities of Cape Town and Port Elizabeth. However it proved to be a major stumbling-block in the smooth path of South African amalgamation, Gijlswijk style. There can be no doubt as to the respect and genuine admiration that the Irish Dominicans had for their German sisters, with the beauty of their celebration of the Divine Office, their practice of the customs of the Order and the variety and success of their apostolate. But just as neither of the two Irish foundations really wanted to join together, so the union of all Dominicans in Southern Africa was totally unacceptable to them. It was to be a battle of wills between Gijlswijk and the Dominican women, who for all their humble submission, had a determination to see that justice was done in their own regard. This was all the more difficult in that Gijlswijk returned to South Africa in 1923, as Apostolic Delegate and consequently was the highest ecclesiastical authority in the country. Opposition to his far-reaching plans for the Church and religious institutions in Southern Africa was firmly rebuffed. Indeed it was not considered proper for religious women or indeed clerics or Vicars Apostolic, to question either his expertise in Canon Law, or the Roman authority which he wielded.

Early in 1923 all the Dominican sisters in Southern Africa were placed under the direct jurisdiction of the Sacred Congregation of Propaganda Fide, with Gijlswijk as their immediate ecclesiastical superior. This opened the way for the smooth and speedy implementation of Gijlswijk's plans for the amalgamation of all the Dominican communities of women in Southern Africa. Or so he thought. Not a sensitive man, he saw no reason why the plans of the church should be hindered or delayed by national prejudice, unnecessary debate or minor differences of opinion. His enhanced authority as Archbishop and Apostolic Delegate, was difficult to withstand. In 1925 he imposed a new book of *Constitutions* of his own composition on all Dominican sisters in Southern Africa. When the Cabra version was sent to the Irish Dominican Houses in South Africa in February 1931, Gijlswijk's *Constitutions* had been in practice for over five years, and remained in force until after amalgamation with the Irish Congregation of Dominican Sisters, in February 1938. Mother Teresa Coleman, the newly elected Prioress General of the Dominicans of the Western Cape thanked Mother Colmcille Flynn, first Prioress General of the new Irish Congregation, and noted both similarities and differences between the two versions:

> I do not know whether a copy of our Constitutions drawn up by the Apostolic Delegate Archbishop Gijlswijk and afterwards corrected by His Excellency on the model of the Schema by the Very Reverend Father Nolan, has ever been sent to you, but if it has you will see by it that, except on two important points, we are now following the same Constitution as those you have sent. The two points referred to are, the saying of the Divine Office and the question of Lay sisters.[33]

On the question of lay sisters Mother Teresa wrote: " I think I may say that we all thank God that in this country we are all one class. There were, of course, difficulties in the beginning, but these have passed or are passing away and we look to the future with great hope and confidence in carrying out God's will".[34] The same was true, in theory at least for the Port Elizabeth Dominicans, though Mother de Ricci would have been happy to maintain the position she had taken from the outset on the question of lay sisters.

> We do not anticipate any very great problems in solving *our* Lay-Sister problem. None of those converted into Choir sisters in April 1925, made their Novitiate again (as Canon 558 requires they should have done), hence those particular Sisters *are* Lay-Sisters in very fact this moment. Only two of

the Class have made vows as Choir sisters, and from my
knowledge of them, they will consent to whatever is legislated
for them. We have not had any of those Sisters (who should
be lay sisters) saying the Choir Office, they have kept to the
Paters & Aves.[35]

Mother de Ricci did not enter into any discussion on the Divine
Office, which had been celebrated by the Port Elizabeth
Dominicans from 1887 until 1922, when Gijlswijk insisted that
they change to the Little Office of the Blessed Virgin. This was
the Office said by the Cape Town Dominicans, and Mother Teresa,
not without justification, defended the right of the community to
retain the custom, especially in view of the pressure of work and
the shortage of personnel. Neither Mother Teresa nor Mother de
Ricci commented on a third difference in the new Constitutions,
that of status, still a matter of great concern in Ireland. In a
letter informing the Prioresses in Ireland of the papal approval of
the Constitutions Mother Colmcille had written: "You will notice
with gratitude, I am sure that the title 'Third Order' has been
deleted from this Decree, which deletion seems that our original
Status has been recognised and approved; again may God be
praised".[36]

In 1924 Gijlswijk wrote to inform the Mothers superior and
all the Dominican communities in Southern Africa that the new
Constitutions were being printed and would soon be promulgated:

> They are compiled in accordance with the present Code of
> Canon Law, and at the same time I have complied with the
> wish of the S.Congregation of Propaganda, which desires that
> all the Dominican Sisters in S.Africa should be governed by
> the same Constitutions. In the Preface of these Constitutions
> there is mention of their coming into force on May 1st. But
> on account of the great delay in printing this has become
> impossible; the date must be postponed in order to give the
> Sisters sufficient time to acquaint themselves with the
> constitutions. Therefore I notify and *give order* that these
> Constitutions shall come into force on and be obligatory on
> all Sisters from July 1st of the present year.[37]

Gijlswijk was so sure of his authority that he had made no
attempt to consult those most nearly concerned in the new
Constitutions, the sisters themselves. Nor did he expect any
hesitation on the part of the nuns in submitting to his authority:

> I have no doubt but that the Sisters will gladly and obediently
> accept, knowing, as they do, that they will be obeying and
> fulfilling the wish of the highest authority of the Church, which

has already been informed of the most important regulations laid down in the constitutions, and approved by them. Moreover, I am sure that their observance will tend towards the greater spiritual perfection of the Sisters and add considerably to the success of the missionary work in S. Africa.[38]

In his efforts to bring about uniformity and prepare the ground for the union of all Southern African Dominican congregations into a single body, he not only imposed *The Constitutions of the Third Order of St. Dominic* which formed the "African Congregation of St. Catharine of Siena", on the Cabra and Sion Hill foundations but cancelled all their pretensions to Second Order status. For the King William's Town Dominicans whose missions originated in Augsburg, this made no change, but for the Dominican congregations founded from Cabra and Sion Hill it was seen as a denial of their historical status.

In 1924 however the Superiors of Cape Town and Port Elizabeth had more immediate concerns than the academic question of status. They knew that they were safeguarded by the constraints of Canon Law and the customs of the Order, but they resented the fact that they were not consulted about the new *Constitutions.* They felt that they had been dragooned with undue haste into accepting and putting into practice a body of laws about which they were not well informed. Although in the convent it was not an age in which the day to day decisions were arrived at through a process of democratic consultation, nevertheless it had been an honoured custom in the South African Dominican communities of Port Elizabeth and Cape Town that all major changes were submitted to the conventual chapter. This gave to each professed choir sister the opportunity to discuss major issues and vote according to her conscience. Gijlswijk did not honour this custom, if indeed he was aware of it. In the final analysis he was the only authority, under Rome, to effect the legal changes which would bring the lives of the sisters in line with the New Code of Canon Law, and he as a member of the First Order, saw himself as an expert in all matters Dominican. His initial criticism of the two congregations had weakened their opposition and his reiterated claim that to resist his plans was to resist the will of the Supreme Pontiff himself, convinced them of the inevitability of the loss of independent participation in legal changes governing their own lives. In addition they were without influential friends in Rome, and they like their sisters in Ireland, did not count among their numbers a single nun well versed in either canon law or theology. Nor indeed were these areas of expertise readily available among the local clergy.

Gijlswijk firmly believed that a uniform book of Constitutions and a single Directory and Customary would insure both conformity to the laws of the church and uniformity in conventual practice. This would facilitate an easy transition from separate congregations to a single amalgamated body of Dominican women, a process he hoped to complete without delay. But the Apostolic Delegate had underestimated the women in the case. Although the deadline for the implementation of the new Constitutions had been extended from May to July, this two month's grace did nothing to make the change more acceptable. Mother Rose Niland who had been working for Roman approval of her Constitution long before Gijlswijk came on the South African scene, was prepared to sacrifice neither the independence of her Congregation nor her own freedom of action to an ecclesiastic, however exalted, who treated his own Dominican sisters in so high-handed a fashion. The stand taken by the Newcastle Congregation was a valuable lesson to the other Dominicans in South Africa. Although the Irish Dominicans accepted the *Constitutions* and *Customary*, and it appeared to Gijlswijk that they at least could be pressurised into supporting his amalgamation plans, this was not to be the case.

The ideal goal proposed by the Rule of St Augustine, "unity of heart and mind amongst those who dwell in the holy House of God", was the basis on which Gijlswijk developed his argument in support of amalgamation. In a draft letter, Mother Reginald Lyons noted the situation in South Africa: "I understand that the Cape Town nuns will take up the new Constitutions from July 1, but "under protest". The respective Bishops and Vicars Apostolic over the other Dominicans have put a suspensory veto on their adoption. Dr. McSherry and De Lalle and Mgr. Browne S.J. are particularly incensed at such treatment being meted out to their nuns. The position is a very critical one". Mother Reginald wondered whether Rome would recall Gijlswijk "because of other grievances of their own which the Bishops and Vicars have in plenty and which have been represented to the Holy See".[39] It was a difficult time for the Council in the Western Cape. Mother Berchmans Cotter had visited each convent under her jurisdiction and held meetings with local prioresses to prepare the sisters for the implementation of the new *Constitutions*. However recurrent illness made her task almost impossible. Once the new dispensation had been initiated she asked to be relieved of her office, thus leaving the community with an acting superior. The Council, which was both strong and experienced, made a fair and critical appraisal of the situation, bided their time and waited for the election which took place in December 1924. The electors choose well and Mother Benvenuta O'Donoghue, the second Provincial of the Dominicans in the Western Cape could rely on the support of her councillors and especially on that of Mother Bertrand Dowling, secretary to the Council, who in controversial issues was forthright in her approach, and never afraid to oppose what she believed to be detrimental to the good of the Congregation.

The Council expressed its dissatisfaction on a number of matters arising out of the new *Constitutions*. The first point at issue was the title, Mother General, which the Council found to have no justification in terms of the new *Constitutions*. This does not seem to have been a problem with Mother de Ricci Harkin, who first assumed the title in 1925 and used it until 1938, when amalgamation with the new Irish Dominican Congregation was achieved. The minutes of the Provincial and later General Council of the Eastern Province are singularly lacking in detail on the matter of the new Gijlswijk *Constitution*, or indeed on any other controversial matter, consequently it is difficult to determine the attitude of the sisters there to the changes that were taking place. However Mother de Ricci was a powerful woman whom even the authority of an Apostolic Delegate could not, and did not overwhelm. Mother Berchmans Cotter, before her resignation on the 30 July 1924, had been keenly aware of the fact that the new *Constitutions* were a major cause for concern, not so much in terms of universal ecclesiastical law, but because of the possible effect it might have on the Dominican status of her community. At a meeting of the Provincial Council in June 1924 the councillors asked for reassurance that they were not "forfeiting under the new arrangements their share in the spiritual privileges granted by His Holiness Pope Pius the tenth to the Cabra community and its foundations". For the Cape Town Dominicans this was not a matter of status. They accepted their position as belonging to the Third Order, but it was a question of spiritual membership of an Order to which they had dedicated their lives and mission.[40] Archbishop Gijlswijk may have given them a Dominican *Constitution*, but it was not a simple matter to restore the confidence which in the traumatic meetings of January 1922, he had undermined.

That the Council also resented the fact that Gijlswijk had given no opportunity, either to the councillors or to members of the communities concerned, to participate in the process of change, is reflected in the minutes of the Council, recorded succinctly by Mother Bertrand Dowling:

With regard to the new Constitutions the Council are unanimous in thinking that they should have been shown and read by the Community before being printed, but that seeing that they become compulsory on the 1st July and as, within five years, appeal is allowed on any point that may be found unworkable, and as it is recognised that the old Constitutions needed revision to bring them into accordance with the present requirements of the Church, they accept the new ones and will put them into practice from 1st July 1924.[41]

Despite this compliance, Mother Berchmans and her Council, over the months following the official promulgation of the *Constitutions*, made it plain to Gijlswijk that they were not satisfied with the way in which he had excluded them from participation in the formulation of a body of laws which would affect every aspect of their lives. Gijlswijk quickly came to his own defence: "Re the Constitutions and Directory it has always been my desire to submit them to the Sisters before having them printed. But experience taught me that such would be impossible, as there are so many Sisters consequently so many sentences". The sisters regarded this as a lame excuse for his high-handed approach to so important a matter, but as an argument it was not without merit. There was a large body of Dominican women in Southern Africa, and the participation of all would have raised many queries and led to disagreements, a process that would have delayed Gijlswijk's own plans. He did meet with strong opposition, but among the various independent groups of Dominican women, those in the Western Cape were probably the most compliant. It was necessary to retain their compliance, and Gijlswijk hastened to reassure Mother Berchmans: "But my dear Mother, are the sisters afraid, that I will put on them too hard things? Are some of them not yet convinced, that I will not in the least trouble them? That my activities on their behalf are only for the purpose to make them happy?"[42] In the circumstances however it was difficult to believe that his aim was as disinterested as he claimed it to be. Nonetheless who would dare to question his authority or challenge his right to impose his will on the sisters under his control? Certainly not the Dominicans of Cape Town, though in the case of Mother de Ricci, he met his match. He did not seem to realise that his authoritarian approach and hasty actions were in themselves a threat to nuns not accustomed to undue interference from ecclesiastical superiors.

The acceptance of the Gijlswijk *Constitutions* and later of the *Directory* by the two Irish communities, while it was a sincere concession to the principle of obedience and submission to lawful authority, did not imply a blind acceptance of regulations and interpretations of the law, which made daily life and apostolic work more difficult. Two days before the deadline date of July 1, 1924, the Council expressed doubts on a number of issues, the first shots in the battle for revision:

> Careful note is to be taken of those portions of the Constitution which may be too hard on Sisters teaching in this climate, such as wearing cloaks during the summer months in Choir, constant wearing of woollen garments etc., and of those which the Community by no means can afford seeing the importance of building suitable classrooms, such as building and supporting guest-houses etc. These points to be laid before [the] Apostolic Delegate.

Mother Bertrand also noted the terminology used in Gijlswijk's letter, "*ordering* observance to be begun on 1st July on *every possible point*".[43] The Council secretary frequently used the verb "ordered" when recording the communications from the Apostolic Delegate, a clear indication of her disapproval of Gijlswijk's forceful manner of expression. In response to a protest as to the impossibility of implementing the whole Constitutions from the first day, Gijlswijk moderated his original demands:

> That the Constitutions are obligatory from July 1 does not mean that everything must be arranged according to the Constitutions on the 1 of July. But it means that from this date the Sisters must *count* with the Constitutions. Therefore what they know they must do and what they don't know, they cannot do and cannot be blamed for. But as soon as they find out their mistake, they should try to correct it. And as to the government, how can everything be arranged on July 1? Do you think that I require impossibilities of the Sisters? I only ask goodwill to work according to the Constitutions from July 1, and to reorganise matters according to our human capacity.[44]

Unfortunately some of the superiors did think that he was demanding impossibilities, and this did nothing to reconcile them to the manner in which he had enforced the new laws. As soon as they began to put the new *Constitutions* into practice fresh queries arose, and the Council, meeting on August 9, 1924, in order to forestall a similar situation arising with the promulgation of the *Directory and Customary*, noted that the Delegate had been asked "to allow the Council to see a copy of the new Directory" before it was printed.[45] As the meeting was recording its wishes, a letter from the Apostolic Delegate on anticipating some of the points raised by the Council at Cape Town, was already in the post.

> After all the Constitutions and Directory (which is only an explanation of the Constitutions), have been given as a foundation upon which we are going to build. If experience teaches, that something must be changed, I will be the first to suggest such an amendment. Only after a fair trial and after having heard the opinions of the communities through the different councillors I will compile them again for the final approval of Rome. Therefore don't worry and have patience.[46]

Clearly if anything was to be done *he* would do it and no one else, certainly not the sisters. Whether he realised it or not he had already lost the support of the Irish Dominican communities for his centralisation project.

In the Prologue to the new *Directory and Customary* promulgated in 1925, he inserted his plan for the union of all Dominican women of Southern Africa. "To attain this unity of heart and mind the Sisters have already been united by the same Rule and Constitutions". This in fact was not to be the case, but the statement alone indicates his confidence in his power to form a single Dominican body of women, a goal he never achieved despite his authority as Apostolic Delegate. His appeal was not only to the law but also to the aims of Dominican men for Dominican women: "For this same end the Dominican Fathers in their different Chapters have been urged to promote this conformity in customs amongst the Sisters of the Order of St Dominic, and have expressed the desire that all the Sisters of St Dominic should form among themselves one great federation". It was a strong argument, especially in the 1920's when the nuns were most anxious to be, and to be acknowledged as, authentic Dominicans, and Gijlswijk did not hesitate to use it, exerting all the pressure at his command:

> Complying, therefore, with this desire of the Chapters of the Dominican Order and with the express wish of the S.Cong. of Propaganda, in my quality of Apostolic Delegate having been given jurisdiction over all the Sisters of the Dominican Order in S. Africa, I hereby publish the following Directory and Customary which is based on a similar work compiled by the late Fr. Hyacinth Cormier, Master General of the Dominican Order, for the use of the Sisters of the Third Order.[47]

These new and detailed regulations governed the minutiae of daily life in the convent and in the schools. For the apostolic work of education the regulations are on the whole reasonable. The temporary professed sisters were to remain in a House of Studies to prepare for their future work. It was to be a convent where the young sisters would be "trained in the science and art of teaching, in languages, both European and Native, in manual work, housekeeping and in all practical knowledge required for work in the mission fields". Gijlswijk was clear as to his own role in this as in all other matters pertaining to the daily life of the Dominican nuns under his jurisdiction:

> In this House, therefore, there must be a staff of Sisters who are eminently fitted to educate these professed 'Novices in the way just indicated in accordance with a syllabus and horary drawn up by the Prioress General and her Council *and approved by the Delegate Apostolic.* If for any branch of study the Sisters have to attend lectures elsewhere the Prioress General should ask permission from the Delegate Apostolic, giving at the same time *an exact account of the reasons for permission.*[48]

Pride in academic or professional attainments had no place in Gijlswijk's plans for the sisters. It was the duty of every teacher "to attain the highest possible skill in the branches she ... [had] to teach and to turn her *modest talent* to best advantage". Of course the nuns were not to "aim at brilliancy", but to apply themselves "to what obedience requires". In all of the strictures imposed and the regulations spelt out in old maidish detail, the authority of the ecclesiastical superior was stressed. Although there was nothing unique or revolutionary in his approach to religious women and the ecclesiastical laws governing their lives, Gijlswijk implied that until his coming they had known little or nothing about religious or Dominican life, and that they were sadly lacking in academic qualifications, professional skills and spiritual maturity. There could be no denying the importance either of well qualified teachers or of a sound Catholic education for Catholic children. Nor was the missionary role of teachers ever questioned by the sisters. The superiors were the first to support in principle at least, the Apostolic Delegate's views on education:[49]

> The whole atmosphere in our Schools should be a Catholic one, with Catholic prayers said, Catholic books, and in games, in exhibitions, concerts, dramatic performances and the like the Catholic idea and sentiment of modesty and moderation in all things should be safeguarded. So, also, the teachers in regard to the children entrusted to their care must be like fathers and mothers in kindness toward them, yet tempered

with a certain amount of severity, the two ways hand in hand,
thus preventing either from going into extremes. Only thus
will the School be a replica of a really good Catholic home,
and at the same time a Catholic School in the truest sense.[50]

Regulations concerning the employment of lay teachers,
whether Catholic or not, imposed considerable strain on the
schools. The *Directory* spells out in detail the regulations
governing the employment of staff. Under no conditions were
non-Catholic teachers to be employed either for class teaching
or to give private lessons on the school premises. Catholic
teachers offering themselves for posts, were first to be examined
on matters of faith by a priest. He would then issue a certificate
which had to be forwarded to the local Ordinary.[51] But on the
practice of admitting non-Catholic pupils to Catholic schools,
Gijlswijk was most adamant: "Moreover there is a danger, and a
great danger, which threatens the Catholic character of our
Education, and which in fact may even affect the right ideas of
the Sisters themselves on Catholic Education, viz the presence
of non-Catholics children in our Schools". This, according to
Gijlswijk, made the schools "like a home or a family of a mixed
marriage, where the members being of different religious
convictions live together", a state of affairs that was "detrimental
to the Catholic children" and condemned by the church. No
reason, however persuasively presented could justify the
admission of pupils other than Catholics into church schools.
Indeed the Apostolic Delegate saw in arguments supporting the
admission of non-Catholic an indication that the "pure Catholic
educational principles of such advisors ... [had] been sadly
infected by the prevailing circumstances".

The sisters concerned with the running of schools, were
familiar with the stand taken by the Church on this matter and
understood the sound religious principles involved, but the
application of such regulations would have placed the educational
work of the Dominican sisters in jeopardy. A strong advocate of
missionary work, Gijlswijk nevertheless surrounded the teaching
apostolate with petty restrictions. Had these been applied, many
Church schools which depended financially on the support of
Protestants and Jews as well as of Catholics, would have been
closed. If there was no immediate promise of conversions why
admit Protestants or Jews? Gijlswijk even advised that the School
for the Deaf in Cape Town be closed, since in his view, it no
longer served what was in his eyes its primary apostolic purpose,
the conversion of children to the True Faith. Such a narrow view
of the role of Catholic schools was in direct contradiction to the

educational policy of the Dominican teachers in Cape Town and Port Elizabeth. Not only would it limit the apostolic thrust of the sisters in respect of schools for European pupils but it would make economic survival impossible. Without entering into debate or indeed even challenging Gijlswijk's regulations, the sisters perforce continued as before, and as far as possible increased the percentage of Catholics on the roll. These regulations did not apply to non-Catholic pupils attending the "Native and non European schools" where it was to be expected that conversions would be the norm.[52]

Gijlswijk was aware of the financial constraints under which the South African Dominican communities worked and of the contribution they made to every missionary project. At the 1924 Kimberley Meeting of ecclesiastical authorities, he noted in respect of religious communities of women throughout Southern Africa:

> The Sisterhoods do not need to be admonished to give financial support to the Missions, since they have always been very generous in this respect in supporting the local Priests, in building Chapels which also serve as parochial Churches, and in spending large sums of money on Native Missions. ... Now we know that the Canon Law does not give to the Ecclesiastical Authorities the right of taxing these religious for this purpose (Canon 1355), and even if Canon Law allowed us to tax them thus, it would hardly be fair and reasonable seeing that of their own free will they have already been so generous in this regard.[53]

Clearly Gijlswijk realised that even for the greater good of missions throughout his territory, the communities under his jurisdiction had to be solvent. Consequently he made provision for this. If children of other faiths had to be admitted to European Catholic schools, certain regulations had to be honoured. Catholic teachers could not stand *in loco parentis* to such pupils, and Catholic doctrine had to be taught and Catholic liturgy celebrated. Encouraging Protestant or Jewish pupils to attend their own place of worship was not to be permitted. In this regard the teachers were to "remain passive, merely allowing them to attend their different churches', if they wished to do so. Other prescriptions governing the treatment of non-Catholic children were detailed and specific:

> The non-Catholic children should be kept separate both in the class-room and in the dormitory. Games to be played, or entertainments given, wherein Catholics and non-Catholics

must mix, should be avoided. No piano-playing, games, nor recreation should be allowed when Catholic pupils are obliged to attend religious instruction. No Protestant ministers or lay-persons replacing them should be allowed to enter our schools to give religious instructions. It should not be allowed in the Prospectus of the school to emphasise the neutrality of education. The annual records published to keep up and foster friendship with old non-Catholic pupils should be abolished. But to keep in touch with and to foster friendship with old Catholic pupils is, on the other hand, to be highly recommended.[54]

These and similar restrictive rules, often impossible of application, did nothing to reconcile those communities, which out of a sense of obedience and loyalty to the Holy See, had accepted the *Constitutions* and *Directory* in the form dictated by Gijlswijk. It was impossible for sisters, with so long and honourable a tradition in the field of education, either to isolate children or past pupils on the grounds of religion, or to deny them the friendship of their Catholic friends. Indeed an important area of apostolic work carried out by the Dominicans ever since their arrival in the Cape Colony in the 1860's, had been the spiritual and practical support they had given to past pupils, irrespective of religion. Consequently for reasons of charity and the exigencies of financial constraints, many of the minor regulations concerning the policy laid down in the *Directory* were never seriously put into practice.

The new *Directory and Customary*, so meticulous in detail, so authoritarian in tone, so obviously the work of one man, and so lacking in the spirit of Dominican freedom, was accepted by most of the Dominican communities in South Africa, but not without protest. Sisters, other than superiors, had been informed only in a general way about the new *Constitutions* and the *Directory and Customary*, and this aroused resentment, and gave reasonable grounds for some members of the community to seek alternative fields for their apostolic work. In 1926 Mother Benvenuta O' Donoghue, during her second year as Provincial, discovered that five sisters had planned to leave the community and found a new congregation of their own. This evidence of a spirit of criticism and unrest among some of the sisters was judged to be a serious sign of the influence of the modern world on life in the cloister. However the departure of nuns from the convent, although infrequent, was no rare or unexpected event, but the fact that they had plotted among themselves, and to forward their plans, had written secretly to members of the Catholic hierarchy both inside and outside of Africa, was regarded by both the Provincial and the Apostolic Delegate, in a very serious light.

The history of religious communities, including that of Cabra itself, has instances of such secret, organised departures. Or perhaps they were courageous ventures into new apostolates, depending on the success of the new foundation, and the support of or repudiation by the ecclesiastical authorities involved. For the five sisters who planned the exodus, the general sense of unease brought about by the changes imposed by Gijlswijk, together with a major clash of one of the ring-leaders with the Provincial, Mother Benvenuta, may have been contributing factors in the decision to leave the community and strike out on their own. What is of special interest in this plan is the fact that they were determined to remain in the Order, evidence that it was not Dominican life that they rejected. Whether they hoped to found a missionary congregation in Africa or in America, is not clear, but whatever their plans, they had to face the restrained wrath of their superiors. In November 1926, the Provincial, Mother Benvenuta, on visitation of the convents in the Western Cape, discovered the plot:

> I heard from one Sister that she had been approached by another Sister, with a view to her joining a party of Sisters who thought of forming a New foundation elsewhere by breaking away from the Community. The reason alleged by the "Foundress" was that the new Constitutions were put upon the Community without their being asked whether they wished to accept them or not. These Constitutions were accepted by the Community in general, although they felt certain restrictions embodied in the Constitutions rather trying, but not impossible or impracticable.

The five sisters "signed a petition to Rome asking permission to found a branch house in America. This proposition was not broached to the Superiors of our Community, all of whom were in ignorance of it. ... A letter in reply from a Vicar Apostolic [of Kilamenjaro] was put into my hands by Mother Prioress". With a persistence worthy of Miss Marple, Mother Benvenuta investigated the case, first seeking advice from Bishop O'Riley.

> I asked him to come down to Star of the Sea Convent so that we might discuss this disruption of our Community ... . His lordship did not come and I had to postpone the interview until such time as his Lordship found time to call on me; he did so about a week after I had asked for the interview, but his Lordship's suggestions did not seem to me the best for the Community, and I told his Lordship so. I returned from

Star ..., and fortified by all the information I had, I determined
to speak to two Sisters in Cape Town, who were to my mind
deeply dyed in intrigue against the Community - in fact I
looked on them as being the prime movers in the plot.

She interviewed two of the culprits "separately at first and
afterwards jointly; they both flatly denied the charges I preferred
against them". The younger of the two, who "had approached
her Prioress with a view to *her* joining the insurgents owned up
... that she would have been pleased to go elsewhere, that she
had tried to get the sisters to join her party". After a further
interview Mother Benvenuta had "the threads" in her hands, and
was ready to face the culprits. "I interviewed in turn each of the
other Sisters. They were obstinate in their designs of leaving the
Community and I told them that I should give them every
opportunity to go whilst safeguarding the interests of the
Community at the same time".

However the application for dispensation from vows to Rome,
made through the Apostolic Delegate was refused, and with one
exception they withdrew their application, did penance and were
restored to their place in the community.[55] Although the ring-
leader who had absented herself from the convent without leave
and was later refused re-admission, had other motives for her
actions, quite unconnected with the question of Constitutions,
nevertheless the threatened departure of members of the
community and the disruption this caused, was a warning to
the Provincial and her Council of the need for adaptation and
more frequent consultation with sisters in the ranks.[56]

Superiors who had given nearly fifty years of service, found
the younger generation much more outspoken on questions of
their rights, than would have been acceptable in their day.[57] Such
attitudes created problems for the Dominican superiors, Victorian
women who were responsible both for the formation of the young
aspirants joining them in the novitiate at Potter's Bar and
Tamnaharrie, and for the smooth running of convents and schools
under their care. Despite their political and economic acumen
they were not in touch with the new post-war world. Mother de
Ricci, not ten years out of the conservative environment of Sion
Hill, held the reins tightly and imposed a discipline and promoted
a work ethic that left little time or energy for the disruptive
machinations of the disaffected. The probability of sisters
challenging her decisions or authority was slim, and while she
became the model and inspiration for some of the sisters, she
was approached by the majority with awe, sometimes with fear
and generally with diplomatic silence.

The superiors in office in the Western Cape during the 1920's had given a lifetime to the mission. They had come up through the ranks and were conversant with every aspect of community interaction, including the conflicts that even the well regulated life in the cloister with its high ideals of Christian perfection, could not exclude. The admission of a relatively large number of candidates in the previous decade had brought its own problems, but the disaffection of some would not be allowed to interfere with the preparation for a possible union with Cabra. In the meantime schools were being built or extended, new foundations were being planned and in money matters, especially the complex arrangements between the Congregation and the local bishop, the patience of Mother Benvenuta was wearing thin. But by 1928 the matter of the revised *Constitutions* soon to be available, and the plans, still on course for a South African Congregation, could be viewed with a measure of detachment.

For other Dominican congregations the situation was different. The path taken by Mother Rose Niland, foundress of the Congregation of the Newcastle Dominicans, and a past pupil of Holy Rosary Convent Port Elizabeth, is a case in point. From the outset she simply rejected Gijlswijk's domination, and refused openly either to accept his *Constitutions* or the *Directory and Customary*, or to comply with his demand for an immediate amalgamation of all the communities of Dominican women in Southern Africa. She was in a strong position, supported as she was by her own *Constitutions*, the final form of which was approved by a decree of Pius XI in August 1925. She also had the approval of Father Louis Theissling, Master General of the Order, and these benefits together with her strong conviction of the rightness of her stand and the legality of her position as superior of an independent congregation, armed her against the importunity of the Apostolic Delegate. For the Irish communities in the Western and Eastern Vicariates the acceptance had been a matter of expediency, since the superiors of both Congregations, though they balked at mutual union, had a common hope that once the Irish Mother Houses reached some form of consensus and amalgamated, they would invite their South African missionary foundations to join them.

The two Irish congregations used more subtle ways to thwart perceived tyranny. They would not have considered aggressive confrontation a valid option. They followed the classic example of Quintus Fabius Maximus. "*Unus homo nobis cunctando restituit rem*".[58] Mother Berchmans Cotter, and in 1925 her successor, Mother Benvenuta O'Donoghue together with Mother de Ricci Harkin, with their respective Councils, listened with due respect and well disguised dismay to Gijlswijk's plans for their immediate future. While graciously bending to the demands of their ecclesiastical superior and professing their undoubted loyalty to the Holy See, they were determined to delay entering into a hasty union while the amalgamation movement was still under debate in Ireland. The implications of the campaign waging between Sion Hill, Cabra and their foundations in Ireland, were not lost on the two major superiors in South Africa, Mother de Ricci, Mother Benvenuta, nor on their councillors. All official minutes and related documentation were sent to them for their information, but despite the goodwill which existed between the Cape Town and Port Elizabeth Dominicans, and the sisterly welcome experienced in the two mother houses, mutual prejudice divided them, as it did their mother houses in Ireland. Not only was union among themselves quite unacceptable, but under no condition would they consider joining up with the King William's Town Dominicans or any of their independent South African foundations. It was an impasse from which the Apostolic Delegate was to find no escape route.

Nevertheless Gijlswijk, convinced of the necessity for immediate amalgamation of the Dominican sisters in South Africa, presided at a Council Meeting held in St Mary's, Cape Town on 21 March 1925 and put his plan to Mother Benvenuta and her councillors. Since the Newcastle Dominicans were not prepared to consider his policies, he saw in the Congregations of King William's Town, Port Elizabeth, Cape Town and Rhodesia, the nucleus of a greater union of Dominican women under his control. His plan provided for a single province consisting of the Irish foundations in the Eastern and Western Vicariates with a Mother House in Cape Town and a common novitiate, already flourishing, at Potter's Bar, England. The realisation of such a plan would necessitate the calling of a Provincial Chapter, preferably in Cape Town and the election of a Mother Provincial. The province would be called the Western Vicariate Province, since the Mother House would be St Mary's, Cape Town, the first foundation of Dominican women in Southern Africa. He envisaged three additional provinces: the Eastern Province consisting of the King William's Town convents, the Rhodesian Province and the Natal Province. He hoped that these four provinces would unite ultimately under a single Mother General. It was a vain hope and the councillors recorded no enthusiasm for the proposed union. According to minutes recorded in Cape Town "Mother Provincial and her Council agreed to consider the matter and to become acquainted with the wishes of the Community in general, and as soon as a decisive opinion was formed to communicate with the Apostolic Delegate". It was also noted by the Delegate that since these communities had accepted and were putting into practice the same Constitutions, the process of amalgamation would be simplified. And Gijlswijk gave an even stronger reason for immediate compliance with his plans: "The Delegate said that he had been sent to South Africa from Rome to carry out this amalgamation. The wishes of the Pope are in favour of it, and these have to be considered as most important".[59]

It is not surprising that Gijlswijk had so little understanding of the complex politics dividing Dominican communities in South Africa. In his haste to reform a system which in more favourable circumstances could have benefited greatly from his help, he alienated those whom he had to convince and win to his way of thinking. Because of his manner, he appeared to members of communities to whom he was a virtual stranger, as an agent of disruption and dispossession. In his dealings with the sisters, he seldom had time to consider the implications of his actions or the historical barriers that separated communities. To be so imprudent as to suggest a hasty amalgamation of the Cabra and Sion Hill foundations in South Africa, argued either ignorance of the historical relationship that divided them, or a level of insensitivity inappropriate in one holding a position of such vital importance to the Catholic Church. To add insult to injury he gave preference to the Cape Town Dominicans over the Port Elizabeth community.

There was however one point of agreement between the two Irish congregations. Mother de Ricci, writing to Mother Pius in Sion Hill, expressed the feelings of her community in this matter: "We would not at all wish to live with either King or Natal. It is most desirable that the Colonial Convents should have their Mother House at home in Europe".[60] It was of the greatest importance to the "Colonial Convents" that while the South African communities played a delaying game, the Irish Dominican communities were moving slowly, and with considerable difficulty, towards union. By September 1926 Gijlswijk's ire was aroused. His plans for amalgamation were no nearer to realisation and he expressed his grave displeasure at the "inconstancy, selfishness, and love of temporal possessions" of the nuns, and practically ordered Mother Benvenuta to send all the postulants to the novitiate at Chingford, a foundation of the Oakford Dominicans in England. This novitiate had been opened in 1924 and the two congregations of King William's Town and Salisbury had been forced by Gijlswijk to send their postulants there. However in view of the fact that Potter's Bar was less than two years in existence and that a joint novitiate might be the first steps to a contrived union, it was a forceful suggestion that had to be resisted. The matter was discussed by the members of Council, and it was agreed that they would inform Port Elizabeth of the stand they were taking. They also decided to ascertain by vote, the opinion of the communities as to whether or not the sisters agreed to the Apostolic Delegate's pressing demands for their immediate amalgamation with the German Dominicans.[61]

Mother de Ricci seems to have held herself aloof from the debate on the subject, but her position in respect of amalgamation with German communities had always been clear. In 1930, almost two years after the Irish houses had united into one Congregation, and hopes were high for an ultimate union with Ireland, the minutes of a Council meeting held at Holy Rosary Convent make a rare allusion to Gijlswijk's plans for a single South African Congregation:

> In the Year of Our Lord 1930, on the 23rd day of May, Mother Prioress General convened a council to consult regarding the reply she should send to a letter received from the Apostolic Delegate on the subject of the Amalgamation of all the South African Dominican Congregations. This subject having been previously discussed, it was decided that His Excellency should be reminded of our unanimously expressed wish to be included in the Irish Dominican Congregation of St. Catherine of Siena, this desire being still maintained.[62]

On August 4, 1930, Mother Benvenuta forwarded the individual replies of the entire community to the Apostolic Delegate's more recent proposal; the "Amalgamation of ...[the] entire Community with the Dominicans of Port Elizabeth". Since Ireland had not yet moved in the matter of amalgamation with their South African foundations, the superiors in Cape Town could no longer resist Gijlswijk's importunity. Of the ninety-four sisters who replied 92 submitted to the "will of the Holy Father in their regard", though in some cases not without qualification. One sisters wrote: "I wish to inform you that I personally in no way favour Amalgamation, yet I firmly believe that in complying with the wishes of the Holy Father, we will draw down upon ourselves, and upon the whole Community untold blessings". However she found herself "utterly incapable" of making any suggestions as to how a closer union among the Dominican sisters (Port Elizabeth) could be affected, a sentiment no doubt re-echoed by Gijlswijk himself. "I shall leave to others the question of settling re Amalgamation, by thus doing it will save me, perhaps, many regrets later on. It would be a desideratum if we could get settled." [63]

The price to be paid for such a union was in the minds of a number of the respondents. "Possibly the 'closer union' His Excellency asks for may be established easily enough, if we individually get deep down into the spirit of self-sacrifice, then with God's help we shall have a 'close union', and we can leave all the rest to Him", wrote one sister, but others were prepared to give a helping hand to Divine Providence by making practical suggestions. Among these was the expressed hope that "amalgamation with the German Dominicans up-country" would not be expected of them, because it was considered that "such an arrangement would be detrimental to the peace and happiness of Religion". One sister wisely pointed out: "Personally I love my own Community, whilst I know nothing at all about Port Elizabeth; and, very probably most of their Sisters feel likewise with regard to us". Those who were more experienced in government proposed conditions, such as a Mother House in Cape Town, the rights of senior sisters to remain in their own Provinces, the establishment of a common novitiate, and the separate appointment of Prioresses from each Province for each Province. While such provisos reflected current attitudes, they did not augur well for the future realisation of a true union. Perhaps the most telling reply of all was the simple sentence, "Let His Excellency's will be done", a politically correct *fiat,* but in the event not the choice of the Supreme Will.[64]

About three weeks later Gijlswijk's answer was received. He found the sisters' replies "very satisfactory, and showed a good spirit", but he did not move into immediate action. "Now I will postpone further proceedings till the next Chapter at which I suppose you will invite me to assist", he wrote.[65] Less than four months later, and immediately after the election of Mother Teresa Coleman to the office of Prioress General of the Dominican Province of the Western Cape, her Council agreed to apply to Cabra to accept them as part of the new Congregation:

> By the express desire of his Excellency, Archbishop Gijlswijk, and with the advice and consent of my Council, I write to make a formal request to you to adopt us as a Province under you as Mother General. Seeing that our Community originally came direct from Cabra and that in adopting us you will be sharing in our efforts to spread the knowledge of our Holy Faith throughout South Africa, we earnestly hope you will grant our request. We have now over 2000 pupils in our schools, of whom about 800 are Coloured. ... I am sending a copy of this letter to the Rev. Provincial of the Irish Dominicans and another to Rev. Father Nolan, asking them to help us in supporting our request.[66]

While the Council at Cabra thanked Mother Teresa "for the great confidence" reposed in them, they felt that the new Congregation was "still very young and perhaps hardly in a position to take up such extensive work". But they wanted statistics regarding the communities of the Western Cape, to assist them in coming to a decision.[67] The Apostolic Delegate, though he expressed some reservations about the Divine Office and the question of lay sisters, was now positive in his approach to this possible union with the Irish Congregation. "I hasten to say that the Constitutions adopted by Cabra are by no means an impediment to the forthcoming amalgamation", he wrote. "If the Constitutions drawn up by me must be put aside and replaced by those of Cabra, I don't mind a bit. My aim has always been and still is to secure the more stability, prosperity and happiness to your Congregation".[68]

Clearly this move had the support of Father Louis Nolan, a Dominican deeply involved in the unification movements, and with valuable Roman connections which he willingly put at the service of the sisters of the Order.[69] Towards the end of 1931 another famous Dominican, Father Finbar Ryan, visited South Africa on the invitation of a good friend of his, Mother de Ricci Harkin. He gave a retreat to the Dominican communities in Port Elizabeth and then visited Cape Town. Mother Teresa in her letter to Mother Colmcille Flynn expressed the delight of the community at his visit:

> He spent two entire days with the General Councillors, another day - Sunday - he devoted to two lengthy lectures delivered to the Sisters from six houses. The first lecture took nearly two hours the subject being the Dominican Order, its status in the church and in God's design, the essentials for true Dominican life. It really lifted us all up to heaven. The second lecture was a development of the proverb "Unity is strength", the application of this to the Dominican Order and the consequent necessity for Amalgamation.

He also spoke so persuasively of the importance of the Divine Office, its essential role in Dominican life and the fact that it took little more than ten or fifteen minutes than the Little Office, that the sisters were willing to adopt it.[70] He proposed that the councillors in both South African Provinces should take immediate action:

> He strongly advocated the idea of forming immediately a new Province with the Dominican Sisters of Port Elizabeth under the Mother General of the Irish Province resident in Dublin.

> ... The Rev. Father said he saw no reason for delay, that the
> decree of Amalgamation could be issued in January 1932
> and that the Mother General when she comes as she proposes,
> to South Africa in November, could in consultation with the
> authorities of the communities of C.Town and Port Elizabeth
> definitely lay down the local arrangements for the new order
> of things.[71]

For a master of diplomacy such as Finbar Ryan, a man well
versed in the intricacies of the almost century old political rift
between the Irish Mother Houses, this was ill-timed advice. He
returned to Ireland enthusiastic about amalgamation but he was
to have second thoughts. In the event there was little likelihood
that his advice would have been followed. Even in 1938 when
eventually this union was achieved, and the sisters were being
congratulated on the amalgamation between the two South
African Congregations, one superior replied, " We did not
amalgamate with Cape Town we amalgamated with the
Congregation in Ireland".[72]

But in 1930 the Irish Congregation was new, and the
achievement of true union was a daunting task which left little
immediate energy for the incorporation of missionary
communities, the problems of which could only compound
difficulties. While the architects of the Irish amalgamation set
about forming a Congregation of perfect observance, a body of
women that no Dominican of the First Order could reproach, the
South African houses waited with confidence until the 1934
General Chapter agreed to accept them into the Congregation in
1937. This was not a decision made without investigation and
mature deliberation. The South African Congregations had to be
observed from every possible angle. Many questions had to be
answered before a decision could be reached. Did the personnel
meet the accepted criteria as religious, as professional teachers
and as potential superiors? Were the buildings and property held
by the communities adequate and in good repair? Were the
finances secure for the upkeep of the communities and the
development of schools? And finally was the motive behind the
request for amalgamation, material or spiritual? The answer to
these and other related questions depended on the mature
judgement and keen powers of observation of those religious,
preferably women, who understood the intricacies of the situation.
Since to ask a Dominican from the South African Congregations
to fulfil such a task would be impracticable, the solution lay in a
fact-finding visit by delegates from the Irish Congregation.

Chapter Twelve

The Visit

By 1933 the need for a formal investigatory visit to Cape Town and Port Elizabeth had become a matter of urgency for the Council General of the new Congregation of Irish Dominican Sisters. Preparations were already in hand for the second General Chapter to be held in the summer of 1934. At that meeting an answer to the request for the amalgamation of the two South African communities with the Irish Congregation would have to be considered and a decision made. Since 1928, when the amalgamation of eight of the Dominican houses in Ireland was achieved, both of the South African Prioresses General, Mother Teresa Coleman and Mother de Ricci Harkin, had visited Ireland and personally, though separately, had put their case to Mother Colmcille and her Councillors. It was agreed that nothing short of a personal visit by the Irish Prioress General or her delegates, would give all parties an opportunity to come to a mutual understanding as to the wisdom or otherwise of union between the Irish Congregation and the two South African Congregations. For Ireland this would mean assuming responsibility for eight houses in the Western Cape and three in Port Elizabeth, together with their respective schools. Since in 1932 the Eucharistic Congress in Ireland delayed the Prioress General's promised visit to South Africa, and she was also hindered by poor health and pressure of work, she delegated Mothers Reginald Lyons and Alberta Grant to act on her behalf.

Mother Reginald, a great personal friend of that notable Dominican, Father Finbar Ryan, and one of the architects of amalgamation in Ireland, was fifty-five years old when, in 1933, she first visited South Africa. She was a woman of sound common sense, with a genuine love for and loyalty to the Order. Her long years of experience as a teacher and her knowledge of every aspect of secondary education, placed her in a strong position to assess the educational work being done in Dominican schools in South Africa. Both her diplomatic skills, evident in every phase of the amalgamation debate, and her social ease of manner, made her a wise choice as a member of the Cabra delegation to South Africa. During the struggle for union among the Dominican women in Ireland, she had gained insight into the political, social and economic problems that beset those involved in the amalgamation movement, and an understanding of the uncertainties that might surround the ultimate outcome. Despite the fact that she held certain entrenched positions from which she could not easily be moved, her personal detachment and discretion usually won the confidence of those with whom she came into contact. Despite this she had those qualities essential for a task that could well arouse suspicion and resentment among the South African sisters, superiors and subjects alike. Indeed it was a mission where diplomacy and not confrontation would serve as a winning tactic and both delegates were keenly aware of this.

Her companion, Mother Alberta Grant, an experienced teacher and a geographer of note, had entered St Dominic's Convent, Belfast and was professed in 1919 at the age of thirty. She prized highly the perfection of Dominican life and observance, and saw in the brethren of the Order, the guardians and purveyors of all that was most authentic in the heritage passed down by St Dominic himself. For her this perfection of sacred custom and practice was personified in Fr Finbar Ryan to whom she and other members of the General Council in Ireland turned for guidance and reassurance. However she had her own strength and as one of the prime movers, outside Cabra, in the process towards amalgamation in Ireland, she realised that to promote unity, some sacrifice of preconceived ideas as to what was and what was not essential to Dominican life, had to be made. For her, good social standing, refinement of manner and sound academic status, were important criteria in the choice of recruits. However she could appreciate the worth of those who did not meet all of these requirements, and was the first to acknowledge virtue in the simple, and potential in those whom lack of opportunity had repressed. She was no respecter of persons, and with her sharp mind, keen powers of observation, and formidable journalistic skills, little escaped her notice or remained unrecorded. Her diary and letters paint a picture of the life and work, the strengths and weaknesses of members of the communities which she visited, and also of the progress and viability of the South African missions and new foundations. But above all these written records lay bare the ideals, virtue and shortcomings of both the young and inexperienced, and of the older women who had spent a lifetime cut off from the mainstream of Dominican life. Some of her observations are unduly harsh and others reveal her ignorance of the new world which bore little resemblance to the sheltered conventual life to which she was accustomed. Nonetheless her diary and letters cast a new and vivid light on the Dominican missions and especially on the women holding high office in the community. In the early 1930's these superiors, by reason of their office, were forced to defend their position and rights in the highly complex and volatile political situation within the Catholic Church in Southern Africa.

Of the Prioress General in Cape Town, whom she had met in Ireland the previous year, Mother Alberta wrote: "Mother Teresa, whom I always liked, improves steadily on acquaintance. She gives me a strong impression of 'absolute truth', with great courage and simplicity of soul. She is a very holy woman, very shrewd & prudent, and though wanting in the polish of accent and manner that so many others have here, she is extraordinarily refined in mind and soul".[1] Whatever might have been the social shortcomings of Mother Teresa, she did not fail in her determination to find the best solution for her sisters and for the Church. In addition she was a woman of her times, the first new blood in the Council for many decades. Mother Alberta recognised this and noted her strictness in the application of such regulations as would win the approval of the visitors and so ensure amalgamation with Ireland. Mother Alberta and Mother Reginald "laughed with Mother Teresa over her terrible anxiety, her white worried face". They realised that she was "taking this whole amalgamation terribly to heart, and is frightfully upset lest anything ... [might] happen to prevent it". However the visit had its lighter moments, and Mother Alberta longed for "the pen of a Mrs. Gaskell" to describe some of the other councillors in the Western Cape:

> M. Columba [McAuliffe], M. Pius, M. Bertrand, and M. Berchmans belong, each in her own way, to the early Victorian generation and on that first evening I felt myself back in the days of 'Cranford'. They are all exceedingly nice, and you would love them all - but as a body they are not altogether suited for modern life. We have constant and prolonged 'Council Meetings' - highly formidable affairs with M. Bertrand and M. Columba as spokeswomen. M. Bertrand on all occasions plays the 'devil's advocate' (she has been doing this for the past 50 years!) and M. Teresa warned us what to expect.

In the event it was an advantage that every possible objection arising out of the amalgamation debate was aired, as this cleared the ground for more positive discussion at a later date.

Mother Pius McLaughlin, 85 years of age, was a "true Northern" and might still have been "part and parcel of Moville". Though she said little her mind was clear and her contributions to the discussions, though few, were very much to the point and showed insight and sound judgement. She died while the visitors were in Port Elizabeth and Mother Teresa sadly missed her support.[2] Sister Mary of the Angels Donnellan was co-opted as fourth councillor.

Much to their delight, the Irish visitors, were entertained in the parlour by Mother Columba and her priest brother, Dr McAuliffe. The "two together are unique", wrote Mother Alberta. "How I wish that you were here just so that we three might retire to a 'desert place' and sit down and enjoy it all".

> Mother Columba is a perfectly wonderful woman with the mind and *gait* of a *modern* early Victorian lady of about thirty. Did I tell you that I hear her proceeding to her daily cold bath at 5 a.m. each morning. She is in the Chapel after it not later than 5.40 a.m! And she is 81! ... As I write I can hear M. Columba talking rapidly on the verandah outside and she has all the polish of accent, grace of bearing and dignity of manner of a great Court lady - combined with a wonderful spontaneity and childlike freshness. Altogether, we wished again only this evening for the pen of a Mrs. Gaskell.[3]

However it was not all social elegance and polite entertainment and the real work of Mothers Alberta and Reginald was in the Council room rather than in the parlour. The task of the visitors was to consult the Prioress General and councillors of each province, to visit the 12 convents, talk to each sister, and to familiarise themselves with problems and needs of the local Church. By close observation and detailed reporting on the daily life, the professional work, and spiritual fervour of the nuns, and the attitude of the sisters towards union with Ireland, they would be able to advise the members of the General Chapter, on the wisdom or otherwise of admitting the communities of Cape Town and Port Elizabeth to the Congregation of Irish Dominican Sisters. It was a mission that demanded diplomatic reserve since the two delegates could make no promises nor could they pre-empt the decision of the General Chapter.

By the end of October 1933, after having spent a considerable time with both the Cape Town and Port Elizabeth communities, Mother Alberta could not "personally ... see any reason of substance" against amalgamation.

> My summing up of the Cape Town situation is that they have had grave trouble in the past due (1) to want of intelligent

government and (2) to a certain spiritual starvation, and (3) to a few clever, restless and unbalanced spirits in the Community. But that trouble is over. The poison has come forth and there is nothing now but immense good will, a real mission spirit and a craving for things Dominican.[4]

Mother Reginald writing to Mother Colmcille, confirmed her companion's views. "All the younger Sisters are in the Schools and all are very nice. The Communities are very simple and nice and very fervent, I should say. And the religious life is exceedingly well observed, and ceremonies well carried out".[5] She also found the older nuns to be "exceedingly nice". But as she moved from one congregation to the other and visited each convent and its schools she realised that there were too few Sisters to meet the growing demands of work for the local Church.[6]

On the question of religious life and observance in Port Elizabeth, Mother Reginald judged it to be excellent but "almost too strenuous and the Sisters are *very* hard working". Mother Alberta was more forthright in her opinion in respect of the situation in the Dominican houses in Port Elizabeth:

> Here the problem is other. It took me aback at first but I think I have sifted the community and now understand. It is a 'one-man show'. M. De Ricci is *all* things - nun's kitchen, parlour, school and Community - and *no* one else anywhere is anything. I need not explain the dangers and difficulties of such a Prussian regime, but the Community is alright - they understand, ... but 'Mother' has done so much for them in the past that nothing can be done till she dies. I am telling you this for yourself. 'Observance' is literally perfect - so much so that no one may be ill! But all are 'dying' for amalgamation and will do anything (especially now) to achieve it.[7]

Mother Alberta recognised that the sisters in the Eastern Cape were "extremely good and regular life is tuned up to concert pitch by M.De R! We hardly approach it at home". Perhaps there was a little envy in this observation and it seems likely that she and Mother de Ricci had more in common than Mother Alberta herself realised. Both were strong, opinionated women certain of their right judgement and of their ability to assess character, command respect, and propose and put into practice the highest ideals of religious life.

Of the two Mother de Ricci was the more restrained. She resisted the temptation to put on record her honest opinion of the visitors and the manner, not always palatable, in which they carried out their mandate. Nor did she reveal her misgivings about the union between her own Congregation and that of the Western Cape. However after a long conclave lasting almost five hours Mother Alberta was to claim, mistakenly it can be argued, "that 'both sides' i.e. M.de Ricci and M. Teresa ... [were] in perfect accord".[8] But whatever her shortcomings as a superior, Mother de Ricci respected those who stood up to her. And the majority of those who had experienced the new hope and reform she had brought with her in 1915, felt that she had earned the tolerance, gratitude and support of her community. Their acceptance of her political control was based, not simply on fear, but in many instances on love, gratitude, genuine admiration and respect. Later the two Irish General Councillors were to find that "she was entirely simple about the whole S.African situation and talked most freely" about it. She too was "in dire straits between the Delegate and Dr. Mc [Sherry]".[9]

Both Mother de Ricci and Mother Teresa co-operated with the visitors in their task of assessing the religious and professional life of the sisters, as well as the financial viability of their schools and convents. But it was in the area of constitutional differences and contradictions that the main focus lay. Indeed whatever could hinder the amalgamation of the South African congregations with Ireland was the subject of debate. It was also important for the delegates to ascertain whether or not the proposed union was really wanted not just by the superiors, but by the sisters in the ranks. While these were the official reasons for the journey of Mother Reginald Lyons and her companion, the reality was much more. It was not simply *the Visit*, it was an orchestration of visits with an underlying theme and variations. The whole production expressed the anxiety and hope, joy and despair, simple interaction and complex diplomacy, of the people concerned. The two superiors of the South African provinces had planned thoroughly for the ordeal, and their agendas were well prepared. They, like the Irish delegates, analysed personalities, judged motives and debated issues according to a preconceived set of criteria, many of which were more appropriate to the last decades of Victoria's reign than they were to the Church and society of Southern Africa of the early 1930's. The two eminent visitors, with a little over five months at their disposal, were anxious to do full justice to the task assigned to them, despite the pressure of long, hot journeys by sea and land, interminable receptions and concerts, an unaccustomed diet, spiritual and material, and the effort to serve with equanimity and patience the god-like role assigned to them. They let nothing hinder their mission, as their records show. Not only do they present a sympathetic picture of two Dominican communities, but they distinguish the differences that divided them and the ecclesiastical context in which they lived.

In both Cape Town and Port Elizabeth the visitors asked three questions, the first posed by Mother Alberta: "Was amalgamation with Ireland still desired by (a) the whole Council: (b) [the] whole Congregation?". While the answer of the Cape Town Council in favour of Amalgamation with Ireland was unanimous, that old warrior Mother Bertrand Dowling raised objections and "discussed advantages to be gained from amalgamation with the Germans". The points she raised were not without merit. If the South African communities were seeking stability, uniting with the German congregations instead of the Irish would be just as effective. As an added advantage the Germans were doing the same kind of work, and would understand the problems facing the Irish communities in the Cape Province. The fact that the "seat of government" would be in South Africa was an added advantage, and since the King William's Town postulants were coming from Germany "in batches of 40 or 50" there would be no shortage of recruits. "You can imagine Mother Teresa and the others!", wrote Mother Alberta: "We sat silent and left it to them - and of course even Mother Bertrand herself would not want amalgamation with the Germans, but (1) she likes to air opposing views and (2) she believes the Apostolic Delegate wants it and she thinks to oppose him is to oppose Rome. ... Mother Bertrand ... is a shrewd far-seeing woman, ... and her arguments are sound enough.[10] Whatever the merits of the argument, amalgamation with the German communities "was no longer an option". In 1932 when the Superior of the Dominican Convent at King William's Town had written to Mother Teresa "to ask her if she would join" she replied "in the negative" as did the other independent Dominican congregations in Southern Africa. Mother Teresa and her Council believed that had they accepted the invitation, the "Irish section" would have been "swamped" by the Germans. "Nobody wanted this; nor did they believe it to be for the greater glory of God who *willed the personality of nations*". That Christ also prescribed unity among all of His followers irrespective of national differences, did not enter into the discussion. The final word went to Mother Teresa who felt that it was a "mere waste of time to discuss such a question".[11]

While in Port Elizabeth, where the state of war between the Apostolic Delegate and Bishop McSherry affected every aspect of missionary development, opinions on amalgamation with the Irish Congregation went unopposed by Mother de Ricci and her Council. When Bishop McSherry made a "state call", Mother

Alberta and Mother Reginald "explained to him generally the Amalgamation proposition and asked his opinion and advice!".

> He expressed himself as altogether favourable and praised the Community in every way assuring us that with his large experience of Religious Convents he knew few to touch it. Amalgamation made for strength, ... and in particular he advocated a central Novitiate, and the longer the training the Sisters got therein the better *he* would like it. Then he turned to what he called 'the German invasion' of South Africa and his eyes lit up and his face hardened as he talked. On that subject and on the subject of the Delegate I should say Mother, that he is not normal. The Delegate is disliked of course, for himself, but primarily because he is a Dominican.

This latter is a political opinion difficult to substantiate, but whatever the reasons put forward for Gijlswijk's unpopularity, the two General Councillors from Ireland felt obliged to call on him. Bishop McSherry "would not hear of it. The Delegate did not deserve it, and it was not necessary".[12] It would demand considerable diplomatic skill to overcome this obstacle, but in the event they travelled to Bloemfontein with the old Bishop's blessing.

The second question, posed by the visitors concerning the Divine Office, was handed back to Mother Reginald and Mother Alberta for comment and explanation. Legislation for the daily recitation of this official Prayer of the Church was one of the main differences between the Constitutions of the Irish and the South African communities. In this debate the visitors were on familiar ground since it was a battle that had been fought and won in Ireland during the 1920's. They realised that although the Latin Office was long and time-consuming, it could be celebrated and with great spiritual benefit, even by those sisters overburdened by teaching and school administration. As a foundation direct from Cabra, the communities in the Western Cape had from the beginning recited the Little Office of the Blessed Virgin, but the situation in Port Elizabeth had been different. After the restoration of the Divine Office in 1887 the sisters of Holy Rosary Convent and its branch houses had retained it until 1925, when they were forced by Archbishop Gijlswijk to substitute the Little Office. The Apostolic Delegate on an official visit to St Dominic's Convent, Emerald Hill in 1925, "made a visitation and enforced on us a new book of constitutions. Divine Office [was] discontinued".[13] Subsequently Mother de Ricci petitioned a number of times for permission to resume the recitation of the Divine Office, but her requests were refused. "Our own Fr N [Louis

Nolan] told her it was 'spiritual pride on her part! So she went to the Master General and he told her to get it back at any cost! This she told to the Delegate".[14] For Mother de Ricci Harkin and her sisters therefore, the resumption of this practice would be seen both as a vindication of the rightness of their earlier position and the restoration of a precious privilege.

Although Mother Teresa and her Council were unanimous in accepting the Divine Office, and immediately began to practise the chant and study the rubrics under the guidance and instruction of the two visitors, Mother Bertrand again forced them to reconsider the matter. She reminded them that in a missionary context there were valid reasons against the recitation of the Office. Mother Alberta sums up the main points of her argument. In the first place the sisters were "overburdened with work", a fact noted by Mother Reginald on her visit to Sacred Heart School and also St Agnes', Woodstock:

> Of course the work in the schools is very heavy. All the classes we saw (except in the Deaf Schools where 10 or 12 is the maximum) are very large. Yesterday we went to the Kindergarten ... here 52 were present in it. At St Agnes' Primary School, Woodstock there are nearly 600 pupils and 17 teachers; 8 nuns and 9 lay teachers. Some of the classes had 40 children.[15]

Mother Bertrand's second reason expressed well the feelings of the some of the older and more conservative members of the community. "The Delegate who represented Rome said that the Divine Office was not 'inherent' in the Third Order of St Dominic. She also argued that the recitation of the Divine Office would also introduce a "principle of division into the Community, some having higher [educational] advantages". The fact that Mother Bertrand voted against the introduction of the Divine Office indicated that she was not, at the outset, convinced by the arguments of her colleagues.[16] She finally came round to the wishes of the majority but stubborn though she may have seemed, there was considerable wisdom in the stand she took. The daily choral recitation of the full seven hours of the Divine Office, together with the weekly Office of the Dead, was in practice an exhausting exercise more appropriate to a enclosed contemplative community than to an active missionary congregation. Within less than three decades, Rome itself was to begin a process of radical, liturgical change which would introduce the vernacular into the liturgy and reduce the length of the Divine Office. However in 1933, when the Irish Congregation was in its first fervour and the Divine Office was the expression of its renewed status in the Order, such ideas would have counted as a betrayal of much that both Mother Alberta and Mother Reginald had worked so hard to secure. The latter addressed the assembled communities both in Cape Town and Port Elizabeth, on the historical links between the recitation of the Office and nuns of the Order, and its spiritual value in the religious life of the sisters. That not all were equally equipped to follow the rubrics or indeed understand the Latin texts, was not only evident to the visitors, but was seen by others as a clear indication that Gijlswijk's solution to the lay sister situation had been ill-conceived and hastily put into practice.

Before amalgamation with Ireland could be considered, the question of lay sisters had to be solved. Mother Teresa and her Council were clear on the issue. They agreed that the arrangement imposed by Gijlswijk was the "best for a coloured country". Mother Teresa suggested that in future "only those capable of being educated be taken into the Novitiate and taught at least English and Latin". Mother Bertrand wanted an appendix to be added to the *Constitutions* stating that in South Africa there was only one class of sisters. The visitors objected, pointing out that this would create trouble at home among the lay sisters in Ireland. Although the other councillors saw the validity of Mother Alberta's argument, Mother Bertrand was not convinced. She pointed out that the *Constitutions* "must be taken as a whole, or not at all. If at a future date any Sister in S.Africa might say that according to the Constitutions the material work of the House was to be done by Lay sisters. She was not such and therefore was not obliged to do it". Mother Alberta acknowledged the soundness of this argument. The question was left open and the meeting adjourned, but that was not the end of the debate in Cape Town. It was felt by some that the levelling down of the community which resulted from the acceptance of lay sisters on equal footing with the Choir nuns, had resulted in a "loss of tone and culture". This, it was argued was "contrary to the Dominican ideal which seemed to demand and to aim at an intellectual standard. Recreation had now (as a matter of charity) come down to the level of the less educated".[17] This opinion was corroborated by Mother Augustine, of the King William's Town Dominicans, but despite this she felt that the single class of sisters suited the "democratic age abroad" and that it worked better. Her solution to the problem was to ensure that the Novitiate house at Schlehdorf selected the candidates with great care.[18]

On the question of lay sisters, Mother De Ricci supported neither democratic ideals nor a lowering of the intellectual or social level of the community. Her interpretation of the 1925

Constitutions in respect of lay sisters was unique, as Mother Reginald noted:

> The lay sister problem is in a somewhat different position from Capetown, as all the Domestic Sisters young and old say the Pater and Ave Office. There are 8 Domestic Sisters here, 7 of whom are still in the Novitiate; there are 7 at Emerald Hill and 1 at Uitenhage; i.e. 16 altogether. None of those at Emerald Hill go to community Recreation - and in everything except the scapular and rank they are like lay sisters. M. De R's proposal is that the old sisters should go on as they are - but that the young sisters should be established as laysisters by giving them a year's Canonical Novitiate. Both she and M.Magdalen say that there would be no trouble with the Sisters concerned over this. However it is too soon to give an opinion on this, and there are many side issues, and pros and cons to be considered. You may rest assured that we shall go slowly about everything and not commit ourselves to anything.[19]

It was clear that Mother de Ricci and her Council were prepared to restore the class of lay sisters. Mother Alberta, on the other hand saw the changes imposed by Gijlswijk as merely cosmetic. She maintained that although there were no lay sisters 'by name' in the two South African Congregations, Cape Town had "Domestic sisters - neither one thing nor the other", and Port Elizabeth presented the reality while giving the lay sisters the white scapular, without in practice changing their status. This statement does not distinguish the essential differences between the two Congregations on the lay sister question. Mother Teresa and her immediate predecessors in office had approved of the change in status for this group of sisters and did not intend to change them back to their former position in the community. This was clearly not the case in the Port Elizabeth Congregation. Mother Magdalen, in a private conversation with Mother Reginald, later assured her that there would be no difficulty in re-introducing the class of lay sisters, that the young sisters knew that they were domestics, which was "another word for lay", and she was "quite definite that they ought to be separate for recreation even if the *class* of laysisters" was not restored.[20]

During one of the most significant of the visits made by Mothers Reginald and Alberta, that to the Apostolic Delegation in Bloemfontein, he made clear his position on the question of lay sisters. He considered that such class distinction was not appropriate in the social climate of South Africa:

1. Such Sisters were treated in fact as slaves - always engaged in heavy manual work, with little time for prayer or the cultivation of the religious spirit.

2. They were looked down upon by the children - because of this manual work done in Africa exclusively by natives - and they were insulted by them.

3. They were never employed in any Mission work. Their position had given rise to much trouble and great unrest. Revolution was, he said threatened in the Cape and there was equal trouble in King.[21]

These points were not of universal application, since from the earliest days, some of the lay sisters in the Cape had done valuable mission work, especially among the most neglected of the Coloured and African children. These they gathered together and taught the rudiments of the Faith and in some cases elementary school subjects as well. Nor is there any evidence on record that lay sisters were ill-treated by pupils attending Dominican schools in Port Elizabeth and Cape Town. On the contrary they were often much loved by the children, who recognised both their kindness and their devotion to work. But whatever the truth of the allegations made by Gijlswijk, his solution to the dilemma was reasonable. He proposed either that the Congregation send no lay sisters to South Africa, or that those coming to the mission should be given the white scapular in order "to establish them on a certain footing". In the event the Congregation chose the former solution, thus taking measures to prevent an upsurge of dissatisfaction among the lay sisters in Ireland, while at the same time leaving intact the arrangement made by Gijlswijk for the South African communities. He was less successful in finding acceptance for his missionary approach to the matter of egress and enclosure.

By 1933 the Dominican sisters had been in Cape Town and Port Elizabeth for 70 and 66 years respectively. During most of that period they had been subject to episcopal enclosure, the application of which varied according to the attitude of the local bishop and the conventions to which continued practice had given the status of law. Since both communities made their first foundations in towns, where small gardens provided very limited space for walking in the fresh air, the custom grew of having vacations at holiday houses other than convents, and occasional picnic excursions to country places or to the seaside. In addition the sisters attended public churches with their pupils, or when a diocesan celebration demanded their presence. It was also necessary for sisters who taught botany, to bring their classes on periodic visits to botanical gardens, and for some of the nuns, daily egress to schools at a distance from the convent was the norm. Of equal importance, were the necessary visits to doctors and dentists. Although enclosure was respected, and where possible maintained, it had never been imposed contrary to the dictates of prudence and good sense. For the members of the young Congregation of Irish Dominican Sisters on the other hand, strict enclosure was one more pledge of their integrity as Dominicans, and an additional proof of their membership of the Second Order. Mother Alberta and Mother Reginald viewed the whole question of enclosure and the more liberal approach to egress in the South African convents, with grave concern, and this despite the fact that they saw for themselves the missionary need for home visiting, and the apostolic value of close interaction between the nuns and families in the vicinity of their schools and convents.

At this time when, under the vigorous leadership of Archbishop Gijlswijk, the Church in Southern Africa was placing more and more emphasis on missionary work and the promotion of Catholic Action among the indigenous majority, the Dominican Congregations of Cape Town and Port Elizabeth were opening new schools and steadily increasing their work among the Coloured people. From the 1860's onwards the promotion of Coloured education had been a familiar part of the professional work of the sisters, but in the 1930's and 1940's, the development of Coloured schools became a matter of urgency. In July 1933, shortly before the beginning of the Visit, when St Teresa's School for Coloured children was opened in Buitenkant St, Cape Town, the question of daily egress caused considerable anxiety, possibly because of the anticipated disapproval of the two Irish visitors:

> Opinion was divided on the opening of a school for the Coloured in Cape Town owing to the necessity for Sisters teaching there to leave St. Mary's Convent and take a five minute walk to and from it every day, but on account of the urgency of the case and the necessity of such a school for such Coloureds as those parents who are actually Catholics or are receiving instructions in preparation for their being received into the Church, a unanimous vote was recorded in its favour.

This would not have been a problem in the previous decade but visits to Cabra after the Irish amalgamation had convinced both Mother de Ricci and Mother Teresa of the necessity to conform as closely as possible to the Irish Constitutions in the matter of egress and enclosure. For the Prioress General of the Cape Town communities the real problem was financial. The economic depression which had tumbled major economic structures world-wide did not leave South Africa untouched. In many cases boarding schools were the first to suffer, and in private day schools pupils of families long connected with the convents were often kept on at reduced fees. Mother Teresa was fortunate that a benefactor donated £100 "for the cost of preparing and furnishing the house" which was on mission property, and which they were given rent free.[22] Mother Alberta was in admiration of the first principal of St Teresa' School.

> The new school has been given into the charge of Sr. M. Augustine [Barry] who is now 71 years of age! She is a Colonial, and it is the first time she has touched coloured people. Apparently she has found her true vocation. She is a woman of the M.De Paul type with extraordinary energy and vitality. All the parents of the coloured children come up to her and she is instructing 25 converts (adults) and marrying the dear knows how many more![23]

The adult apostolate, always an important part of the work of the Irish Dominican in South Africa, was steadily growing. Every member of St Mary's community in Cape Town, with the exception of Mother Teresa, was involved in adult catechetics. The same was true in Port Elizabeth where evening classes for converts and lapsed Catholics were, for the sisters, a regular feature of after-school activities. The increased involvement of the sisters in this work was due in no small measure to the encouragement given by the Apostolic Delegate, and the emphasis he placed on direct evangelisation. The visitors were to gain some perspective on the potential for missionary activity when in August 1933 they spent a few days at Holy Trinity Convent, Matroosfontein, a microcosm of the vast missionary territory as yet neglected by the Catholic Church. To the Irish visitors it was a "new world":

> It is not a town, or a village, but a district - a portion of open veld with one 'made' road through it, the rest being sandy tracts as in sand-dunes, odd (very odd!) paths being hardened to sea-shore sand. It is covered with sea mat grass, heather-like plants, and tall (4 to 6 feet high) veldt bushes. The whole region is flat and hemmed in on all sides by glorious, high, jagged mountains. The Convent is a cottage by the roadside, and a few feet from the back door is the famous Shamrock Church - of which there is surely not a second in the world. The whole place is unique.

For sisters who such a short time previously, were living within the enclosure at Cabra, a large formal convent, it was indeed a unique experience. Mother Alberta and her companion "went to sleep to a chorus of thousands of croaking frogs, ... woke off and on to the sound of horses and donkeys clattering along the road, got up amid the uproar of hundreds of crowing cocks and singing birds". This other world where poverty prevailed among a vibrant people was a far cry indeed from the solemn silence and peaceful isolation of the cloister.[24]

The Cape Flats was a district where the need for Catholic schools and apostolic work among the Coloured families was clearly evident, but it was not an area where it would be possible to reconcile the urgent demands of mission, with the strict application of the laws of enclosure as envisaged in the Irish Dominican Constitution. The work of the sisters involved three things, the teaching of the Coloured children, the instruction of adults and visiting the poor and troubled people in their homes. For this work a dispensary in the convent, and a sound knowledge of first aid would be needed. This latter would enable the sisters to deal with common ailments and provide remedies for the housebound sick. It might also involve them in household work for those too ill or disabled to help themselves.[25] There was certainly ample opportunity for social work:

> All along the 'Flats' ... the people are simply swarming - all Coloured - and there is an immense field of work amongst them. ... So Mother Teresa is not far out in building for 500. It is a hard struggle to live as the Catholics appear to be all poor. These Coloured people live on next to nothing; the 'land' on the Flats is just sea sand with scrub bushes growing all over it. The people live by cutting it into 'kindling wood' which they sell for a few pence, and by eggs from the hens they keep. And there are literally hundreds of houses all over the place - just little sheds covered with corrugated iron or thatch.[26]

The small community at Matroosfontein consisted of five Choir nuns and one sister in charge of the domestic work of the convent. The school which had been opened on the arrival of the sisters in 1931, had by 1933 about 200 pupils some of whom were taught in the church, others in a small cottage beside the convent and the rest in the bush. This was only a temporary arrangement and Mother Alberta noted : "M.Teresa has plans for a very fine new School but she is being held up by the Government who (like the N.Ministry) do not want to recognise it".[27] Despite the delay, the work of the mission was making good progress and the "whole district [was] tending to come to the Sisters, and with approximately 500 lapsed Catholics in the area", Father Jerome was confident that the nuns would "draw hundreds to the faith". The school and church were built in 1935 at a cost of £7500 of which £1300 was contributed towards the church by Bishop Henneman. This foundation remains a vital centre of Catholic life on the Cape Flats, no small tribute to the sisters and teachers who taught there and to the Holy Cross sisters at Parow who gave many of them such excellent professional training.

The fascination of the Matroosfontein experience was repeated in Port Elizabeth when Mother de Ricci brought the visitors to St Finbar's and the Kabah. But there was sadness as well. The people were poor, many illiterate, and there were few opportunities for a Catholic education for their children They made a visit to St Finbar's on a Sunday afternoon. It was to be one of the highlights of their visit to the Eastern Province:

> The 'pupils' ranged from 7 days to 70 years and I must say their knowledge of the Catechism was wonderful. Which reminds me that the Religious question out here, Mother, would make you weep. Practically *nothing* is done for the Coloured or the Native, and they are living and dying all round in thousands. It is appalling. Some of the priests are furious - but helpless. I suppose the older generation just cannot see things in a new light. Dr McS[herry] will do nothing. No one can move him. The only solution seems to be a German successor.[28]

It was the plight of the indigenous people and the urgent need for the implementation of an effective missionary policy that had led Gijlswijk to subdivide the large Vicariates and introduce German Vicars Apostolic who, with their priests, would put in hand the evangelisation of the people. And it was also his firm conviction that the urgent needs of the mission demanded freedom from enclosure for the Dominican teachers. It was a conclusion that neither Mother Reginald nor Mother Alberta could approve of, though they did accept as inevitable the daily egress, for catechetical purposes, to schools, as well as to churches and other centres.

Both of the Irish visitors gained personal experience of the work being done at local Sunday schools when they accompanied the three sisters from St Dominic's Priory on their Sunday afternoon visit to St. Finbar's.

> It was just crowded out with men, women and children when we arrived. One old man of 92 had made his 1st Holy

Communion that morning and 2 babies (Chinese) had been baptised also. Both the old man and the babies were there as well as a couple of hundred of all kinds of people, some nearly white and some as black as ink. Sr. Columba asked me to question the grown-ups in Catechism and Mother Alberta went to the children in another room. You would have laughed over strange answers in strange languages - but the fact is these poor people really did know the Catechism - a short one in both English and Afrikaans. Later Sister Ceslaus got them to sing 'Hail Glorious St. Patrick' to the accompaniment of a tinny piano. Then we presented them with rosary beads and pictures and the children with buns and sweets made at the Priory and finally one of the women gave me a box of fudge ... and we all got bouquets of wild flowers before we moved away.[29]

St Finbar's School, one of the first post-amalgamation foundations in South Africa and at the outset served from St Dominic's Priory, was finally opened in 1939 "in a quiet area amongst a simple congregation of Coloured". Mother Teresa wrote seven years after the formal opening of this school:

Every morning a donkey trap bearing one Dominican Sister accompanied by a coloured teacher goes from Priory to Fairview, a distance of about two miles. Here dear old Sr. M. Columba has unostentatiously reaped a harvest of souls for Christ during the past seven years. She looks after the needs spiritual and temporal of the poor. She is the Principal of the school with a roll of 170 pupils about fifty per cent Catholics. She has with her a faithful band of coloured teachers.[30]

Later there were two nuns and three teachers but no government subsidy, and apart from an annual grant from the Holy Childhood fund, the salaries for the teachers had to be found each month. The application of the Group Areas Act forced the Coloured people out of Fairview and the school, by then 100% Catholic, was closed in 1972. The provision of schools for the Coloured community was viewed with special interest by the General Council in Ireland, and was the fulfilment of the wishes of the two visitors after their experiences in the Cape during 1933.

Mothers Reginald and Alberta spent some time in Mater Admirabilis Convent a "true missionary house", from which the Sisters travelled daily by motor to the Kabah location to teach in the fine one-storey school built by Mother de Ricci. While the Government and private Junior schools won praise for the high standard of work being done, the fact that a large number of the pupils were Protestants was a matter of concern to the visitors.

This was a common complaint in most of the European schools, primary and secondary. The case of Coloured and African schools was different. It was to be expected that many of the pupils and their parents would join the Church and this justified the admission of pupils who were not Catholics. The Kabah situated "on the side of a hill consisted of rows of huts made of wretched bits of old corrugated iron, or else of mud hovels. Hundreds are born and die daily without ever hearing of God. The whole thing is amazing in view of the fact that there is a surrounding 'civilisation' ". Mother Reginald and her companion after visiting the Kabah and some of the other locations in the vicinity of Uitenhage, were convinced of the wisdom of opening a convent next to the school at the Kabah. This would solve two problems: it would limit egress, and provide greater apostolic opportunities for work among the African people of the area. Marymount Convent was finally opened in 1942 and the secondary school offered to the young Africans in that area, the only opportunity for higher education. This foundation has survived many vicissitudes and today offers excellent service to the pupils and to the community at large.

The situation in the Eastern Vicariate stunned the visitors as Mother Alberta explained to Mother Colmcille Flynn:

> Next to nothing is being done by the Church for the Natives or the Coloured, and with a teeming native population in twelve to twenty Locations in the Vicariate, not a single Catholic Church is put up or anything whatever done for them. ... The Bishop is too old to do anything, and he cannot face the responsibility of touching the problem at all, or letting anyone else touch it. I suppose the only remedy at present is prayer. But the situation is, to us, almost inconceivable.

They drove through Korstan, at the North End of Port Elizabeth and found it "truly a dreadful place, of evil repute and with not a single evidence of Catholicity".[31] Mother de Ricci's plans to open a convent at the South End, Port Elizabeth, had been thwarted by Bishop McSherry, who with only 30 priests for such a large Vicariate, could not guarantee a chaplain. It was not until 1937 that this foundation could be made. In the meantime seven or eight sisters from Holy Rosary Convent drove daily to teach in the two schools, one for White and the other for Coloured children. In the Coloured and European schools, each of which had an enrolment of approximately 250 pupils, the majority of the children were either Catholics or under instruction.[32]

In the South African context the ideal proposed by the Church, Catholic schools for Catholics was as admirable as it was unrealistic. In a few cases Gijlswijk had applied a simple remedy; he insisted that children of other faiths be dismissed from the schools. When these institutions were forced to close he realised that until the Catholics could support their own schools the admission of Protestants was inevitable. Nevertheless, whether or not the presence of children of other faiths attenuated the Catholic atmosphere of the schools, the allegation could not be ignored. Mother Reginald felt very strongly on this matter and about fifteen years later when as Prioress General of the Congregation she made visitation of the Region of South Africa, she "denounced" the practice of admitting Protestants. The criticism implied in this denunciation was one of the reasons why some of the sisters resented amalgamation and what was seen as the condescension of those superiors living in a secure, insular, Catholic environment. The complete exclusion of Jews from the schools, demanded by Mother Reginald, was another ground for criticism. That this refusal to admit Jewish pupils to Irish Dominican private schools coincided with the violent anti-Jewish pogroms in Europe, and the death or exile of many innocent people, was unfortunate. However for the sisters in South Africa it was not the international implications of this exclusivity that caused resentment, but the betrayal of good and loyal friends who had contributed to the rich diversity that characterised convent schools in Southern Africa. They had also been a strong source of moral and financial support for Dominican institutions in times of need, and as loyal past pupils had remained valued members of the Dominican "family" in the Cape.

In a record that is noteworthy for journalistic frankness of criticism and sharp delineation of the characters of sisters with their strengths and weaknesses, neither of the Dominican visitors found anything negative to write about the Catholic education given in the schools. Indeed the Protestants were often among the most devout pupils. They valued the moral and spiritual training given by the sisters, and found in them support and friendship in adult life. While Mother Teresa, Mother de Ricci and their councillors were well aware of the feelings of many of the sisters in this regard, they believed that they had no choice but to accept the policy both of Church authorities and of the Council General in Ireland. It was a matter that was to weigh heavily on principals of schools and the Regional Vicar and every subsequent report of the Region of South Africa to General Chapters reflected the percentage of Catholics on the roll. In the Report of the Regional Directress of Schools to the General Chapter of 1948, Mother Thecla Wilmot wrote: "It is probable that some of our Secondary Schools will decrease in numbers within the next few years as we readily comply with the instructions of the Apostolic Delegate[33] and the Bishops of South Africa to strive to make the enrolment 100% Catholic, but the spiritual gain we hope will accrue from this measure will more than compensate for the loss".[34]

It was not a sentiment that expressed the true feelings of many of the sisters involved in the schools and in practice the private schools have never reached the 100% goal. However, despite criticism of admission policies, Mother Alberta and Mother Reginald were impressed, indeed delighted by the high standard attained in Dominican schools, both in religious education and in academic subjects at primary and secondary level. Since there was nothing to choose between curricula and official examination systems in Ireland and South Africa, they seldom commented on such matters, except in a general way.[35] The main focus of attention was on the cultural attainments of the pupils in fine sewing, crafts, music and singing, dancing, drama, and public speaking. In Springfield the president of the Debating Society welcomed the Provincial and the Irish Mothers in "simple, fluent, well-chosen words". The poise, social ease and openness of the pupils was noted, as well as the excellence of the music, singing and sewing, embroidery and art. They were invited to Wynberg for a display and small sale of the children's handwork. "The standard, tone and taste, ... is very high - astonishingly so. And imagine, they have actually Dominican Inter-School Examinations with printed Papers, Prizes etc. - the whole worked by a Mistress General of Studies. I am taking home specimens of all for our mature consideration".[36]

On their return from Port Elizabeth the visitors again went to Wynberg to attend the High School concert and distribution of prizes. Mother Alberta judged the whole affair to be excellent. The children were "extremely well trained". Each item was of a "very high standard - especially the Piano Duo". This was brilliant, and the school song was "martial and stunning". The stage discipline, as well as the acting, singing and playing of the children of St Augustine's Coloured Primary School was "especially good - as good as a Secondary School".[37] St Michael's Rondebosch, judged in terms of the building to be the "best Convent of the lot", and the Primary School across the road was "in tone and standard ... altogether Secondary. Only better class pupils seem to go there", Mother Alberta wrote, "Rondebosch being a rising district near the University".

The visitors found Star of the Sea Convent, St James "a bit of a surprise". Mother Alberta, thought that since it was "at the sea and that the nuns owned a portion of the mountain" it would be "something of the Wicklow type". The reality, as she noted with a keen geographer's eye, was quite different:

> It is utterly other. The mountains drop almost perpendicularly to the coast road about 50 feet wide, and all the houses, including the Convent are built into the mountain side. The view from above is undoubtedly superb - but the ascent is practically perpendicular and the older Nuns or M.Reginald could not even attempt it. The view from the cell window where I write is glorious - the Indian Ocean - stretching to the South Pole in front and the Bay (some hundred miles round) shut in by mountains. The western curve is dotted with towns that cling to the mountain sides, and at night there are myriads of lights that make the place look like fairyland.[38]

The visits to schools and the receptions, speeches and concerts given by the pupils convinced the Irish Mothers of the refined manners and self confidence of the secondary pupils in all the Dominican schools. In Priory the girls who "gave a very nice little concert", were "very nice, well-mannered [and] more developed than our own". The boarding school, had 83 pupils, and there were a few day girls, less than was usual because of the depression. Of these 22 were Catholics. Mother Hyacinth Lamont was Head Mistress, and the school which offered all grades up to and including Matriculation, was very successful. Mother Hyacinth, "a Colonial" was judged by Mother Alberta to be "very good, very loyal and efficient, unsurpassed in rectitude, zeal and religious spirit".[39] Mother Alberta gave the Priory girls a lesson "on the working of God in human things - an outline of the greater civilisations up to the birth of Christ showing the preparation made by God for the New Law and the coming of Our Lord". She chose this topic because it had bearing on Religion "since they were mainly Protestants - and yet it could not be altogether religious". This is not a distinction that the South African sisters would have made. Nor indeed would the pupils, well accustomed as they were to Catholic ideals, doctrine and liturgy. Mother Alberta was also "practically forced" by Mother de Ricci to speak to all the sisters on any topic of her choice:

> I gave them 'Dominicanism' according to Fr. Finbar i.e. a hash up of all his Lectures and talks the first day; and 'Dominican Education' according to F. Finbar and Fr. Cussens the second day. I had all the Novices and the whole Community - about 43 or 44 in all. They are clamouring for a third, and if they keep on I will talk on 'Catholic Action'.[40]

The chapel at St Dominic's Priory, Port Elizabeth.

An interesting comment on the dependence of a well read, clever woman with a creative mind, on the ideas and pronouncements of her Dominican brethren.

As an observant reporter however Mother Alberta needed no model, Dominican or otherwise. Her description of St Dominic's Priory proves this point:

> The Priory is on top of a hill surrounded by about 100 acres of land. Oranges, lemons, figs, bananas etc. grow in the grounds in what are really clearings in the bush. The Convent is fairly large and a new wing has just been completed. You would just love the teak and jarrow wood floors - and doors; and I think you would like a new and very unusual Chapel. It was not designed as a Chapel and is unlike anything I ever saw. The windows (largely of amber glass) are about 18 feet high and the colour scheme is in various shades of brown, with cream walls and a blue ceiling! It looks astonishingly well.[41]

Mother Alberta and Mother Reginald did not limit their interests to the Dominican communities of Port Elizabeth and Cape Town. They visited institutions run by other congregations, and especially the King William's Town Dominican convents and schools. This Congregation had 500 sisters in South Africa, and an additional 100-150 at Schlehdorf. There were 16 Priories and 24 mission houses, and with financial aid from Germany, it was possible to support poor missions. The well planned buildings, the "magnificent" churches and properly equipped schools, the science museum, and especially the African missions, deeply impressed the visitors. But the celebration of the Dominican liturgy at King William's Town, with a choir of almost 150 sisters, was the "most perfect" they had experienced. The kindness and courtesy of both the Prioress General, Mother Augustine Geisel and the local Prioress, Mother Ignatius, was incomparable. They discussed matters of common interest including the difficulties between the Bishop and the Apostolic Delegate, and the pressures put on them by Gijlswijk to make foundations, such as that at Klerksdorp, "a remote upland village with no facilities". The scheme was a failure as the Dominican sisters had foreseen from the beginning. When Mother Augustine closed the house without the permission of the Delegate he was incensed at her temerity. Clearly in this as in many other matters Gijlswijk made exorbitant demands on the Congregation and expected complete obedience, even when wiser counsels would have cautioned delay.[42]

Both Mother Alberta and Mother Reginald deeply appreciated the openness and hospitality of Mother Augustine and her sisters, and if the revelation of Gijlswijk's many clashes with the Congregation made the projected visit to him less appealing, at least the two Irish visitors were warned. In the event the Apostolic Delegate was as charming as the long interviews with him were exhausting. He gave them a detailed analysis of the situation of the Church in Southern Africa, of the school situation, and the need for a strong Catholic Action movement. He discussed the problems surrounding the Catholic Training College for Coloured students and the need for many more schools for Coloured and African children.[43] He needed money for all of these projects but above all he needed workers.

> The trouble in the country was that there was so much work to be done, and so few hands to do it. The Vicariates must be divided and re-divided, and priests, Nuns and Brothers got in - for the future of Africa lay with the Black and Coloured Races and it was for us to build up the Faith in them. The opposition of the Government and the competition of the other innumerable sects was so great, and their work so heart-breaking, that if we were just another sect he would say 'Pack up and go home to Europe'. But as we were not a sect, but the Church of Christ, we were going to triumph - and so - come and help.[44]

Gijlswijk, in the long hours he gave to the two Dominican visitors, talking and smoking incessantly throughout each session, made a strong impression on them. They both liked him very much. He was "perfectly straight and entirely sincere, and consumed by two great desires - to save souls, and to promote the glory of the Dominican Order. For these two ideas he ... [would] go to any trouble and make any sacrifice". As the hours passed the two sisters became more and more impressed by the Delegate, as Mother Alberta confessed in her Christmas letter to Mother Colmcille: "Altogether ... we found him an eminently reasonable man, a great Dominican and a really holy Priest. He is also a great fighter - and will tackle governments, and educational authorities, or anything else - and all for the glory of God".[45]

He reinforced his opinions on the apostolic necessity for egress in South Africa and insisted that the recitation of the Divine Office would place a heavy burden on the nuns. On the lay sister question he stood firm though his argument was focused more on uniformity of dress than on equality of status. He also supported the request of the Dominican sisters of the Cape for a single, central novitiate in Europe. Variations on these topics were by 23 November all too familiar to Mothers Reginald and Alberta, but they listened to his forceful and masterly presentation and reserved comment on controversial matters. He spoke highly of *his* Dominican sisters and defended his stand on the amalgamation of all the Dominican congregations in Southern Africa. However he expressed himself satisfied that Cabra was seriously considering reunion with its missionary foundations.

> Amalgamation, he says is an absolute necessity for Cape Town and Port Elizabeth. The Dominican Nuns were pioneers in the country and have done great and magnificent work, but because they had no Mother General in Europe they 'fell under the thumb' of various Bishops who made them Diocesan for their own purposes and split them up into various Congregations (as with the German Dominicans) or else let them stagnate as in C.Town and P. Elizabeth.[46]

"It is all exactly as we see it and feel about it at home", wrote Mother Alberta. "The Bishops and priests in places, he says, make slaves of the Nuns - one Bishop actually wanted to stop them saying the Little Office because it took up too much time".[47] Gijlswijk saw himself as the protector of the nuns and wanted to make the most of his opportunity to ensure their status. In this letter to Mother Colmcille Flynn, Mother Alberta captures the determination of the Apostolic Delegate to bring stability to the two Irish Dominican Congregations in Southern Africa.

> Whilst a Dominican Archbishop is here in Africa as Delegate ... the Dominican Nuns are safe as the Bishops know that he will give them no hearing where 'his Sisters' are concerned; but Rome may recall him tomorrow, and almost certainly a Dominican will not succeed him. The Dominican Nuns will then fall back again as they have no support and no real touch with the Order. Realising this he wants to save the Order and stabilise it in the country at any cost - and so he is willing to make any sacrifice to bring about the amalgamation of P.E. and Cape Town with us.

He told of his earlier attempts to bring about an amalgamation of all the Congregations in Southern Africa and of its "failure - and of the hatred with which he was regarded". While as Apostolic Delegate he was obliged to deal with all the different congregations, he felt a special concern for the Dominican communities, those of his own religious family. Talking about the sisters in general, he had found the Dominicans in S. Africa "in a bad way", and he tried to implement his own strategies to solve their problems.

> With his own it was different. He was convinced personally that it was fatal for a Convent or Congregation to be in the

hands of a Bishop - and even if Communities were banded into a Congregation and had a Mother General, little was achieved while she lived in Africa in the Diocese and 'under the thumb' of any one Bishop. Living in his Diocese it was almost impossible to oppose him - and this might be a real necessity at times.[48]

The Delegate reiterated what he had said so often and with so much force to the Dominican Congregations throughout Southern Africa, that Amalgamation was not a matter of choice:

It is very necessary, the Delegate says, that the General Chapter be made to understand that the Amalgamation of the S.African Sisters with Ireland - and if not with Germany - is the wish of the Holy Father - and therefore not an open question. He begged that Fr. Finbar Ryan be brought to the Chapter to explain the needs of the Order in Africa and the immense field of Missionary labour open to nuns. As the Holy See had ordered the amalgamation of Dominican Sisters and it was given to the Delegate to carry it through in Africa, M Rose Niland took alarm. She did not want any such amalgamation as having entered at King she caused so much trouble that she left. She asked to be taken in Port Elizabeth but was refused. Oakford accepted her. There again she became a storm centre and being sent to do hospital work during the war trouble broke out in her community at its close. A Visitation was held as a result of which Oakford offered to give her the House and whatever Sisters wished to stay with her.[49]

Gijlswijk attributed his failure to bring about the amalgamation of the various Dominican Congregations in Southern Africa to the intransigence of Mother Rose. "In consequence neither King, nor Oakford, nor P.Elizabeth will have anything to do with her. Rather than be forced into any amalgamation scheme with other Dominicans in Africa she got her own Constitutions approved and flouted the Delegate". It was a long and complicated series of events, a battle of wills by two accomplished strategists, and Mother Alberta's comment aptly sums up the situation: "A very clever woman and one who has triumphed over the Delegate".[50] If she had been a "storm centre", so indeed had he. They were well matched and Mother Rose's opposition to a total amalgamation of Dominican women in Southern Africa, proved to be the opportunity for the other communities to stand out against a hasty and ill-considered union.

Gijlswijk saw the plan for amalgamation between Cabra and the two South African Congregations to be mutually beneficial. He considered that benefits would be considerable:

The contemplated amalgamation is of vital importance for the religious and disciplinary improvement, and also for the establishment of well-organised government in the aforesaid Congregations, while your province in an easy and simple way will have its members increased by more than 200 subjects and the number of houses multiplied, thus acquiring the honourable name of a province having a large mission field attached to its activities, for which other religious Congregations desirous of complying with the wishes of Rome, have to bring enormous sacrifices in money and in personnel as well.[51]

Although there is little proof that the General Council in Ireland had any imperialistic aspirations, this amalgamation did indeed confer on the Congregation the undoubted advantage of loyal compliance to the wishes of the Holy See. But it was more than a unilateral "taking up" of the South African communities. It introduced a new phase in the history of the Irish Dominican women, although for many of the nuns in Ireland the Region of South Africa remained a *terra incognita*, peripheral to the real life of the Congregation and little more than an incidental responsibility from which little could be expected.

Whatever the ultimate outcome of this projected union, late in 1933 the two Prioresses General informed their respective communities as to the progress already made and the need to confirm their formal request for amalgamation with Cabra. When all the legal steps had been completed the decision of the 1934 General Chapter was anxiously awaited. Each of the South African Congregations wanted to form a separate vicariate, each with its own vicaress and council. They also sought a general dispensation "in the matter of necessary and habitual, desirable, and non-recurrent egress in the interests of our schools and the health of ... [the] Sisters". In addition, Port Elizabeth requested the right to substitute the office of the lay sisters, for those "not capable of reciting the Divine Office".[52] In the event the South African Dominicans as well as the Cabra Congregation were to have sufficient time to reconsider their options. At the General Chapter of the Congregation of Irish Dominican Sisters held at Cabra, Dublin in July 1934, the amalgamation requested by the two Dominican congregations of Cape Town and Port Elizabeth was approved in principle, but would be delayed for a period of three years. In a time of rapid missionary development, with the opening of new schools and the urgent need for recruits to fill in the many vacant posts, this was an unwelcome delay. Gijlswijk for his part could not understand the need for a period of waiting. He called together the combined Councils of Port Elizabeth and Cape Town for a conference under his chairmanship, to consider the matter. The letter from Mother Colmcille was ambiguous and in some cases self-contradictory. It was implied, though this was not the intention of the General Chapter, that in the interim period the Irish Congregation would have some authority over the South African communities. In South Africa the scheme proposed by the Irish Chapter was discussed and amendments proposed. The Apostolic Delegate wrote to Mother Colmcille Flynn:

> Paragraph 2 suggests a re-organisation of the government. But this can be done only after the amalgamation has been effected. Any re-organisation or alteration of the present government anticipating the amalgamation would be against their present Constitutions, thus unconstitutional and unlawful. And what would be in this case the canonical position of the two Congregations? Now, having their Constitutions approved by Rome and being of pontifical right, they would lose this canonical position by forming two vicariates and by neglecting those articles of the Constitutions which regulate their government. By so doing, they would be practically dependent on Cabra, although not amalgamated, whereas only the fact of the amalgamation can place them under the authority of the Superior General of Cabra. To such an ambiguous canonical status Rome will never consent.[53]

Mother Colmcille, in suitably gracious and apologetic tone assured Gijlswijk of the rightness of his conclusions on points of law, but stood her ground on the question of the three year delay. Indeed since this was a Chapter decision she had no alternative, a point of law with which the Apostolic Delegate should have been familiar.

> I regret very much that certain phrases in my letter ... to your Excellency were not as clear as we had intended them to be, ... I fear we wrote too hurriedly, and, in consequence, some clauses in my letter were open to misinterpretation. With regard to ... the postponement of the Amalgamation for three years, the General Chapter, after much consideration, decided that this period of time was essential for the adjustment of the affairs of our own Congregation, some of which have to be brought to maturity. While most anxious to meet your Excellency's wishes we regret very much that it is not possible in the circumstances for us to delete the words 'for three years' from the Scheme.[54]

By 1936, Father Louis Nolan also wished that the "Cabra negotiations went more briskly". So did Mother De Ricci and Mother Teresa who in the meantime were involved in plans to have a common novitiate at St Catherine's Convent, Tamnaharrie - their first tentative step towards closer co-operation. This was done in view of the fact that the Irish Congregation would not be able to accommodate candidates for the South African mission at Cabra, and until the opening of a large central novitiate, the house at Warrenpoint, though not ideal, would suffice. In Ireland Mother Colmcille Flynn, with the help of Father Nolan, was drawing up the documentation for the legal process of amalgamation, while in South Africa Mother De Ricci and Mother Teresa with their communities, were preparing to hand over their independent foundations to the authority of a distant Congregation in Ireland. It was the end of an era, which was seen by some as a time of new and creative opportunity, by others as a regressive step into a restrictive life of Irish Dominican fundamentalism.

But for the Prioresses General and their Councils in Port Elizabeth and Cape Town the immediate feeling was one of relief. It had been a long and arduous campaign, with the displeasure of Rome and with the constant threat of enforced amalgamation with other Dominican congregations held over their heads. By August 1937 Mother Teresa could write with honesty to the Prioress General in Ireland:

> We are confident now ... that the Decree will soon be passed and that we can take a definite step forward. It will be a great comfort to us to get a *fixed* book of Constitutions into our hands, instead of one which is always subject to change. Yes I feel amalgamation will bring with it for us a sense of great spiritual stability, and with this guarantee the Sisters are prepared to launch forward in safety.[55]

The legal process of amalgamation was completed by 25 January 1938, and by early February Mother Teresa and Mother de Ricci had the letters in hand informing them of their new status as members of the Irish Congregation of Dominican Sisters. The next step, the appointment by the General Council in Ireland of a Regional Vicar and four councillors, two from each area, was completed by May. It was a new regime, but those placed in authority locally were women familiar to all the sisters. Mother Teresa Coleman was the first Regional Vicar, an office she was to hold for ten years. Her first councillor was Mother de Ricci who had asked for a Regional superior to be supplied by Ireland. Mother Thecla Wilmot from Holy Rosary Convent, Port Elizabeth was second councillor and Mother Mary of the Angels and Mother Clare Martin represented the Cape Town interests on the Council.[56]

The process of amalgamation begun in 1919, had at last caught up with the South African communities. For better or for worse the sisters, as a corporate body were part of a greater Congregation, the membership of which brought changes into their lives, some perceived as positive and others as obstructive and unnecessarily severe. However no one expected that real union, between the Western and Eastern Cape would be effected by a Papal Brief or the rigid application of Constitutions. What was not foreseen was the negative influence of geographical isolation on the process of true amalgamation with Ireland. The intervention of the 1939-1945 war excluded the South African Region from participation in the third General Chapter of the Congregation, a circumstance that did nothing to promote a strong sense of belonging. But the times were changing and this was already being felt both in secular society and in the religious and clerical life of the Church. The Congregation of Irish Dominican Sisters buttressed and enclosed by so many precious customs and laws and secure in its heritage was, with the rest of the Catholic Church, on the eve of an era of rapid and radical change that would put in question much that seemed most precious and desirable in the two decades preceding the outbreak of war. It was in these circumstances that the true wisdom of amalgamation would be evident to those who had doubted its relevance or value. The immediate future, while it saw the normal continuation of religious life in the Dominican communities recently united with their Mother House in Ireland, also witnessed a new missionary phase in the Catholic Church and more specifically in the Cabra Congregation in South Africa.

Chapter Thirteen

St Rose's Congregation

1938-1974

During the period between the two world wars the Church constantly urged the promotion of the indigenous church in missionary territories throughout the world. This is reflected in the work of Archbishop Gijlswijk who sub-divided and re-organised the large Vicariates in Southern Africa and introduced German Vicars Apostolic and priests, with a strong missionary bent. He based his policy on that prescribed in 1923 by the Sacred Congregation of Propaganda. This policy emphasised the need for the appropriate training of those destined for work in foreign missions, renewed vigour in the preaching of the Gospel, the acquisition of African languages, and familiarisation with the "manners and customs" of the regions in which the missionaries were to work. A sound preparation together with an appropriate methodology "best adapted for the work of evangelisation in each country, would ensure the success of their mission". But even appropriate training for those destined for foreign missions would not be enough to ensure the firm establishment of the Church in a country:

> It is of the highest importance that the Superiors should see ... that the formation of indigenous clergy be taken in hand in the Missions entrusted to their Institutes. This, indeed is necessary, since the various territories have been committed to them precisely in order to found and establish the Church therein. Now the conversion of the infidel is only the beginning ... ; following this must come the formation of Christian communities ... with their own Chapels or Churches, and the institution of schools, orphanages, refuges, hospitals and other works; and there must follow ... the formation of indigenous religious of both sexes.[1]

The dangers of a purely European Church was clearly recognised, in theory at least, as inappropriate to the African culture, and in his encyclical letter *Rerum Ecclesiae* of 28 February 1936, Pius XI exhorted the Bishops of missionary territories to "institute native religious Congregations ('Sodalitates') of both sexes in which aspirants may profess the evangelical counsels". In an *Instruction* issued by the Sacred Congregation of Religious in 1937, bishops were given precise information as to the various steps to be taken to establish such "a Congregation of Natives ... on the model of an Institute flourishing with religious life in the Church".[2] It was not a simple process as time was to prove, but for the Dominicans of the newly formed Region of South Africa it had practical as well as spiritual significance.

Mother Teresa Coleman, the new Regional Vicar, was at heart an enthusiastic missionary, and she was well aware of the practical need for Coloured sisters to teach in the growing number of mission schools which the Dominican communities had opened in the Eastern and Western Cape. In addition Coloured aspirants would not be part of the Congregation of Irish Dominican Sisters but would form a diocesan congregation, free from the restrictions of enclosure. They would be competent in Afrikaans, their mother tongue, and would have a good understanding of their own people. The General Council in Cabra, Ireland also recognised the need for such a development and saw no reason why the Region of South Africa should not give to the local bishop the help he needed to establish a new Coloured institute on a firm religious and professional footing. Support also came from the clergy who saw in the promotion of indigenous sisterhoods an obedient and inexpensive work force which they needed in schools and parishes.

Father C R Murphy, who in 1933 had brought Mothers Reginald and Alberta on a guided tour around the African Locations in the vicinity of Uitenhage, and had pleaded the cause of the neglected people there, wrote in 1940 to Mother Reginald, newly elected Prioress General of the Congregation of Irish Dominican Sisters:

> One thing seems very clear in our S. African educational system. It is this. If this Church is to keep step with our modern trend in school affairs we must have Coloured Sisters. Every day the difficulty of getting European Sisters appointed to Coloured schools grows more difficult. The slogan is Coloured teachers for Coloured schools. The Dept. of Education is acting on that policy. You are high up in the

Councils of the Dominicans at home, you must throw in your influence and weight towards its accomplishment.

He saw in institutions such as the newly founded Coloured Vocational School at St Colmcille's Mission, Kirkwood the promise of future vocations. It was evident to him that the human potential was there. "Training and discipline will bring into the field a good reliable class of Coloured Sister". He quoted the example of the King William's Town Dominicans who had "after years of patient trial got some very good Native Sisters". He could not see that the problem of getting Coloured sisters was so different since they were of "European descent", a fact that would make the "formation of their Religious Life easier".[3] In a letter written at the same time to Mother Colmcille Flynn whom he had met during her visit in 1938 to the newly amalgamated South African Region, he again pleads for a Coloured foundation basing his argument on his familiarity with St Colmcille's School and Convent of Mary Immaculate, Kirkwood:

> The Church of St Colmcille and also [the] grounds [are] a thing of beauty. It looks really a picture. It is supposed to be one of the best buildings in town. The class of children is just surprising, bright, happy, and intelligent, only awaiting the development of character which the Sisters' tuition is securing them. Mother Vicar's [Teresa Coleman] scheme for a Domestic Science Course will just complete the bill. We are up against great odds in our schools for Coloureds. If we are to retain our hold in the struggle, it seems to me, the best way to meet the new situation is to get Coloured nuns for the posts. ... The children who go through the Sisters' hands, should with extra post-school care make a success of the new life. ... It will take time and careful training, but will succeed. I am not alone in this thinking. Many of our Priests see no other way.[4]

Bishop Henneman together with Mother Teresa and her Council who, in terms of the Roman Instructions of 1923 and 1936, collaborated in the foundation of the diocesan Institute of St Rose of Lima, had little realisation of the extreme force of new apartheid legislation which, following the Nationalist victory at the polls in 1948, would be used to constrain and oppress the African, Coloured and Indian people of the African sub-continent. It became increasingly difficult to accept, in a climate of severe oppression and injustice, that any form of authority wielded by white men or women, under whatever guise, was anything other than the by-product of racial discrimination. Many young women, virtuous and eager though they were to accept a life of dedication to the service of God, often saw in the novitiate training further evidence of the oppression by White against Black. Nor had the Dominican sisters of the Cape surrendered the inherited snobbery that was part of their impedimenta from 1863 onwards. They had become part of colonial society, serving both the wealthy and the poor with equal devotion but not in the same institutions, and certainly not in contravention of contemporary norms and social divisions, including the separate education of Europeans and indigenous peoples. While the sisters of the Dominican Region of South Africa had, prior to 1938, long experience in Coloured schools and in the instruction of adults, often parents or family members of their pupils, they had never, with one or two possible exceptions, received recruits from the Coloured sector of the population. There is no overt mention of any Coloured applicants being accepted by either of the two congregations, nor is there any comment on the acceptability or otherwise of such recruits. The Catholic schools had followed in principle the accepted practice in South Africa of separate schools for European, Coloured and African pupils. However the latter two groups were often mixed in Catholic schools.

Although the sisters had no Coloured members in their communities, in their schools they promoted lay groups including that of Dominican Tertiaries. This was one way of sharing Dominican ideals and religious teaching with lay men and women, and for the young women concerned it also served as an introduction to the possibility of life-long commitment as Dominican sisters. In 1938 two pupils of St Augustine's School at Wittebome, Angeline Fortes, and Mabel Meyer, 17 and 15 years old respectively, asked Mother Emelia, the much loved Principal of St Augustine's School, Wittebome, to help them to fulfil their wish to become religious sisters and devote their lives to the service of God. Since the Irish Congregation had no Coloured foundation, the two aspirants applied to the Holy Cross at Parow, where a Coloured novitiate had just been opened. It was not however their first choice and when Mother Teresa was approached she promised to do all in her power to solve their problem. She realised that all aspirants, without exception, needed a sound education. As she had done in the case of most of the novices who had come from Potter's Bar in the 1930's, she set the two young girls to study, housing them in the School for the Deaf at Wittebome, and sending them to the Secondary School nearby. There they spent two years completing their studies for Junior Certificate. In 1941 they were sent to Holy Trinity Convent, Matroosfontein and from there they attended the Catholic Training College run by the Holy Cross Sisters at Parow.

Although Mother Teresa was full of zeal for the new undertaking there were many canonical and practical points to be considered. By 1942, when decisions had to be made as to the nature of the new Institute and its relationship with the Irish Dominican Congregation, the political situation in Europe precluded interchange of visits or personal exchange of ideas between the Prioress General in Cabra and the Regional Vicar in Cape Town. Already the South African Dominicans, the newest member of the Congregation, were, in relation to their Irish houses, at a political disadvantage. The outbreak of war in September 1939 had prevented the South African delegates from attending the third General Chapter of the Congregation of Irish Dominican Sisters. This would have been the first opportunity of the newly constituted Region of South Africa to present its case personally, through its own delegates, and to share with the representatives of the eleven Irish convents, the urgency of the missionary needs in the Region of South Africa, and the importance of a foundation for Coloured aspirants. Nevertheless the step was not taken without consultation and a careful survey of the work done by other congregations for the promotion of indigenous religious in Africa.

Such indigenous foundations were not without precedent in Africa and one of the models considered was that used by the Killeshandra Sisters in Nigeria. This was a natural choice since the Sisters of the Holy Rosary were themselves foster children of the Cabra Dominicans. Admission to their "Native Sisterhood" in Nigeria depended not only on perceived motivation and the suitability of the aspirant's temperament, but they had to be "sufficiently well educated to be able to follow instructions on the religious life (given in English) and read simple books", as well as having the potential for training for professions such as nursing and teaching.[5] The Institute of St Rose of Lima placed educational standards of aspirants somewhat higher, initially making Std VI the minimum requirement for admission. This was about the same level as that demanded of quite a number of the Irish girls from rural areas, who in the three decades prior to amalgamation had entered in Cape Town and Potter's Bar. Indeed the same level of academic attainment also held good for some of the choir sisters and postulants who were sent from Sion Hill and Cabra during the nineteenth century. That in both cases a number of postulants were already qualified teachers or were at least ready to begin a qualifying course, is evident from the records, but the relatively low academic standards required for admission to postulancy, did not always augur well for the future development of the young institute. During the short life of the

Institute of St Rose of Lima the education and training of the sisters was the object of constant concern to the Dominican superiors, often with excellent results.

Not so easy to determine and make acceptable to the members of the Institute was the question of status. Neither the Nigerian model nor that of the King William's Town Dominicans was acceptable in every respect, though sound guidelines and useful alternatives were suggested. The former provided for a separate congregation guided at the outset by the Sisters of the Holy Rosary, and under the direct jurisdiction of their Vicar Apostolic. It was envisaged that such communities would become independent in the course of time.[6] On the other hand the indigenous foundations made by the Congregation of King William's Town Dominicans, enjoyed full membership of the founding body, with the same Constitution, but the Native sisters lived separately in Districts, under Vicaresses, and not in European communities.[7] Fr Thomas Garde OP, writing from Rome in September 1943, proposed to the Prioress General, Mother Reginald Lyons, three ways in which she could proceed:

> I received your important letter of July 31st. This time I approached the S. Congregation of Religious, and explained your project. They pointed out that you may proceed in *three* ways: (1) The Native Sisterhood to form an integral part of the Irish Dominican Congregation. ... I don't think we need dwell on this project, as, apparently, you have no idea of making the native Sisterhood a party to the Cabra Congregation; and in this you are, I think, quite right.
> (2) The native Sisterhood be aggregated ... to the Cabra Congregation. ... there is no need of any special permission from this Congregation at this stage, as the vows the native Sisters will take, though taken publicly, are not considered as canonical vows. So you may proceed with the approval and under the direction of the Vicar Apostolic.
> (3) You may, in these early stages, consider this group of native Sisters as a pious sodality, which later will be developed into a separate Congregation. In this case you need no other authority than that of the Vicar Apostolic. [8]

The unreliability of the wartime postal services made it very difficult to conclude any business between Rome, Ireland and South Africa. Almost two months and two lost letters later, Father Garde made the position of Rome clear in respect of new indigenous sisterhoods:

> I approached the S. Congregation of Religious on the matter. They informed me that the Holy See is opposed to separate

(modified) Constitutions for native Sisters as this would seem to put them in a position of inferiority. I pointed out how difficult it would be for the coloured Sisters to conform to the Cabra Constitutions - the Divine Office for instance. Anyhow the Congregation thought it better that you should proceed for the present with the permission of the Vicar Apostolic, so that the Native Sisterhood should be for the present 'Juris diocesani'. They refused *for the present*, permission for a native Sisterhood, which would be part of the Cabra Congregation, but with modified Constitutions, and advise you to proceed with the permission and authority of the Vicar Apostolic.[9]

The St Rose's Institute was to adopt part of the Constitution of the founding Congregation and substitute the Little Office of the Virgin Mary for the Divine Office. As with the Region of South Africa there was to be only one class of sister. The postulants wore a "steel grey" dress which had "proved very satisfactory for the Tertiaries". For professed members of the Institute there was a white habit and scapular, a black veil and a cappa. The guimp and coif were to be "soft, and differently arranged from those of the Sisters of our Congregation".[10]

For the two aspirants the four years of study, culminating in the attainment of a Primary Teachers Certificate, prepared them for the next important phase in their new life. Indeed it was the second major step towards their goal. On 10 February 1941, Father Oswin Magrath OP had received them as Dominican Tertiaries. This was a familiar road in the history of Dominican women, many of whom moved from the life of lay Dominicans to the conventual life, though not without many vicissitudes. On the Feast of the Epiphany, 6 January 1943, the two aspirants were admitted as postulants by Mother Teresa, and immediately began teaching in Holy Trinity School. It was the beginning of a new era for the sisters themselves and for the Coloured community. It also opened up fresh vistas for the Irish Dominican Vicariate and for the Congregation of Irish Dominican Sisters as a whole, since St Rose's Institute, when it was given formal recognition, was placed under the jurisdiction of the Mother Vicar of the Region of South Africa. Sisters Mabel Meyer and Angeline Fortes found in Holy Trinity Convent inspiration, living as they were with women such as Mother Colmcille Nagle who, during the first years of the new Institute, combined the offices of local Prioress and Mistress of Postulants. Her untiring work for the spiritual and material development of the poor on the Cape Flats, and her sympathy with the aspirations of the young Coloured postulants, made her a convincing role model for those at the beginning of a life devoted to apostolic work. To her Dominican sisters and to the local community she became a legend even in her own lifetime both for her charitable works, and for her uncompromising approach to and forthright condemnation of the unrepentant delinquent.

By the *Decree of Erection of the Institute of St. Rose of Lima, affiliated to the Holy Order of St. Dominic*, issued 15 January 1944, under the seal of Francis Henneman, Titular Bishop of Coptus and Vicar Apostolic of Cape Town, the new Coloured community was given official recognition by the Church.[11] Eighteen days later, on 2 February 1944 the two founding members, Sister Dominic Fortes and Sister Catherine Meyer, received the habit and under the guidance of Sister Francis Carton, entered into their formal year of canonical novitiate. After a second year of novitiate, during which they taught in Holy Trinity Mission School, they were professed. On the 20 January 1946 a Pontifical High Mass was celebrated by Bishop Henneman with a choir of Dominican nuns. Father Ninian McManus preached, just one more example of the constant service given at this time by the Dominican Fathers of Stellenbosch to their Sisters in religion. It was a day of rejoicing but of sadness too. There was little sign of growth in the new community. Between 1944 and 1950 five aspirants joined the novitiate but three, for one reason or another, returned home. It was to be the pattern which became all too familiar in the two decades that followed.[12]

In December 1947 Dorothy Kotze, a trained primary teacher, and a gifted musician, entered and began her postulancy. Two years later she received the habit and the name Sister Rose. In March 1949, a third recruit, Sally Louw, 34 years old, a convert to Catholicism and a qualified teacher, who had taught in St Augustine's School, Wittebome prior to her acceptance as a postulant, joined the novitiate. These sisters were fortunate to have the guidance of Mother Catherine Dixon during the first crucial years of their religious training. She had just completed a term of office as General Councillor in Ireland, and had experience in the charge and training of novices in Tamnaharrie, Ireland. An eminently suitable choice, she was installed as Novice Mistress at Matroosfontein on 15 June 1948. This was the decision of the 1948 General Chapter:

> The inception of a new Congregation is a work requiring prayer and sacrifice as well as training by an experienced Mistress. It was agreed that the best efforts of the Congregation should be put into this great work. The proposal of the Council General to send Mother Catherine Dixon to Africa for a few years to train these Coloured Sisters was unanimously

approved. On these Sisters rest our hope of an apostolate in
the Coloured Schools.[13]

Mother Catherine spent less than three years as Novice
Mistress in Matroosfontein. In September 1951 she was appointed
Regional Vicar, replacing the much loved Mother Colmcille Flynn
in that office. However her interest, concern and work for the
Coloured sisters found a new and powerful outlet. As Prioress
General of the St Rose's community she could do much to ensure
that they were given every opportunity to further their secular
and religious training, and their ministry in the schools. The
task of recruitment was also given primacy of place though St
Rose's never became a sizeable body of sisters. However, many of
those who came, and after a period of time returned to the secular
life, as lay women, later rendered valuable and willing service to
Catholic education in South Africa, and some later became
Dominican Tertiaries.

At the beginning of April 1951 three new recruits were
welcomed by both Mother Catherine and the two novices, Sister
Rose Kotze and Sister Agnes Louw. Of the three, one left after
eight months, the second after two years of temporary profession
and one, Letchmy Pillay, in religion Sister Martin who was in her
twenty second year and a qualified teacher, persevered. Between
1944 and 1967, 49 candidates entered the postulancy of the
Institute of St Rose of Lima. Of these 37 returned home and 12
persevered. Of the total number that entered, only 18 reached
Final Profession and of these six ultimately left the Convent. Of
the other 31, at least 15 returned home in their postulancy, nine
after the reception of the habit and seven in temporary vows. It
was a small harvest after so much effort, and the onus of apostolic
work fell on those who persevered.[14]

With remarkable speed, considering the length of novitiate
training, the St Rose's sisters moved into the Coloured schools
originally founded and staffed by members of the Congregation
of Irish Dominican Sisters, and supported by lay teachers. In
1959, Sister Catherine Meyer, after teaching in Holy Trinity and
St Augustine's, was appointed Principal of St Joseph's Coloured
Primary School in Cape Town, and four years later she took up
the same post in St Augustine's, Wittebome. Sister Dominic Fortes
taught in Holy Trinity, in St Teresa's Cape Town, and in Ida's
Valley, Stellenbosch. In January 1963 she was assigned to the
Convent of Mary Immaculate in Kirkwood and in December of
that year was appointed Principal of Blessed Reginald's Mission
School. The St Rose's Sisters made their first foundation in
Uitenhage in January 1953. It was there in 1959 that Sister Rose

Kotze took over the principalship of St Joseph's Coloured Primary School. Sister Martin Pillay also taught for a number of years in the Uitenhage school, and in 1965 she was appointed Principal of Holy Trinity School, Matroosfontein.

Sister Assumpta de Villiers, commenced her postulancy in 1953, the year of the Uitenhage foundation. She received the habit in 1954 and made her Final Profession in 1959. In 1954 Sister James Williams joined the novitiate, and the Report of the Regional Vicar for the period June 1947 to January 1954 records there were four professed of St Rose's Congregation, two in final and two in temporary vows. These together with five novices and four postulants constituted the St Rose's community. Of these, three professed sisters were stationed at the new convent at 11 Dale Street, Uitenhage, with Mother Martin Tuohy as Prioress. The St Rose's Sisters taught in St Joseph's Mission School under the principalship of Sister Alvarez Magee until 1959 when Sister Rose Kotze was to be appointed principal. Seven years later, in 1966 Sister Rose was made Prioress of the Dale Street Convent. This foundation, though it did not involve the opening of a new school, created fresh opportunities for missionary work in the area. Mother Teresa reported:

> Since their arrival in Uitenhage a new impetus has been given to the growth of the Catholic Church in that district. They have organised the Parish Choir so that both adults and children take part with the Sisters in singing Mass on Sundays and Benediction on two days a week. ... It was providential that the Settlement of fifty T.B. patients, Coloured and Natives, should have been started at the same time as our Convent in Dale Street. The Sisters have been asked to help and have begun in a small way.[15]

In December 1960 St Joseph's Convent, Ida's Valley, Stellenbosch, was formally opened by Archbishop McCann, the ecclesiastical superior of St Rose's Congregation. Because of the shortage of sisters only two of the St Rose's community were available for this new foundation.[16] For 21 years the Catholic Mission School at Ida's Valley had been served from Aquinas Convent and all the Dominican communities in the Cape Peninsula had contributed financially to its support. This had been done directly and through support of the annual school bazaar. It was in Ida's Valley that the valuable interaction between the Dominican brethren of St Nicholas' Priory and the community of Aquinas Convent found a rich missionary outlet. The influence of the Sisters of St Rose of Lima soon made itself felt. "We hope to increase their number as more sisters become available", wrote the Regional

Vicar, Mother Jordan Keary. "Already the effect of their presence in the Valley and the visitation work done by them, accompanied by our sisters is evident in the greatly increased numbers at Holy Mass and the Sacraments". In the Valley as in other areas where St Rose's sisters contributed to the missionary work of the local Church, the "instruction of Converts, visiting the houses, training parish choirs, organising days of Retreat and recollection ... [were] all being carried on as successfully as before".[17]

Between 1957 and 1960 five aspirants entered, Sister Immaculata da Rocha in 1956 and Sister Paul Cloete in 1957. Three years later, in 1960, Sister Vincent Saldhana, Sister Annunciata Veitch and Sister Raymund (Gloria) September joined them. The 1960's was a period of intensive work and development in the schools, and the pressure to improve academic and professional qualifications was increasing in both the Irish Congregation and in the Institute of St Rose of Lima. In the case of the former, most of the sisters from Kerdiffstown had entered after completing their secondary education and only a minority were qualified teachers. Of those admitted to the novitiate at Matroosfontein, five were trained teachers with some professional experience, and of the remainder, the majority had reached Std 8 level or lower. Sister Martin Pillay completed her Senior Certificate through private study in 1963, and in 1965 with Sister Catherine Meyer, began to study for a BA Degree at Belville University College, later the University of the Western Cape. Most of the sisters attended Parow Catholic Training College but two, Sisters Vincent Saldanha and Annuntiata Veitch completed their Senior Certificate and were sent to Hewat Training College where they obtained their Senior Primary Teachers' Certificate. At a time when pre-school education was developing in the South African system, the need for competent teachers was felt in all the schools, and those run by St Rose's Congregation were no exception. In 1965 Sisters Assumpta de Villiers and Immaculata de Rocha attended Athlone Training Centre for Nursery School Teachers, and three years later Sister James Williams successfully completed the same course.[18]

But by the mid-1960's the Congregation of St Rose of Lima had other concerns besides those of running schools and achieving academic and professional excellence. The growing pressure of the apartheid system focused attention on the inequalities experienced by the Coloured, African and Indian sectors of the community, and this no less in the cloister than in secular society. The Coloured sisters, were living in a mixed society where the European members, seconded to St Rose's, trained the Coloured aspirants in religious life, and generally held most of the positions of authority. In view of the perceived inequalities inherent in such a situation, the St Rose's community found it difficult not to interpret the roles of European sisters as evidence of the acceptance and application of apartheid principles in religious life. And feelings of discontent with the system were not one-sided. Not all of those who, for a time at least, became part of the St Rose's community, were at home in the environment so different from that for which their own training had prepared them. And for some the temporary substitution of the Little Office of the Blessed Virgin for the Divine Office, was a loss too great to sustain. It was an undeniable fact that the two cultures, though each was rich in itself, did not always blend. This was most likely to occur when, due to adverse circumstances, negative aspects and points of difference concerning professional work or conventual practice were stressed, to the detriment of mutual tolerance and charity. Sometimes in a time of racial tension it was inevitable, despite goodwill, to misinterpret an appointment to office, a simple reprimand or word of advice, as attempts to denigrate or deliberately to insult.[19]

Added to cultural and social differences was the fact that in terms of Canon Law there was a clear legal distinction between the two Congregations, one was of pontifical and the other of diocesan right. Such a difference in status could lead to unfortunate conclusions not complimentary to the Irish Congregation. Such was especially the case in a political milieu where harshly applied laws imposing "separate development", fuelled hatred and mutual distrust in society at large. This danger was recognised both by the nuns of the Irish Dominican Congregation and by the Sisters of St Rose of Lima. It was one of the factors that contributed to the loss of valuable members of the latter community, some of whom in their short time in the convent, had made a generous contribution to the Dominican apostolate, both in the schools and among the adults who came within their sphere of influence.

The contrast between the two congregations was great. In September 1963 the Congregation celebrated in Cape Town the centenary of the first foundation made by Dominican women in Southern Africa, while the affiliated Institute of St Rose of Lima had from its formal inauguration, completed only 19 years. In the period between October 1961 and July 1965, 24 Dominican sisters, among whom were four South Africans, came out from Kerdiffstown, the novitiate in Ireland. These were ready to take up their work in the schools or to continue their academic and professional training.[20] There were 264 sisters in the Dominican

Region of South Africa of whom only 13 were incapacited by sickness or old age.[21] During the same period St Rose's had a total of 21 sisters. Of these, 11 had made final and seven temporary profession and three were in their postulancy.[22] Compared with that, the Dominican Congregation was a formidable body, both in itself and in its union with the Congregation in Ireland. It is little wonder then, that the St Rose's sisters sought in the latter the status and support that they needed to promote their mission and their own spiritual and intellectual life. Both the St Rose's sisters themselves and their superiors in the Dominican Congregation, wanted to see the Institute develop, not in isolation as a diocesan congregation, but linked in some way to the Irish Congregation. This was a logical step since the "spirit of the Congregation ... [was] wholly Dominican and the Rule [was] based on that of the Cabra Sisters with appropriate modifications".[23]

When in 1957 the Regional Vicar, Mother Catherine Dixon successfully applied to the Master General on behalf of the sisters of the Institute of St Rose of Lima, there was no question of amalgamation.

> The Congregation has diocesan status and while in no way wishing that this should be changed, it is our wish to petition Your Paternity for aggregation of the Congregation to the Dominican Order so that the Sisters may be members of the Dominican family. The Constitutions have been approved by His Grace Most Reverend Archbishop McCann. The enclosed printed leaflet will explain the character of the Congregation which we all feel will grow and prosper all the more surely if it has the benefit of unity with the Order and can live by the Order's life and spirit. In view of the trend of civil legislation in South Africa it is becoming more and more imperative that vocations should be fostered among the people of this country of all races so that the work of the Church and the Order may go on unimpeded.[24]

In January 1964, Mother Jordan Keary, Prioress General, visited South Africa to hold formal visitation. At the same time the Regional Council consulted her about the vexed question of the status and future development of the Institute of St Rose of Lima. At a meeting held on 24 March 1964 the question of the "establishment of St. Rose's as a separate Congregation and the constitutional changes which this would bring about", were discussed. It was agreed that a Prioress General and General Council of St Rose's would be appointed by the Mother Prioress General of the Congregation of Irish Dominican Sisters. The new higher superior would issue assignations, and the members of the Institute would be answerable to their own Prioress General, and not as in the past, to the Regional Vicar. In addition the former would be responsible for the appointment of prioresses to St Rose's communities. It was also agreed "that property should be registered in the name of St Rose's Congregation, and debts transferred to them", and also that the newly appointed head of the St Rose's Sisters in all her official actions, would be directly responsible to the Prioress General in Cabra .[25]

In April 1964, a month after these important decisions had been taken, but not put into effect, the *Constitutions of the Institute of St Rose of Lima* were approved by Rome. The new *Constitutions* were a compromise. The early drafts based on the model of the 1947 Constitutions of the Congregation of Irish Dominican Sisters had to be adapted, a task in which Father Oswin Magrath OP gave valuable assistance. In April 1956 he had offered some "rather radical criticism" of the draft document.

> In view of the present situation, which may soon lead to these Sisters ceasing to benefit from the close living together at present part of their training, it is important that they have definite lines, where necessary different from those of the Irish Sisters, of training and development. Both the apartheid policy and the rapidly growing independence of the Coloured people, will probably bring this greater separation about. A second consideration is that wherever they are placed, they will need both to be able to assist in any and every work of the church, and may also have to earn their own living by other ways than education, which may be largely closed to them. Their purpose must therefore be of the widest possible.

Magrath also proposed the curtailment of the "choral and devotional exercises". He quoted the King William's Town Dominicans' example in respect of suffrages for the dead and he also pointed out that Rome did not favour the practice of weekly recital of the Office of the Dead. On the question of enclosure, he like Gijlswijk before him, took a broad view: "Enclosure - again on the Fathers' lines - should apply only to the convent, not to the Sisters, and the local superior should have all powers to allow egress. This I think is essential if they are to be free to do mission work properly."[26] The Constitutions approved by Rome in 1964 reflected most of these amendments, but like the 1947 revised Constitutions of the Congregation of Irish Dominican Sisters, they were not only to have a short life span, but in many respects they were inappropriate in a rapidly changing society.

For some of the European sisters seconded to the Institute of St Rose of Lima, the application of the new regulations to their own lives was a positive step into the second half of the twentieth century. For others the reduced liturgy was a betrayal of all that their training had conditioned them to hold most dear. Although European sisters could not be assigned to St Rose's without their own personal consent, most would hesitate to question an assignation given to them in the name of obedience. Consequently there was a growing need to define their own status as seconded members of the Irish Congregation and to clarify their voting rights within the Institute of St Rose of Lima and at Regional Chapters.[27] Despite community problems exacerbated by the spirit engendered by oppressive apartheid legislation, the Roman approval of the *Constitutions* was a milestone in the history of St Rose's community. The major superiors of the Irish Congregation were prepared to do all in their power to support and develop the young foundation. Indeed it seemed that the road ahead was clear for the St Rose's sisters to expand and move towards greater freedom in their chosen mission. While the implementation of the March proposals might take some time, the goodwill was there. But Mother Jordan Keary had scarcely returned to Ireland after her visit to South Africa when a crisis arose.

Later in 1964 a group of religious men and women had planned secretly to set up a Secular Institute. These included two of the St Rose's sisters, "seven European Teaching Brothers in South Africa and five elsewhere", together with "at least two European Sisters who eventually withdrew". The participants applied for dispensation from their vows, the Brothers to Rome and the St Rose's sisters to their local bishop. The Brothers would seek ordination and, "in the guise of seculares", would work in State Schools and in factories or other places where their apostolic thrust would be most effective. The sisters would have their own convent and would share in the mission of the priests. They would initiate their project in Boston, USA and later return to South Africa. In the event the Holy See refused to grant dispensation to the Brothers, and the plan, not without merit in its vision of the needs of the contemporary Church, had to be abandoned. The whole affair had a profoundly deleterious affect on the Institute of St Rose of Lima. In 1964 two finally professed sisters obtained dispensation from their vows and in the same year three sisters in temporary vows and two postulants left the Institute. This was at a time, when the St Rose's sisters, of whom five held the position of principals, were responsible for approximately 2800 pupils in five Coloured Primary Schools. It was a crippling loss, not just in terms of personnel but in the threat it posed to the very survival of the Institute.

Mother Damian Madden, Regional Vicar, and Prioress General of the Institute of St Rose of Lima, knew that drastic action would have to be taken without delay:

> This movement caused uneasiness throughout St Rose's Congregation and many of the Sisters were becoming unsettled. We discussed this crisis at a Council Meeting at St. Mary's and it was decided that the matter should be referred to Reverend Mother Prioress General. It was felt that her presence was needed at this critical time and she was asked to return to South Africa to be on the spot in case major decisions regarding both Congregations had to be made.

Mother Jordan Keary, who had just returned to Ireland when this request came, laid aside her onerous work at Cabra and willingly returned to Cape Town. She had held office as Regional Vicar in South Africa from 1960-1961, prior to her election as Prioress General at the 1961 General Chapter. Her personal experience of the Sisters of St Rose's had given her an understanding of progress made and the tensions and problems created in the two Congregations as a consequence of differences in culture and the influence of the application of apartheid policies of the Nationalist Government. She had sympathy for the sisters who had lost loved and respected colleagues and friends with whom they had lived and worked. She realised that this had aroused in the diminished community a sense of insecurity, and the need to define more clearly the status of the Institute of St Rose of Lima as a religious body affiliated to the Dominican Order, and its relationship with the Irish Congregation. But she was also realistic. In June of 1964 she had written to Mother Damian: "I was glad to get all the news and especially of St Rose's. Please God the unsettled Sisters will settle down or decide to go - their unsettled state of mind is bad for all - not only themselves".[28] That some had left the convent came as no surprise to her, but the needs of those who remained became her first priority.

In late December 1964, Mother Jordan Keary together with Mother Damian Madden, the Prioress General of the St Rose's Institute, spent three days with the community at Matroosfontein, where St Rose's sisters had come together for the holidays. Time and opportunity for private and public discussion ensured that the community could consider the options best suited to their own situation. On 9 January 1965, when all the ideas and proposals had been considered, the Regional Council together with Mother Jordan discussed every aspect of the question. Until their numbers increased it was considered impracticable to give the St Rose's sisters a Prioress General, but the establishment of a separate Council would give them some direct participation in their own affairs. The Regional Council nominated the two founding members, Sister Dominic Fortes, as first councillor and Sister Catherine Meyer as third councillor. The positions of second and fourth Councillor were to be held by Sister Dympna Carew and Sister Ambrose Doherty respectively. The latter was a recent and much loved volunteer from Sion Hill, Ireland. "There was great rejoicing when this news was heard", wrote the annalist, "We were very glad that Mother Teresa, who had done so much for the Congregation in its infancy, was here to join in the rejoicing and congratulate the new Mothers on their appointment. It is a sign that the Congregation is 'coming of age' as it will be twenty - one years founded on January 16, [1965]".[29]

A minimum of two statutory meetings were to be held annually but St Rose's Council could meet more frequently if necessary. It was realised that St Rose's would not be financially viable if the Regional subsidies were withdrawn.[30] Though it was a small start and did little to increase the actual independence of the Institute of St Rose of Lima, it took place in a period of great change in the Church. The immediate post-Vatican period of *aggiornamento* was for women religious the dawn of a new spring, and the Dominican Congregation to which the St Rose's community was closely linked, was to become deeply involved in the searching process of constitutional change and spiritual renewal. This would include a reconsideration of the position of the Institute of St Rose of Lima, a process in which all the sisters would be personally involved.

The next most significant stage was discussed at the 1967 General Chapter in Ireland. While the slow growth of the St Rose's foundation was noted with regret, the sisters needed to be given more responsibility for their own government as the Regional Vicar of South Africa noted:

> Mother M. Angels Donnellan reminded the Chapter that up to this the Mother Vicar of the Region has been the Mother General of St. Rose's Congregation. This arrangement, in her opinion, is no longer desirable. It would be better for them to have a Mother General who would be entirely their own - not also Vicar of our Congregation, - but not necessarily either a Sister of St. Rose's Congregation. ... The Chapter commissioned Mother Vicar and her Council to discuss the major issues with St Rose's Congregation.[31]

When she returned to Cape Town later in the year, Mother Angels immediately set about the legal process of appointing Mother Martina Lennon Prioress General of the St Rose's sisters.[32] Three days later she informed St Rose's and the Region of the closure of the Dale Street Convent in Uitenhage, and later of the mutual decision of St Rose's and the Regional Council that the local apostolic work would be carried out by the sisters of the Irish Congregation.[33] As the result of a strong representation made to Bishop E Green, three sisters were left in Uitenhage to maintain St Joseph's Schools, but the house in Dale Street was sold to raise funds for building a Nursery School. At the same time negotiations were begun with the Bishop for the building of a convent for St Rose's sisters but in the event, no such convent was ever built.[34]

By two separate Decrees issued by Cardinal Owen McCann in January 1968, the new Congregation of St Rose of Lima was established. Mother Jordan Keary spoke to the assembled communities:

> His Eminence Owen Cardinal Archbishop, having held consultation with the Sisters, had decided that St Rose's is to function as an independent Congregation for the present. In order that ample time may be given for further consideration of the sisters' expressed wishes for a Region and of the possibility of implementing this later on, He has appointed Mother Martina Lennon to the office of Prioress General of the Congregation. ... - subject only to the Cardinal - and that she has all the authority attached to the office in all that concerns the Convents of St. Rose's Congregation, including the Sisters seconded to it. The Sisters seconded retain, however, their rights to their own Congregation - this is Canon Law - and each sister is free to be returned to it, at any time.[35]

Four sisters were appointed to the General Council: Sisters Dominic Fortes, Imelda O'Hara, Agnes Louw and Josepha Mullen. It was the completion of the 1964 plan and the opening phase of the last years of St Rose's Congregation as a separate, potentially independent entity. At a meeting of the Council held on 31 March 1969, the question of the future of the Congregation was discussed. The choices were clear. Theoretically they could choose to form a separate and independent congregation, but in reality without the seconded Cabra sisters and the subsidies contributed by the Irish Dominicans in South Africa, they had neither the numerical strength nor the financial means to support such a body. Their economic situation would not have been sound even with the benefit of teachers' salaries they could earn by working in the schools that had been founded, staffed and maintained by the Irish Dominicans, and handed over to the St Rose's Congregation. A second and more viable alternative was to form another South African Region of the Congregation. This implied that the St Rose's sisters would fall under the jurisdiction of the Irish Congregation, and gain pontifical status, but it would not solve the economic problems nor was it likely that in the absence of local aspirants, it would attract recruits from Ireland. The final proposal was complete integration into the Congregation of Irish Dominican Sisters which would make St Rose's part of the Dominican Region of South Africa.

A Capitular Conference of St Rose's Congregation commenced during the last week of September 1969. Besides being an opportunity for spiritual renewal, it was also for the elected delegates, a time for serious discussion on and decisions about the future of St Rose's. Some of the sessions were open and this ensured the widest possible consensus of opinion. There are few detailed records of the meetings of the delegates but the arguments for and against the various options were well summarised in September 1969, by Mons J P Murphy, Vicar General of the Diocese of Port Elizabeth. Of the eighteen sisters he interviewed in the course of visitation, 13 were in favour of amalgamation, four preferred a separate region and one a separate congregation. Mons Murphy summed up the reasons for each choice. How would the public view religious apparently divided on racist terms?

> A separate region would smack too much of separation in the sense of apartheid. It is virtually impossible to explain to the general run of people how Sisters can be the same and yet separate. A separate region is even less acceptable than a separate Congregation. A separate Congregation could not exist on its own for any length of time because of lack of finance; and also a lack of personnel who would be capable of taking charge of various offices, particularly in the Novitiate. All in favour of amalgamation wish to be Dominicans, sharing everything, everything except where prohibited by Civil Law. Charity demands amalgamation. Amalgamation would secure a higher standard in the Novitiate, greater opportunities in the academic life of the Sisters.

Those who favoured a separate region also had valid arguments on their side. It was seen as an easy step to future amalgamation "or even to a separate congregation". The sisters had not entered the Dominican Congregation but that of St Rose's, and if becoming a Dominican meant going through another novitiate, that was unacceptable. And some had real doubts as to their welcome in the Dominican Congregation. Indeed it would not be a happy solution to find oneself "tagged on to another congregation".[36] On 3 October 1969 the Capitular Conference of the Congregation of St Rose of Lima, in which at this time there were 17 professed sisters, two who had made promises, and two postulants, made a formal petition to the Prioress General of the Congregation of Irish Dominican Sisters.[37]

> After much deliberation, prayer, weighing of all the advantages and disadvantages of amalgamation, discussion of the subject with His Eminence, Cardinal Owen McCann and after the unanimous vote of the members of the Capitular Conference of the Congregation of St. Rose of Lima in favour of amalgamation. We ... petition most humbly and earnestly for total amalgamation with the Irish Congregation of Dominican Sisters ... We members of the Capitular Conference realise, that owing to the apartheid laws of this country of South Africa, that there of necessity must be two Novitiates and that Coloured Sisters must reside in declared Coloured areas; nevertheless, we are of the opinion, that it is only through amalgamation with the Irish Congregation of Dominican Sisters that we can develop spiritually, culturally and numerically. Therefore, we humbly present our petition, profess our loyalty and our readiness to accept and abide by the decision of the Irish Congregation of Dominican Sisters.[38]

In view of the growing violence in South Africa and the stubborn intransigence of the Nationalist Government in the face of national and international opposition to and criticism of the apartheid system, Mother Isidore Collins, Prioress General of the Irish Congregation had serious reservations as to the wisdom of immediate amalgamation, and she had a number of serious questions demanding well-considered answers:

> Did the Sisters consider what would happen should the Irish Congregation be forced to leave? I'm sure they did, but at the moment rational argument is drowned in a surge of emotional desire for present security. Let us take some time for further thought and prayer; but assure them, Mother, that their request is being sympathetically considered.[39]

Mother Isidore put the matter to a Canon lawyer, Father Ambrose Duffy OP, and in November 1969 wrote to Mother Martina Lennon:

> He thinks we would hardly be justified in going further than the setting up of a Region since the other type of integration

had not been considered by the General Chapter. Would the St. Rose's ever be convinced that a Region *is* complete integration but of a different kind from what they visualise, especially if it were put to them that we have the power to give that but not the other. In the event of their pushing for the other now we should have to get at least the consultative vote of each Sister of the Region. That might not be in their favour. On the other hand if we try out the region, sisters may, later on, be convinced that they could go further. As far as possible we would wish to have goodwill on both sides in the case.

She had also consulted Cardinal McCann on the matter of region vs integration. "The Cardinal called one day and talked over the matter of St. Rose's. He would prefer to give a Region but sees difficulty in getting the Sisters to accept it".[40] By the end of the year it was clear that "nothing short of complete amalgamation" would satisfy the members of St Rose's Congregation. This, according to Mother Isidore, was the opinion of Mother Genevieve Hickey, Regional Vicar of the Irish Dominican Congregation in South Africa.

> Are the Sisters prepared to work towards that till the next [General] Chapter? I now see how the present climate has to be taken into account and I feel sure that the sooner amalgamation is possible, the better. The anti-apartheid feeling, even here in Ireland has waxed very strong especially as the day for the Springbok match is getting near.[41]

While the sisters concerned anxiously waited the outcome of their formal request for amalgamation, Mother Isidore was exploring the possibilities of hastening the procedure. "I personally feel" she wrote, "that the matter is urgent and that decisions should be reached as soon as possible in such a complex situation. Conflicting opinions reach me from SA. ... Some favour a kind of experimental amalgamation - I don't know that the Irish Congregation would agree to that".[42] However, agreement was reached and the Sacred Congregation for Religious and Secular Institutes gave formal approval to the trial amalgamation in August 1970.[43]

On 11 November 1970 Cardinal Owen McCann issued a Decree of Trial Amalgamation, to be put into effect from 1 January 1971 to the 31 December 1973. This was more than the legal bringing together of two separate congregations, it was also a political statement, an earnest penny of mutual good will, and a rejection of the principles of apartheid. Although the situation was open for review at the end of the trial period, in 1971 the Congregation of St Rose of Lima ceased to operate as an independent body, and became part of the Dominican Regional Vicariate with its Mother House at Cabra, Dublin. Of the 250 sisters of the Irish Congregation in South Africa who voted on the question, 204 approved of trial and 18 of full amalgamation, while 20 voted against the proposed union - a 92% positive vote. For the sisters concerned it was not a move into a totally unfamiliar social or canonical environment. Members of the St Rose's Congregation had been trained in religious life by the Cabra Dominicans, had lived and worked side by side with them in their well-established mission schools, and in the final battle for amalgamation the St Rose's sisters had been given the support of those Dominicans who had been their colleagues and superiors. What was even more important, from mid-1969 the Interim Directives, the first draft of the post-Vatican II Irish Dominican Constitutions, had been followed by the St Rose's community.[44] In December 1973 Mother Isidore Collins announced the results of the poll on amalgamation. A majority of sisters voted in favour of the complete and permanent union of the two congregations. With the exception of 154 sisters in Ireland, who knew little or nothing about South Africa and 16 South Africans who were probably absent when the votes were cast, the results were almost unanimous. Of the 601 votes cast, 589 were for amalgamation and 12 were against it. The Sacred Congregation of Religious, approved the amalgamation which would soon become a legal reality. "Therefore as from 1st January, 1974 the Congregations merge completely and the former Congregation of St Rose of Lima becomes one with ours", wrote Mother Isidore to the sisters in Ireland and South Africa. "This union of the two Congregations is particularly consoling in an age when the world is torn with divisions and conflict".[45] It was also an age of great and for some disturbing changes in the Church which by 1974, were already engaging the time and energy of men and women religious throughout the world. An age of hope and renewal for some, of deconstruction for others.

Chapter Fourteen

The Congregation

It was hoped that the Decree of Amalgamation of the 17 November 1937, the final seal on a long and stressful period of negotiation, would be the beginning of a new and constructive era in the life of the Congregation of Irish Dominican Sisters. The South African superiors envisaged, not without trepidation, a creative interaction and the opportunity to be part of a wider, more traditional body to which they could contribute their unique missionary experience, and from which they would receive Dominican inspiration, a stable Constitution and practical support. Above all they anticipated a regular supply of young sisters well versed in Dominican life and academically and professionally prepared for work in the rapidly expanding educational system in Southern Africa. Both Mother Teresa Coleman and Mother de Ricci Harkin had few illusions. They were keenly aware that there was a price to be paid for the union with Ireland, and that whatever the benefits, the act of amalgamation would deprive them of their domestic autonomy. What no one had anticipated was the fact that during the ten years immediately following amalgamation, they would be denied active and immediate, personal participation in the business of the Congregation. However in the euphoria of March 1938, none of this was evident and Mother Teresa was clearly happy to be able to record the unanimous support of the South African communities for amalgamation with Ireland:

> I am sending by this weeks surface mail 149 Declaration Forms duly signed by every member of the Congregation. ... Everybody is happy and not by word or sign is there any indication of the seven who dissented from voting last October. We are all looking forward to a new era in the history of our Congregation, a new impetus to Dominican life. My visit to Port Elizabeth ... was a very *happy* one. Complete sympathy will easily exist between the two portions of the Region. I was

quite edified with the lovely spirit of the Sisters and with the splendid work being done up there.[1]

In the event neither legal union nor goodwill could bridge the gap created by almost three quarters of a century of the independent existence of the two missionary Congregations of Cape Town and Port Elizabeth. And it was even more difficult to create strong bonds with a distant Irish Congregation to which the South African communities owed a debt of gratitude. Or was this union not perhaps the greatest political error made by the Irish Dominican communities in South Africa? Finbar Ryan, writing to Mother Colmcille Flynn towards the end of 1938 noted: "I take it for granted that there are probably some of the sisters who are not quite enamoured by any change in the S. African system and who might (without any malice ...) have expressed their views".[2] While Mother Teresa would not have entertained any criticism disloyal to the Congregation, the rank and file had no such scruples. Some sisters found aspects of the new regime restrictive and narrowly oppressive and did not hesitate to express their opinions in private if not in public.[3] For this reason it was essential that the choice of a Regional Vicar should be acceptable to the two legally united communities in South Africa. Although for the first time within living memory in South Africa the higher superior was to be appointed, not elected, and the final decision rested with the General Council in Cabra, Ireland, the members of the two pre-amalgamation Councils were asked to suggest candidates.

In accordance with a long held tradition in both Port Elizabeth and the Western Cape the members of the former Councils looked to their own ranks for suitable officials, as Mother Teresa informed Mother Colmcille Flynn:

> In both places the Councillors elected by the vocals of the last General Chapters seemed the most appropriate persons to return to office now. Mother De Ricci and the Councillors of P.E. informed us that at their "postulation" last August Mother De Ricci accepted the office of Prioress General only on condition that she would retire from same when the Decree of Amalgamation would bring about fresh changes of offices. I suggest either Mother Thecla [Wilmot] of P.E. or Mother Mary of the Angels [Donnellan] for the office of Regional Vicar. They are both well known to me as good, zealous religious; both are possessed of common sense, well-balanced minds and clear reasoning powers. ... I consider Mother De Ricci admirably suited to the office of First Councillor because of her great zeal for the interests of the Congregation and her long years of experience in government, the other members I

would suggest are Mothers Clare [Martin] and Benvenuta [O'Donoghue].

She also suggested Mother Thecla as Secretary to the Council, since she belonged to the "other Vicariate" and her knowledge of the Eastern District would be a real help to the Regional Vicar. Since Mother Thecla was an excellent teacher and well versed in school matters she could combine the roles of Secretary to the Regional Council and Regional Directress of Schools. Finally Mother Teresa, looking for financial expertise, proposed Mother De Sales Ryan as Regional Procuratrix.[4] The combined Councils, at a meeting held at St Dominic's Priory on 20 February 1938, approved all of these proposals with one exception. For the office of Regional Vicar, Mother Teresa Coleman was the unanimous choice.[5]

The General Council approved the South African choice and on 28 May 1938 Mother Teresa Coleman and her Council were formally installed in Office for a period of three years. The previous day Mother Teresa had written to Mother Colmcille Flynn:

> Your kind letter, letters of appointment, and Ceremonial reached me this afternoon. ... May I humbly say "*Benedictus deus in donis suis*". I promise Mother, to the best of my ability, to give you Rev. Mother Prioress General, that "loyal obedience" which you asked the Sisters to give Mother Vicar, and 'in a great spirit of faith and trust to support you and the members of your Council in all that concerns the government of the Vicariate'.

Mother Teresa was to serve as Regional Vicar for almost ten full years, and a further twenty years as Regional Councillor, not retiring from office until 1968. She, together with her immediate successors in office, had a profound influence on what was a period of missionary construction and gradual adaptation, in the Congregation and in the Church in general. Developments were often carried out in the face of frustrations, delays and misunderstandings.[6]

For the new Regional Vicar the prospect of an immediate visit by the Prioress General was viewed with a combination of joy and panic. She knew her own sisters and was aware that opinions would be voiced that might not meet with the approval of the more conservative Irish superiors. Writing to Mother Alberta Grant she revealed her concern:

> You may be sure we shall take care of dear Mother General's health while she is with us. We shall send her back a 'new

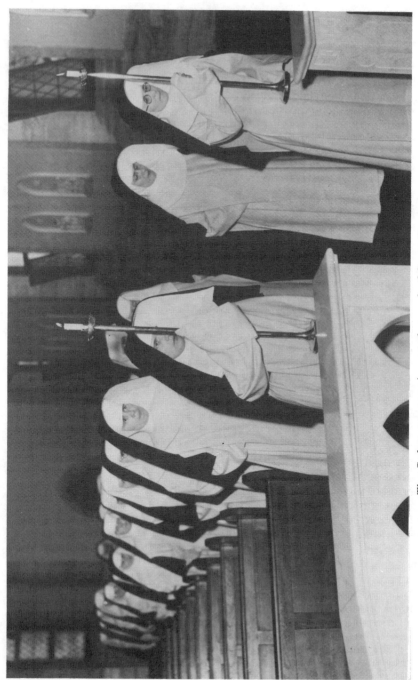

The Salve procession at the end of Compline,
at Springfield Convent, Wynberg, Cape, in the early 1950's.

woman'. I hope she will not be shocked at many things, but I do believe if she stays long enough to see us well she will find we are not too bad. You and Mother Reginald did not return with too bad an opinion of us! Mother will hardly approve of as much 'outspokenness' as is amongst us, but I think they are all very good. Dear old Mother Columba used always to say to me when there was question of Sisters filling certain posts, especially if they had been old novices of mine, 'They are all swans in your eyes'.[7]

The ability to see the good in others was also a characteristic of Mother Colmcille, who during her friendly visits and formal visitation, won the goodwill and appreciation of the sisters. This ensured her a genuine welcome when in 1948, she returned to South Africa as second Regional Vicar. Her departure for Ireland early in 1939, after visitation, had left the Region more secure in the knowledge that their efforts at conformity to the Irish Dominican model had met with official approval. But it was also the beginning of a period of isolation and of frustrated attempts to maintain practices that bore little relevance to the missionary situation of Southern Africa. What created even greater practical problems was the lack of aspirants to meet the growing need for personnel in all parts of the Region. But whatever the problems created by the obligation to appeal constantly to a distant Prioress General, the Constitutions were available to all and the Regional Vicar and her Council had their own agenda, their specific aspirations as to what was and what was not of high priority for the mission and the progress of the Congregation. What they often lacked was the legal power to act.

True unity, implied in legal amalgamation, was much more difficult to achieve than conformity in clothing, in the minutiae of daily life, or in liturgy and government. To the hierarchy and to the religious superiors it was the establishment of new missionary foundations that gave concrete expression to the willingness of religious women to meet the needs of the local Church. It was appropriate therefore that 1939 should see the foundation of two new houses, Stellenbosch in the Western Cape and St Colmcille's Mission in the Sunday's River valley in the East. Santa Sabina, Stellenbosch, later renamed Aquinas Convent, had Mother de Ricci Harkin as its founder and first Superior. It was funded and staffed at the outset mainly by Holy Rosary Convent, Port Elizabeth. This house gave excellent service to student sisters attending Stellenbosch University, and through the school at Ida's Valley it provided pre-primary and primary education and later vocational training for the Coloured community. But it did not become a symbol of unity of heart between the East and the West, one of the motivating forces behind the foundation. When the young sisters from the novitiate at Kerdiffstown came to Aquinas Convent to qualify as teachers, they learnt for the first time the story of amalgamation, and the difficulties encountered by those who tried to bridge the gap between what had formerly been the two independent communities of Cape Town and Port Elizabeth. During the 1950's young nuns were well advised when visiting other houses on the Cape Peninsula, to keep references to Kerdiffstown and Aquinas Convent out of their conversation.[8]

The Convent of Mary Immaculate in Kirkwood was a Cape Town foundation which during the first years was staffed and funded mainly by the Dominican houses in the Western Province. It was a mission begun and sustained in great poverty and the lives and experiences of the sisters created myths and legends of another heroic age. It provided a field of active missionary involvement outside the normal conventual experience of many of the sisters who were assigned there in the founding years. Visiting the rural Coloured communities, baptising babies, helping the terminally ill to die well, clothing children so that they could attend school, instructing adults for admission into the Church and feeding the poor; these were all part of the sisters' tasks. Gradually the staffing of this and other houses became congregational rather than regional. This was especially the case with the post-Amalgamation sisters who were assigned to the Region of South Africa after 1945. These knew little or nothing about past divisions or historically defined differences between the East and the West, except what they learned from casual conversation. They were the direct products of a strict Irish novitiate, consequently the regulations controlling enclosure, egress, sacred liturgy and the rigid application of the law of silence were familiar and not seen as an imposition of an outside agency. For those who had lived a lifetime in South Africa or had come to join one or other of the communities prior to amalgamation, many of the new regulations irked, and some, though minor, were rejected on principle, though often perforce obeyed in practice. Among those who felt the pressure of certain changes in customs and practices was Mother Teresa herself.

Immediately after amalgamation with Cabra, the new Regional Vicar was faced with a dilemma. In May 1938, for the first time in their 75 years at the Cape, the sisters were being asked by political parties to cast their vote in the elections. Sixteen months earlier Mother Teresa would not have hesitated to give her permission, but the sacred nature of enclosure and the rigours of the new dispensation in respect of egress gave her pause. She sent the politicians to the Bishop who "though he approved in principle of the Sisters using their vote, he took on no public responsibility" for the matter. But the canvassers were importunate. "It was only yesterday the utmost persuasion was brought to bear on me". wrote Mother Teresa, "and I was left with no loop-hole when the candidate offered to send [a] cable and answer prepaid. The wording of the text was mine". She knew that such a permission demanded sound justification:

> This is the first time we are using our votes, Mother. Tomorrow - 18th inst - the Sisters of St Agnes' Convent and of St Michael's Convent will be conveyed in a Private car to their respective polling stations. They will go in the early morning, and the members will see that the utmost privacy will be observed, no party colours will fly from the cars. The candidates are not Catholics but they are friendly towards us. The time has come when it is 'Catholic Action' to help good men against a Socialist or Communist opponent. I am sending you the *Southern Cross* this week so that you may see how Catholics are now becoming more self-assertive in the government of the country.

Mother Teresa acknowledged that the matter must have been a "little shock" to Mother Colmcille since it was a "new departure" for the sisters.[9]

The question of egress always dominated discussions on regular observance, especially when the Prioress General visited the Region of South Africa. While necessary egress for mission work would be permitted, there should be " no egress to shops or business houses, and no pleasure drives".[10] The necessity for a more flexible approach to egress was as evident to sisters themselves as it was to the priests in whose parish the Dominican convents and schools were situated. These latter condemned as impractical, a policy of strict enclosure for missionary women in South Africa. It was unfortunate therefore that the intervention of World War II prevented delegates from the South African Region from personal participation in the Third General Chapter of the Congregation scheduled for 1940. Matters of extreme urgency could be presented to the Prioress General only through letters and cables rather than discussed face to face at the Chapter. This was the correct forum for the solution of problems experienced in South Africa in the immediate post-amalgamation period. For this and other reasons it seemed to Mother Teresa that a General Chapter should not be held in the absence of representatives of the Region of South Africa. In May 1940, she wrote to Mother Colmcille Flynn:

> I was in hopes ... that the Chapter would be postponed but
> the Cablegram ... has brought great disappointment.
> Simultaneously with it came the special news that Holland
> and Belgium were invaded and this menacing news seems to
> thwart the designs of even the most courageous travellers.
> We are still confident that you will consider our position and
> postpone the Chapter, as there are sanguine hopes that with
> vigorous conduct of war now, operations will cease in a few
> months.[11]

In the event the Sacred Congregation of Religious permitted
the postponement of the General Chapter,[12] but since the war
was prolonged it was held the summer of 1941, in the absence of
Mother Teresa and the South African delegates. It was not until
1947 that the Region of South Africa had the opportunity to send
representatives to the General Chapter at Cabra. This period of
almost ten years between the issue of the Decree of Amalgamation
and the active, personal participation of the Region of South Africa
in the affairs of the Congregation, resulted in a certain loss of
confidence in the full membership of the Region in the
Congregation. It also delayed the process of adaptation to new
laws and customs. Although the 1941 General Chapter did not
make decisions concerning the Region of South Africa without
prior consultation with the Regional Vicar and her Council, there
was little sympathy for legitimate requests for adaptations to
Constitutions and customs, which in many respects were
unsuited to a missionary environment, and indeed even to the
life of active educationists working in Ireland.

Another result of isolation enforced by war was the shortage
of recruits from the novitiate at Kerdiffstown. The last group of
sisters to be sent from Ireland, arrived at Cape Town on the
Warwick Castle towards the end of January 1940. Sisters Alvarez
Magee, Athanasius Melican and Christopher Cormack remained
in St Mary's and taught part-time in St Teresa's Coloured School,
while Sisters de Montfort Dempsey and Henry Costello were sent
to Matroosfontein to teach and to study Afrikaans in preparation
for College in 1941. These were to be the last sisters to be sent to
South Africa until 1945, when peace was established in Europe.
The war had presented other personnel problems in missions
throughout Southern Africa. Mother Teresa while noting the
delight with which in 1940, the Apostolic Delegate, Archbishop
Gijlswijk viewed the progress being made in the building of the
convent in Stellenbosch, warned Mother Colmcille of growing
pressure for religious men and women to fill in gaps in missions
depleted by war. "He was very strong on our preparing ourselves
now to fill the mission places all over S. Africa when Germans

and other aliens will be refused admittance. He said he had written to you, Mother, about it. God knows we are short-handed here".[13] By July Mother Teresa needed 15 postulants for the growing mission,[14] and three months later she pointed out that with 16 convents in the Region, 16 sisters each year would constitute a very small increase to the communities.[15]

It could well be argued that Mother Teresa expanded the work of her Dominican communities in South Africa far beyond the limits of their resources. This criticism could be applied equally to her immediate successors in office, Mother Colmcille Flynn (1948-1951) and Mother Catherine Dixon (1951-1960). These women were caught up in a process of rapid missionary development, expressed appropriately by the Irish Dominican Congregation in the opening of new schools, especially Coloured primary, vocational and later secondary schools. This expansion became a matter of greater urgency as the application of apartheid regulations and the growing intransigence of the Nationalist Government, made the running of Coloured and African schools by European principals, increasingly difficult. The local, hierarchical Church for its part made greater, more insistent, and often unreasonable demands on women and men religious to open schools for all racial groups in a radically divided society. But apart from outside pressures to expand the scope of educational services, the Dominican sisters who had worked a lifetime in South Africa, or the women who, though still young, had volunteered to do so, were all aware of the magnitude of the task ahead and the urgency to provide educational services wherever possible. In such circumstances the need for additional sisters was always a matter of priority.

In January 1940 there were 234 sisters in the Region of South Africa. Twenty-four of these had died by 1947, one of whom was a young South African, Sister Callista Symonds who had made her final profession in Holy Rosary Convent, Port Elizabeth in January 1946 and died only 16 months later. Of the rest, three finally professed sisters in the Western Cape planned together to leave the Congregation. Although on their own written testimony they had no complaints against the Dominican community, they decided to find a new life outside the cloister.[16] At that time such a departure was well within the experience of most religious communities, but for the Irish Dominicans in South Africa it was, during the 1940's, that first faint breeze, presage of a mighty wind that would destabilise religious life throughout the Church in the decades to come. Indeed change was already in the air, and in the Region of South Africa, Mother Teresa and her

Councillors were already expressing, however politely, the right to have their voices heard. They wanted the Region of South Africa to play a responsible part in the Congregation and to have its apostolic needs met.

The fundamental weakness of the Irish Dominicans of Cape Town and Port Elizabeth both before and after amalgamation, was their inability to attract and hold a sufficient number of South African recruits to maintain their own foundations. This indeed represents in microcosm the entire missionary Church in the region during the nineteenth and early twentieth centuries. Europe and not Africa, was seen by both the hierarchy and by religious superiors, as the ideal recruiting ground for priests, brothers and sisters. Even when the recruitment and training of indigenous priests and religious was being promoted by Rome, the hierarchy continued to build the local church on a Eurocentric foundation with European personnel. Like the modern novice in a traditionally conservative congregation such as that of Cabra and her South African foundations, the Coloured, African and Indian aspirants were forced by accepted tradition into an alien social and religious mould which bore little relation to their cultural needs or spiritual aspirations. It is little wonder that the history of indigenous women religious in South Africa forms in many instances, a sad and cautionary tale.

The Regional Chapter of 1947 did however indicate that attitudes were changing in the Congregation. For the first time individual convents submitted petitions to the Chapter. This was clearly approved of by the Prioress General, Mother Reginald Lyons who, prior to the meeting of the Regional Chapter, had spent five months visitating the Dominican houses of the Congregation in the Eastern and Western Cape. The petitions provide clear evidence that matters of importance to the Region were being given serious consideration, not just by the Regional superiors, but by the Irish Dominican Congregation as a whole.[17] Since the Region of South Africa did not accept lay sisters, and those coming from Kerdiffstown were usually potential teachers, the need to recruit young women for domestic work had become a matter of urgency. This matter was addressed in the 1947 Regional Chapter:

> We declare that, in view of our urgent need of Sisters for domestic work it was decided by unanimous vote to petition the General Chapter to consider the question of collecting and preparing candidates without High School education for entrance into the Novitiate.

> The Chapter commissioned the Delegates to the General
> Chapter to petition for facilities to address and collect such
> candidates.[18]

In pre-amalgamation days this kind of recruitment drive had ensured a steady flow of aspirants. The Region also needed teachers and since the Irish novitiate was proving to be an unreliable source of recruits for the Region, the Chapter "expressed a unanimous wish that volunteers from home Convents would be allowed to come to South Africa to help in the present shortage of Sisters".[19] When Mother Teresa and the other Delegates went to Ireland in 1948, for the General Chapter at Cabra, they were permitted to visit Dominican schools and speak to the pupils about the South African mission. In the event this proved to be no substitute for the recruiting drives carried out in rural Ireland in pre-amalgamation days. Nor was the petition to the Regional Chapter, that "Postulants on entering in Ireland be given the choice of coming to South Africa when professed", given effect in Kerdiffstown. Unless the candidate made it clear from the outset that she had entered for the missions, she had little hope of receiving permission to come to South Africa.

This was part of the price the South African communities had to pay for membership of the Cabra Congregation. But despite goodwill and a desire to make amalgamation work, the spirit of the times influenced the attitudes of individuals and groups within the Region of South Africa. This was reflected in one of the community petitions, that "the question of a Wireless in the Community room be discussed".[20] Although this was not an unreasonable request it was seen as an indication of a growing worldliness among the younger sisters, especially in view of the fact that normally, newspapers were made available to superiors only, and not to community members at large. To entertain such a concession was clearly going too far too fast, and there is no record of the matter in either the Acts of the Regional Chapter or in the memorandum sent out by Mother Teresa on the eve of her departure for Ireland. Another petition "that there should be a change in the Headdress", was for the Dominican sisters the first shot in the sartorial battle that was to lead by the 1980's, to changes in dress beyond the imagination of the first architects of the Congregation of Irish Dominican Sisters. In one other significant way the trends of the professional world were penetrating into the cloister. A memorandum issued after the 1948 General Chapter warned the sisters of the Congregation against worldly standards and personal ambitions:

> The Chapter drew attention to the growing tendency among some Sisters to place emphasis upon 'academic qualifications' as making Sisters valuable in the community. Such an outlook is to be deplored. A Sister is truly useful in a Community in proportion to her true religious spirit and the virtues she exercises in her daily intercourse with others. A religious vocation is essentially supernatural and its value can be estimated by God alone.

Despite this admonition, superiors were under considerable pressure to ensure that student-sisters were prepared for their work in the schools. The growing demands of Departments of Education in South Africa for teachers proficient in Afrikaans and qualified academically and professionally, ensured that whether or not individuals were tempted to take undue pride in their academic achievements, the survival of Dominican institutions depended on the teaching sisters being given the opportunity to study at Colleges of Education and at Universities offering appropriate courses.

While the future of the schools depended on the wise provision of well qualified teachers, the recognition of the Region of South Africa as an equal partner in the Congregation of Irish Dominican Sisters was the hoped for result of attendance at the General Chapter, held at Cabra, Dublin in January 1948. But it was not an equal situation. With the exception of four or five major superiors who had come on official business to South Africa, on visits that were often more in the nature of royal progresses than a realistic experience of what life there was really like, the Irish delegates knew little or nothing about the country. Nor indeed had they occasion to concern themselves with so distant a mission. The Irish communities had quite enough to do to promote their own interests, protect their own rights, and ensure that their convents maintained that measure of autonomy consonant with membership of the Congregation. The 1948 Chapter, while it dealt fairly with the requests and proposals from the Region of South Africa, was essentially an Irish Chapter, dealing with Irish affairs. The re-election of Mother Reginald Lyons as Prioress General, was to have considerable influence on the South African Region.

Mother Reginald, after two visits to South Africa was familiar with the strengths and weaknesses of the communities there. For a woman of vision and generous spirit she failed to reconcile those sisters in the Region who saw in her refusal to condone any form of recreational egress, an act of excessive authoritarianism by a outsider, one who did not understand the

Dominican sisters of the Western Cape taking part in an Eucharistic procession through the streets of Cape Town in 1951.

needs of the missionary sisters, or respect their customs and privileges. But egress was not the only bone of contention. In common with the Church, she could not condone the continued policy of admitting non-Catholic children to the European schools, and her forthright condemnation of this was another ground for dissatisfaction in South Africa. Such judgements were less than fair to a woman who in the process of amalgamation in Ireland, had been willing to make any sacrifice to achieve unity. Nevertheless it was an indication that the Region of South Africa though legally bound, was still a separate entity, aware of its subordinate position in the Congregation, but in many respects *unable* to comply with customs and regulations emanating from a fundamentally conservative body working in the security of a Catholic environment.

As the result of years of isolation another point of difference had arisen between the Region of South Africa and the superiors in Ireland. This was the question of maintaining a separate novitiate in South Africa. The delegates from South Africa argued that a novitiate in Cape Town or Port Elizabeth would not only encourage local girls to enter but would reassure parents who hesitated to send their children to Ireland, with its cold, wet climate. If the aspirants did not persevere, it would be less expensive to return them to their homes. It was also pointed out that all the other Dominican congregations had novitiates in South Africa. In addition it was clearly the wish of the Church that the indigenous clergy and religious be developed to take over the evangelisation of their own people, and where better could they be trained than in their own country? The arguments were weak. The South Africa Region did not have a large enough number of aspirants to justify the establishment of a novitiate, on a scale and at a standard possible in Ireland. Nor did it reflect the mind of Mother Teresa and her Council when they had made their formal request for union with the Irish Dominican Congregation, and this the Chapter pointed out:

1. One of the major reasons for the request for Amalgamation given by South Africa (1931) was the necessity for training young Religious in a Catholic atmosphere, and in a large Novitiate where numbers would allow of efficient training by competent staff.

2. The number of candidates offering themselves in South Africa at present would not allow of such training being given, nor are the facilities conducive to the best formation available.

3. A Central Novitiate in which all receive the same formation makes for unity and for that common heart and mind

necessary in the pursuit of a common ideal in South Africa
and in Ireland. This unity is of the utmost importance in
these early days of Amalgamation.[21]

No one could deny the cogency of these arguments, and the
South African delegates accepted the decision of the Chapter
that local postulants would spend a few months on trial in South
Africa and then join their Irish counterparts in the novitiate at
Kerdiffstown, from which the exigencies of war had excluded
them.

The war which had isolated the Dominican Region of South
Africa, had not hindered the progress of the mission of the
Dominican sisters in the Western and Eastern Cape. The Report
of the Regional Directress of Studies gave the Irish capitulars
some insight into the educational developments in the Region
during the preceding six years:

1 The expansion of educational work in South Africa.
2 The establishment of new Schools for White, Coloured and
Native children, and addition to existing schools.
3 The establishment of Vocational Training Schools for Native
and Coloured girls and for Deaf Pupils, boys and girls.
4 The inauguration of Retreats for Past Pupils, both White
and Coloured.
5 The establishment of the Catholic Secondary Schools'
Association.[22]

The Chapter did not consider that expansion of work in South
Africa should be limited to African and Coloured areas as there
was " a strong movement among Afrikaans speaking (Dutch)
people towards the Church".

Mother Vicar proposed that as efficient teaching, especially
in Coloured Schools, could only be done by Sisters who had
been trained through the medium of Afrikaans, young Sisters
should receive their Primary training in the Afrikaans-
speaking university of Stellenbosch. As a preliminary course
in Afrikaans of at least one year would be necessary for the
Sisters before entering the University, Mother Vicar asked
that Sisters suitable for Primary training be sent to South
Africa after leaving Kerdiffstown.[23]

The foundation of Aquinas Convent in Stellenbosch was
conceived not only as a symbol of unity between East and West,
but as a House of Studies for sisters attending the Afrikaans
medium University of Stellenbosch. Sisters from the community
went daily to teach in the Coloured Mission School in Ida's Valley,

and Stellenbosch became the centre of missionary interaction between the Dominican nuns and their brethren of St Nicholas' Priory. The dream of Father Bede Jarrett OP for a Dominican Priory of full observance in the heart of Calvinist Stellenbosch, was only in its early stages of realisation when the Irish Congregation made its first foundation there in 1939. And it was the sisters, the women of the Order, not the brethren who made the first impact on the Dutch Reformed academics of the University of Stellenbosch. The Afrikaans apostolate began in Stellenbosch, not as the result of the persuasive teaching of great Dominican men, scholars who could overwhelm the local academics with their brilliance, but through the courage and obvious need of young religious, missionary women, studying through the medium of a foreign language in an alien social and religious environment. This aroused the sympathy and admiration of the Dutch Reformed professors and lecturers, who in the decades following the opening of Aquinas Convent, accepted Dominican sisters, many within a day or two of their arrival in South Africa, and helped them to survive the babel experience during their first year of study. Soon, with such generous assistance, Afrikaans with its local flavour, its rich developing literature and its colloquial directness of expression, became a familiar vehicle of thought and conversation for these Dominican students, as well as a comfortable means of academic expression.

In 1957 the local press reported the prowess of some of these nuns:

> The soft Irish brogue changed suddenly to fluent, idiomatic Afrikaans. Sister Sixtus [Lenaghan], a Dominican nun at the University of Stellenbosch was obviously at home in her 'adopted' tongue. She is one of nine Roman Catholic nuns who are students at Stellenbosch. Seven are from Ireland, one from Germany and one is South African. All are being taught through the medium of Afrikaans. From the Stellenbosch Roman Catholic Convent where these somewhat unexpected 'Maties' are living comes this comment: 'They are quite at home and very happy at the university'.

Not only did they feel at home in the Dutch Reformed environment but apparently they were accepted there:

> Their lecturers and fellow students could not be more friendly and co-operative. Stellenbosch was chosen especially for the nuns to help them to understand the language and the Afrikaans people. The experiment has been a marked success. Dr. F. J. Malherbe, who teaches Afrikaans at Stellenbosch

said: The nuns are ideal students. They work exceptionally
hard and do very well. It is amazing how quickly they master
the Afrikaans language.[24]

According to this report, four of the student nuns were working
for primary and high-school teaching diplomas, and the rest were
studying for BA and BSc degrees. "Two of them, Sister Augustine
and Sister Marianus, both B.A. students majoring in Afrikaans,
have won bursaries for the second successive year".[25] The former,
Sister Mary O'Driscoll, after a number of years spent teaching in
South Africa, studied at the Gregorian University for a doctoral
degree in spiritual theology and presently is Professor of Spiritual
Theology at the Angelicum University in Rome. Her companion,
Sister Marian O'Sullivan, was Principal of Springfield Convent
School and later taught at Sint Paulusklooster, the Afrikaans-
medium school outside Pretoria. At the Regional Chapter of 1977
she succeeded Mother Genevieve Hickey as Regional Vicar, an
office she held with distinction until her election as Prioress
General in 1986. For two Dominican Maties these were giant
steps, and the University of Stellenbosch must be given due credit
for the contribution it made to their education and training, and
to that of many other members of the Congregation of Dominican
Sisters, Cabra.

Already in 1939, Father Oswin Magrath OP, writing to Mother
Philomena Kelly at Cabra, was enthusiastic about the
developments at Stellenbosch:

> I find great changes here. A small Kindergarten in the Sacristy:
> a flourishing coloured school: sisters at the University.
> Everything is progressing rapidly and just along the right
> lines. It is small yet: but the likelihood of big developments,
> especially among the coloured, is already visible. I have hardly
> had time to come to grips with it yet. We are arranging to give
> monthly conferences at all convents in Cape Town after the
> July holidays. So in future we shall see plenty of the sisters.
> I have not yet seen very much of the sisters here. ... Sr Baptist
> [Jameson] seems to be a very great success with the coloured
> school.[26]

In 1947, during a visit to South Africa, Mother Reginald Lyons
and her companion Mother Catherine Dixon, Directress General
of Studies, were both deeply impressed by the progress made in
the Coloured and European schools attached to Aquinas Convent.
They found it consoling to be able to record that "in a very bigoted
Dutch Reformed town and district of Stellenbosch the number
of both Catholics and non-Catholics has steadily increased in

the European School and the influence of the Nuns is evident by the conversions in the district". Mother Reginald expressed her appreciation of prime movers in the formation of this Afrikaans apostolate: "The Foundation of the Convent and Schools is due to the Apostolic zeal, faith and courage of Mother Colmcille Flynn, Prioress General in 1939, and of Mother Teresa Coleman, the revered Mother Vicar. The wisdom and fortitude of Mother de Ricci Harkin, first Prioress of the Convent, carried through the whole undertaking to its successful issue".[27]

The opening of St Nicholas' Priory saw the beginning of a good working relationship and friendship between the Dominican Fathers at Stellenbosch and members of the Congregation of Irish Dominican Sisters. Father Bernard Delaney writing to Father Oswin Magrath in 1938, advised him to meet Mother Colmcille Flynn, while she was in South Africa. Magrath was to pay his respects but not "rush her into schemes" about a foundation in Stellenbosch. Delaney was in Dublin and was "concerned to urge the Cabra Sisters to do something at Stellenbosch". He received the support of Archbishop Finbar Ryan who had "interested himself most kindly, and he *cabled* to the Mother General urging her not to let the opportunity slip". Delaney quoted Finbar Ryan on the Stellenbosch issue:

> 'If there is to be an Africa *vere Dominicana* both Fathers and Sisters must go to work thoroughly and begin to build up. The pioneering stage has lasted too long'. He agrees with me that we must aim at a *bona fide* Priory and real Dominican Life, as a kind of 'heart' sending out the warm blood of a truly spiritual and Dominican life to the Fathers. Look what the Sisters have achieved because they have safeguarded and established their religious life. We must aim at a central house in S.A. if we are to have permanence as Dominicans.[28]

The close collaboration and mutual support between the English Dominicans and the sisters of the Irish Congregation lasted until the 1960's, when the forces of change, in society in general as well as within the Church, resulted in the departure from the Order and the priesthood of a considerable number of the brethren. The theories of religious life and practices propounded by some of the young Fathers at Stellenbosch, who later left the Order, were unacceptable to the sisters and this caused a rift between them which took a considerable time to heal. By the time old wounds had healed there was no longer a Priory, a novitiate, or House of Studies for the brethren at Stellenbosch. Consequently Regional Vicars turned to Ireland for retreat masters, or participated in less Dominican but more available, and for some more creative forms of annual spiritual renewal. When in 1974 after long and careful thought and negotiation, the Federation of Dominicans in South Africa was formed, the Dominican brethren did not become formal members, although they gave it occasional support.

In reality the missionary work of the sisters, while it was greatly enhanced by the spiritual support of the brethren, never depended on it for the practical business of life, in the professional, academic and economic spheres or indeed in matters of government. Of far greater importance was the decision made by the 1948 General Chapter. In a letter addressed to the Prioresses of the Congregation Mother Reginald Lyons wrote:

> During my recent Visitation in South Africa I was overwhelmed by the sight of the teeming millions to whom the Catholic Church has not yet reached out because of the dearth of 'labourers in the vineyard'. At a great sacrifice to the Congregation in Ireland we are sending Mother Colmcille Flynn and Mother Catherine Dixon to South Africa in the near future to help in the Apostolate there. It would be the dearest wish of my heart to send many others, and many I know are eager to go, but the needs of our work at home are also pressing, and so at the moment we are unable to send as many as we would wish.[29]

Despite the condescension implied in the "great sacrifice" being made by Ireland in sending *two* sisters, these first volunteers to offer their services, conservative women though they were, became eloquent advocates for the mission which they had adopted, and in a very real sense helped to bring the Region of South Africa into the Congregation. Although it could have been no easy task for nuns who had lived a lifetime in Cabra or Sion Hill, to assume high office in South Africa, both Mother Colmcille as Regional Vicar and Mother Catherine Dixon as Novice Mistress of the first recruits for the Institute of St Rose of Lima, showed no hesitation in taking up their responsibilities. For them strict enclosure was part of their tradition. Placing them in positions of authority in the Region of South Africa, would ensure greater observance of this and other regulations laid down in the 1947 *Constitutions*. Mother Reginald Lyons had made it clear to Mother Teresa in 1948, that she expected strict adherence to the law of enclosure. In the eyes of some of the younger sisters, this ban against occasional recreational egress and other minor freedoms, had done much to exacerbate the local situation, and cast doubts on the wisdom of amalgamation. Mother Teresa, during her ten years in office as Regional Vicar, while respecting the ideal of enclosure, did not see it as a rigid law precluding holiday celebrations in the country or at the seaside. She had permitted the traditional community picnic and the occasional country walk. She believed that even attendance at special religious performances held outside the confines of convent and school premises, fell within her dispensatory powers.

An excellent example of the broad view she took on the question of egress was the attendance of the sisters at a special screening of the film, *The Song of Bernadette*, held in the Bioscope Hall in Wynberg. At the eleventh hour Mother Teresa wrote to Mother Reginald Lyons, the Prioress General: "I presume dearest Mother, it will be all right for us to go. If *not* I think a cablegram would reach us before the event would come off".[30] Fortunately for the sisters no cable arrived and they had the rare treat of joining other religious for a happy afternoon at the *Curzon*. That Mother Teresa was called to justify this breach of regulations is evident from the ensuing correspondence. "We went to *The Song of Bernadette* on April 7th, all the nuns of the Peninsula were there. It was just as if we had been in church. We all liked the film very much. Bernadette in Convent Life was not *true* to life. The attitude of her Novice Mistress was quite unreal and very harsh".[31] This was clearly not the end of the matter and three months later the Regional Vicar once again attempted to justify the visit to a public place of entertainment:

> Another matter I feel I should like to mention to you dearest Mother, is this. We Dominicans are in the majority of Religious Orders here in the Cape Peninsula. When there was a question of showing a Catholic picture - a certain number of Religious was necessary. It was our *big* number that made it possible for the Religious of other Orders (it was a *special* show for Nuns only in the case of *The Song of Bernadette*) *all* Religious in the Peninsula went, H Cross, Nazareth Sisters, Holy Family and the out-Sisters of the Good Shepherd and the Loretto. There may not be another Picture, but should there be the O.P's by standing out, would be in great disfavour with the others who by this action would be deprived. I only mention this so that you may know.[32]

For Mother Reginald Lyons, re-elected to the office of Prioress General in 1948, any unnecessary egress was anathema. The appointment of Mother Colmcille Flynn as Regional Vicar in 1948 was in a sense, a guarantee that the more liberal practices still prevailing in the South African Region would be curbed. It could also be hoped that the arrival of young nuns from Kerdiffstown, would ultimately be a stabilising factor. These temporary professed sisters had trouble enough adapting to a new climate and country, and to community life and work, without becoming involved in local convent politics. They had no knowledge of local traditions, and heard the murmuring of those who resented the changes brought about by amalgamation, without understanding the reasons behind the criticisms. And if it could be argued that the training given in Kerdiffstown did little to promote openness and outgoing social relations, it could not be faulted in the matter of loyalty. At the outset at least, the young generation of religious were members of a Congregation, rather than adherents to communities or groups of convents within the boundaries of Southern Africa. Many of them in their early years in the Region, worked or studied outside the convent precincts and did not feel the loss of social outings or other activities, the lack of which they had accepted as part of the sacrifice demanded of them as members of an enclosed community. For some of the Kerdiffstown generation, time and a measure of stability, moderated attitudes and promoted regional loyalties. And with a few exceptions, there was little or no possibility of sisters who had emigrated to South Africa, revisiting their homeland. For almost a hundred years, the Eastern and Western Cape had become home to generations of Dominican women whatever their country of origin, and as the years passed, the sisters of the Region, whether from the Western or Eastern Cape had become family.

In the early 1950's the forces of change were already at work in the Region of South Africa. During the term of office of Mother Catherine Dixon, who was installed as Regional Vicar on 26 October 1951, the Dominican women of the Region were moving into new fields of action.[33] Between 1956 and 1962 three foundations were made in the Transvaal (now Gauteng Province). Already in March of 1951 the Apostolic Delegate, Archbishop Martin Lucas SVD, had proposed that the Irish Dominicans open an Afrikaans medium boarding school. Mother Colmcille and her Council approved in principle of his suggestion but did not look beyond their traditional area, the Cape, as the ideal setting for such a foundation. "Some thought Stellenbosch would be the best place, others suggested dual medium classes in Springfield". No immediate decision could be made, but the seed was sown.[34] Among the Council recommendations to the Regional Chapter of 1954, was the proposal that the foundation of an Afrikaans-medium school should be considered. The Chapter decided to "leave the matter in abeyance" until Archbishop McCann should clarify the position as to the number of Afrikaans - speaking families who would support such a school and the best location in which to establish it.[35]

In the meantime two building projects were in progress, a new school in Ida's Valley and St Anne's Convent in Walmer, Port Elizabeth. In both cases the money had to be found to meet the mounting debts. As the Acts of the 1954 Regional Chapter testify, the established houses responded to the call for financial help to meet the monthly repayments on the two buildings.[36] The Convent at Walmer, was opened in 1954, with Mother Dympna Byrne as its first Prioress, and now eyes were turned to Vanderbijlpark, a developing industrial centre in the Transvaal. In July 1955, the Regional Council considered a request from Bishop Boyle that the Cabra Dominicans would take over a small primary school in Vanderbijlpark, previously run by the Sisters of the Holy Rosary. This offer was accepted and Mother Vicar set off for the Transvaal to visit the Bishop and the Holy Rosary Sisters and to inspect the property.[37] The formal opening of Sancta Maria Convent, Vanderbijlpark was held on Rosary Sunday, 7 October 1956. For Mother Emily O'Keefe and her community Sisters Jordan Byrne, Virgilius Dennehy, Placid Walsh and Catherine-Joseph Scott, and indeed for the whole Region of South Africa, this new foundation was another step into the modern world. By 1962 three additional foundations were made in the Transvaal. St Catherine's Convent in Florida, a suburb of Johannesburg, was opened in 1957. The Afrikaans apostolate was to be served by Sint Paulusklooster, situated on a farm at Brummeria, outside Pretoria. This was founded in 1961, and the following year Mother Alexius McGonigle and four sisters arrived at St Dominic's Convent, Hammanskraal, prepared to open their new school for African deaf children[38]. Without delay they admitted the first pupils and the school was soon flourishing.

What was remarkable about the first three Transvaal foundations at Vanderbijlpark, Florida and Pretoria was the development of close and lasting interaction between the sisters and the people, parents and parishioners, they had come to serve. Their welcome as religious and teachers was never in doubt, and they were given encouragement and practical assistance by friends and virtual strangers. Gradually the nuns became closely involved in the life and concerns of the people, and found in mutual friendship and help the support they needed in the early years of the new foundations. On the eve of major change in the Church there developed for many of the sisters in these relatively small and economically straitened communities, a freer spirit and a renewed sense of mission. Unlike the convents in the Cape, they had no Government schools and consequently received no state subsidies or salaries. With the income from school fees and some help from the central fund of the Region, they had to pay lay teachers and support staff, maintain buildings, supply educational equipment, and provide for the Dominican community. With the help of Parents Associations and other voluntary bodies these schools flourished.

Mother Teresa Coleman, despite advancing years, had lost none of her enthusiasm for the missionary apostolate. While in Vanderbijlpark in June 1956 she wrote to the Prioress General, Mother Benignus Meenan:

> Vanderbijlpark is flat and open. One can see far away to the horizon as, so far in its history, scarcely any of those sky scrapers or flats have arisen. There are factories galore as this is an industrial place, nice farms too - worked by Hollanders, Italians, Germans etc., so our school is multi-racial. The children have the advantage of being far away from busy city-life and are unsophisticated. About 50% of our 185 pupils are Catholics. ... Mother Emily and her little community are kept busy, all have to turn their hands to teaching, to cooking and laundering, etc. They don't seem to mind if occasionally one feels inclined to look for a hammer to break the pastry of an apple-pie. This part of life will improve gradually D.V. They will be better off when they go into the new Convent which they expect will be ready on Sept. 12th.[39]

Mother Teresa was impressed at the apostolic opportunities in the area and noted the catechetical work for children and adults already being done by the sisters, the lessons being given in Afrikaans as well as in English. During this visit she and Mother Catherine went to Florida to view the site of the new convent and school. They were "very pleased with the prospects of Florida". There was no Catholic school for girls in the area and they found in Father McNicholas, the parish priest, a willing helper in the project. "We are being offered a beautiful site - valued £10,000, free. It is certainly the most beautiful spot in the whole area".[40]

They next visited Archbishop Garner who took them to Hammanskraal, about 25 miles north of Pretoria. Even in the dry winter dust and cold of the bush Mother Teresa's enthusiasm did not fail her.

> To me it seemed as if Almighty God had just prepared the spot to give us every facility for educating (for life) our Native Deaf. ... The place is ideal. There are 38 acres of ground in [the] European area just adjoining the Native Territory, in such a way that we could have the nun's choir on one side and the remaining part of the church across the border line. We could build our Convent there and on the Native Mission ground build our School and Hostel for the Deaf.[41]

Mother Teresa never failed to recognise a missionary opportunity, and she constantly reminded the Prioress General and her Council of the need for additional sisters to secure the apostolic life of each new foundation. The close of this long letter was a cry for help: "Mother please don't forget that it is the Irish Sisters who can help the Afrikaners. Well educated bi-lingual Irish Sisters backed up by a sanctified life is what our dear Lord is calling for. Please Mother do something about it".[42] In her long life either as Mistress of Novices, Provincial, Prioress General, Regional Vicar or Councillor, Mother Teresa was always keenly aware of the need for new recruits and the importance of expansion of work, best provided for, in her opinion, by the establishment of new foundations. She lived to experience the changes in liturgy and religious life, begun in the 1950's and given impetus and direction by the teachings of Vatican II. She rejoiced that many of the restrictive regulations imposed on the South African Region after amalgamation, had been revoked. But she also experienced sorrow during the last years of her life. A community woman and a loyal supporter of the Church and of the Congregation, she regretted the departure of the eleven fine young sisters who, for whatever reason, returned to secular life. When Mother Teresa died on 7 August 1974 at the age of eighty-one, the Cabra Dominicans in the Region, in common with religious congregations throughout South Africa, were to face a period of decline in personnel. But it was also a time that saw members of the community directly involved in the political struggle for justice and reconciliation, and many of the sisters moving into more diversified apostolates, both within and outside the formal school system.

Chapter Fifteen

The Struggle: Senzenina?

Cry mercy for the men who built the wall
between the races
who brought the stare of hopelessness
the look of torment and the anguish
to a million faceless faces.
Cry mercy on it all.[1]

During the ten years following Mother Teresa's death, there
was a need to do something, not only to ensure the provision of
new aspirants to religious life, but also to retain those in final
vows. This was to become a growing concern for the Church and
for each religious Order or Congregation, in South Africa and
throughout the world. In the era of rapid change following Vatican
Council II, some of the most fundamental principles of religious
life as it had developed over the centuries, were being put into
question. Nuns, priests and brothers were returning to secular
life, and few aspirants were entering novitiates. This state of affairs
threatened not only the survival of Catholic schools, but also
put into question the validity of running institutions for the
benefit of a privileged white minority. Statistics show that the
Cabra Dominicans in South Africa were no longer in a position
to staff the many schools under their care. Between 1969 and
1976 the number of sisters in the Region of South Africa fell
from 251 to 224. Of the 27, seventeen had died, and thirteen
were dispensed from final vows. Another two sisters, who had
entered and made their profession within this period were
dispensed from their temporary vows. Twelve volunteers joined
the Region from Ireland of whom six returned home after a short
term of service. During the same period sixteen members of the
Region returned to Ireland for various reasons.[2] However in the
mid-1970's the question of recruitment and retention of staff
was to be by no means the only problem, or even the most

immediate concern facing those Cabra Dominicans for whom South Africa was home. Following the student riots in Soweto in 1976 and the subsequent deterioration of the political situation, the Interim Regional Chapter of 1977 considered the need for emergency planning for their Dominicans nuns in South Africa. The Prioress General, Mother Jordana Roche, assured the capitular sisters that " in the event of an escalation of violence, each sister ... [would] be given personal consideration. She extended a warm welcome to any sister who felt she could not remain in a revolutionary situation, but no sister would be compelled to make decisions repugnant to her".[3] With the growing unrest and the escalation of violence there was sufficient justification for some at least of the nuns to seek refuge in Ireland. However for the majority of the sisters this was not a viable option. As political tension increased and the press reports revealed the harsh and repressive measures being used by the police to suppress student demonstration, even those sisters who were less politically aware, decided to remain and continue their work in a country so rent by division, violence and injustice. But whatever the personal choice made by individuals, the decision whether to stay or to leave South Africa, was not an easy one and purity of motive could neither be claimed nor taken for granted.

While the official stand taken by the Congregation in respect of the Region of South Africa was sympathetic and supportive, this did not reflect the attitude of a significant number of Dominican nuns in Ireland. Some of these sisters had gained their knowledge of South African politics not only from the press, but also from the growing anti-apartheid movement in Ireland. They judged that the continued participation of Dominican sisters in government schools and in the prolongation of an apartheid system in private European Catholic schools, was at worst an act of collaboration with a repressive Nationalist government, at best a culpable blindness which condoned gross racism and injustice under the guise of missionary zeal.[4] But it was easy for the arm-chair critics, far distant from the centre of conflict, to take a high moral tone. For those born South Africans and the immigrant sisters, either silent observers or in the thick of action, and committed to the maintenance of their educational institutions, the issues were not so clear. In South Africa, religious communities, like families, were deeply divided on what was and what was not appropriate action in the face of escalating violence and increasing police brutality. Emotional arguments for and against personal and institutional involvement in the "struggle" did little to promote a sound understanding of a situation so far removed from the experience of many of the nuns. For South African Catholics, priests, religious or lay people, there could be ignorance but not neutrality.

Already in June 1952, when the Nationalist Government was getting into its stride, the South African Catholic Bishops' Conference expressed in discreet terms, its disapproval of the official apartheid policy and, without directly condemning the ruling Party, stressed the fundamental rights of all peoples:

> With regard to fundamental rights, no person or society may deprive the individual of their exercise. The State, though justified in controlling the exercise of rights to the degree required for the common good, cannot abolish them; for the Person is superior to the State, which exists for his benefit. Contingent rights, too, cannot be arbitrarily denied or restricted. They are frequently the expression or adaptation to particular circumstances of fundamental rights; and it would be unjust to refuse them to persons capable of exercising them and of contributing their share to the welfare of society .[5]

But in the 1957 plenary session of the SACBC, the tone of the hierarchy had changed. They expressed their strong condemnation of the apartheid system.

> The basic principle of apartheid is the preservation of what is called white civilisation. This is identified with white supremacy, which means the enjoyment by white men only of full political, social, economic and cultural rights. Persons of other race must be satisfied with what the white man judges can be conceded to them without endangering his privileged position. White supremacy is absolute. It overrides justice. It transcends the teaching of Christ. It is a purpose dwarfing every purpose, an end justifying any means. ... From this fundamental evil of apartheid flow the innumerable consequences, for men must be hurt and injustice must be done when the practice of discrimination is enthroned as the supreme principle of the welfare of the state, the ultimate law from which all other laws derive.[6]

While at this time the Catholic Church in South Africa did not give *formal* approval to the policy of segregation, the bishops acknowledged that it was not without blame in this respect: "The practice of segregation, though officially not recognised in our churches, characterises nevertheless many of our church societies, our schools, seminaries, convents, hospitals and the social life of our people". The bishops were clear, in theory at least, on the need to change this situation. "In the light of Christ's teaching this cannot be tolerated for ever. The time has come to pursue more vigorously the change of heart and practice that the law of Christ demands. We are hypocrites if we condemn apartheid in South African society and condone it in our own institutions".[7] The sin of racial discrimination had to be avoided but it was to take almost twenty more years to bring the Church into open and uncompromising confrontation with the State in this regard. And it is significant that it was the women religious, and more specifically the Cabra Dominican women who were in the vanguard when it came to putting theory into action in their own private white schools.

It is not without interest that it was during the 1950's and early 1960's, that young Irish sisters who had been trained in the novitiate at Kerdiffstown, came to serve the Church and the Congregation in the Region of South Africa. Aspirants made a deliberate choice of the missions, and reminded the Prioress General and her Council of this throughout their years of formation, and this despite the fact that in Kerdiffstown they received neither direct encouragement nor specific preparation for their future mission. And they had expectations. These expectations were raised during their schooldays when visiting nuns gave lectures and exhibited photographs of Dominican missionary work in South Africa. These had always focused on the activities of Black and Coloured children in Marymount, Kirkwood, Matroosfontein or Ida's Valley. In addition, some of the senior girls in Dominican secondary schools in Ireland were encouraged to correspond, on a regular basis, with pupils at Marymount.[8] This encouraged mutual sharing of news, ideas and ideals and aroused in some of the Irish school girls a keen interest in South Africa. Most Dominican schools also encouraged regular fund-raising efforts for the missions, an added incentive to those aspiring to the life of a Dominican missionary. However these school activities did not prepare the young sisters for the reality of life in the Regional Vicariate. Even after three years in the novitiate they knew little or nothing of conditions of life in South Africa or of the history of the missionary foundations of Cape Town and Port Elizabeth. Consequently many were surprised, some even dismayed, that the teaching and evangelisation of Coloured and African people, the most urgent task at hand, while it was not neglected, formed only a small part of the educational work being done by Cabra Dominicans in South Africa. In 1958, Mother Benignus Meenan, after her official visit to South Africa as Prioress General, warned sisters on the eve of their departure, that they had little hope of being assigned to work in a Coloured or African school.[9] Many young sisters found themselves in private schools teaching white pupils from a relatively prosperous section of society. And it was not an era when criticism of the conventual system or its educational policy was either welcomed or wise. For young nuns, while the ideal of *blind* obedience was never expected, *silent* obedience was expedient. Nor did the Kerdiffstown nuns find it politic to criticise the *status quo*, at least during the first 25 years after amalgamation. But the greater freedom of speech within religious communities after Vatican II, together with the growing racial tensions in South Africa in the early 1970's, found expression in open criticism by some sisters, of a school's policy that concentrated on white education, a luxury freely available in government schools.

The *South African Catholic Education Survey*, (SACES), carried out by Sister Augusta Neal, SND, despite its inherent weaknesses and its lack of appreciation either of the role of Catholic education or of the complexity of the South African situation, made a considerable impact on the Cabra Dominicans. While for some its implementation was a significant milestone, for others it was a stumbling block. This is not the place to offer a comprehensive critique of Neal's report nor does it fall within the expertise or scope of this study. However because Neal's recommendations, and the survey and report of Canon Verryn, were in one way or another to influence community policy for the next 25 years, their impact cannot be ignored. Father L H Hughes SJ in a critique of Neal's recommendations, arising out of the survey, highlights a number of salient points, the facile acceptance of which created strong divisions of opinion among religious. In his critical analysis of the recommendations of the Report, Hughes noted the "recurrent theme of criticism of any form of satisfaction with religion as taught in the schools; if people feel satisfied with Catholic education on this score, the inference is - and for that matter the statement is - that this is associated with some form of narrowness and being closed off against change".[10] The pejorative assigning of labels such as 'conservative', to those who found little validity in many of the sociologically based policy changes proposed by Neal, and later implemented to promote either correct political involvement in the struggle, or in active participation in spiritual renewal, did little to promote unity and a process of a peaceful transformation of religious life As Hughes pointed out:

> It would be hard to find anything more offensive to the conservative person (as so termed) and her personal integrity than the suggestion that she should drum up funds to enable the free spirits to pursue *their* line in good conscience because

> the old and infirm will be looked after. But as the funds are to
> be stable and protected, the free spirits will themselves benefit
> from them in time to come. Is there a lack of consistency in
> this sort of attitude?[11]

Those sisters who moved from the classroom to other areas of apostolic work, including new ventures in the field of education, in their turn faced the criticism of the nuns who stayed at their posts in Dominican schools. The former were seen to have "opted out" of the work of the community, to have "abandoned the schools", to be "doing their own thing". The perceived attitude of their condemnation of white education, is well expressed in one of the more offensive topics for discussion proposed by the AWR in 1972, after the publication of Augusta Neal's report. This reads: "White Catholic schools, being an implicit acceptance of apartheid, of white privilege and oppression, constitute a counter-witness to the Gospel, and should be closed as soon as possible".[12] While such propositions were for debate and had no personal target, they opened wounds that were not easily healed.

Towards the end of 1973, with the Regional Chapter only a month away, the debate on mission, especially with regard to white schools, had become a major bone of contention among the sisters. Some advocated that since white schools could not in any sense be considered as mission, they should all be closed immediately. Others maintained that white children were as much in need of evangelisation as anyone else and that with the emphasis of the Church on social teaching and justice, it was essential that European children should be properly instructed in these matters. This debate was not confined to the closure of existing Dominican institutions for Europeans. It also focused on the possibility of redeploying sisters to teach in white government schools. It was argued that in public schools nuns would have a wider influence and come into direct contact with an even greater number of Catholics than was possible in the Dominican private schools, then flourishing. In an age of rapidly growing interest in more varied apostolates and smaller communities, the younger and very vocal minority of sisters, wanted radical change, and that without delay.[13]

Canon Verryn made his first proposal in respect of the apostolic priorities of the Cabra Dominicans in mid-1974. "A provisional verdict, based on the practical difficulties of high school work, and the *prima facie* case for the Church to make greater efforts among Blacks, is that white schools should close first".[14] In the New Year of 1976 Verryn noted that since the Dominican white schools were integrating the above recommendation was no longer valid.[15] The opening of white private convent schools to all races was not a step that found favour either with all the sisters or with all parents and children. Apart from differences in language, cultural background and educational opportunity, there was the law of the state to contend with. Legal registration of schools could be withdrawn and that would bring to an end the existence of institutions which for more than a 100 years, had been a strong force in the educational mission of the Church in South Africa. For some of the sisters the main objection to open schools was not racial, although the century-old British colonial policy of separate education, had been accepted by them without question. They would have welcomed, or at least tolerated, educational integration, had it been carried out in terms of the law. Most of the Catholic institutions were deeply in debt and the repayment of bonds as well as the survival of the private school system depended on a regular income from school fees. Would the opening of Catholic schools to all racial groups in South Africa undermine the financial stability of Congregations committed to formal education? Would White parents withdraw their children if Coloured or African pupils were admitted? These and many other questions created divisions of opinion, and for some a debilitating sense of insecurity.

However the ongoing preparation of parents and pupils for the change in admission policy and the education for justice in the schools, did much to reconcile those who at the outset, experienced the contravention of apartheid laws enforcing separate education, as a threat to their work as Catholic educators. As circumstances changed, sisters were themselves witnesses to injury, dispossession and too often the death of innocent men, women and children. When they, like their friends and professional colleagues involved in the struggle, were held in Pollsmoor Prison, when fugitives from the forces of apartheid had to be housed and hidden, and when school children declared themselves willing to die for the cause, and meant it, and died - only then could the reality of the situation no longer be denied. Even when conditions grew more threatening, the inauguration of the open schools policy justified the continued efforts to maintain private schools. From 1863 onwards the work of the sisters had never been limited to formal education, and as the need for the conscientization of the people in all sectors of society grew more urgent, the nuns found a new outlet for their zeal among children and adults. This was a task well suited to Catholic schools, where staff, parents and pupils could work together to promote greater understanding of the problems and needs of all. When in 1976 the struggle for justice entered the classrooms and campuses of schools and tertiary institutions across the country, and violence threatened the lives of teachers, pupils and students alike, adaptation to the new demands being made on the whole school community, had to be accommodated.

Some of the Cabra Dominicans in South Africa disapproved of the active involvement of nuns in the struggle, but even these either by deliberate choice or by force of circumstances, were drawn into political activities, if only for the protection of their pupils. For some of these sisters, especially those directly involved in Coloured, African or open schools, and tertiary institutions, personal involvement in the struggle was to become an inevitable component of the work to which they were committed. It was not enough to awaken the consciences of the community to the evils of both the theory and application of the apartheid system. There were other urgent reasons for personal and institutional support for just laws in a just society. For the Dominican women of the Region of South Africa, as for many other groups and individuals, there could be no choice. Until integration of schools had been achieved, most sisters teaching in European private and government schools often had little direct knowledge of or contact with life in townships and informal settlements. Nor had they experienced at first hand the growing anger and potential for violence of a people trapped in a system that denied them respect and the most basic of human rights. For these Dominican women and those connected with their educational institutions, the years 1975 and 1976 were significant.

The need to face the reality of the apartheid situation, especially in respect of education, was becoming more and more a matter of urgency to both the Catholic hierarchy and to members of the Association of Women Religious (AWR). This was especially the case since many congregations of women religious in South Africa were deeply involved in Catholic education. It had also become an issue of debate in the press and the results of an opinion poll published in *The Star* in 1975 indicated that 75% of White South Africans voted against involvement of the Church in political matters.[16] Those most deeply concerned with the restoration of peace and justice in South Africa recognised that the churches had a special role to play, and women and men in positions of responsibility had to be prepared to take action. According to Dr C F Beyers Naudé, Director of the Christian Institute, " The Church is probably the only agent left in South Africa to bring about peaceful change".[17] But it was not a process of transformation that could be carried out in secret, nor could its political implications be ignored. *Resolution 2* passed by the Executive Committee of the AWR on 15 September 1975 stated:

That the time has come for those Catholic Schools which had hitherto accepted only white pupils to give practical Christian witness to social justice by accepting non-white Christians into their schools. The policy should be one of quiet infiltration, with no sought-after publicity, and that it should be adopted by all Convent Schools. A.W.R. requested the Bishops' Conference to give this resolution explicit support and approval.

Mother Genevieve Hickey, a woman of great integrity and determination, was among those most deeply concerned about the need for positive witness in this matter, both by the Church and by her own Congregation. As Regional Vicar of the Cabra Dominicans in South Africa, and as a member of the Executive of the AWR, she gave her full support to the policy of integrated education. Although the matter of admission of Coloured and African pupils to Catholic schools was still under debate by the SACBC, the AWR, and the ECAR,[18] no decision had been made by the Catholic hierarchy. However Mother Genevieve believed that *Resolution 2* should be put into force without delay, at least in private schools under her jurisdiction. For the first assay against educational apartheid she chose one of the most prestigious of the Dominican private secondary schools, Springfield Convent, at Wynberg in the Western Cape. Towards the end of 1975 she wrote to Cardinal Owen McCann:

I wish to express my thanks, and that of the members of the Regional Council, for the interview which you granted us on the 18th inst., in connection with our plans for the immediate racial integration of our private schools. As educationists we feel that this is the best and most practical contribution we can make in response to the call of the South African hierarchy to promote the cause of peace and justice. We are convinced that the time is ripe and opportune for radical action, and as this is a major decision of our Congregation, we wish to place it officially on record, and to thank you and Bishop S. Naidoo, for the promise of your support in its implementation.[19]

In January 1976, for the first time in the history of Catholic education in South Africa a European private school run by religious, officially and illegally admitted children who were classified in terms of apartheid law, as Coloured.[20]

The unilateral response of the Regional Vicar and Council of the Cabra Dominicans and the immediate opening of schools, potentially to all South African people, precipitated the inevitable confrontation with provincial and central government authorities, and served as a test case for the Church and more specifically church schools, Catholic, Anglican and Methodist in South Africa. The Rev A Hendricks, President of the Methodist Conference of Southern Africa saw the move of the Roman Catholic Church in opening schools to all races as " most commendable" and he pointed out that it was "the church's ministry continually to heal the country. Our divided education system causes pain, and the Catholic gesture is aimed at healing that pain. ... At our last conference in Kimberley the subject was raised, and it was said we believe people of all races should attend the same school".[21]

All official bodies representing the Church agreed that neither confrontation nor publicity should be sought, and indeed the first intake of Coloured girls into Springfield Convent School was small, and statistically, made no major impact either on the school or on the educational system in general. However its witness value far outweighed its academic or social impact on those of the Coloured community who at the outset, gave the open schools their support. The move could not escape the notice of the press or of the Provincial Administration of the Western Province. Indeed the reaction of a small number of Catholic parents made official intervention inevitable. These resented the new policy of admitting Coloured pupils to Springfield, a policy, they claimed, that had been initiated without any consultation with parents. They immediately withdrew their own children and informed the Provincial Administration of the breach of law. In the face of such civil disobedience by the Dominican sisters one official of the Education Department asked, "What has happened to these nuns? All through the years they have always been co-operative and obedient. Why have they changed now?"[22] The reaction of individual members of the Provincial Administration who made investigatory visits to the school, was significant. While defending the apartheid policy in their official capacity, and clearly defining the laws which were being breached, most of the representatives of the Education Department and the Provincial Administration who came to Springfield during 1976, its first year as an "open" school, privately assured the Principal that they admired the step the Dominican community had taken and considered it to be a courageous, Christian response to the needs of the children from all sectors of the community. They also warned that the nuns were putting their institutions, teachers and pupils at grave risk, not only in terms of the law, but as a consequence of public resentment which brought with it the possibility of retaliatory violence.[23]

Government officials were not alone in viewing as unwise the integration of schools without proper negotiation. Not all members of religious congregations of women and men, approved of the precipitate way in which the new admissions policy had been implemented. Some feared that such a breach of law would lead to the withdrawal of official registration and the eventual closure of the schools concerned. It also drew unwanted political attention to the Church and put at risk Catholic institutions outside the school system. Others, the majority of those directly involved in the launching of the open schools policy, were critical of the fact that the change had been imposed from above, without suitable consultation or the opportunity to prepare for so radical a step. Was this an error in judgement, a failure to recognise the need for the preparation of the nuns, teachers, parents and pupils directly involved in the implementation process? Or was it perhaps part of a well-planned strategy? Whatever the reasons, it can well be argued that Mother Genevieve, a woman of sound judgement, seized the opportune moment for action and succeeded, where a more cautious approach might have derailed the whole project. The element of surprise and the absence of protracted discussion before the event ensured that the impetus was not dissipated.

Sisters, lay teachers, parents and children were plunged into a situation which captured the imagination and won the wholehearted support of all, but especially of those who were more adventurous, more politically 'aware. After so much high-minded discussion, so much verbal protest by the Church, it was a relief to be involved in real action on however small a scale. All of the participants, whatever their political stance, nuns, teachers and parents, advanced into the educational arena where this major battle for human rights was to be fought, with considerable trepidation but not a little courage. However it was clear to all concerned that in future adequate preparation should be provided to all participants in a process that would involve them as individuals and as members of an institution, in direct contravention of civil law, however unjust the specific law might be. The political and social problems which arose out of the first experience of educational integration served as a timely warning to the hierarchy, the AWR, ECAR, and other concerned bodies which were working to redress the injustices of the apartheid system.

Springfield's anti-apartheid admission policy had provided a test case, not only to relevant government departments, but also to those responsible for private schools, Catholic or otherwise. At a plenary session of the South African Catholic Bishops' Conference held in January 1976, the policy of open schools was endorsed. While the Springfield experiment was in its first critical year, a meeting was held at Hammanskraal in July 1976 to "discuss the question of opening Catholic Schools to pupils of all races, in accordance with Resolution 7.0. 9. of the 1976 Plenary Session of the Southern African Bishops' Conference". This resolution made the position of the Catholic Church clear:

> Realising that the Church must give witness to the Gospel in its institutions, the Conference favours a policy of integration in Catholic schools, encourages individual schools and association of schools to promote the implementation of the policy according to the circumstances, and directs that the Department of Schools continue to study the question with a view to enabling the Conference to confirm and concretise the policy.[24]

Present at this meeting were major superiors of religious congregations, a number of lay men and women, and clerics, including representatives of the SACBC and of the Executives of all the main official clerical bodies. In the first instance the conference was "to provide education and information on every possible level with regard to the possibilities of integration".

> Secondly, to receive the advice and suggestions of all concerned about the next steps to be taken and the best methods of proceeding, including whether or not to approach the government with a view to negotiations, bearing in mind that the policy of integration has been accepted by the Bishops, and that delay in implementation will result in the fact that the Church will have lost all credibility.[25]

The aim of the meeting was to assist the Department of Schools of the SACBC by shedding light on the legal and financial implications of the policy, and by advising the hierarchy and making suggestions as to the timing and procedure for the opening of Catholic schools to all races. It was abundantly clear that the Church should act without undue delay, but in the case of schools it would not force the implementation of integration. While the participants rejected any compromise or "soft approach" to the government, it was pointed out that the meeting was "merely consultative and had taken *no decisions*".[26] It was unfortunate that while major superiors of women religious and brothers, together with bishops, priests and some lay men and women were represented at the meeting, principals of schools were not. The Executive of the AWR noted the same situation in respect of the relevant SACBC Commission:

> There was a general agreement that there was insufficient representation of those actively engaged in schools on the

Commission for Christian Education. Sister Louis Michael H.C., was the only such Sister representing the contemporary teachers. It was ... agreed that an approach be made to Archbishop Hurley [Chairman of the Commission] requesting further representation of those directly engaged in teaching.[27]

Archbishop Daniel agreed that "considering the weightiness of the problem, that there be on the Commission people actively engaged in schools particularly during the time of crisis", and the president stated that it was " imperative that those engaged in schools should be consulted when plans were being made so that their reactions could be presented to the Commission before matters were finalised".[28]

The meeting was to be an educational process, the more meaningful in that one institution, Springfield Convent, at Wynberg in the Cape, which had been an exclusive school for white pupils for over 100 years, was already deeply involved in the hazardous but also exciting process of educational integration. The Interim Regional Chapter of the Irish Congregation of Dominican Sisters gave full credit to Mother Genevieve Hickey, at the end of her term of office as Regional Vicar, for her courageous role in the open schools question: "The Committee expressed admiration and gratitude for the way in which Mother Genevieve and her Council had launched the desegregation of our private schools".[29] The capitular sisters recognised that as Dominicans the role of the Congregation aimed at the "evangelisation of all mankind. ... As an integral part of South African Society at present deeply disturbed by social and political unrest, we have a special and urgent duty to promote justice and bring together in Christian brotherhood a distressed and divided people. Our effort towards the desegregation of schools is a positive step in this direction". There was also a need to "intensify apostolic efforts among staff, pupils and their parents", not only to prepare them for the integration of schools but also to promote mutual tolerance and goodwill among the peoples of the African sub-continent.[30]

During 1976, a vigorous process of preparation was begun in Holy Rosary Convent, Port Elizabeth. Sister Margaret Kelly later described the experience:

> We began to prepare as a staff by opening ourselves to the Scriptures, to the African aspects of our South African history, and to the riches of different languages, cultures and traditions. But while the new knowledge helped, we became aware that the real problems lay in what Yeats called 'the foul rag-and-bone shop of the heart' where the junk of wrong attitudes and feelings of superiority cluttered our openness

to others. Fortunately our white pupils had less time to accumulate such junk and received with enthusiasm the new insights into the life and literature of coloured people which Adam Small described to them.

The school community shared sports days, concerts and choirs, and in this way learned to be at ease together and to develop a mutual appreciation of and respect for each other. In January 1977 the first 33 African pupils enrolled in the school, joining classes from pre-primary to secondary level. It was not a move that met with the approval of the Provincial Administration. Accepting Coloured pupils was one thing, the admission of Blacks was quite another.[31] The *Cape Times* reported the latest official response to the open schools debate:

> Administrator of the Cape, Dr L A P A Munnik, yesterday warned that he would consider closing two Port Elizabeth Roman Catholic schools 'forthwith' if they continued to admit Black pupils. Dr Munnik said that Holy Rosary Convent and St Dominic's Priory should ask the Black pupils they had enrolled to leave immediately. Otherwise he would consider withdrawing the registrations of the two schools and closing them.[32]

Sister Marian O'Sullivan, the newly elected Regional Vicar of the Cabra Dominicans in South Africa, stood her ground. She made it clear that all the Cabra Dominican schools had become "open schools" and children would now be accepted "without reference to so-called race classifications". In this she was acting in accordance with the decision of the SACBC taken at their plenary session in February 1976 and with the approval and support of her own sisters. It was a field day for the press. The *Weekend Argus* noted the position of the papacy in respect of the open schools question. "The growing clash between the Roman Catholic Church and the Government over mixed schools took on a wider implication today with the disclosure that Pope Paul VI fully supported South Africa's bishops".[33] This was to be the beginning of a protracted debate on an issue, which for the Church in principle and for the sisters in practice, was not open to compromise. According to the *Sunday Times* of 30 January 1977:

> It was the pressure from nuns that helped to open Roman Catholic schools to black children. ... Nuns everywhere began re-thinking their role after the Vatican Council of Pope John in the Sixties. The Council led to open discussion of many problems in the modern church - in South Africa on education

especially. Young nuns in particular had become increasingly
unhappy about the intolerable situation of segregated schools.
They believe that it is against the whole Christian ethos that
they should teach only whites. The hierarchy, which generally
tended to be conservative, was increasingly affected by
pressure from these nuns'.[34]

While the Church did not seek confrontation and according
to Father Dominic Scholten, secretary-general of the SACBC, it
should act "quietly, positively and decisively, he agreed that there
was no merit in interfering with private schools and believed
admission should be on the basis of merit, and not race". After a
week of debate following the admission of Black pupils to the
two Dominican schools in Port Elizabeth, the Minister of National
Education, Dr P G J Koornhof together with the administrators
of the Cape and the Transvaal, Dr Munnik and Mr S van Niekerk,
issued a statement partly threatening and partly conciliatory:

> The Minister of National Education and the Provincial
> authorities are prepared to discuss problems of Church
> institutions and help to find solutions, taking into account
> the standpoint of the parents. The Government must
> nevertheless warn that continued disregard for the law
> contains serious implications with regard to non-recognition
> of schools and non-recognition of education taking place in
> such schools. But the Government cannot allow chaos to be
> created in education which would ultimately badly affect all
> race groups, and harm the education of the children.[35]

The situation was defused but not settled and the negotiations
continued well into the 1980's. The religious women and men
running the open schools would not retreat before government
threats. Consequently, short of closing schools, which would have
been a very provocative act in a time of great racial tension, there
was little the Government authorities could do. In reality the
open civil disobedience demonstrated in the contravention of
three specific apartheid laws; the *Group Areas Act,* the *Bantu
Education Act* and the *Bantu Urban Areas Consolidation Act,* was
a continuation of a long term admissions policy, not in private
schools but in those that fell under the jurisdiction of the relevant
government department. In the Archdiocese of Cape Town alone
there were 55 Catholic primary and secondary schools, run by
religious congregations. Most of the primary schools could not
have survived without government subsidies, and it was these
that at the outset had to approach a non-discriminatory policy
with caution. Institutions such as St Agnes' Convent Primary
School, Woodstock, were situated in mixed areas and had never

been able to apply strict adherence to the racial laws controlling admissions. From 1976 onwards proof of legal classification was no longer sought by the Principal, Sister Justina Nutley, or if offered by parents, was not accepted. Official letters demanding information based on racial criteria were ignored and left unanswered and children were accepted, irrespective of official racial classification. This was a practice consonant with the ideal of "quiet infiltration" which though less dramatic, was just as effective as the integration policy of the private schools.[36]

In September 1981 a meeting was called at St Anne's, a Dominican Primary School at Southfield, Plumstead. Parents were informed that a number of Black pupils had applied and would be admitted the following January. This decision aroused the ire of some of the parents and a few threatened to withdraw their children from the school. "As a European ratepayer in Plumstead I have a right to object to the school being opened", one man protested. "In times of unrest we will be hit first". Generally the parents were not concerned about the admission of Black children to the school but they were worried about the safety of their children in times of political and civil disobedience. Another objection was that the low school fees, only R15 per term, would open the school to an undesirable element. However it was explained to them that in practice Catholic schools had been open for a number of years but neither Coloured nor African pupils had applied to St Anne's for admission. Father Nicholson reassured the parents: "I really feel that we ought to point out that parents shouldn't worry too much since many black people are just as opposed to integration as some whites may be. They also have their pride". Most of those who applied to St Anne's in 1981 "had been turned down by Marist Brothers College when the school was threatened with closure".[37] Acceptance of the admission of pupils of all races was the common response by parents, the majority of whom gave their full support to the school and benefitted from the new opportunities for social and cultural interaction.

The non-violent defiance of the apartheid laws implied in the early stages of the open schools system, increased the political awareness of those Principals and teachers, religious and lay, whose task it was to put into effect a policy that was potentially a direct threat to the continued existence of the schools. It also made them more sensitive to the need for mutual tolerance and support among parents and children, the first step on the way towards a fully interacting, multi-cultural society. The work of active conscientization of parents and children was seen by the Cabra Dominicans as one of their most urgent tasks, especially in a time of division and institutional violence. In schools such as Holy Rosary Convent, Port Elizabeth and Springfield Convent School in the Cape, meetings and activities were organised to promote ideals of Christian responsibility for the promotion of justice, peace and racial harmony. A main focus of the meeting of Dominican Principals to be held at Springfield in July 1978, was the evangelisation of all mankind, especially through the apostolate of the schools. The implementation of Article 25 of the Acts of the Interim Regional Chapter of 1976-1977, was the focus of this meeting. It states:

> As an integral part of South African Society at present deeply disturbed by social and political unrest, we have a special and urgent duty to promote justice and bring together in Christian brotherhood a distressed and divided people. Our efforts towards the desegregation of schools is a positive step in this direction. While recognising the value of our schools, we realise that the time has come, not only to intensify our apostolic efforts among staff, pupils and their parents, but also to reach out to the thousands of South Africans who need our help. ...The school, in addition to its formal role, should be a centre from which the Sisters penetrate into the local community. This can be achieved by means of family catechesis, pastoral activities such as prayer groups, adult education and literacy courses. The training and involvement of lay staff, parents and pupils in well organised programmes will both deepen their own personal commitment to Christ, and enrich the lives of many.[38]

In this challenging work the sisters would be helped by community renewal to "accept necessary changes with courage and generosity". This programme was carried out with remarkable dedication in most of the Dominican primary and secondary schools, and it is clear from the records, that while the nuns were keenly aware of the needs of the schools and the wider community, there were not enough to go round.[39] Financial aid to private schools would do much to solve the budgetary problems, but in the late 1970's and through the next decade, there were more immediate pressures. When threats of arson and violence, at one time from the White right, at another from the Black left, angry at the lack of support by private institutions for school boycotts, even the sisters and lay teachers of convent schools might have been justified in asking, with their African brothers and sisters, *"Senzenina?* What have we done?"

For all of those directly involved in education and in the process of conscientization one thing was clear. South Africa was the place for action. It might be dangerous but it never lacked interest and excitement. However, in the circumstances, it was not always easy to achieve consensus within communities, especially on the question of the political involvement of the sisters. Some disapproved of the active, and sometimes aggressive, political involvement of some of the nuns. And the opening of Dominican schools to all South Africans had presented its own problems, both for the children who found themselves in schools where the majority of pupils were classified as white, and for the Coloured and African parents. These had to be prepared to face official harassment and the resentment and threats of their own neighbours. The need to educate sisters, teachers, parents and pupils in their responsibilities to promote justice, not only in the wider political sphere, but in the day to day living and working together, was recognised and as far as possible implemented. Some of the Dominican schools did not suffer directly from the class boycotts and absenteeism which from 1976 onwards, were mainly the result of compulsory attendance at political rallies. The disruption in regular schooling which these activities caused, affected every group, and few could hope to escape the consequences of ongoing violence in the confrontation between pupils, students and police. In many such circumstances the sisters could not avoid involvement however trepidatory they might have felt. In the records of the Cabra Dominicans in South Africa, as well as in the living memory of those who were personally engaged in Coloured and Black education, and in open schools, there is abundant documentary and oral evidence of anti-apartheid activities involving sisters and lay teachers. In some cases participation was voluntary, in others by force of circumstances. For the protection of pupils from their own temerity and violence and from police brutality, every risk had to be taken. Even the safe conduct of pupils on their way to and from school, or their safeguarding at church services and in the school playing fields and classrooms, demanded of the teachers careful planning, strategical ingenuity and the acceptance of personal risk.

During the 1980's when school boycotts and illegal protest marches by school children and students were of regular occurrence, some of the sisters and lay staff of schools such as Marian High in Elsies River, and Immaculata High in Wittebome, accompanied the marchers both as unofficial marshals, ensuring the good conduct of their own pupils, and as potential witnesses of and a shield against brutal police action. The Dominican nuns were no strangers to tear gas attacks and the assault of rubber bullets, nor indeed to arrest and imprisonment. Sister Áine Hardiman one of the protestors arrested on 28 August 1985 during the march to Pollsmoor prison, later wrote to Sister Marian O'Sullivan and her Dominican sisters of the events leading up to her arrest:

> The march on Pollsmoor was announced through the media. The purpose of the march seemed to me to be 'spot on' - to march to Pollsmoor and deliver a letter to Nelson Mandela to encourage him and pledge to work for his release and that of all political detainees. The Minister of Police banned the march and detained the leader, Dr A. Boesak. I prayed and fasted the day before the march seeking guidance on whether to participate - the main deterrent worrying me was the likelihood of police brutality on the students. Yet when morning came it was clear to me that I should walk *in solidarity* with others to say *peacefully* and with determination that real leaders must be freed to speak for their people and that the sham of 'negotiations' with puppet leaders must be dropped. Four Sisters in our community took part.[40]

A group of twenty, including the four sisters, two students and fourteen teachers left Holy Trinity Convent en route to the Athlone stadium where the marchers were assembling. Sister Áine's description of the situation there and the show of power by the army and the police is representative of so many similar occasions occurring throughout South Africa at that time:

> There we found an array of caspirs and other military vehicles that reminded me of a military tattoo. All men aboard the caspirs, hypos, buffels were at the ready with guns pointed. The police were deployed in relays in front of the army but at ground level. As we arrived police baton-charged a group of youths down a side street. ... The loud hailer ordered us to disperse. We stood. The command to charge was given and people started running helter skelter with police in hot pursuit brandishing shambuks, quirts, batons. The teacher beside me said: Sister just stand. ... One man as he passed us raised his baton and brought it down on the head of my companion. Patrick lost his balance and fell. I bent down to help him up and the TV crews were on top of us. A TV man asked him if he was alright. I shall never forget the dignity and strength of Patrick's answer. 'I'm OK and I want to tell you this. We *shall* overcome'

The protestors moved off quietly to regroup at another venue, and at Hewat College joined forces with about 1000 students. "It was a joy to find Sister Feargal beside me as we started the march", wrote Sister Áine. The two Dominicans were invited to join the clergy in the first two rows of the 2000 strong body of marchers.

> We linked arms and silently wended our way round the side
> streets that lead to Kroomboom Road. The caspirs etc. were
> there ahead of us, about 500m. The silence deepened as we
> walked towards the massed array of force. ... we clung to one
> another more tightly as we advanced and prayed softly. It
> was for me a moment of vision - what the new SA could be -
> all races, all creeds, and none, walking arm in arm into danger
> for justice.

The two thousand people knelt on the ground "in silent prayer"
before the military force of apartheid. The crowd was ordered to
disperse and the twenty-nine leaders of the march in the two
front rows, including Sisters Áine and Feargal were arrested.
According to Sister Áine "The march in itself and our being in jail
was a small thing relative to the whole struggle but it was
significant because it revealed that peaceful demonstration was
being repressed, and secondly, it showed the large number of
clergy ... on the side of the struggle".[41]

It was clear to all witnesses of this march that the large crowd
of protesters had made no attempt to resort to violence. For some
of the Dominican sisters the risk taken by their colleagues in
this demonstration was a foolhardy act. Sister Feargal accepted
that opinions on such matters differed but stood her ground on
the action she and the other Dominicans had freely taken:

> I know there are some people who would frown on our
> participation in that march on the 28th August. It set out to
> be and continued to be until dispersed, a peaceful, prayerful
> demonstration, led by clergymen. Not a stone was thrown.
> The only violence was on the part of the police force, as they
> charged the crowd behind us. I am not sorry I was part of the
> happenings of that day as I am convinced that people saw
> the Church of Cape Town willing to take the lead and not
> satisfied with bringing up the rear.[42]

At the time of their prison detention it was little consolation
that the two Dublin born Dominican sisters were under the same
roof as Nelson Mandela. During the bail hearing on the Thursday
and Friday following the arrest of the 29 marchers, it was claimed
that "some of the black detainees among the group had been ill-
treated, 'stripped and humiliated' ". The Irish press was kept
well informed of the course of events, the *Cork Examiner* being
one of the papers to make direct contact with Sister Marian
O'Sullivan, at that time Regional Vicar of the Cabra Dominicans
and herself a native of Douglas, Cork. Among those chosen by
the group to give evidence was "Sister [Áine] Hardiman, [who] in
her testimony, told the court that she had been working with the

oppressed people for 16 years. She regarded the protest march as one way in which they could release tension in a peaceful fashion". According to Sister Marian, she "presented a very courageous, strong statement for peace and for understanding of the frustrations which exist in South Africa. ... If bail is not granted, then it will be clear to anybody that the hearing has been a whitewash. It is obvious to anybody listening to the evidence that the accused people did not have any violent intentions".[43]

Peter Barry the Irish Foreign Minister, who was "greatly concerned at the detention of the nuns" intervened on their behalf.[44] He asked the Foreign Minister of Luxembourg, Mr Jacques Poos, who was leader of an EEC delegation on a fact-finding visit to South Africa, to raise the matter with the Foreign Minister, Pik Botha. In the event, those detained after the attempted march on Pollsmoor were given bail, but only after they had been held in prison over the weekend. This was not the last time that Cabra Dominicans, and indeed religious women of other congregations in South Africa, experienced the reality of imprisonment. At the 1986 Annual General Meeting of the Association of Women Religious the involvement of sisters in the struggle was noted:

> During this year a number of Sisters have made public stands and have been arrested and imprisoned. Others have been negotiating - sometimes day and night - with the authorities to get them to see another point of view over education, or to release people taken into custody; others have been dealing, sometimes daily, with the SAP or SADF in trying to avert violence. Still others have been 'around' to console, advise, to heal and to take affidavits. I am sure that for many Sisters this is becoming part of the Apostolate. Some Sisters because of their action or involvements against the system get heard about - this is good, we need to expose the evil - others are fighting the system without getting heard about; each of us has her role to play when her time comes.

This was indeed the case among the Cabra Dominicans. Some worked in the front line but for the majority it was a hidden battle. As in the case of many other topics touched upon in this study, the history of the role of women in the struggle is still to be completed. During the second half of the 1980's when the State of Emergency gave the police, in practice at least, almost unlimited powers of action, those involved in adult education or in development projects in African townships and squatter camps were inevitably caught up in the daily life of the people among whom they worked. On most occasions of potential violence such as protest marches, mass meetings and funerals, sisters, ministers of religion and others who formed part of working teams, were present. For those such as Sister Clare Harkin and Sister Áine Hardiman, who lived at one time or another in shacks at Nyanga and Guguletu, the results of excessive police action were all too evident, and very personal to them. In such dangerous times, who would seek direct confrontation with the police? Certainly not Sister Clare, but circumstances challenged her and she reacted to protect a youth she did not even know. Early in July 1986, she had accompanied parents who were searching for their son. Finally they found his body in the police morgue. He had been beaten up and killed in Nyanga. Sister Clare attended the civil funeral as a concerned friend of the family, and not as a form of political protest. The burial completed the two sisters started to drive to the home of the deceased young man for the ceremonial washing of hands and for refreshments. However they found themselves with the people surrounded by caspirs filled with armed police. Sister Áine left the car to walk with some of the young people while Sister Clare tried to tell the police that it was not a political funeral. The police ordered the crowd to disperse, which they did. Then Clare saw a policeman raising his quirt to attack a young man and, on the spur of the moment, she came between the boy and the policeman. They were both immediately arrested, bundled into a police van and taken away. Sister Clare was charged with inciting people to violence and with interfering with a policeman in the course of his duties. During the 17 days of her detention in Pollsmoor prison she was roughly interrogated for several days, first about the Anglican ministers of religion who had attended the funeral and later she was questioned by the police about the Kairos document, of which she had been a signatory.[45] The *Case of Sister Thérèse Emmanuel Dempsey vs the State*, was heard in the Supreme Court in Cape Town. The verdict was that Sister Clare Harkin had been unjustly arrested and that she must be released without delay. There was great rejoicing among those most concerned about unjust detention, but when the verdict was brought to the Appeal Court in Bloemfontein, the right of police action was upheld.[46]

But not all interventions of the Cabra Dominicans involved in townships projects, brought them to the attention of the police. Those who worked daily in the townships and on the Cape Flats, either in formal education, pastoral care, or development, could not be ignorant of the fact that many adults needed either academic help, literacy courses or practical skills to improve their quality of life and opportunities to earn a livelihood. The opening of St Francis Cultural Centre in Langa in the Western Cape in the early 1970's, prepared the way for increasing participation by lay people and religious in part-time education programmes for Africans, ranging from literacy classes to matriculation. Sisters from most of the Dominican convents in the Cape Peninsula offered their services in the evenings. In the Transvaal the picture was somewhat different. Beginning in a very small way the sisters at Sancta Maria Convent, Vanderbijlpark, had given tuition to men and women from Sharpville from the mid-1960's onwards. Classes were held at the Convent during the week and in a primary school in Sharpville each Saturday morning. Some of the students were completing matriculation, others were at a lower level, while a few were beginning study for a degree. Courses given included English, history, geography, biology, mathematics, criminology, and Latin for those planning to study law. This was a common spread of academic subjects. In the 1970's the number of adults availing of this service increased rapidly and Sancta Maria school premises were used in the evenings. This evening school provided tuition for up to 300 students, all involved in improving their academic qualifications. St Catherine's Convent, Florida was also involved in work among adult Africans. Sister Feighan Gillooly, a proficient speaker of Portuguese, worked with the miners from Mozambique, more to meet social and pastoral needs than in formal education. The night school is presently flourishing, at Florida, on the West Rand. It is not under the control of the Dominican sisters but St Catherine's Convent School premises are used each evening and courses range from basic literacy to matriculation. In St Dominic's School for the Deaf at Hammanskraal, the sisters followed the tradition of Wittebome in promoting the qualifications of teachers on their staff, most of whom had a professional teacher's certificate but not a diploma in deaf teaching. Sister Finbar Conway, in the best tradition of the two deaf institutions in the Western Cape, devoted her time and expertise to the care of past pupils, while Sister Mannes Daly, for years after her retirement from teaching, worked with Father Cyril Axelrod for the adult deaf in and around Johannesburg.

In Holy Rosary Convent and St Dominic's Priory, Port Elizabeth, the work for adult African students and for justice and peace involved many of the sisters. In the mid-1980's the community of Marymount Convent, Uitenhage, besides their educational work for adults, which had been initiated in the late 1970's, were also deeply involved in the support of those caught up in public protest and police violence. The Langa massacre of the 21 March 1985 left in its wake the wounded, the traumatised, those who had been the victims of or who had witnessed, police violence, and many who were on the run from the law. Sisters Bernadette Flinter and Kathy Gaylor spent long hours at the Catholic Presbytery in Uitenhage helping the wounded, collecting evidence, and assisting those writing affidavits. It was not possible for the sisters to operate from Marymount since at this time the convent and schools were under continuous police surveillance. The sisters also helped in other practical ways: providing venues for protest meetings and safe houses for those on the run. They also copied and circulated pamphlets giving information to squatters as to their rights. Sister Rita McMeniman, a woman of principle, spent her last years in Marymount, and in her old age wrote letters of protest against the inhuman treatment being meted out to the African people in the locations around Uitenhage. Remembered for her gentle spirit, for her musical skills on the violin, always played for the delight of her sisters, and for her wit and humour as a public speaker, she, with all the other members of her community, played a hidden part in a violent situation so foreign to her peaceful spirit.[47]

It is not possible to measure statistically in terms of reconciliation and the application of true Christian justice, the value or success of the various projects initiated for the protection of the beleaguered people involved in the struggle, or for the promotion of educational opportunities for children as well as for mature African students. However as violence escalated in South Africa it became clearly evident to the Catholic hierarchy that there was also a urgent need for direct Christian education in the sphere of justice and reconciliation. In 1972 the SACBC in plenary session noted:

> Only last year in Rome, the World Synod of Bishops again declared the Christian's duty to work for social justice in the public life of his community, of his nation and of the world community. ... So, wherever citizens are capable of influencing their own destiny through active participation in community and national affairs, they are bound to carry their Christianity fully into public life. This means that, in the human situation, there must be involvement of all Christians, and an involvement in all situations. The Synod itself said of this love: it 'implies an absolute demand for justice, namely a recognition of the dignity and rights of one's neighbour'. Let us also remember that Pope Paul's theme for the year is that if we want peace we must work for justice.[48]

The full history of the work of the Catholic Church in South Africa for justice, peace and reconciliation during the 1980's and early 1990's, has not yet been written. In society at large there was no corporate body, religious or political, that could claim the monopoly of effective action in the promotion of justice and reconciliation. Within the Catholic Church the SACBC made a strong appeal for active participation by the laity and by clerics and religious men and women. In 1984 the AWR delegated to its Executive the task of an in-depth study of the integration of justice and faith in the work of evangelisation. A sub-committee specifically for that purpose, met in January 1985. Its task was to "look at certain issues of justice and reconciliation facing major superiors in South Africa today and to do necessary research to be able to conduct workshops" on these issues at the Annual General Meetings of the AWR. This was one of a number of initiatives taken to educate religious in the matter of justice and reconciliation. A little over three years earlier, in September 1981, Sister Bernard Ncube was appointed by the SACBC to promote an understanding of the principles and practical application of justice and reconciliation, among women religious. In January of the following year Sister Margaret Kelly OP of the Cabra Dominicans joined her on a part-time basis.

This was not Sister Margaret's first experience of work for justice and peace. In 1974 she was the first Chairman of the Justice and Peace Committee in the Diocese of Port Elizabeth, a position later taken by Sister Dorothy Balfe. The Newsletter of 14 October 1982 issued by Sisters Bernard Ncube and Margaret Kelly gives a clear picture of their work and experiences:

> Part of the time we have spent on our own on-going education in the area of Justice and Reconciliation. We visited re-settlement camps and other areas of crisis. We also attended workshops to help us to learn methods of community development and economic, social and political analysis. To keep us in touch with the problems of daily life we also are involved in our local situations. Sr. Bernard works with Y.C.W. Youth Groups, Women's Federation Group and Interdomination Self Help Projects. Sr. Margaret works mainly in the sphere of education .[49]

The two sisters responded to invitations from Bishops or religious superiors. In some cases they visited each house of a diocesan Congregation in order to "help to update ... [the sisters] on the situation in South Africa". This could be part of preparation for a Chapter or perhaps a one-day or weekend workshop followed by visits to some convents. They dealt with such issues as the work of the Justice and Peace Commissions and the scriptural basis of the Church's teachings on justice. An analysis of the economic, social and political situation in South Africa helped participants to come to a greater understanding of the main issues of justice, and the role and responsibility of religious sisters in this work. Both Sister Bernard and Sister Margaret were convinced of the importance of the work they were doing.

> For our part we feel that as sisters we experience the pain, the fear, the guilt and all the other emotions involved in facing these issues both in ourselves and in our communities and congregations. We also find those we work with feel the need for more help and information. Of course they say that priests and brothers need it too! Many find the message disturbing and confusing and some find our presentation of the message less than perfect but nearly all express the wish to travel further along the road together.[50]

Within the first year of this Sisters' Project, Sisters Bernard and Margaret had worked with 500 of the 4 500 women religious in South Africa. Some of the participants submitted their individual or group evaluation of the seminars given, and most of the responses were positive. The clarification of the scriptural base of justice and reconciliation was of great value to those who had seen the work for justice as simply a political response to the apartheid regime. One opinion expressed made this clear: "There is need of deep theological foundations and a good understanding of history and culture before people can see the full implications and demands of the Church's teachings on justice and reconciliation. Slogans or mere counter-propaganda will not suffice". Another perception was that the sisters were attempting to fight the evils in the South African situation with the "weapons of the world" rather than with the "weapons which Jesus used and passed on to us". For others the "content and method of presentation proved a disturbing but healthy challenge to pre-conceived ideas and ignorance".

The women religious who attended the workshops, meetings and courses run by Sisters Margaret and Bernard, learnt not only the importance of social analysis and the urgent necessity for promoting justice and peace. For many of the sisters involved it was the first time that they faced the reality of the social injustices imposed on women, and learnt that in the feminine context they as women had to accept responsibility in the struggle for justice and peace. The interest engendered by this work inspired Sister Margaret to follow a course of studies for a Master's degree at the Irish School of Ecumenics. Her research topic in the field of feminist theology is entitled *South African women and feminist theology*, and the essence of thought on the position and role of South African women is well summed up in the following:

> South African women have long been oppressed but for a long time too they have been committed to fighting racism, classism and sexism. They have joined the black man in the struggle for national liberation but the men often underestimate their contribution and are themselves often guilty of sexism. Feminist theology offers such women a chance to reflect on their own situation in the light of the scriptural teachings on women and liberation. It exposes the patriarchal bias in scripture itself and develops the secondary story of women: some women are oppressed and evoke our compassion, others call forth our admiration by their liberating lives. It portrays the ideal of Jesus that the church should be a discipleship of equals ... ; it provides a meaningful spirituality for the present and it helps women to portray their own ideal of liberation for the future.[51]

This study was a valuable preparation for the work Sister Margaret was to do between 1987 and 1994, as Secretary of the Justice and Peace Commission of the SACBC. This involved among other things the education of the people for participation in the 1994 elections.

There were other methods of challenging pre-conceived ideas and combatting ignorance in the spheres of justice and reconciliation, and the involvement of the Cabra Dominicans as of other religious congregations was not limited to either membership of commissions or formal projects for the instruction of specific groups in the community. The practical *doing* of justice by the nuns, many of whom had retired either from full-time teaching or from household management, was and remains one of the most remarkable expressions of the Congregation's commitment to local, practical justice. For a significant number of sisters in South Africa the challenges of the last two decades of the twentieth century have provided a new vocation arising out of a strong Dominican urge to use every moment of active life as missionaries among the local people. Age, seen by social analysts and by the sisters themselves to be the main stumbling block to apostolic effectiveness, has proved in the event to be one of the great emancipators of many of the nuns. Rather than limiting the work of those above the age for retirement, it has freed many seeking greater apostolic involvement. Sister Stephana Ward who had spent most of her active life in St Dominic's Convent, Wittebome overseeing the laundry and household work, became a much loved visitor, friend and spiritual guide to the old, the sick and the lonely. Despite her age and increasing deafness she brought Communion regularly to her friends and supported them by her prayers. In some ways a formidable woman, she recognised no parish boundaries but moved freely to those who needed her help. Work of this kind has been the choice of many of the sisters, who find in pastoral interaction fresh opportunities to fulfil their Dominican vocation.

In 1972 Sister Louis Rudden, after almost a lifetime involved in household work in St Mary's Convent, Cape Town, was assigned to Holy Trinity Convent, Matroosfontein. With Sister Geraldine O'Driscoll, the new principal of St Mary's School at Nyanga, she began a creative phase in her life as a Dominican missionary. This so-called "unstructured apostolate" focused mainly on adult catechesis which included informal instruction, encouragement, spiritual guidance, shared prayer and friendly support. It was a dangerous and difficult time in which to travel around on the Cape Flats or indeed to visit people in their homes, but it was also a period when this service was of great value for building up the morale of the community. A sister reporting on the needs of Guguletu, indicates the problems arising out of this kind of work:

> One of the difficulties in this field is that there is no precedent to measure by so there is difficulty in recognising achievement or evaluation even of work, as compared with the classroom situation. ... To belong to a team ministry seems to be one of the important ways of finding support. The needs of Matroosfontein: Sisters [who are] free to visit parishioners in their homes. [This is] already being done by Sister Louis, also distributing Communion, visiting the hospital, instructing converts. Sr. Louis has made tremendous changes in the relation of the convent to the parish through her quiet, consistent work.[52]

Visiting the poor, the sick and the old became part of the apostolate of many of the Cabra Dominicans in South Africa. In 1990 Sister John Lavelle was assigned to Holy Trinity Convent, Matroosfontein and she immediately began the work of visiting the local people in their homes. When Nazareth House was opened in Elsie's River, she added this to her visiting schedule. She brought to all her friends, spiritual comfort, material assistance and a wealth of amazing stories. One of her main tasks was to organise the distribution of food donated weekly by main supermarkets in the Cape Peninsula. Her friends rallied to her call for assistance and many families in and around Elsie's River, benefitted from her work.

Two retired Sisters in the Western Cape studied reflexology, another way in which service could be provided for the wider community. Sister Oliver Connell, a music teacher by profession, qualified towards the end of 1991 and Sister Columbanus O'Mahoney, a teacher, at the beginning of 1992. Both run small clinics, Sister Oliver in Springfield and Sister Columbanus at St Mary's Convent, Nyanga. From 1998 onwards the latter is offering her services in St Dominic's Priory, Port Elizabeth. They serve the sisters, priests and lay people from the community, and both the sisters and their clients can enjoy a quiet talk together. Ms Maria Msebenzi, also followed the course in reflexology and did her practical training under the supervision of Sister Columbanus. She is now a qualified reflexologist working in the clinic at Nyanga. Sister Columbanus brought her services beyond the limits of the township. She made weekly visits to the sick in St Michael's Convent, Rondebosch and to the Region House in Cape Town.

Many other members of the Dominican Region in South Africa, too numerous to mention, moved from professional teaching to an apostolate among the sick, the poor, the educationally deprived. Their clients were those who needed some help to face life and responsibility in a complex and often violent society. Among those who accepted the challenge of this apostolate were Sisters Assumpta Carey, Philip Ryan, Colette Kenny and Madeleine Corcoran, all of whom on retirement moved from the classroom to work as chaplains or visitors among the sick. Sister Assumpta is a welcome and familiar visitor in Victoria Hospital, Wynberg and in Wynberg Military Hospital while Sister Philip moves between Groote Schuur Hospital and Medi City, Kenilworth. Sister Colette, who lives at St Agnes' Convent, Woodstock, visits the sick in Woodstock Hospital,[53] while Sister Madeleine visits the old and the lonely of all religious persuasions in and around Woodstock bringing friendship and prayer to the lonely. In this work the sisters find opportunities to give expression to their apostolic zeal in the spirit of their Dominican vocation. In the professional field Sister Jennifer Alt has served the church for many years as a clinical psychologist. Others answering the call of Vatican II, combined full-time professional work with service to the community in liturgy, adult education, catechetics and development work. These nuns had experienced their own "long walk to freedom" as Dominican women, and they were anxious to share with others the freeing experiences of renewal that had given them the opportunity to follow their Dominican vocation more fully.

Chapter Sixteen

A Time to Change

The history of the first hundred years of the Cabra and Sion Hill Dominicans in South Africa illustrates the varying phases in the life and development of the missionary foundations begun in the second half of the nineteenth century. After initial dispersal, each group moved from a temporary sense of isolation into a period of adaptation. For the women involved it was a time to build, a period of construction, when the Sisters built convents and enlarged schools to meet the growing needs of a developing educational system. They also trained teachers and prepared young women, for the most part Irish and South African, for their religious life as Dominican missionaries. Both for the nuns and for the young boys and girls they were training as teachers, the growth of the examination system demanded more rigorous academic and professional qualifications. The new criteria were met, and the excellence of convent education, whether for the financially straitened attending mission schools or for the more affluent in private academies, was recognised and appreciated both by parents and by the official representatives of the Department of Education. Gradually the Dominican Sisters made good friends and became part of the colonial society in which they had settled.

Fading memories of life in Cabra and Sion Hill remained for many the ideal, and in times of discouragement, a nostalgic reminder of the security and comfort of a traditional mother house. Involvement in the amalgamation debate in the early 1920's, and in the long process of union, offered future hope to the South African superiors. Amalgamation with the Cabra congregation was seen as a guarantee of survival, of a steady influx of young, educated Irish recruits. It would mean also the restoration of the true Dominican spirit which, Ireland assured the South African Dominicans, they sadly lacked. Eminent clerics such as Archbishop Finbar Ryan had expressed real doubts as to the motives of the sisters in the Region of South Africa in seeking amalgamation, and he did not hesitate to communicate his uneasiness to the Dominican superiors, his very good friends in Ireland. Mother Teresa Coleman and Mother de Ricci Harkin and their respective Councils chose what to them at the time seemed to be the lesser of two evils, a solution not unfamiliar to the Irish communities which in the 1920's moved hesitantly, and in many instances with strong reservations, to the implementation of amalgamation in 1928. Given the variety and often incompatible ingredients in both Ireland and South Africa, it would have been impossible to create a perfect, foolproof recipe for that perfect unity of "heart and mind in God", proposed by St Augustine. However the Prioresses General and the Regional Vicars could impose, and as far as possible, did impose, the ideal of exact conformity to customs and monastic practices which to them represented an outward sign of inward Dominicanism in its purest form.

In the event the union between the South African and Irish Dominicans which took place in 1938, was not to be the precursor of a return to medieval Dominican ideals and practices. World War II, which brought rapid development in almost every area of science and technology and created new work and career opportunities for women, also left as its legacy to a battle weary world, the Cold War, with its constant threat of nuclear destruction. In the circumstances, where life was potentially on the verge of extinction and every moment was precious, young men and women could argue the case for a life style that concentrated on self-fulfilment now, with present pleasure taking precedence over future reward. Such aspirations of a secular society could not be excluded from the cloister, and of this the Church was keenly aware. Nevertheless many religious superiors, including the Prioresses General of the Cabra Dominicans, strove to maintain the old order through the strong imposition of conformity and uniformity. It was the safest way to ensure the preservation of that perfect Dominican practice proposed by Finbar Ryan and other Dominican brethren.

Whatever the forces of age-old tradition, the legitimate needs of women religious had to be met. Many young people inside and outside the cloister, were restless and often resentful in the face of virtually meaningless, petty restraints. In April 1943, Pius XII speaking to the Italian Women's Diocesan Associations of Catholic Action, noted the radical change in the common perception of the role of woman in society, as wife, home-maker and nurturer of children:

> Today ... this traditional type of womanhood is undergoing rapid transformation. You see women, young women in particular, leave the retirement of their homes and enter almost all of the professions - fields of life and work formerly confined exclusively to men. The beginnings of this revolution, at first tentative, then gradually growing in strength, have been in evidence for quite a while and have been caused chiefly by the industrial development of the modern world. But for some years now - like a torrent which overflowing its banks overcomes all resistance - women seem to have penetrated the entire field of social life.[1]

This might have been the case in civil society, but for the Dominican Sisters in the Region of South Africa, the first 25 years following amalgamation with the Irish Congregation in 1938, while it was a time of hope and development, was also characterised by a policy of constraint and control. This arose out of a need to meet the criteria for perfect Dominican practice laid down by the Congregation in Ireland. Some of the Sisters who had entered and were trained for the Cape Town and Port Elizabeth missions prior to amalgamation in 1938, tended to see the imposition of certain regulations, especially those restricting egress, as retrogressive. Clearly they had been made by higher superiors who did not understand the South African situation. Those who criticised the new system were well aware that by amalgamation with the Congregation in Ireland, the Dominican Sisters of the Region of South Africa had gained status. They were members of an international body, and one that had the support and respect of eminent churchmen. But they had also lost many of the traditional freedoms which had evolved in the Cape Colony during the 1860's and 1870's. These had been granted to meet the needs of the missions, and to provide opportunities for reasonable recreational facilities. As a result of accepted practice in the earliest years of the Dominican foundations in South Africa such concessions had come to be regarded as sacred rights handed down to them from their foundresses, and not, as the Irish superiors seemed to infer, as signs of decadence. There was an even more serious obstacle to the realisation of a true spirit of amalgamation. Young Irish sisters, in the training and preparation of whom the South African Dominicans had no part, and were in no way consulted, arrived from Kerdiffstown. Their very presence and their training in Dominican life and liturgy, served to emphasise the marginalisation of the Region which it was believed, was outside the mainstream of the Congregation. Rightly or wrongly the perception was that the Congregation was in Ireland and the newly formed Region of South Africa was an adjunct. The struggle of the 1920's and 1930's, which led to union with Ireland and not with German communities in South Africa, was clearly not the solution to all problems. Nor could the sisters of the Region of South Africa claim to be alone in the battle for reasonable change in a system that in many respects did not meet either the aspirations or the needs of the modern world.

The process which brought about fundamental changes in the lives of Catholic religious, women and men, involved another struggle initiated by the Church, conscious of the growing conflict between the traditional ways of religious life and the modern mentality. "We can then take it that the disease from which religious life is suffering is that of institutional crisis, of a lack of adaptation of the ever-creative ideal of the order to the claims of modern life, an insubordination of the letter to the spirit".[2] This malaise was evident in many religious congregations and the Cabra Dominicans were no exception. For those religious superiors and their spiritual guides who had fought for an authentic revival of the old and revered principles of monastic laws and practices, and who themselves belonged to another more conservative age, it was difficult to recognise the needs of the young. However the question, "What is to be done?" was asked, and at the highest level:

> Ought we to remain obstinately faithful to the letter of the law and to details of observance as well as methods of formation, and to be content, if need be, with making use of individual dispensations such as were foreseen by the maker of the rule? Or is it not wiser to see the finger of God in the legitimate needs of our time and without eliminating it completely to interpret in the manner best suited to its special purpose an observance that has grown less efficacious?[3]

In 1952, at the International Meeting of Mothers General convened by the Sacred Congregation of Religious, attention was focused on a "better understanding of the movement known as *aggiornamento*, or the adaptation of religious life to present needs, its necessity, its meaning, and its extent; a deeper sense of the need for collaboration and coordination of active forces too often scattered, and dispersed". The founding of Associations and Federations of Superiors General, linking the many congregations of nuns and sisters throughout the world, would give the major superiors a united voice in the transformation of religious life.[4] This Congress also considered the founding of a School for Higher Religious and Social Studies and other institutions "intended to impart a university culture to Sisters and apostolic workers".

The record of the proceedings make this point clear: "The need for higher studies in literary, scientific and professional matters is generally recognised, but there is a tendency to regard higher studies in religion as the special sphere of the priest".[5] The establishment of a Roman college of higher studies for nuns, and women involved in apostolic activities, did not exclude the establishment of similar schools for the same purpose in different parts of the world.[6] The agenda for the three-day meeting anticipated many of the areas of concern, change and co-operation which were to engage the attention and energy of women religious for the next forty years. The changes popularly attributed to the vision and courage of Pope John XXIII were already there in the programmes of renewal proposed in *Sedes Sapientiae* and *Sponsa Christi* by Pius XII. Indeed the renewal process was already making an impact on religious life in the decade preceding Vatican II, though the pace was slow and in some cases reluctant.

In the *Concluding Instructions* of the 1952 International Congress, the extent of the task of adaptation was spelt out for the Mothers General. What is of great interest here are the areas for adaptation and change proposed by the Sacred Congregation of Religious. These reflect the growing discontent among religious and particularly nuns and sisters. The major superiors were to look critically at the 1922 Constitutions and propose to Rome what modifications they considered necessary. What was envisaged by the Sacred Congregation of Religious was a "genuinely vital evolution ... without jolts or shocks". All modifications of Constitutions were to be submitted to the General Chapter, and approved not only by an absolute majority, "but even by the moral unanimity of the capitulants".[7] Pius XII was clear on the areas of special concern in the revision process:

> For your part this is what We counsel: make sure that nothing in your customs, your manner of life or your ascetical practices raises a barrier or causes loss of vocations. We have in mind certain usages which were, no doubt, suited to the times and surroundings in which they were instituted but are out of place today, so that even a good girl with courage would find them an obstacle to their vocation ... To return for the moment to the question of dress: the religious habit should always be expressive of the consecration to Christ; that is expected and desired by all. For the rest, let it be in keeping with hygiene ... To sum up, then, in all that is not essential, make the adaptations called for by reason and well-ordered charity.[8]

On the question of moderation of the religious habit, Rome advised that where a minority found this unacceptable, but were "not unduly obstreperous in its opposition", superiors should "go ahead with the changes", otherwise the Church counselled patient waiting.[9] The first sartorial concession made by the 1954 General Chapter of the Cabra Dominicans was no more than a minor move, a first tentative step in what was to be a relatively slow process of change. Many of the sisters in the course of time, laid aside the habit and wore secular dress without the veil. However during the late 1960's and 1970's the shortening of sleeves, the raising of hemline and the simplification of veils, which led to the exposure of hair and ankle, were seen by some sisters as grave breaches of monastic etiquette. For others it was both a legitimate expression of femininity, and a simplification of dress more appropriate to life in the modern world. It was also a healthy substitute for the habit in a hot climate. The radical change from adapted habits, to complete secular wear for local travel, holidays and home visits, was slower in the Region of South Africa than in Ireland. It was not until 1977 that permission was granted to sisters in South Africa, in very special circumstances, to wear a discreet form of secular dress for travel purposes only, but for some time after that the wearing of the veil remained *de rigueur.*

In 1952 however the concept of adaptation of dress, especially the substitution of a grey ensemble for the white Dominican habit, was hardly conceivable. The General Chapter of 1954 recommended that there should be "as far as possible, uniformity in clothing - cappa, travelling cloak, underclothing, and bedclothing". In 1947 a petition for a simpler form of head-dress was approved by the Regional Chapter, and submitted to the 1954 General Chapter .[10] This concession had not been granted by the 1948 General Chapter, but when it was put to the vote in 1954, two years after the approval given by the Pope for the adaptation of the religious habit, thirty-four out of the thirty-five capitulars, accepted the proposal. The heavily starched head-dress and guimp were to give way to a simpler, softer form of cap and veil. In 1955, after experimentation in the novitiate at Kerdiffstown, the new style, still constrictive, was adopted by the Congregation.[11] The question of dress though not an issue in the 1950's, became a matter of greater importance in the post-Vatican II period of renewal. The *Decree on the appropriate renewal of religious life,* laid down the general guidelines to be followed in this matter:

> The religious habit, as a symbol of consecration, must be
> simple and modest, at once poor and becoming. In addition,
> it must be in keeping with the requirements of health and it

must be suited to the times and place and to the needs of the apostolate. The habits both of men and of women, which are not in conformity with these norms ought to be changed.[12]

This process of adaptation of dress, as of more fundamental matters affecting religious life, occupied the interest and attention of the sisters. Since distances between houses in the South African Region were great, no formal commissions were established. Nevertheless the sisters, in local communities and at regional meetings, explored the Constitutions and answered the numerous questionnaires, sending in their recommendations to the Generalate. Until 1978 when the Regions of Ireland, Louisiana and Latin America were formally established, South Africa had the unique advantage in the Congregation, of its own Regional Chapter. This ensured that proposals could be submitted not only by communities but also from the Regional Chapter, a forum where all proposals could be debated before submission to the General Chapter in Ireland. Freedom of dress and the opportunity to participate in a creative process of adaptation and transformation of religious life, became for some of the sisters in the ranks, symbols of the rights of consecrated women to legitimate self-expression and of participation in policy-making.

However conservative an individual sister might be, in the various processes of post-Vatican renewal, there could be no passive observers or armchair critics. Women religious took the matter of renewal very seriously and embarked on a period of training in community discussion, decision making, liturgical experimentation, and the revision of Constitutions. This demanded of each participant that she take a critical view, not only of her own personal life and of conventual life in general, but also of the society in which the whole community was immersed. It required of each person that she look critically at the real world in which she lived and worked. For the Cabra Dominicans of the Region of South Africa, this meant involvement of one kind or another with the women, men and school children in their struggle for peace and justice. In the Church as a whole, it was also a time of challenge for superiors. For the first time they were expected to consult, on a wide variety of subjects, not simply their Council but the whole body of sisters. In the past, even the most authoritarian superior was obliged to consult the community chapter on matters of great moment for the community, but generally this had been little more than a formality. Rome was aware of the problems that arose out of an inappropriate exercise of authority on the part of women superiors. In 1952 Pius XII had two urgent points to make to the Mothers General:

> First motherly affection in the guidance of your Sisters. Psychologists say, and it is probably true, that when in authority it is harder for woman than for man to find the exact balance between severity and kindness. ... Remember that for your Sisters, as for yourselves, religious life demands a great sacrifice. They have given up their families, the joys of married life and a home of their own. It is a sacrifice of great worth and importance for the apostolate of the Church, but it is none the less a sacrifice, and those possessed of greatness of soul and delicacy of sentiment feel it most keenly.

Pius XII's second plea to superiors was for a "broad-minded and liberal approach " to the education and training of Sisters in preparation for their apostolate, also giving them the "opportunity and the means to keep their professional knowledge up to date".[13] This was a policy familiar to the Cabra Dominicans, though limited in scope in the pre-Vatican II era. According to the 1947 Constitutions: "The official work of the Congregation of Irish Dominican Sisters is to maintain and teach schools of all grades, both for boarders and day-scholars; as well as Training Colleges, Hostels and other institutions for the promotion of education and instruction according to the law and mind of the Holy Catholic Church".[14]

The maintenance of schools had always been given priority by the Cape Town and Port Elizabeth Dominicans, but with the rapid opening up of apostolic opportunities in the renewal era many sisters were attracted to missionary work outside the classroom. To meet the need for specialisations, sisters returned to the lecture room, upgrading academic qualifications or attending courses in catechetics, theology, spirituality, peace studies and psychology. Members of the Region of South Africa would have found it difficult to fault the approach and attitude of Regional Vicars in the promotion of sisters, both in providing for spiritual renewal and making possible study at undergraduate and post-graduate levels. During the 1970's Sisters Genevieve Hickey and Marian O'Sullivan encouraged those who wanted to specialise in academic areas of interest. It was for many of the sisters a time of spiritual renewal, personal development, academic enrichment and preparation for new apostolates. If there was an area of contention it arose, not out of any reluctance to promote the development of those who had the ability and the desire to meet different apostolic needs in the local church, but because it appeared to the sisters still maintaining schools, the main source of community funds, that they and the institutions founded and maintained with such devotion and sacrifice, were being abandoned for greener and freer fields of action.

By 1964, the adaptation and renewal process which had begun in the 1950's, was popularised by Pope John XXIII, who was elected in 1958. This entire process of renewal, which was given formal definition in the legislation of Vatican Council II, found many of the sisters ill-prepared for the heavy demands it made on their time, courage and creativity during the next twenty-odd years. The majority of the nuns, despite their professional expertise and managerial skills, had rarely been consulted formally on major matters of conventual policy, much less ecclesiastical law. In the case of the Cabra Dominicans, even major superiors had no previous experience in the re-writing of Constitutions, one of the main tasks in the renewal process. As has already been noted, the 1922 Constitutions had been imposed on the majority of Dominican women in South Africa, much against their will.[15] In 1947 as a result of amalgamation with Cabra, the Cape Town and Port Elizabeth Dominicans once again found themselves recipients of a book of constitutions, in the formulation of which they had no part. These were the women, at every level in the community, who in the 1960's and 1970's found themselves active participants in regular discussion and working groups dealing with subjects ranging from the revision of Constitutions, the implementation of ecclesiastical laws, the new liturgy, and the adaptation and renewal of religious life, to the absorbing questions of sartorial change, and the wisdom or otherwise of allowing sisters to visit their family homes.

For the Cabra Dominicans of the Region of South Africa, for whom in the past the maintenance and success of educational institutions had taken precedence over all other apostolic activities, and indeed over the legitimate personal needs of individuals and groups of sisters, this was a welcome and life-enhancing change. It is not without interest that one of the essential preparations for this new process of community consultation was training in techniques of group discussion, evidence enough that this had been of rare occurrence in the past. It was assumed that because the nuns had not been officially involved in conventual discussion and decision making, they had no experience or expertise in this field. This was a serious error of judgement on the part of superiors who should have been aware of the covert body, normally referred to as the 'junior council', which in South Africa debated many issues and held strong opinions about policy matters in which they had no voice, and certainly not even a consultative vote. At this time involvement in the transformation of religious life was a learning experience, as much for superiors as for subjects. In all congregations and local communities there were a number of religious women who, whatever their formal status or lack of practical leadership experience, had the personality, exceptional skills and professional expertise which placed them in a favourable position to influence conventual policy. But in the past, in respect of internal community matters, the majority of sisters had kept a low profile, a defence mechanism well learnt in the novitiate.

The promulgation, on 28 October 1965, of the Decree *Perfectae Caritatis* initiated the process of adaptation and renewal of religious life, a radical movement, the final consequences of which are still in the future. This decree, and those that were issued in the five years that followed, proposed to "deal with the life and discipline of those institutes whose members make profession of chastity, poverty and obedience, and to make provision for their needs, as our times recommend".[16] The Cabra Dominicans world-wide studied the Vatican II documents and responded with enthusiasm to the call of the Church, both for spiritual renewal and for practical adaptation of conventual and professional life to the needs of the modern world. Every aspect of the life of religious institutes was to be scrutinised in terms of the Congregation's "own proper character and functions", with the "spirit and aims of ... [the] founder ...[being] faithfully accepted and retained".[17] Rome, ever cautious of its authority, adds a warning:

> Effective renewal and right adaptation cannot be achieved save with the cooperation of all the members of an institute. However, it is for the competent authorities, alone, and especially for general chapters, to establish norms for appropriate renewal and to legislate for it, as also to provide for sufficient prudent experimentation. The approval of the Holy See and of the local ordinaries must be sought when the law requires this. Superiors, however, in matters which concern the destiny of the entire institute, should find appropriate means of consulting their subjects, and should listen to them.[18]

This opportunity for debate and consultation at all levels, gave to the sisters a new understanding of their unique vocation as consecrated women in the Church. It also opened up a whole treasury of apostolic opportunities, some new, but many a flowering of traditional work freed from the petty restrictions of out-dated norms and practices. Initially, for many of the Dominican sisters in the Region, the right to participate freely and with effect in the adaptation of laws governing their own lives, was of greater importance than the final outcome of discussions. The ongoing debate gradually brought about a greater understanding of the mutual responsibility of all the sisters for the local communities, and for the mission of the Church. In respect of the re-writing of the Constitutions, the Acts of the General Chapter of 1980 noted: "It has been our privilege during the past twelve years to share in this work. Constitutions are a clear expression of the way of life to which we have been called".[19] From 1965 onwards each succeeding General Chapter had examined revised drafts of the Constitutions in the light of proposals submitted by all communities throughout the Congregation. Amendments, to be incorporated into the final draft, were immediately put into practice on an experimental basis. In 1977 the General Chapter provided for the appointment of a team of sisters to rewrite the Constitutions.[20] This group did not include any member of the Region of South Africa.[21]

The nature and mission of the Congregation is clearly stated. It is of "pontifical right and of simple vows and is part of the Dominican Family", a definition which would have won the approval of such stalwart Dominican women as Mothers Teresa Coleman, Colmcille Flynn, Reginald Lyons and Alberta Grant. There would however have been one important query, not easily answered even in terms of the Basic Constitution; for Dominican women, what does the term "Dominican Family" really imply? In respect of the mission of the Congregation, the architects of amalgamation would have been in accord with the 1983 Constitutions: "Within the general purpose of the Dominican Order the special mission of the Congregation is the proclamation of the Word of God through living our religious consecration and through education".[22] The new 1983 Constitutions while they incorporate the main tenets of ecclesiastical law, clearly express the Congregation's commitment, as a body of women, to the ideals of Dominican community life:

> 2 The essentials of our life in common are put before us in the gospel: that we come together in the name of Christ, that we love and forgive each other, and that we share what we have with one another. Inspired by St. Dominic's vision we live in communion, contemplating, celebrating, studying and proclaiming the Word of God.
>
> 3 The quality of our community life and our apostolate depends on the responsible participation of each one.

Sister Marian O'Sullivan, Regional Vicar in South Africa, 1977-1986; Prioress General of Cabra Dominicans 1986-1998.

> 4 Following the example of St. Dominic 'who was a father and consoler of the sick and those who suffered trials', the sisters and especially the prioress should have a loving concern for all in special need of care. Our concern should likewise extend to the sisters' families especially in times of joy and sorrow.

These opening Articles of the Constitutions express the growth and mature understanding of the whole Congregation of its religious and Dominican vocation. It was the fruit of years of intensive community prayer, discussion and creative interaction, a process of communication which did much to create a common vision and a strong sense of each sister's ownership of the Congregation and its policies. All the questions and criticisms that had been levelled against one or other of the changes in customs and the valued traditions of another age, found their answers and justification in these statements which were in direct contradiction to all that was petty. The detailed application of the laws embodied in the *Constitutions* is to be found in the *Directives*, but even here the ideal is spelt out and the Sisters are reminded that all true religious communities are "founded on mutual re-affirmation of faith which alone accounts for our call", and that religious life demands of each member of the community, compassion, co-responsibility, mutual respect and affirmation.[23] The years that led up to the promulgation of the final version of the *Constitutions* certainly showed strong evidence of the spirit of co-responsibility in the tasks imposed by the renewal of religious life, the common concern of all sectors of the Congregation.

For the members of the Region of South Africa it was thirty years of rapid change, of intensive and extensive debate on every aspect of Dominican life, and of dialogue, a verbal interchange easier to define than to achieve. In 1967 one community annalist noted : "The big word today seems to be dialogue - easier than it sounds, but a little fresh air blowing through the religious house will bring death to no member. The pains may be severe but the final cure should be worth it all".[24] Two years later the same scribe, discussing the retreat on the renewal of religious life, felt that there had been too much discussion, and "a rather lurid press had convinced some of us that if religious life had any meaning in the modern world, it was difficult to find".[25] Despite the ongoing debate and the negative press it received, the Cabra Sisters continued to work for peaceful transformation of religious life, while around them an apartheid-ridden society was wracked with injustice and violence.

It was in this environment that new apostolates emerged, and those traditional to the Congregation were re-defined and brought into line with the needs of Church and of society in South Africa.[26] These new apostolates were often, though not exclusively, the response of sisters who had retired from teaching or from full responsibility for household management, and who wanted to help to meet the apostolic needs of local communities. Where special preparation was needed, and full-time involvement by younger sisters in the pastoral ministry was envisaged, study opportunities were provided both in South Africa and abroad. The need to promote higher studies for religious women, especially in the field of theology, had been a matter of concern for the Church in the decade preceding Vatican II, although not all clerics were in agreement as to the level of courses suited to women. In an address given at the First National Assembly Consortium *Perfectae Caritatis* in 1974, one cleric suggested remedies that would counteract "the forces tending to undermine the faith of the religious" woman:

> If she is to cope with the Modernist ideas she is almost certain to meet in her reading or at seminars, she will need a sound formation in doctrine. This does not call for a course in dogmatic and moral theology, such as seminary students used to follow, but some systematic teaching that will give her *at least an elementary grasp* of Christian apologetics, an understanding of the role of the magisterium, and a knowledge of the teaching of the Church regarding the principal mysteries of faith and man's moral obligations.[27]

This implies that nuns mainly because of their limited intellectual capacity needed no more than a superficial knowledge of doctrine, and this at the very time when the paramount, intellectual position of priests was already being challenged by religious and lay women. However it is also a fair reflection of the differences in the education and training of women religious and that provided for seminarians. Despite serious efforts being made, religious women had emerged from initial formation with little or no theological or scriptural expertise. It was a lack that became more evident in the challenging post-Vatican II era, and a significant number of religious women were eager to undertake serious study in these disciplines. Beginning in 1960 when at the instigation of the AWR, a three-year diploma course in theology was launched, many of the Dominican Sisters of the Region of South Africa registered and at the end of three years, completed the diploma course.[28] This provided excellent opportunities for reading, discussion and debate and proved to be a very stimulating and enriching experience. For some sisters it was the beginning of a renewed interest in sacred study at a level that was generally regarded as the monopoly of the clergy. From the 1970's onwards members of the Region of South Africa attended and completed courses in catechetics, sacred liturgy, philosophy, theology and scripture. Some courses followed at tertiary institutions and centres for renewal in Rome, Ireland, Britain, the USA, Australia and South Africa, led to formal qualifications, such as PhD, MA, BD and Licentiate degrees as well as diplomas. In a number of cases nuns on renewal courses preferred to follow lectures and participate in work experience as a preparation for catechetical and pastoral work.

Not all of the Sisters went abroad to follow renewal courses or to upgrade academic and professional qualifications. The AWR helped to provide for the renewal of religious women, of both international and diocesan congregations in Southern Africa. The work of this organisation of major superiors covered a wide field, from the adaptation and facilitation of initial and ongoing formation and renewal, to the needs of diocesan congregations and the provision of courses for superiors and formators. Fons Vitae and Maryville Centre of Spirituality, established to meet the needs of women religious, were both initiated by and were responsible to the AWR. The well-documented history of these institutions, which in a period of adaptation and change were active forces in the Catholic Church in South Africa, should be told in full. What is relevant to this study is the influence these bodies had on the spiritual and professional development of the individual sisters, and on their re-orientation to pastoral work and facilitation. In addition some were engaged full-time and at all levels, in the field of catechetics. The training received has also inspired sisters to do voluntary chaplaincy work, in prisons, hospitals and in tertiary institutions which are both within and outside the jurisdiction of the Church.

It is also of interest to the Cabra Dominicans in South Africa that Maryville, established by the AWR at St Dominic's Priory, Port Elizabeth, was initiated under the leadership of Sister Genevieve Hickey, who for two years held the double office of Directress of Maryville and Prioress of the local community. Sister Evangelist Quinlan, President of the AWR, could justify the choice of Sister Genevieve to lead this project:

> We are fortunate to have been able to obtain the services of Sister Genevieve, OP, as Directress of the Centre. Sister Genevieve has spent many years in South Africa. From 1969-1976 she was Regional Superior of her congregation and during that period trained [at Fons Vitae] with Father Gillick for giving Directed Retreats. From 1977-1981 she was in Rome

as Assistant Directress of an International House of Studies for Dominican Sisters. She also obtained a B.D. and Licentiate in theology from the Angelicum University. Sister Genevieve will be assisted by a well qualified staff recruited from South Africa and overseas.[29]

Maryville was formally opened on 2 March 1983, and during the four years of its existence it served 69 Sisters from 32 congregations, both international and diocesan.

The general enrichment of life which the Cabra Dominicans received was common to other congregations in Southern Africa. However there were also serious questions being asked by some of the sisters of the Region as to the possible danger of losing their specific Dominican charism. Interaction between the various Dominican congregations was seen to be one way to promote the spirit of the Order. This was confirmed by Father Brian Farrelly OP, representative of the Master General, who in preparation for a General Chapter of the Order, visited all the Dominican congregations in Southern Africa. In compliance with his mandate from the Master General he proposed that for the sake of greater unity and more effective apostolic action, the six congregations of Dominican Sisters of the Third Order should form a federation. He could point to the example of Latin America where a similar policy had been very successful. It was a proposal that had to be presented circumspectly to members of the six congregations since not all of the sisters favoured this form of interaction. And did not historical precedent indicate that high-ranking Dominicans who had come from Rome in the past, had used undue moral pressure to gain their ends? Mother Genevieve Hickey's letter, circulated with the express permission of the Prioress General and informing the Sisters of this proposed federation, was diplomatic:

> Father Farrelly ... is visiting the various countries in order to encourage different Congregations to co-operate more closely and effectively in the interests of the Church and of the Order. This co-operation by no means implies any kind of diminution of the authority of the Major Superiors or the autonomy of the members of the various Congregations. The identity of each Congregation is to be strictly respected in the form of a loose Federation which Father Farrelly proposed to the Convention.[30]

The discussion at the Dominican Convention, which besides Father Brian Farrelly, involved 35 sisters from the six Dominican Congregations, including the six major superiors. From among the brethren was Father J L Brenninkmeijer OP, Vicar Provincial, together with Fathers Damian Magrath, Gregory Brooke, Emil Blaser, Louis Peters and Bernard Connor. It was clear from the discussions that "the best way towards such a growing co-operation would be one which respects the *juridical independence* of each Congregation on the one hand, but which asks on the other hand for *voluntary co-operation* of each Congregation in the establishment and on-going work of a Federal Commission".[31] All of the Dominican sisters throughout Southern Africa were asked to vote on the wisdom or otherwise of forming this federation, taking cognisance of the purposes for which it was being founded:

> To foster unity and co-operation among Dominican Congregations and with the brethren in Southern Africa.
>
> To promote a common search for inspiration and renewal in our Dominican way of life according to the character of each Congregation.
>
> To maintain contact with the General Secretariate for Dominican Nuns and Sisters in Rome.
>
> To examine apostolic priorities and to co-operate in certain areas of the apostolate.
>
> To promote indigenous vocations.
>
> To provide formation personnel.
>
> To arrange for an annual Dominican Conference.[32]

Of the 216 votes cast by the Cabra Dominicans, 202 were in favour of federation. The six congregations formed the Federation of Dominicans of South Africa, with Sister Marian O'Sullivan the first elected representative of the Cabra Congregation and Sister Majella Keary appointed by the Regional Council.[33] It is not without interest that while the brethren, as was their custom, gave the Dominican women their full clerical support in this new venture, they did not become formal members of the federation until five years after it had been founded. The incongruity of their position became increasingly clear to those of the brethren who were involved in the promotion of the Dominican Family, and in 1977 they became full members of Fedosa.

Among other services to the Dominican community in Southern Africa, Fedosa organised a renewal course for its members. If the Dominican major superiors were planning to build an Arc in Rome, then South Africa, on a more modest scale, could launch a Canoe. Under the Directorship of Bernard Connor OP, and with the support of the Dominican Fathers who offered lectures in their fields of expertise, Canoe was initiated in 1975 and served the Fedosa communities until 1979. It helped to promote both spiritual renewal and unity of mind among the members of different Congregations who shared the experience. Together they studied, prayed, lived and recreated as a single community, creating a sense of unity of purpose which was to find expression in undertakings planned and carried out together. This presents a very different picture from the situation in the first half of the twentieth century, when the question of unity among Dominican women in Southern Africa was viewed with suspicion, and was strongly resisted.

One of the main areas of collaboration is the common novitiate opened in 1992 in Geluksdal, a move not without precedent in Southern Africa. Twice weekly meetings of novices men and women, from different congregations had been organised by the AWR, and the Dominican Congregations also held regular meetings in Gauteng and Natal. The YOPS, young Dominicans, women and men, also meet together at regular intervals to share ideas, pray together and gain greater insight into the ideals of the Order in which they hope to serve God and the Church for the rest of their lives. As in the case of many other topics briefly discussed in this chapter, the impact of the various forms of interaction among members of Congregations of the Dominican Family, cannot yet be assessed. However, the vision statement formulated by the major superiors in February 1991, sixteen years after the founding of Fedosa, reflects its aims and ideals:

> As Dominican women and men in Southern Africa united in our witness to the liberating Word of God, rooted in the values of Contemplation, Truth, Justice to the whole of creation and Compassionate Action as expressed in our respective mission statements, open to on-going growth and transformation, we commit ourselves to develop inter-Dominican Collaboration
> - in the formation of our members
> - in our common mission and ministries
> - in our prophetic role within a fragmented South Africa.[34]

The maintenance and development of the contemplative element fundamental to Dominican life, was a cause of concern to members of Fedosa and to the Cabra Dominicans. Although all Dominicans, whatever their professional work, are by vocation bound to an apostolic life based on and flowing from the contemplation of Divine Truth, it was felt that in the age of renewal when the values and demands of secular society obtruded on conventual life, a need was felt for a place and a community totally dedicated to prayer and contemplation. The closing of the private primary school at Simonstown in December 1972, provided a suitable venue for a House of Prayer, to be run at the outset, on an experimental basis. The simple aim of the foundation was " to enable Sisters to live their Religious life more fully and to renew themselves from within".[35] The House of Prayer was opened privately on 2 February 1973, with an all-night vigil. There was a core community of three, Sisters Immaculata Lavery, Benvenuta Connolly and Fabian Doyle.[36] This foundation was resited to St Michael's Convent Rondebosch in 1978 and over the years other sisters joined the staff. Sisters Thecla McGowan who formed part of the group in Simonstown and in St Michael's, gave retreats and spiritual direction, instructed adults in the faith, and prepared young men for the diaconate. As a gifted and enthusiastic teacher of English, Latin, history and mathematics, she had influenced the lives of generations of young women in the Western Cape and in the Transvaal. Mother Thecla was noted for her integrity both in the classroom and as a member of the Regional Council. This she brought to her work in the House of Prayer.

Among the Cabra Dominicans, the dynamic force behind the establishment of a House of Prayer in the Western Cape, was Sister Genevieve Hickey. In this she was inspired by Father Bernard Haring CSSR, who in 1973 spoke to the major superiors about his work in promoting the House of Prayer Movement in the USA. After her years of study in Rome Sister Genevieve was assigned to St Michael's House of Prayer. Over the last twenty years she has given directed retreats and spiritual direction to priests, to men and women religious and to lay people. For twenty-five years the House of Prayer has provided for many Christians of different persuasions, a quiet place for prayer, contemplation, spiritual direction, directed retreats, or for a poustinea experience. It has also provided peace and creative silence for Hindus and other peoples who find in its contemplative atmosphere an opportunity for renewal of spirit. This House of Prayer, a place apart, has been for the Cabra Sisters in South Africa, one of the significant influences in the ongoing renewal process.[37]

In May 1993 Sister Agnes Finn joined Sister Genevieve and both continue to give spiritual direction and retreats. They also attend a monthly ecumenical meeting for spiritual directors, and for the last four years Sister Agnes has been chairperson of this group.[38] One of those who saw to the comfort of the visitors and the community in the House of Prayer was Sister Lelia Lynch, a retired primary teacher, who expressed her contemplation through art and crafts, culinary skills and cheerful hospitality. The transfer of invalided Cabra sisters to Rondebosch in 1984 and the provision for their professional nursing and spiritual care, added another facet to the work of the community. In this work Sister Giuseppe Largey has promoted the peaceful atmosphere in which old and sick sisters have found rest and loving support. Many retired sisters have shared this task. One of these is Sister Raymund Delaney who gave many fruitful years of cheerful service helping to care for the frail and the incapacitated. The prayers and patience of the sick and the loving care they are given, both promote the spiritual aims of the house and influence those who come to pray or to visit old friends.

For the Region of South Africa, visits to home and family brought about fundamental change both in communities and in the outlook of individual sisters. The capitulars attending the Regional Chapter of 1960 were well aware that home visits for nuns had Roman approval. However, for enclosed communities this was a controversial issue, and certainly for Mother Catherine Dixon, it was not a move to be taken lightly. This Regional Chapter which petitioned for the revision of constitutions dealing with egress to suit South African conditions, also debated the wisdom of permitting home visits. It was a conservative age and many of the capitulars agreed that a sacrifice once made by sisters and by their parents, should not be revoked. Nor could it be claimed that the South African climate was injurious to health as was the case in other parts of Africa. Ideals apart, a strong and valid argument against home visits, was the financial burden it would impose on the Region where there were over 200 sisters who had been more than ten years in the country. It was argued that if five sisters went overseas per year, "it would be forty years before one circuit could be completed". To send five Sisters to Ireland would cost the community a total of £1,000. It was pointed out that it "would hardly be just to use for our pleasure money which is badly needed for the support of our missions". There would also "be the disorganisation caused in our schools and Communities and in addition the inconvenience to Convents overseas". On the other hand it was argued that a visit to parents and families would be of spiritual and physical benefit to the sisters and would promote vocations. Other congregations had solved the financial problems entailed in sending their Sisters overseas to visit their families, and so could the Region of South Africa. After all, sisters working in Government schools were paid a holiday bonus and this could form the basis of a fund into which each house could contribute monthly. However when the capitulars voted on the question, as to whether or not the Sisters should be given an overseas holiday, the result was 14 in favour and 19 against.[39] But this was not the end of the story. Ireland also debated the question and one sister was emphatic in her opinion: "Holidays at home: no emphatically. Sisters from Africa are in an exceptional position".[40] Another argument found its justification in tradition:

> I think the question should be *thoroughly* examined by the Chapter, and the problems arising from it for the Congregation, for Superiors and for Subjects themselves, carefully investigated. The *difficulty* of emotional involvement will arise - probably also that of Chastity. Our Sisters would need to be thoroughly committed to the Religious Life - whose 'mission and grace' in our case has not been to go abroad .[41]

In the light of past legislation and practice these misgivings were not without merit. Would a radical revision in the laws governing egress which would open the way for home visits, change the whole character of the Congregation? Or would refusal to grant this request result in a loss of a valuable apostolic experience for the Congregation? "The *arguments* for going home, are, to my mind, *fallacious*", one of the nuns asserted and another reiterated the argument made in South Africa: "We left home and our people *because* we loved them - and this was part of the holocaust. To wish to return now is to withdraw a major part of the gift".[42]

It was perhaps easier for Sisters in Ireland to view home visits with such detachment, but for the nuns in South Africa, some of whom had not seen their relatives in over forty years, the matter was more urgent. But it was a battle that was not to be won immediately. At the Regional Chapter of 1961, when the request for overseas holidays was once again put to the vote, 14 were in favour, 15 against and there were two abstentions. It was a bitter disappointment to those who had hoped for a positive response, but the whole tone of the Chapter and its concentration on imposing conformity and uniformity in minor matters, indicates that more than 50% of the capitulars were neither ready, nor free enough to make such a decision. The future political urgency to elect delegates to the Chapter who would give strong support to the promotion of overseas holidays, was not lost on the Dominican constituency in South Africa. It was clear to superiors that generally the growing freedom of movement and the consequent threat to regular life and enclosure being experienced in the Region, had to be dealt with. While sisters living in convents with no grounds could take a walk in quiet areas, the Chapter agreed that in the case of the Transvaal convents the "Rules of Egress and Enclosure should be enforced". Mother Jordan Keary, who as a relatively new Regional Vicar had little knowledge of South Africa, never succeeded in bringing this about. In many respects the convents in Vanderbijlpark, Johannesburg and Pretoria were the first true amalgamation houses. Sisters whose traditional homes had been either Port Elizabeth or Cape Town worked together to develop new institutions and to seize apostolic opportunities in the communities which had made them welcome and continued to give them support. The differences, though indefinable, anticipated some of the freedoms that were to emerge slowly throughout the Region during the 1970's. But for superiors of the early 1960's, this was a threat, an indication that proper control was not being applied. The Transvaal houses were far from the centre of government, and this freed the new communities, to some extent at least, from the constraints and prejudices of their own past as separate Cape congregations, and also from the constant surveillance of the Vicar whose views on egress were not those of the average South African sister.[43]

The responses of the Cabra Dominican in Ireland and South Africa in 1967 on the matter of vacations, reveal many attitudes to home visits. One respondent quoted Fr Séan O'Riordan CSSR speaking to the sisters attending Regina Mundi in Rome: "Sisters should visit home for reasons of the apostolate, e.g. at a time of illness, or to see aged Parents, - but never for relaxation- and not for holidays".[44] Cardinal Suenans, in his book *The Nun in the world*, first published in December 1962, and soon a best seller, placed equally exalted ideals before women religious:

> The religious has chosen a new family; her house is her convent, and her fellow-nuns her sisters. Being at home means in the first instance being in her convent, and that is how she sees it. Visits to families must not be regarded in the same light as boarders' holidays, but rather as a reconciliation of two duties: that of maintaining a certain distance from the world, as properly desired by every religious, and that of *pietas*, family charity ... towards one's own people.[45]

He stated, while offering no proof to support his opinion, that the "modern world ... [was] more sensitive to a refined expression of filial piety" and that home visits would probably be more appreciated by young religious than by their elders. These latter might view the whole matter as a sign of laxity. But the Cardinal was confident that once the older sisters had been assured that home visits tied in with the policy of the Church, they would accept them "wholeheartedly".[46] It was an opinion, in respect at least of the sisters of the Region of South Africa, that was quite unfounded. The older sisters did nor need any persuasion, and in the event it was the senior members of the community who had been most firmly opposed to home holidays, who were most eager to avail themselves of the permission, once it had been officially granted.

The exhaustive preparations for the Renewal Chapter of 1967-68, in which all the members of the Congregation participated, brought about a change of heart in South Africa. When the capitulars of the 1967 Regional Chapter, voted on the question of overseas holidays, the result was unanimously in favour of home visits, proof positive that whatever opposition had existed in 1961 had been overcome, and that the sisters were making progress in public debate as well as in political acumen. It was without doubt a happy decision but there was one further constitutional problem to be solved. Where would the Sisters stay, inside or outside the enclosure? Could they stay in their own homes if they so wished? With a majority of 34 to 1 the Chapter agreed to petition the General Chapter to allow those who wished, to stay with their families.[47] In the region of South Africa the permission for family visits was greeted with enthusiasm and joy by young and old. All were eager to visit their own people, and for many this real holiday was the first, and perhaps the most significant step in the way towards the official closure of the egress debate, and an opening into a more sensitive approach to the joys and pains of family life. Travel and exposure to a wider world also developed interests in more varied apostolates and in renewal programmes available outside Southern Africa.

In a time of change the Dominicans had other less happy consequences to accept. At home in South Africa, in the debate and questioning of some old and firmly held ideals of religious life, there was the added pain of losing those valued Dominican friends and colleagues, who returned to secular life. It was also a time that saw the reformulation and re-assessment of the apostolate of the Dominican schools in the Region, when, it was claimed, risks had to be taken and sacrifices made for the sake of justice and reconciliation. Some institutions were either closed or handed over to secular principals. It was asserted that this was done, often too hastily and without due consultation with the sisters of the Region. The closure of schools was a painful experience for those who, in accordance with the 1947 Constitutions, had given their entire lives and service to the promotion of Catholic education. In the circumstances it is not surprising that for some members of the community the movement of their professional colleagues into "self-chosen areas of work", in tertiary institutions, in parishes or in informal African settlements, seemed to be more in the nature of a betrayal of the educational mission of the Congregation rather than an innovative approach to the "real" mission of the Church. This loss of professional teachers to informal or even formal work outside the Dominican school system was strongly deprecated. This is understandable since there were never sufficient nuns to meet the needs of the schools, and it was these institutions on which the economic stability of the communities depended.[48] It became increasingly difficult to reconcile conflicting staff needs in a community where the results of professional surveys confirmed the obvious fact that Sisters were growing older and that there was a dearth of vocations.[49]

The rapid and comprehensive changes were neither recognised as essential for renewal nor accepted with equal enthusiasm by all the Sisters. Indeed for women such as Mother Alberta Grant, who had reverence for every Dominican custom and practice, and who had worked with such devotion for the amalgamation of Cape Town and Port Elizabeth to the Irish Congregation, the gradual lifting of the strict rules of enclosure and the general growth of freedom within the cloister, presaged the deterioration of religious life as she had known it. Writing in December 1967 to Mother Ambrose Doherty, at that time in Holy Trinity Convent, Matroosfontein, she mourns the standards of the new age.

> The problems with which we are all faced are somewhat staggering - but as you say, the whole world is in a ferment and we cannot expect to escape. ... Father McNicholl seemed to emphasise in his Chapter Retreat that the Holy Spirit was now speaking through the young. That was taken to mean that He was not speaking at all through the old. Do you agree with this? The young all seem to want 'Adaptation' - but 'Renewal'? How much of the idea of Monastic life should we retain? Is it possible to hold on to the idea and ideal of *'contemplari et contemplata aliis tradere'* without some degree of silence and cloister? The idea of penance and mortification is entirely out of fashion. Yet control of the senses is absolutely necessary for contemplation. The idea of the young seems to be to get out: and the excuse or argument is 'the apostolate of communication'.

Mother Alberta, at this time 79 years old and within a little over two months to her death, noted that it was not the very young who wanted sweeping changes "but the 28's to 45's. And the very good - and there are many - are silent, being brought up to Obedience and reverence for Superiors". She quoted two American Mothers General as saying that enemy number one was *authority* and the watchword was *freedom*.[50]

Not a few of the South African Sisters within and outside the dangerous years, would certainly have agreed with Mother Alberta. Some judged it to be an iconoclastic age which was carrying out the swift and irresponsible dismantling of much that was best and most sacred in Dominican life. It was argued that the main incentive for change came, not from the teachings of Vatican II, but was the result of an uncritical acceptance of aggressive feminist propaganda emanating from the USA, and the even more insidious influence of the secular philosophies of the day. Neither was liturgical adaptation without its critics. For some it was an opportunity for self-expression and creativity and a source of spiritual inspiration. Others however, considered the occasional or regular substitution of subjective prayer for the Divine Office as a trivialisation of the sacred liturgy. The official prayer of the Church which, in the living memory of most of the sisters, had been one of the signs of true Dominican status, was being replaced by popular devotions, often at the whim of individuals. Since during the 1970's the charismatic movement attracted many devoted followers from among the Cabra Dominicans in South Africa, there was opportunity for endless debate and a degree of polarisation.

There were bound to be many areas of disagreement. The sisters were not all equally at ease with the new techniques being used for the promotion of social and spiritual interaction, nor with the implementation of theories and practices, which they judged to be foreign to their inherited Dominican culture. Certain books from the USA, mainly by women feminists, analysed, in terms of current psychological and sociological theories, every aspect of the vowed life of consecrated virginity. Many of these works set trends and fashions which found expression and approval in local and international conferences, in regional and general chapters, in retreats and prayer groups and in community discussions. In such gatherings it appeared to some participants, that these studies were often given the status of divine revelation and carried undue weight in the realisation of renewal programmes. For others they opened up new horizons, both in terms of the potentially important contribution that an understanding of the social sciences would bring to the renewal process, and as a source of spiritual enrichment.[51]

But these were not the only influential factors in the renewal process. The proliferation of Catholic journals of high quality, provided all religious women belonging to international congregations, from major superiors to the sisters in the ranks, with detailed analyses of a great variety of topics, from the revision of constitutions to critiques on every aspect of the religious life and practice. Many of the articles were written specially, but not exclusively, to meet the needs of consecrated women. The writers who put their expertise, theological, scriptural, psychological, sociological and sartorial to the service of sisters world-wide, were mainly men, clerics with impressive academic records. These claimed, at least by inference, to have inside knowledge of the experiences, feelings and ambitions of women living a conventual life. In this at least little had changed since pre-Vatican II days, and it is not surprising that for some of the sisters a touch of the feminine was a welcome relief from the weight of clerical patronage and scholarship. While among the Dominican sisters in the Region of South Africa there are few feminist fanatics, strong support of women's rights has become increasingly evident, and many of the nuns have rejected paternalistic condescension, however clerically eminent the source from which it comes. Nevertheless the Catholic journals of the post-Vatican II times have provided a rich source of legal guidance, theological analyses and spiritual upliftment. This has helped to keep communities in touch with the on-going debate on religious life.[52]

Within South Africa another important source of inspiration and mutual support for congregations, including the Cabra Dominicans, was membership of the Association of Women Religious, (AWR). This was established in 1955 in response to the wishes of the Sacred Congregation of Religious. Membership included major superiors of congregations established in Southern Africa, and the AWR as a body, after a relatively slow beginning, gradually became a force to be reckoned with in the South African Church. It offered courses in initial and on-going formation, and contributed to the spiritual education and development of African Diocesan sisters. It provided for renewal courses in the Fons Vitae Institute and Maryville Centre for Spirituality, both of which were founded by and responsible to the AWR. Among those who have served to date on the Executive of the AWR were the Regional Vicars of the Cabra Dominicans, Sisters Damien Madden, Angels Donnellan, Genevieve Hickey, Marian O'Sullivan, Raymunda Brennan and under its new title and extended membership, Sister Margaret Kelly, the present Cabra representative. Sister Damian Madden held the office of Chairman from 1964 to 1965, when she returned to Ireland. In 1968 Sister Genevieve Hickey was elected Regional Vicar and represented the Cabra Dominicans on the Board of AWR for eight years. As a member of the Executive from 1971 to 1976, she was noted for her "insight and humour which had been so beneficial to all".[53] Sister Marian O'Sullivan served on the Executive from 1979 to 1986, when she was elected Prioress General of the Cabra

Dominicans with her headquarters in Dublin, Ireland. In June 1987, Sister Raymunda Brennan was elected on to the Executive, where she served until the end of her term as Regional Vicar in 1994.

Among the events organised by the AWR were special conferences and retreats for superiors and for those working in formation. This was part of the response to the call of Vatican II for the adaptation and renewal of religious life. But it was also a necessary re-education of superiors in the light of criticisms levelled at the traditional interpretation and practical application of their powers, role and functions. In the on-going debate on the revision of constitutions there was open and forthright discussion on every aspect of conventual law and practice, including the office of superior. In principle among the Cabra Dominicans, to a greater extent in Ireland than in South Africa, prioresses and higher superiors had a poor press. This indeed was a common phenomenon in many congregations. The responses to questionnaires on the role, functions and short-comings of superiors, reveal attitudes and resentments that would never have been expressed publicly or accepted without recrimination, in less liberal times. The records show that a considerable number of sisters rejected authoritarianism in superiors, and considered it within their rights as mature adults, to be consulted on matters of policy, and to be allowed carry out the work assigned to them without undue interference. Many of the negative responses, often expressing the opinions of an individual rather than a group, reflect a situation where nuns for the first time in their religious lives, were free to make public expression on matters that were hitherto held to be sacrosanct. There is an interesting parallel between the secular trends of the 1960's and '70's and the movement among nuns to express their freedom, as individuals and as members of a corporate body of women, vowed to obedience.[54]

Some critics maintained that superiors themselves often lacked a proper understanding of obedience, that they used their legal authority to the detriment of real communication and constructive dialogue, and gave no scope for individual initiatives. Nor were they prepared to delegate authority, even to those formally assigned to positions of responsibility. However not all the faults and weaknesses of the system could be laid at the door of the superior. In very large communities she was occupied with administration, and consequently had little time for the individual Sister.[55] To the question "Does our practice of Obedience mean for us freedom and maturity?", the following answer, representing a minority view, was given:

That the 'practice of Obedience does *not* mean for us maturity and freedom is due to *the attitude of superiors.*

1 Some superiors treat their subjects as 'teen-agers' and this leads to lack of trust and frustrations and so unhappiness.

2 Excessive 'maternalism' on the part of Superiors robs Sisters of initiative.

3 Some Superiors are difficult to approach: too domineering, not open to new ideas.[56]

In terms of the third point, sisters in the ranks were themselves not without fault. Indeed the office of superior generated its own frustrations, and the prioress often had to walk the narrow, hazardous path between maternalism and the rightful and adult exercise of authority. The fact that in the past new superiors had no training for the work of leadership was recognised, and this led to special renewal programmes which provided courses and retreats for superiors. Indeed this was requested by the Cabra Sisters, who suggested among other things, that the work of administration be delegated to others in order to leave the prioress free for the community, and that annual courses for superiors should be instituted "for *all* present Superiors without exception. Newly appointed Superiors should be catered for".[57] The benefits derived from such courses no doubt gave those women in leadership positions many insights into the qualities needed, and the problems to be encountered, in their difficult task. There were other effective changes which, to some extent, placed the burden of choice of local superior on the community concerned. For the Congregation which emerged in 1928, the appointment of prioresses had been the norm, though this had not been the case in South Africa prior to amalgamation in 1938. The right to a consultative vote in the choice of local prioresses was one of the first indications of a limited transfer of responsibility to the sisters in the ranks. In 1968, during the second session of the Eighth General Chapter, it was agreed that "subject to approval by Rome the Congregation adopt the Dominican tradition of allowing each community to elect its own Local Superior".[58] From 1969 onwards, as the office of prioress fell vacant in a convent, the sisters had a direct vote in the election of a successor, the choice of candidate being submitted to the Prioress General and her Council for ratification.

In 1987, eighteen years after this return to Dominican tradition, a new experiment was launched, the final outcome of which is not yet known. This was the introduction of "responsible participation" which involved the sharing of leadership in the community. Within the ten year period under review a number of communities in the Region of South Africa have chosen this option, and the general consensus has been that in small communities it is in many respects a happier solution than the more traditional, structured form of conventual life under the leadership of a prioress. The General Chapter of 1992 looked at the various forms of community living:

> The Chapter affirms that an attitude of openness in community develops new ways of Dominican living that are challenging and prophetic. This entails the acceptance of a variety of community life-styles within the congregation. The Chapter recognises that the experiment known as 'Shared Leadership' has been a fruitful one. It has promoted personal growth and a richer experience of community life. It is evident that it has functioned best where there has been outside facilitation in working towards right relationships, and a common faith context in fidelity to community reflection and prayer. The Chapter agreed that the experiment should continue and the Leadership Conferences would review it, between now and the next General Chapter.[59]

In October 1997 the Government Commission of the Congregation circulated a questionnaire to assist in the evaluation of this experiment, so that the General Chapter of 1998 might be able to determine whether it should be continued, discontinued or changed.

> Responsible participation and leadership are not synonymous. In our tradition the task of leadership in the community is given to a designated person ... for a limited period of time after which the role passes to another person. The question we have to decide is whether this role can be satisfactorily shared by all members of the community or whether anything gets lost in the arrangement.[60]

Shared leadership, the election, role and power of 'cluster prioresses', and the legal position of those who choose to live alone, represent the different forms of community life within the congregation. While they have raised many questions, as the current questionnaire indicates, especially in the realm of obedience, acceptable solutions are a matter for the future and have no further place in this historical study.

Despite differences of opinion, there were positive benefits arising out of active participation of the Region of South Africa in all aspects of the renewal process. It increased the sense of belonging to an international body with a Generalate situated outside the limitations of the local environment. Creative talents, hitherto lying dormant, could now be used for the benefit of the universal Church and its mission. A survey of congregational documentation produced during the thirty years under review reveals a marked shift, from narrow institutionalism to a broader perspective of the Church, from the imperatives of professional and managerial responsibilities to the needs of the individual sister. Such changes, both personal and institutional were gradual, and they were made by the South African sisters in a political context that denied the most basic, fundamental rights to the majority of the people among whom they worked. It was a situation where both the transformation of religious life, and the political struggle, each had a profound influence on the Cabra Dominicans. And neutrality was not an option in either case. Consequently, when on 27 April 1994, the Cabra Dominicans queued to cast their votes in the first free elections, and with their fellow citizens rejoiced as a single nation, the "new" South Africa, under the presidency of Nelson Mandela, the sisters were no longer voiceless women hidden within the anonymity of the cloister. The period of open and often violent protest from which South Africa had emerged, and the equally intense though bloodless transformation of religious life in the process of which the Dominican community had been active participants, demanded of nuns action, interaction and reactions, which in an earlier political and ecclesiastical climate, would have been judged to fall outside the role proper to consecrated women religious. This 'proper' role for consecrated women in the Church is not yet clearly defined, nor is the process of adaptation and renewal complete. This will be the task of the Cabra Dominican women as they move from the dying century into the hope of a new millennium.

APPENDIX I

ORAL EVIDENCE, 1989-1998

RECORDED INTERVIEWS:

Sisters

Christopher Cormack	St Dominic's Priory, Walmer, PE.	1991
Gerard Crawford	Holy Rosary Convent, PE.	1991
Vincent Drew	St Dominic's Priory, Walmer, PE.	1990 &1991
Juliana Egan	St Agnes' Convent, Woodstock, CT.	1990
Oliver Fearon	St Dominic's Priory, Walmer, PE.	1991
Helen Hatton	Springfield Convent, Wynberg, WP.	1990
Bede Kearns	Sion Hill Convent, Blackrock, Co Dublin.	1991
Rose Kotzé	Holy Trinity Convent, Matroosfontein.	1989
Finbar Lawlor	St Dominic's Priory, Walmer, PE.	1991
Petra Mangan	Sion Hill Convent, Blackrock, Co Dublin.	1991
Lucia McDermott	St Dominic's Priory, Walmer, PE.	1991
Sabina Murphy	Holy Rosary Convent, PE.	1991
Servatius Nyhan	St Dominic's Priory, Walmer, PE.	1997
Cynthia Rice	St Dominic's Priory, Walmer, PE.	1991
Simeon Tarpey	Sion Hill Convent, Blackrock, Co Dublin.	1991
Marie Thérèse Wakefield	HRC, & St Dominic's Priory, PE.	1990-1991
Berchmans Woods	St Dominic's Priory, Walmer, PE.	1991

TELEPHONIC INTERVIEWS AND PERSONAL RECORDS, 1997-1998.

Sisters

Feargal Cassidy	Dominican Sisters, Kirkwood, EP.	1997-1998
Paulinus Conroy	Dominican Sisters, Hout Bay, WP.	1997
Gilbert Dowd	St Margaret's Convent, Swaziland.	1998
Agnes Finn	St Michael's Convent, Rondebosch, WP.	1997-1998
Kathy Gaylor	Marymount Convent, Uitenhage, EP.	1998
Áine Hardiman	St Michael's Convent, Rondebosch, WP.	1998
Clare Harkin	Stellenbosch, WP.	1998

Genevieve Hickey	St Michael's Convent, Rondebosch, WP.	1998
Margaret Kelly	Region House, CT.	1997 -1998
Francis Krige	Dominican Sisters, Hout Bay, WP.	1998
Rose Dominic Laros	St Dominic's Priory, Walmer, PE.	1998
Andrew Maguire	St Dominic's Priory, Walmer, PE.	1991
Basil McCarthy	St Michael's Convent, Rondebosch, WP.	1998
Mairéad McGlade	St Dominic's Priory, PE.	1998
Justina Nutley	St Dominic's Convent, Wittebome, WP.	1998
Amata Tuohy	St Michael's Convent, Rondebosch.	1998
Sally Young	Region House, CT.	1998
Evelyn Waters	St Mary's Convent, Nyanga.	1996

APPENDIX II

HIGHER SUPERIORS AND COUNCILS, SOUTHERN AFRICA, 1863-1998

Elections and appointments to the office of higher superior and assistant/s, Cape Town foundation, 1863-1938.

Name	Dates	Office
Mother Dympna Kinsella	1863-1869	Appointed Foundress / Prioress
Mother Hyacinth Casey	1863-1869	Appointed Sub-Prioress
Mother Dympna Kinsella	1869-1872	Elected Prioress
Mother Hyacinth Casey	1869-1872	Elected Sub-Prioress
Mother Dympna Kinsella	1872-1875	Appointed Prioress[1]
Mother Francis Borgia McDonnell	1872-1875	Appointed Sub-Prioress
Mother Francis Borgia McDonnell	1875-1879	Elected Prioress[2]
Mother Dympna Kinsella	1875-1879	Appointed Sub-Prioress[3]
Mother Francis Borgia McDonnell	1879-1882	Elected Prioress
Mother Dympna Kinsella	1879-1882	Elected Sub-Prioress
Mother Dympna Kinsella	1882-1885	Elected Prioress
Mother Thomas Casey	1882-1885	Elected Sub-Prioress
Mother Dympna Kinsella	1885-1888	Elected Prioress
Mother Pius McLaughlin	1885-1888	Elected Sub-Prioress
Mother Pius McLaughlin	1888-1891	Elected Prioress
Mother Dympna Kinsella	1888-1891	Elected Sub-Prioress

Mother Pius McLaughlin	1891-1894	Elected Prioress
Mother Dympna Kinsella	1891-1894	Elected Sub-Prioress
Mother Dympna Kinsella	1894-1897	Elected Prioress
Mother Pius McLaughlin	1894-1897	Elected Sub-Prioress
Mother Dympna Kinsella	1897-1900	Elected Prioress
Mother Pius McLaughlin	1897-1900	Elected Sub-Prioress
Mother Pius McLaughlin	1900-1903	Elected Prioress
Mother Columba McAuliffe	1900-1903	Elected Sub-Prioress
Mother Pius McLaughlin	1903-1906	Elected Prioress
Mother Imelda Bean	1903-1906	Elected Sub-Prioress
Mother Antoninus McLaughlin	1906-1909	Elected Prioress
Mother Pius McLaughlin	1906-1909	Elected Sub-Prioress
Mother Antoninus McLaughlin	1909-1912	Elected Prioress
Mother Pius McLaughlin	1909-1912	Elected Sub-Prioress
Mother Pius McLaughlin	1912-1915	Elected Prioress
Mother Antoninus McLaughlin	1912-1915	Elected Sub-Prioress
Mother Berchmans Cotter	1915-1918	Elected Prioress
Mother Pius McLaughlin	1915-1918	Elected Sub-Prioress
Mother Berchmans Cotter	1918-1922	Elected Prioress
Mother Pius McLaughlin	1918-1922	Elected Sub-Prioress
Mother Berchmans Cotter	1922-1924	Elected Provincial[4]
Mother Pius McLaughlin	1922-1926	Elected 1st Councillor/Vicaress
Sister Bertrand Dowley	1922-1926	Elected 2nd Councillor
Sister Reginald Boyd	1922-1926	Elected 3rd Councillor
Sister Joseph Glynn	1922-1926	Elected 4th Councillor[5]

Sister Benvenuta O'Donoghue	1926-1930	Elected Provincial[6]
Sister Pius McLaughlin	1926-1930	Elected 1st Councillor
Sister Bertrand Dowley	1926-1930	Elected 2nd Councillor
Sister Columba McAuliffe	1926-1930	Elected 3rd Councillor
Sister Magdalen Horan	1926-1930	Elected 4th Councillor
Sister Teresa Coleman	1930-1936	Elected Prioress General[7]
Sister Benvenuta O'Donoghue	1930-1936	Elected Councillor
Sister Pius McLaughlin	1930-1933[8]	Elected Councillor
Sister Columba McAuliffe	1930-1936	Elected Councillor[9]
Sister Bertrand Dowley	1930-1936	Elected Councillor[10]
Sister Teresa Coleman	1936-1938	Elected Prioress General
Sister Clare Martin	1936-1938	Elected Councillor
Sister Bertrand Dowley	1936-1938	Elected Councillor
Sister Benvenuta O'Donoghue	1936-1938	Elected Councillor
Sister Angels Donnellan	1936-1938	Elected Councillor

Election / appointment to the office of higher superiors and assistants, Port Elizabeth Foundations, 1867-1938.

Mother Rose Whitty	1867-1873	Appointed Prioress\ Foundress[11]
Mother Thomas Kelly	1867-1873	Appointed Sub-Prioress
Mother Rose Whitty	1873-1879	Elected Prioress
Mother Thomas Kelly	1873-1879	Elected Sub-Prioress
Mother Rose Whitty	1880-1883	Elected Prioress[12]
Mother Thomas Kelly	1880-1883	Elected Sub-Prioress
Mother Rose Whitty	1883-1886	Elected as Prioress
Mother Thomas Kelly	1883-1886	Elected as Sub-Prioress[13]
Mother Rose Whitty	1886-1889	Elected Prioress
Mother Thomas Kelly	1886-1889	Elected Sub-Prioress

Mother Rose Whitty	1889-1892	Elected Prioress[14]
Mother Thomas Kelly	1889-1892	Elected Sub-Prioress
Mother Dominic Housley	1892-1895	Elected Prioress
Mother Thomas Kelly	1892-1895	Elected Sub-Prioress
Mother Dominic Housley	1895-1898	Elected Prioress
Mother Thomas Kelly	1895-1898	Elected Sub-Prioress
Mother Catherine Behan	1898-1900[15]	Elected Prioress
Mother Dominic Housley	1898-1900	Elected Sub-Prioress
Mother Dominic Housley	1900-1903	Elected Prioress
Mother Rose Whitty	1900-1903	Elected Sub-Prioress
Mother Dominic Housley	1903-1906	Elected Prioress
Mother Rose Whitty	1903-1906	Elected Sub-Prioress
Mother Magdalen Slattery	1906-1909	Elected Prioress
Mother Dominic Housley	1906-1909	Elected Sub-Prioress
Mother Magdalen Slattery	1909-1912	Elected Prioress
Mother Dominic Housley	1909-1912	Elected Sub-Prioress
Mother Dominic Housley	1912 1915	Elected Prioress[16]
Mother Augustine Keon	1912-1915	Elected Sub-Prioress
Mother Augustine Keon	1915-1918	Elected Prioress
Mother Magdalen Slattery	1915-1918	Elected Sub-Prioress
Mother de Ricci Harkin	1918-1921	Elected Prioress
Mother Augustine Keon	1918-1921	Elected Sub-Prioress
Mother de Ricci Harkin	1921-1925	Elected Prioress[17]
Mother Hyacinth Lamont	1921-1925	Elected Sub-Prioress

Mother de Ricci Harkin	1925-1930	Elected Prioress General
Mother Magdalen Slattery	1925-1930	Elected 1st Councillor
Mother Catherine Behan	1925-1930	Elected 2nd Councillor
Mother Thecla Wilmot	1925-1930	Elected 3rd Councillor
Mother Joseph Scallan	1925-1930	Elected 4th Councillor[18]
Mother de Ricci Harkin	1931-1937	Elected Prioress General
Mother Thecla Wilmot	1931-1937	Elected 1st Councillor
Mother Hyacinth Lamont	1931-1937	Elected 2nd Councillor
Mother Magdalen Slattery	1931-1937	Elected 3rd Councillor
Mother Catherine Behan	1931-1937	Elected 4th Councillor
Mother de Ricci Harkin	1937-1938	Elected Prioress General[19]
Mother Thecla Wilmot	1937-1938	Elected 1st Councillor
Mother Hyacinth Lamont	1937-1938	Elected 2nd Councillor
Mother Magdalen Slattery	1937-1938	Elected 3rd Councillor
Mother Catherine Behan	1937-1938	Elected 4th Councillor[20]

The Congregation of the Irish Dominican Sisters: Appointments / election to the office of Regional Vicar and Regional Councillors for the Region of South Africa, May 1938- 1998.

Mother Teresa Coleman (CT)	1938-1948	Appointed Regional Vicar
Mother de Ricci Harkin (PE)	1938-1948	Appointed 1st Councillor
Mother Angels Donnellan (CT)	1938-1948	Appointed 2nd Councillor
Mother Thecla Wilmot (PE)	1938-1948	Appointed 3rd Councillor
Mother Clare Martin (CT)	1938-1948	Appointed 4th Councillor[21]

Mother Colmcille Flynn (Cabra)	1948-1951	Appointed Regional Vicar
Mother Teresa Coleman	1948-1951	Appointed 1st Councillor
Mother Thecla Wilmot	1948-1951	Appointed 2nd Councillor
Mother de Ricci Harkin	1948-1951	Appointed 3rd Councillor[22]
Mother Angels Donnellan	1948-1951	Appointed 4th Councillor
Mother Catherine Dixon (Sion Hill)	1951-1955	Appointed Regional Vicar
Mother Teresa Coleman	1951-1955	Appointed 1st Councillor
Mother Thecla Wilmot	1951-1955	Appointed 2nd Councillor
Mother Angels Donnellan	1951-1955	Appointed 3rd Councillor
Mother Francis Gunn	1951-1955	Appointed 4th Councillor
Mother Catherine Dixon	1955-1960	Appointed Regional Vicar
Mother Teresa Coleman	1955-1960	Appointed 1st Councillor
Mother Angels Donnellan	1955-1960	Appointed 2nd Councillor
Mother Francis Gunn	1955-1960	Appointed 3rd Councillor
Mother Immaculata Lavery	1955-1960	Appointed 4th Councillor
Mother Jordan Keary (Sion Hill)	1960-1961	Appointed Regional Vicar[23]
Mother Teresa Coleman	1960-1961	Appointed 1st Councillor
Mother Angels Donnellan	1960-1961	Appointed 2nd Councillor
Mother Vincent Drew	1960-1961	Appointed 3rd Councillor
Mother Immaculata Lavery	1960-1961	Appointed 4th Councillor
Mother Damian Madden (Belfast)[24]	1961-1965	Appointed Regional Vicar
Mother Teresa Coleman	1961-1965	Appointed 1st Councillor

Mother Angels Donnellan	1961-1965	Appointed 2nd Councillor
Mother Vincent Drew	1961-1965	Appointed 3rd Councillor
Mother Immaculata Lavery	1961-1965	Appointed 4th Councillor
Mother Angels Donnellan	1965-1968	Appointed Regional Vicar
Mother Teresa Coleman	1965-1968	Appointed 1st Councillor
Mother Immaculata Lavery	1965-1968	Appointed 2nd Councillor
Mother Vincent Drew	1965-1968	Appointed 3rd Councillor
Mother Dympna Byrne	1965-1968	Appointed 4th Councillor
Mother Genevieve Hickey	1968-1972	Appointed Regional Vicar
Mother Vincent Drew	1968-1972	Appointed Councillor
Mother Gonzales Tuohy	1968-1972	Appointed Councillor
Mother Thecla McGowan	1968-1972	Appointed Councillor
Mother Immaculata Lavery	1968-1972	Appointed Councillor
Mother Genevieve Hickey	1972-1977	Appointed Regional Vicar
Mother Vincent Drew	1972-1977	Appointed 1st Councillor
Mother Thérèse Emmanuel Dempsey	1972-1977	Appointed 2nd Councillor
Mother Thecla McGowan	1972-1977	Appointed 3rd Councillor
Mother Majella Keary	1972-1977	Appointed 4th Councillor[25]
Sister Marian O'Sullivan	1977-1980	Appointed Regional Vicar
Sister Thérèse Emmanuel Dempsey	1977-1980	Appointed 1st Councillor
Sister Raymunda Brennan	1977-1980	Appointed 2nd Councillor
Sister Majella Keary	1977-1980	Appointed 3rd Councillor

Sister Macrina Donoghue	1977-1980	Appointed 4th Councillor
Sister Marian O' Sullivan	1980-1983	Elected Regional Vicar[26]
Sister Thérèse Emmanuel Dempsey	1980-1983	Elected 1st Councillor
Sister Majella Keary	1980-	Elected 2nd Councillor[27]
Sister Raymunda Brennan	1980-1983	Elected 3rd Councillor
Sister Macrina Donoghue	1980-1983	Elected 4th Councillor
Sister Margaret Kelly	1980-1983	Co-opted as Councillor
Sister Marian O'Sullivan[28]	1983-1986	Elected Regional Vicar
Sister Thérèse Emmanuel Dempsey	1983-1986	Elected 1st Councillor
Sister Macrina Donoghue	1983-1986	Elected 2nd Councillor
Sister Margaret Kelly	1983-1986	Elected 3rd Councillor
Sister Martin Pillay	1983-1986	Elected 4th Councillor
Sister Raymunda Brennan	1986-1990	Elected Regional Vicar
Sister Majella Keary	1986-1990	Elected 1st Councillor
Sister Martin Pillay	1986-1990	Elected 2nd Councillor
Sister Francis Krige	1986-1990	Elected 3rd Councillor
Sister Brigid Gillen	1986-1990	Elected 4th Councillor
Sister Raymunda Brennan	1990-1994	Elected Regional Vicar
Sister Margaret Wall	1990-1994	Elected 1st Councillor
Sister Francis Krige	1990-1994	Elected 2nd Councillor
Sister Kathleen Keary	1990-1994	Elected 3rd Councillor
Sister Brigid Gillen	1990-1994	Elected 4th Councillor

Sister Margaret Kelly	1994-1998	Elected Regional Vicar
Sister Margaret Wall	1994-1998	Elected 1st Councillor
Sister Sally Young	1994-1998	Elected 2nd Councillor
Sister Jennifer Alt	1994-1998	Elected 3rd Councillor
Sister Kathy Gaylor	1994-1998	Elected 4th Councillor

Prioresses General of the Congregation of Dominican Sisters of Our Lady of the Rosary and Saint Catherine of Siena, Cabra, 1928-1998.

Names:	Dates:	Terms of office
Mother Colmcille Flynn	1928-1941[29]	2 Terms
Mother Reginald Lyons	1941-1954	2 Terms
Mother Benignus Meenan	1954-1960	1 Term[30]
Mother Jordan Keary	1961-1967	1 Term[31]
Mother Isidore Collins	1968-1974	1 Term
Mother Jordana Roche	1974-1986	2 Terms
Sister Marian O'Sullivan	1986-1998	2 Terms

APPENDIX III

SISTERS IN THE REGION OF SOUTH AFRICA, APRIL 1998

WESTERN CAPE

DOMINICAN REGION HOUSE, CAPE TOWN (1863)

Margaret Kelly (Regional Vicar)
Josepha Mullen (Regional Bursar)
Margaret Wall (Regional Councillor)
Sally Young (Regional Councillor)
Alberta Crowe

SPRINGFIELD CONVENT, WYNBERG (1871)

Christopher Brick
Assumpta Carey
Rosemary Commins
Oliver Connell
Caroline Geoghegan
Valerian Grimes
Marcellus Hennigan
Berchmans Horan
Antoninus Kennedy
Pia O'Connell (Prioress)
Mechtilde Purcell
Philip Ryan
Dominica Tobin

ST AGNES' CONVENT, WOODSTOCK (1898)

Madeleine Corcoran
Aloysius Deady
Majella Keary
Colette Kenny
Brona Lagan
Canice McArdle
Catherine Meyer

ST MICHAEL'S CONVENT, RONDEBOSCH (1905)

Bede Carew
Dympna Carew
Finbarr Conway
Nora Deady
Alphonso Denny
Assumpta De Villiers
Ronan Drury
Otteran Fenning
Agnes Finn
Áine Hardiman
Genevieve Hickey
Catherine Kelly
Giuseppe Largey (Prioress)
Basil McCarthy
Alexius McGonigle
Stella Reynolds
Amata Tuohy
Clara Walsh

ST DOMINIC'S CONVENT, WITTEBOME (1937)

Dominique Fortes
Mary Hunt
Agnes Louw
Justina Nutley
Fidelma O'Donnell

Vincent Saldanha
Gloria September
Jennifer Slater
Jacinta Teixeira

DOMINICAN GRIMLEY SCHOOL, HOUT BAY (1980)

Paulinus Conroy
Macrina Donoghue

Francis Krige
Cynthia Thompson

ST MARY'S CONVENT, NYANGA (1987)

Aideen McIntyre

Evelyn Waters

STELLENBOSCH

Ancilla Griffiths
Clare Harkin

Dympna Travers

EASTERN CAPE

HOLY ROSARY CONVENT, PORT ELIZABETH (1867)

Sheila Corcoran
Francis Joseph Cosgrove
Columbia Fernandez

Sabina Murphy
Andrea Murray
Anne Woulfe

ST DOMINIC'S PRIORY, PORT ELIZABETH (1900)

Benignus Atkinson
Jordan Byrne
Colmcille Carr
Josephine Crawford
Stanislaus Deighan
Raymund Delany
Vincent Drew
Carmel Forde
Emily Garry
Baptist Jameson

Rose Dominic Laros (Prioress)
Andrew Maguire
Rosina McGlade
Albertus McGuinness
Servatius Nyhan
Pius O'Loughlin
Columbanus O'Mahony
Cynthia Rice
Gonzalez Tuohy

MARYMOUNT CONVENT, UITENHAGE (1942)

Eileen Acton
Irene Conlon
Bernadette Flinter
Kathy Gaylor (Regional Councillor)

Rose McLarnon
Austin Rooney
James Williams

GELVAN PARK, PORT ELIZABETH (1983)

Carmel Hurley
Noreen Mortell

Cleophas Trant

DOMINICAN CONVENT, KIRKWOOD (1996)

Feargal Cassidy
Paul Cloete

Kathleen Keary

GAUTENG

SANCTA MARIA CONVENT, VANDERBIJLPARK (1956)

Thérèse Byrne
Elizabeth Clifford
Clare Lenaghan

Maria Mackey (Prioress)
Philippine Tuohy

ST CATHERINE'S CONVENT, FLORIDA (1957)

Sheila Barrett

Aimo Eady

SINT PAULUSKLOOSTER, PRETORIA (1961)

Jennifer Alt (Regional Councillor)
Margaret Close
Alvarez Lernan

Athanasius Melican
Siobhán Murphy

DOMINICAN NOVITIATE FOR CABRA, NEWCASTLE, KING WILLIAM'S TOWN AND OAKFORD CONGREGATIONS, at GELUKSDAL

Immaculata Da Rocha

NEWCASTLE DOMINICANS, BOKSBURG

Raymunda Brennan

JOHANNESBURG

Marilyn Marriner

FREE STATE

BENINCASA, SASOLBURG (1980)

Kathleen Boner   Caitriona Owens

SWAZILAND

ST MARGARET'S, MANZINI (1994)

Gilbert Dowd   Deirdre O'Neill
Eileen McCarthy

IRELAND

FANJEAUX, DUBLIN (1988)

Maude Fitzgerald   Brigid Gillen

APPENDIX IV

SISTERS WHO HAVE WORKED IN THE REGION OF SOUTH AFRICA

NAME OF SISTER	PRESENT ASSIGNMENT
Dorothy Balfe	Ireland
Barbara Cahill*	Ireland
Catherine Campbell	Ireland
Marie Thérèse Carvill*	Ireland
Noreen Christian	Ireland
Marie Cunningham	Ireland
Aileen Cusack	Ireland
Pius Donnelly	Ireland
Cora Gaffney*	Ireland
Caitríona Geraghty*	Ireland
Antonina Goonan	Ireland
Mary Kehoe	Ireland
Laura Looby*	Ireland
Ann Maher	Ireland
Celine Mangan*	Ireland
Madeleine McCann	Ireland
Hilda McDermott*	Ireland
Benen McGeown*	Ireland
Casimir McGlade*	Ireland
Kathleen McGlynn	Ireland
Breda Molloy	Ireland
Gabriel Joseph Moore	Ireland
Teresa Morgan	Ireland
Sheila Mullan	Argentina
Vivienne O'Beirne*	Ireland
Claire O'Brien*	Ireland
Geraldine O'Driscoll	Ireland
Mary O'Driscoll	Rome
Gráinne O'Grady*	Ireland
Elizabeth Mary O'Hara	Ireland
Berenice O'Keeffe*	Ireland
Ruth Pilkington*	Ireland
Martin Pillay	General Councillor
Lorna Ridley	Ireland
Lua Tuohy	Ireland
Cynthia Veitch	Brazil
Sarah Mary Walsh	Ireland

* Sisters who volunteered for the South African mission for a limited period of time.

APPENDIX V

OBITUARY OF SISTERS OF THE WESTERN CAPE FOUNDATION 1863-1938

NAME	DATE	NAME	DATE
Alberta Bean	1864-1935	Regis Healy	1864-1904
Anastasia Brophy	1855-1896	Perpetua Helfrich	1818
Bridget Burke	1840-1921	Anne Kearney	1849-1903
Reginald Burke	1859-1915	Anastasia Kelly	1929
Bernard Butler	1838-1884	Dympna Kinsella	1828-1903
Lazarian Byrne	1867-1938	Joseph Leahy	1845-1890
Hyancinth Casey	1843-1872	Benignus Lynch	1870-1893
Thomas Casey	1845-1889	Michael Mallon	1839-1894
Genevieve Clarke	1897-1926	Rose Manning	1846-1873
Stephana Connelly	1871-1930	Columba McAuliffe	1854-1936
Jordan Connolly	1889-1927	Margaret McCabe	1840-1909
Gonzales Cosgrave	1925	Gabriel McCarthy	1865-1901
Berchmans Cotter	1862-1934	Stanislaus McCreanor	1919
Dolores Cotter	1877-1911	Michael McCullagh	1858-1923
Paul Cotter	1860-1932	Borgia McDonnell	1918
Gonzales Cronan	1862-1935	Raphael McDonnell	1859-1899
Ida Dooling	1869-1938	Hyacinth McDonough	1848-1919
Veronica Dooling	1860-1905	Antoninus McLaughlin	1850-1933
Agnes Doran	1840-1912	Pius McLaughlin	1848-1933
Benignus Dowley	1885	Aquinata Mullen	1906-1931
Catherine Enearny	1935	Vincent O'Brien	1850-1891
Brendan Farran	1883-1918	Stephana O'Connell	1913
Ignatius Flannery	1863-1911	Lelia O'Connor	1881-1919
Mechtilde Fleming	1893-1923	Martha O'Flaherty	1931
Aloysius Flynn	1875-1913	Zita O'Reilly	1935
Bernard Flynn	1862-1938	Ida Quinn	1884
Patrick Gallaghan	1877-1938	Patrick Rice	1862-1895
John Gillen	-1898	Kieran Sampson	1876-1913
Agatha Halliden	1876-1912	Francis Sherwin	1846-1919
Aloysius Hart	1866-1897	Catherine Smith	1846-1920
Gertrude Hart	1849-1924	De Sales Wollaston	1892-1927

OBITUARY OF SISTERS OF THE EASTERN CAPE FOUNDATION 1867-1938

NAME	DATE	NAME	DATE
Imelda Best	1874-1903	Clare Linden	1885-1935
Johanna Byrne	1903-1930	Monica Moore	1843-1917
Bertrand Connell	1880-1910	Michael Morton	1836-1899
Dominic Connolly	1891-1925	Patrick Morton	1852-1915
Aloysius Cowley	1821-1900	Rinaldo Mulcachy	1864-1900
Raymund Dowling	1854-1902	Brigid Neville	1863-1930
Martha Flaherty	1877-1913	Vincent O'Donoghue	1864-1923
Xavier Gordon	1860-1907	St Joan O'Kelly	1910-1936
John Heller	1865-1892	Gertrude O'Neill	1895-1926
Dominic Housley	1850-1915	Hyacinth Potter	1837-1896
Frances Kelly	1846-1888	Margaret Rooney	1848-1894
Thomas Kelly	1831-1895	Baptist Taaffe	1838-1902
Augustine Keon	1850-1927	Rose Whitty	1831-1911
Teresa Kilkinger	1854-1884		

OBITUARY OF SISTERS IN THE REGION OF SOUTH AFRICA 1938-1998

NAME	BIRTH	PROFESSION	DEATH
Regis Allen	1874	1912	06.04.1960
Gabriel Allen	1879	1905	02.10.1948
Raphael Anglim	1881		03.12.1943
Stanislaus Barr	1894	1921	05.09.1987
Augustine Barry	1862	1880	27.07.1949
De Chantal Bateson	1909	1942	12.06.1991
Imelda Bean	1858	1881	14.03.1941
De Ricci Bean	1864	1884	07.08.1943
Catherine Behan	1858	1878	27.09.1948
Antonia Bergin (Ireland)	1923	1946	29.12.1990
Aloysius Blum	1873	1910	07.06.1949
Reginald Boyd	1879	1899	22.12.1944
Cyril Brick	1917	1935	03.02.1957
Martha Brick	1920	1938	06.02.1971
Alacoque Broderick	1882	1913	26.06.1973
Paschal Bourke	1912	1934	09.10.1997
Aidan Butler	1897	1917	20.12.1961
Anthony Byrne	1875	1898	07.09.1943
Dympna Byrne	1914	1932	13.10.1989
Thérèse Cahill	1898	1917	05.05.1982
Ursula Campbell	1894	1916	24.12.1968
Monica Carr	1895	1926	28.03.1972

NAME	BIRTH	PROFESSION	DEATH
Francis Carton	1896	1926	28.05.1960
Anne Casey	1911	1933	04.02.1955
Monica Chad	1885	1907	25.06.1959
Magdalen Cheesman	1926	1948	14.07.1992
Paul Clancy	1914	1934	22.08.1986
Teresa Coleman	1890	1910	07.08.1974
Leo Coll	1917	1935	21.06.1988
Benedict Collins	1874	1901	19.12.1953
Paul Comly	1859	1885	29.02.1944
Peter Conlon	1903	1925	27.09.1967
Amata Connolly	1908	1936	24.09.1963
Benvenuta Connolly	1896	1923	21.04.1990
Emelia Corcoran	1898	1919	25.12.1970
Tarcisius Corcoran	1903	1930	27.02.1975
Consilia Cormack	1910	1949	18.05.1990
Christopher Cormack	1906	1935	18.02.1997
Oliver Joseph Cormican	1915	1944	08.06.1988
Bernadette Costello	1909	1929	25.11.1969
Henry Costello	1917	1939	19.07.1993
Dominic Coughlin	1855	1874	07.07.1946
Ceslaus Coyle	1891	1922	15.02.1977
Raymund Crane	1886	1919	30.05.1952
Gerard Crawford	1908	1932	09.05.1993
Cecilia Crolly	1862	1884	09.03.1942
Alphonsus Cummins	1899	1923	16.04.1996
Stephana Cuniffe	1898	1922	20.10.1986
Ignatius Curtin	1875	1901	13.07.1961
Gerard Daly	1885	1908	07.06.1963
Mannes Daly	1914	1933	26.02.1996
De Montfort Dempsey	1915	1939	18.08.1962
Thérèse Emmanuel Dempsey	1916	1941	13.04.1998
Virgilius Dennehy (Ireland)	1909	1930	21.07.1996
Catherine Dixon (Ireland)	1891	1920	10.07.1974
Ambrose Doherty (Ireland)	1899	1923	06.03.1987
Angels Donnellan	1897	1919	29.03.1979
De Montfort Doran (Ireland)	1906	1948	21.01.1988
Bertrand Dowley	1855	1878	02.02.1938
Angela Dowling	1886	1919	27.06.1962
Carina Dowling	1925	1946	13.06.1985
Gabriel Doyle	1935	1956	04.12.1983
Matthew Doyle	1901	1932	25.06.1987
Fabia Doyle	1923	1945	01.01.1993
Osanna Duggan	1896	1929	13.06.1967
Augustine Dunne	1901	1932	17.09.1988
Juliana Egan	1916	1934	03.12.1993
Oliver Fearon	1910	1936	24.05.1993
Felicitas Finnerty	1888	1915	18.08.1970

NAME	BIRTH	PROFESSION	DEATH
Anne Fischer	1879	1924	28.11.1965
Gertrude Flanagan	1893	1926	03.10.1971
Colmcille Flynn (Ireland)	1879	1905	28.06.1958
Patricia Fox	1900	1920	04.08.1989
Paschal Gallagher	1908	1935	21.07.1943
Teresa Gardiner	1873	1896	16.04.1954
Lucy Geelan	1876	1901	04.07.1955
Calasanctius Gibbons	1898	1919	03.08.1987
Benedicta Gillen	1919	1940	28.03.1964
Feighin Gillooly	1918	1943	10.10.1989
Clement Gleeson	1878	1906	08.11.1973
Joseph Glynn	1874	1895	26.05.1961
Reginald Gordon	1859	1879	01.06.1942
Michael Griffin	1898	1934	04.04.1970
Bonaventure Griffin	1906	1927	14.02.1957
Francis Gunn	1890	1914	01.08.1964
Margaret Hagan	1901	1925	14.06.1968
Annunciata Hall	1904	1931	01.02.1983
Ceslaus Hanrahan	1901	1922	26.02.1970
Scholastica Hansford	1881	1905	27.02.1957
De Ricci Harkin	1867	1891	19.10.1950
Helen Hatton	1914	1934	28.08.1994
Raphael Hayes	1887	1906	23.11.1962
Felicite Heneghan	1898	1921	28.12.1974
Agnes Hickey	1890	1916	24.10.1976
De Paul Hickey	1898	1919	11.09.1977
Xaveria Higgins	1870	1896	01.03.1949
Aidan Hogan	1915	1936	03.12.1979
Margaret Mary Hogan	1878	1902	15.07.1950
Caterina Holeman (Ireland)	1873	1895	06.01.1959
Emmanuel Hope	1912	1934	29.03.1989
Magdalen Horan	1856	1880	29.10.1940
Fidelis Hughes	1890	1912	10.07.1962
Ethnea Hughes	1885	1907	26.07.1971
Benvenuta Ivers	1899	1922	02.10.1952
Ethelreda Jardine	1898	1926	14.05.1992
Hilary Kearney	1886	1906	20.06.1965
Teresita Kearney	1899	1925	20.09.1981
Jordan Keary (Ireland)	1900	1924	10.03.1981
Bartholomew Kelly	1912	1935	09.06.1988
Laurence Kelly	1912	1934	08.04.1988
Columba Joseph Kennedy	1912	1950	04.03.1998
Baptist Kirwin	1870	1890	08.01.1948
Rose Kotze	1926	1951	25.07.1992
Hyacinth Lamont	1881	1905	24.05.1956
Colman Lavelle	1913	1934	17.08.1992

NAME	BIRTH	PROFESSION	DEATH
John Lavelle	1916	1934	08.06.1994
Immaculata Lavery	1908	1930	18.04.1982
Finbar Lawlor	1913	1935	20.05.1997
Columba Lawlor	1875	1901	12.11.1951
Germaine Lawrence	1908	1929	06.04.1985
Rose Leahy	1899	1918	28.04.1981
Lewis Bertrand Leahy	1895	1922	08.09.1981
Martina Lennon	1912	1936	27.03.1998
Ruth Lernihan	1924	1943	21.07.1994
Sylvester Liddy	1919	1937	17.03.1976
Ligouri Lowe	1898	1919	22.10.1966
Alphonsus Lynch	1871	1895	22.02.1960
Rose Lynch	1873	1896	04.08.1951
Jordan Lynch	1914	1932	12.12.1990
Lelia Lynch	1905	1928	18.05.1995
Bernard Mackesy	1898	1924	03.01.1991
Kiernan Mackey	1896	1917	16.12.1966
Damian Madden (Ireland)	1910	1931	24.02.1987
Alvarez Magee	1913	1936	26.12.1997
Lucy Maher	1901	1926	23.10.1982
Rosary Mangan	1894	1918	06.08.1983
Lawrence Manweiller	1908	1935	06.07.1976
Clare Martin	1869	1897	08.02.1946
Dorothea McCarthy	1913	1931	06.12.1944
Lucia McDermott	1911	1932	01.05.1995
Imelda McDonagh	1913	1936	18.11.1961
Damian McDonald	1911	1933	06.10.1975
Immaculata McDonald	1896	1918	16.09.1980
Mary of the Rosary McEnery	1906	1931	07.01.1984
Thecla McGowan	1907	1929	05.03.1985
Cosmas McKeever	1919	1942	28.03.1946
Joanna McLaughlin	1906	1929	29.12.1994
Veronica McLoughlin	1874	1914	26.07.1974
Bruno McLoughlin	1896	1920	15.04.1948
Angela McLoughlin	1894	1918	04.08.1958
Aquinas McMahon	1899	1918	20.05.1956
Rita McMenamin	1913	1934	08.07.1992
Mannes McPartland	1900	1930	01.08.1985
Jane McWeeney (Ireland)	1915	1934	25.12.1989
Anthony Melia	1877	1901	07.09.1964
Ceslaus Melvin (Ireland)	1928	1953	20.06.1974
Kevin Molloy	1885	1907	01.10.1949
Sabina Monagle	1907	1936	31.05.1986
Vincent Monson	1874	1902	07.10.1951
Philomena Moody	1880	1901	15.01.1947
Maris Stella Moody	1892	1924	14.02.1984
Thomas Mooney	1888	1908	01.05.1976

NAME	BIRTH	PROFESSION	DEATH
Elizabeth Moore	1865	1898	07.03.1945
Walburga Moscher	1875	1911	21.03.1957
Thaddeus Moynihan	1910	1932	04.02.1984
Ambrose Mulcahy	1886	1910	13.11.1959
Cecilia Mulcahy	1879	1901	27.10.1948
Philomena Mulcahy	1881	1906	11.03.1965
Patrick Mulkerrin	1891	1917	18.12.1973
Martha Muller	1883	1919	03.03.1971
Thomas Murphy	1915	1934	22.04.1992
Peter Murphy	1858	1883	19.12.1944
Anselm Murphy	1892	1919	25.08.1962
Brendan Nagle	1902	1923	26.04.1960
Colmcille Nagle	1875	1905	04.06.1962
Gonzalva Nolan	1891	1918	27.07.1963
Martin O'Brien (Ireland)	1907	1934	19.05.1990
Anne O'Connell (Ireland)	1929	1959	04.02.1996
Rose Angela O'Connell	1876	1897	07.06.1943
Benignus O'Connor	1888	1907	21.09.1970
Malachy O'Connor	1877	1906	06.02.1957
Declan O'Donoghue	1883	1906	28.10.1946
Benvenuta O'Donoghue	1889	1906	01.07.1970
Gertrude O'Hagan	1909	1929	24.10.1952
Imelda Dominic O'Hara	1920	1942	28.02.1990
Emily O'Keeffe	1904	1923	11.08.1989
Aquin O'Mahony	1919	1939	12.01.1983
Agnes O'Neill	1863	1885	15.03.1942
Josephine O'Reilly	1914	1935	26.11.1988
Elizabeth Oldham	1880	1904	04.03.1957
Camillus Orr	1893	1912	06.04.1959
Barbara Power	1890	1920	23.01.1978
Malachy Quinn	1913	1935	11.06.1964
Evangelist Raleigh	1891	1928	06.06.1976
Carmel Reck	1885	1919	25.08.1981
Sebastian Reynolds	1901	1919	14.07.1972
Veronica Rice	1868	1898	20.09.1950
Henrietta Riordan	1914	1935	24.08.1994
Rita Roche	1916	1932	27.05.1950
Louis Rudden	1909	1933	01.11.1986
Thérèse Rudolph	1902	1936	12.05.1981
Ita Ryan	1892	1917	06.09.1984
De Sales Ryan (Ireland)	1894	1919	16.04.1981
Joseph Scallan	1864	1882	05.03.1954
Francesca Schwabel	1858	1878	19.05.1939
Dolores Sheridan	1892	1918	22.06.1975
Magdalen Slattery	1860	1886	16.07.1943
Felix Stapleton	1884	1907	12.04.1966
Martina Stevenson	1911	1931	12.01.1944

NAME	BIRTH	PROFESSION	DEATH
Xavier Sullivan	1864	1887	11.01.1948
Callista Symons	1920	1943	03.05.1947
Bernadette Treacy	1896	1922	05.08.1979
Eugene Treacy	1890	1917	06.09.1956
Martin Tuohy	1921	1941	04.09.1961
Bernardine Voskula	1883	1915	04.01.1951
Thérèse Wakefield	1911	1932	08.03.1992
Joan Walsh	1909	1933	05.07.1996
Jordan Walsh	1909	1928	22.01.1951
Stephana Ward	1912	1935	12.07.1991
Thecla Wilmot	1880	1902	23.04.1971
Dominic Wilson	1905	1923	07.03.1989
Constance Wilson	1912	1934	26.03.1966
Berchmans Woods	1900	1923	11.05.1995

Notes

Preface

[1] Congregation of Dominican Sisters, Cabra, *Constitutions*, Dublin, 1983.

Introduction

[1] Dominican Sisters, Galway, 1994.

[2] Dominican Publications, Dublin, 1994.

[3] Australian Publishing Co, Sydney, etc, 1949.

[4] Columba Cleary OP, Eleanora Murphy OP & Flora McGlynn OP. Published by the Dominican Sisters, Boksburg, 1997.

[5] The preparation of these documents according to subject matter was completed as part of this project and many key texts have been analysed in detail.

[6] Ecclesiastes, 12:12, *Jerusalem Bible*, Darton Longman &Todd, London, 1966, p 990.

Chapter One

[1] See Appendix 1.

[2] Transcripts of interviews are being held in a closed file in the Dominican Archives, Cape Town, DAC.

[3] See Chief Abbreviations, p vii.

Chapter Two

[1] This chapter has been influenced by many publications and by discussion and debate with, and seminar presentations and papers of undergraduate and post-graduate students of the University of the North West. The book that was most influential for this section is, Renate Bridenthal & Claudia Koonz, (eds), *Becoming visible: Women in European history*, Houghton Mifflin, Boston, London etc.

2   M.-H Vicaire OP, *St Dominic and his times*, Alt Publishing Co, Wisconsin, 1964, p 122.

3   See, Fiona Bowie, (ed), *Beguine spirituality: An Anthology*, SPCK, London, 1989; Marygrace Peters, 'The Beguines: Feminine piety derailed', *Spirituality Today*, St Louis, Spring 1991, 43, 1, pp 36-52.

4   C Augustine OSB, *A Commentary on the New Code of Canon Law*, III, St Louis & London, Herder, 1929, pp 20-21.

5   G Huyghe, 'What do we mean by religious?', in G Huyghe *et al*, *Religious Orders in the modern world*, Geoffrey Chapman, London, Dublin, 1965, pp 7- 8.

6   Huyghe, 'What do we mean by religious?', p 7.

Chapter Three

1   De Burgo, *Hibernia Dominicana*, p 357, in Cabra *Annals*, p 12.

2   For a more complete account of the Galway foundation, see Rose O'Neill OP, *A Rich inheritance: Galway Dominican Nuns, 1644-1994*, Galway, 1994.

3   *Hibernia Dominicana*, p 354, in Cabra *Annals*, p 23.

4   40 A, Cabra, 2 March, 1831, APF SOCG 946, f 1170.

5   *Annals*, Sion Hill, *passim*.

Chapter Four

1   Griffith, Letter 2, [Stellenbosch], 20 June 1839, 7a, CAC.

2   Griffiths, Letter to a friend, 25 Oct 1840, 7, CAC.

3   Griffiths, CT, 19 Nov. 1840, 7c, CAC.

4   Griffiths, to a friend, CT, Jan 1841, 7, CAC.

5   Letter, CT, 21 Aug 1861, DCA.

6   *Ibid.*

7   *Annals*, Cabra, pp 123 & 125.

8   *Ibid.*

9   Italics mine.

10   *Book of Annals, Sion Hill Convent*, Browne & Nolan, Dublin, 1904, pp 60-62.

11   Grimley, CT, 20 Jan 1862, DCA.

12 Grimley Episc., I, 20 a, 1861, p 6, CAC.

13 Grimley to Fr John Leonard, CT, 21 May 1862, 18, CAC.

14 Annals, St Mary's CT, 1863, p 2, DAC.

15 Grimley Episc, I, 13 Dec 1862, p 14, CAC.

16 CT, 20 Dec 1862, DCA.

17 Grimley to Leonard, CT, Comm. of St Paul, 1863, DAC.

18 *Book of Annals, Sion Hill,* 1904, p 2.

19 Statistics compiled by Sister Bertranda Flynn OP, Archivist, Cabra, 1991.

20 Annals, St Mary's Convent, CT, p 7, DAC.

21 *Annals*, Cabra, p 129.

22 *The Cape Argus*, 16 Jan 1864, Letter to the Editor, in MAKB, p 1.

23 Annals, St Mary's, CT, pp 3-4.

24 Griffiths, CT, Jan 1841, 7, CAC.

25 Grimley to M de Ricci Maher, CT, 20 Jan 1862, DCA.

26 Grimley to J. Leonard, CT, 18 July 1862, 18, CAC.

27 *Annals*, Cabra, p 169.

28 Grimley to M de Ricci Maher, CT, 12 July 1866, DCA.

29 *Ibid,* 19 Oct 1866.

30 St Mary's, Cabra, Profession Book, DCA.

31 Grimley to Leonard, 20 Dec 1863, CAC.

32 Annals, CT, 1863-1937, p 5.

33 Grimley to Leonard, CT, 16 Oct 1863, 18a, CAC.

34 Annals, CT, pp 5 & 6.

35 *Ibid, 1864,* p 5.

36 Grimley to Mother de Ricci, CT, 10 Feb 1865, DCA.

37 CT, 13 June 1865, DCA.

38 *Ibid,* CT, 1 Jan 1866.

39 Grimley to M de Ricci, CT, 12 July and 19 Oct 1866, DCA.

40 Annals, St Mary's Convent, CT, 30 Aug 1866, p 6.

41 Grimley to M de Ricci Maher, CT, 19 Oct 1866, DCA.

42 Grimley Episc, I, 14 Oct 1866, 20 a, np, CAC.

43 Annals, CT, 8 Oct 1864, p 5- 6.

44 Annals, CT, 1867, p 6.

45 CT. 18, CAC.

46 Dates of Baptisms, etc, 1717-1886, Cabra, p 39, DCA.

47 Official books and records give two spellings of this name McLaughlin, and McLoughlin. The former will be used in the text.

48 Dates of Baptism, etc, 1717-1886, Cabra, pp 39 & 41; Annals, Cabra, 1644-1883, 9 Aug 1873, DCA.

49 Annals, Cabra, 10 Aug, 1881; Leonard, Letter Book & jottings, File 31, p 61, CAC

50 Annals Cabra, 6 Sept 1882. Four professed choir nuns, Sisters Gonzales Cronin, Raphael McDonnell, Magdalen Crolly, Paul Cotter, and one professed lay sister, S. M. Ida Quinn, and three choir postulants, Sisters John Gillen, Rose Rooney, Alberta Bean.

51 Chronicles of the Community of St Mary's Cabra, 1819-1944, np, DCA.

52 Letters, CT, 12 April 1881, 33a, CAC.

53 Margaret Kearns, 'Springfield - A History of the property', 1683-1996, in Rosemary Commins OP, *(ed)*, *Springfield: The First one hundred and twenty-five years*, Wynberg, nd, p 18.

54 See Rosemary Commins OP, *The History of Springfield*, for a full account of this foundation.

55 Letter, CT, 29 Feb 1876, 30, CAC.

56 Letter, Leonard to Ricards, 21 March, 1876, 30, DAC.

57 Letter, Wynberg, 14 March 1883, in MAKB, p 118: SGE 1/71, Misc Letters, 1883.

58 Leonard, 13 August 1884, 34c, CAC.

59 *Report to the Central Council of the Work of the Propagation of the Faith.*

60 Autobiography of Bishop Grimley, 1867-1871: *Ecclesiastical returns*, 1868, p 43, 20A, CAC.

61 MAKB, p 15: *Ecclesiastical returns*, 55B, CAC.

62 Letters, CT, 1877, 1878-1881, 21, CAC.

63 Annals, CT, Easter 1899, p 30.

64 See Appendix II.

65 Letter Book, to Bishop John Leonard, 9 Feb 1890, 77 D (1), CAC.

66 Annals, CT, 1863-1937, p 31-32.

67 See Appendix II.

68 Annals, CT, 1863-1937, Feb 1905, p 32.

69 *Ibid*, p 34.

70 *Silver Leaves*, 1908, p 7.

71 Annals, CT, 1863-1937, p 43.

Chapter Five

1 Annals, St Mary's Convent, CT, 1863-1937, Nov 1867, p 6, DAC.

2 *Book of Annals*, Sion Hill Convent, p 1.

3 *Ibid.*

4 Letter, Belfast, 15 Dec 1902, The Foundresses, 2, DAS.

5 Letter, Mother Ignatius O'Doherty, Belfast, 15 Dec 1902, The Foundresses, 2, DAS.

6 Document confirmed by Dr Murray and notarised on 15 Oct 1839, DAS.

7 Notebook, Sept 1867, DAS.

8 *Annals*, SH, pp 49-50.

9 *Annals*, SH, pp 51-52.

10 Letter, Mother Rose Whitty, On board the *Lady Eglinton*, 8 Oct 1867, File 38, DAS.

11 Letter, Mother Thomas Kelly, The *Celt*, off Plymouth, 9 Oct 1867, File 38.

12 Letter, Mother Rose Whitty, The *Celt*, anchored at Plymouth, 9 Oct 1867, File 38.

13 Letter, Mother Thomas Kelly, The *Celt*, 9 Oct 1868, File 38.

14 Letter, M Thomas Kelly, PE, 14 Jan 1868, DAS.

15 Letter, PE, Nov 1868, DAS.

16 Letter, Sr Baptist Taaffe, PE, Nov 1868, DAS.

17 *Annals*, SH, p 54-55.

18 Annals, HRC, 1867-1923, p 4, DAP.

19 Letter, PE, Ascension Thursday, 1870, File 38.

20 Letter, Mother Thomas Kelly, PE, Aug 1868, File 38.

21 Letter, Mother Thomas Kelly, PE, Aug 1868, File 38.

22 Annals, HRC, PE, 19 Dec 1870.

23 *Ibid*, 29 Oct 1872.

24   *Ibid*, 9 Nov 1874.

25   Annals, HRC, PE, 19 Dec 1875.

26   *Ibid*, Statistics, *passim*, 1867-1900.

27   Annals, HRC, June 1869, p 4.

28   *Ibid*, 1869, p 5.

29   *Ibid*, 1871, pp 7-8.

30   *Ibid*, 1872, p 9.

31   *Ibid*, 17 Sept, 1873, p 11.

32   Annals, HRC, 1873, p 11.

33   *Ibid*, 1881, p 28.

34   Letter, Sr Hyacinth, PE, 21 June 1868, File 38.

35   *Ibid*, PE, Nov 1868.

36   Annals, HRC, School Statistics, *passim*; Closure, 19 Dec 1904, p 123.

37   *Ibid*, 1 May 1895, p 79.

38   *Ibid*, 9 May 1895, pp 80-81 & 257.

39   Annals, HRC, 13 June 1898, p 90.

40   *Ibid*, 6 Nov 1885, p 38.

41   Annals, Mater Admirabilis Convent, Feb 1889, pp 8, 32-33, DAC.

42   *Ibid*, 30 May 1896, pp 37-38, DAC.

43   *Ibid*, 1 April 1898, p 45.

44   *Ibid*, 10 Sept, 1898, pp 46-47.

45   *Ibid*, 1899, pp 50-51.

46   Annals, HRC, 1899, pp 93-94.

47   *Ibid*, p 100.

48   *Confirmatio Electionis Priorissa*, 3 Dec, 1898, DAP.

49   B J T Leverton, 'Wilmot, (John) Alexander', *Dictionary of South Biography*, II, HCRC, Tafelberg, Cape Town and Johannesburg, 1972, pp 849-850.

50   Annals, HRC, pp 101, 103 & 105.

51   Statistics in Annals, HRC, 1898-1920, *passim*.

52   Appendix I, Interviews, 1991-1997, *passim*, DAC.

53   Annals, HRC, p 178.

Chapter Six

1. Mother Berchmans Cotter OP, Necrology of the Dominican Sisters founded from Cabra at Cape Town, 1863, CT, 1925, p 2, DAC.

2. Leaflet, 1889, DAC.

3. Interview, 30-32, Thérèse Wakefield OP, 1991, DAC.

4. Interview, 2, Vincent Drew OP, 9 Oct 1990.

5. Regulations for the guidance of the pupils, St Mary's, Cabra, 1 & 3, pp 28-30, DCA.

6. Notes on the Order of The School, Sion Hill, Sept 1891, p 1, DAS.

7. Notes on the Order of The School, Sion Hill, p 20.

8. *Constitutions*, PE, 1888, Commentaries, p 84.

9. *Ibid*, p 94.

10. Interview, 3, Vincent Drew OP, 9 Oct 1990.

11. *Constitutions*, Commentaries, p 98.

12. *Ibid*, p 99.

13. KB, Oral evidence.

14. Immaculata, Cabra, Rules, 10, 1914, pp 18-19.

15. Immaculata, Cabra, Rules, p 19.

16. Oral evidence, Juliana Egan OP, CT, July 1991.

17. Minutes, Provincial Council, CT, 7 Jan 1917, p 67, DAC.

18. Interview, Sister Finbar Lawlor OP, 19-20, 8/3/91.

19. *Ibid*, 48.

20. Interview, Cynthia Rice OP, 15-18, 7 March 1991, DAC.

21. Interview, 8 March 1991, DAC.

22. *The Rule of St Augustine and the Constitutions of the Sisters of the Third Order of St Dominic forming the African Congregation of St Catharine of Siena*, Bloemfontein, 1925, p 35.

23. *Rule and Constitutions, 1925*, p 35.

24. *Directory and Customary of the Third Order of St Dominic forming the African Congregation of St Catharine of Siena*, Bloemfontein, 1924, p 11.

25. Immaculata, Cabra, Rules, 4, p 31, DCA.

26. *Ibid*, 7, pp 32-33.

27   *First Prospectus of Immaculata School*, in Immaculata Cabra, Rules, pp 67-68.

28   *First Prospectus of Immaculata School, Immaculata*, Cabra, p 68.

29   Leaflet, 1889.

30   J Procter OP, Preface, p v, A T Drane, in *The Daily life of a Religious*, Sands and Herder, London etc., 1896.

31   Regulations for the guidance of the pupils, St Mary's, Cabra, pp 28-31, nd.

Chapter Seven

1   K Boner, The Irish Dominicans and education in the Western Cape (1863-1892), unpublished MA thesis, Unisa, 1976, p 37.

2   Mother Bertrand Dowley, Obits 1872-1936, p 22, DAC.

3   Grimley Autobiography, 1, 1861-1866, np, 20A, CAC.

4   G.9-'91: Education Commission, Minutes of evidence.

5   *The Wynberg Times*, 18 & 25 Aug 1888.

6   Leonard, CT, 13 Jan 1885, Misc letters, 1885-1894, 23, CAC.

7   Re School fees see MAKB, Ch IV, *passim*.

8   Annals, Mater Admirabilis Convent, Uitenhage, July 1920, p 130, DAC.

9   G. 1-'71: *Report of the Superintendent of Education for 1870*, Appendix C, p 122, in MAKB, p 82, footnote 33.

10   MAKB, p 104.

11   Sister Berchmans Cotter, Necrology, 1863-1934, pp 3-4, and 49-50, based on oral evidence, DAC.

12   See MAKB, *re* the training and qualification of teachers, Chapter 3, *passim*; Dowley, Obits, 1872-1936, p 16.

13   Annals, CT, 1863-1937, p 6, DAC.

14   MAKB, p 101.

15   MAKB, p 102.

16   *Educational reports, 1863, The Cape of Good Hope Blue Book*, 1, Y, 48. Quoted in MAKB, p 78.

17   G.75-'80: *Commission report ..., Minutes of evidence*, 1245, p 207. Quoted in MAKB, p 76.

[18] G.12-'83, *Cape of Good Hope, Preliminary Report on the State of Education ...*, pp 4-7.

[19] G.12-'83, *Preliminary Report ...*, p 12.

[20] G.12-'83, *Preliminary Report*, p 12.

[21] *Ibid*, p 13.

[22] *Ibid*, p 14.

[23] Cotter, Necrology, 1872-1934, pp 15-17.

[24] *Ibid, p 20; Annals*, Cabra, Appendix I, p 165.

[25] Cotter, Necrology, 1872-1934, pp 20-20a.

[26] *Ibid*, p 20a.

[27] Published in 1900.

[28] *Silver Leaves*, 1904, p 18.

[29] Annals, Mater Admirabilis Convent, 1887-1937, p 35, DAC; Annals, HRC, 1867-1923, pp 142 & 156.

[30] Annals, HRC, p 160.

[31] *Ibid*, p 34.

[32] G12-'83, *Preliminary Report*, p 35.

[33] These were probably the T3 or T2, but the records give no specific information.

[34] G12-'83, p 34.

[35] *Ibid*, pp 35 & 37.

[36] Springfield, Wynberg, Register of Births, Professions ..., np, DAC.

[37] Letters, 1867-1881, *passim*, DAS.

[38] Annals, HRC, pp 3 &15.

[39] Book of Clothing & Profession, PE, 1867-1943, np, DAP.

[40] 1892, p 39.

[41] Annals, CT, 1863-1937, 1904, p 30.

[42] *Annals*, Cabra, 1644-1883, 6 Sept 1882.

Chapter Eight

[1] *The Nation*, 22 Jan 1859.

[2] Annals, CT, 1863-1937, p 10, DAC.

[3] Catholic Institution ..., *Eleventh Annual Report, 1857*.

[4] *The Standard and Mail*, 22 Sept 1874.

5   *Ibid.*

6   Annals, CT, 1863-1937, p 10.

7   *Eleventh Annual Report*, 1857, p 34.

8   *Ibid*, p 35-36.

9   For a clear and detailed history of deaf education in Ireland and its development in the twentieth century see Sister Nicholas Griffey OP, *From silence to speech*, Dominican Publications, Dublin, 1994.

10   *Encyclopaedia Britannica*, VIII, p 886.

11   *Ibid.*

12   P. E. Biesenbach, 'Ons Instituut te Worcester', *Die Kerkbode*, *LXXVIII*, 12 Sept 19, 1956, p 538.

13   Springfield, Wynberg, Account of the Cape foundations, p 39.

14   Letter, 28 June 1881, SGE 1/6, Misc Letters, CA.

15   *Ibid.*

16   Letter, J J O'Reilly, 3 July 1882, 33C, CAC

17   Letter, CT, 26 July 1882, SGE 1/65, Misc Letters, CA.

18   Annals, CT, 1863-1937, p 41.

19   Annals, CT, 1867-1937, 1896, p 26.

20   St Gabriel's School for the Deaf, Draft of a letter, M M Maher to Canon Kennedy, 24 May 1882, DCA.

21   Letter, 21 Dec 1900, SGE 1/246, R 126/986, CA.

22   Letter, 15 Oct 1902, SGE, 1/317, R146/770, CA.

23   Letter, 29 Dec 1902, SGE, 1/317, R148/852, CA.

24   Letter, 13 Dec 1904, SGE, 1/423, R174/211, CA.

25   Diary, 1888, pp 10 & 12, 71D, CAC.

26   Address, Deaf Mutes of St Joseph's, nd, DAC.

27   Letter, J J O'Reilly to Dr Muir, 3 Jan 1899, SGE, 1/120, R 106/514, CA.

28   Letter, 3 Jan 1899, SGE, 1/120, R 106/514, CA.

29   Interview written in pencil, 17 Jan 1908, SGE, 1/689 CA.

30   Sister Bertrand Dowley, Obits, 1872-1936, 8 April 1919, p 43, DAC.

31   G39-'82, p 42, CA.

32   Annals, CT, 1863-1937, p 45.

33   Annals, CT, 1925-1954, Report of the Prioress ..., 1925-1927,

pp 18, 20, 21.

[34] *Ibid*, p 38.

[35] Oral evidence, Sr Basil McCarthy OP, 28 May 1997.

[36] Oral evidence, Sister Amata Tuohy, 30 May 1997.

[37] Annals, I, Wittebome, 1937-1948, p 7, DAW.

[38] Annals, II, CT, 1925-1954, pp 47-91, *passim.*

[39] Annals, I, 1937-1954, Wittebome, p 8, DAW; Annals, II, CT, 1925-1954, p 90.

[40] Oral evidence, Sister Francis Krige, 29 Dec 1997.

[41] Oral evidence.

[42] Oral evidence, Sister Gilbert Dowd OP, Feb, 1998.

Chapter Nine

[1] Annals, II, Galway, p 74, DGA.

[2] *Rule and Constitution of the Sisters of St. Dominic*, Dominican Convent, Cabra, O'Toole, Dublin, 1843, 3, p 66.

[3] *Ibid*, pp 66-67.

[4] *Rule and Constitution*, Cabra, 1843, p 67.

[5] *Constitutions of the Dominican Sisters of the Second Order*, HRC, PE, 1888, p 112.

[6] Letter, File 18, CAC.

[7] Annals, CT, 1863-1927, p 8, DAC.

[8] Mother Berchmans Cotter, Necrology, 1872-1934, pp 13-14, DAC.

[9] Cotter, Necrology, 1872-1934.

[10] Cotter, Necrology, 1872-1934, pp 21-24, DAC

[11] Grimley Episc., II, 1874, File 20a, p 291, CAC.

[12] Cotter, Necrology, pp 37-39.

[13] Cotter, Necrology, 1863-1934, p 5.

[14] Sister Bertrand Dowley, Obits, 1872-1936, p 14.

[15] Cotter, Necrology, 1872-1934, p 8.

[16] Annals, HRC, 1876-1924, p 179.

[17] *Ibid*, p 86.

[18] *Ibid*, pp 95, 98 & 102.

19   *Rule and Constitutions*, Cabra, 1843, pp 67-68.

20   *Ibid*, pp 68-69.

21   The Divine Office was restored to the Port Elizabeth Dominicans in 1888, when their new *Constitutions* were approved.

22   *Constitutions*, HRC, PE, 1888, p 112.

23   A. Devine, *Convent life; the duties of Sisters dedicated to religion to the service of God, intended chiefly for Superiors and Confessors*, London 1889, p 298.

24   *Ibid*, p 299.

25   *Constitutions*, HRC, PE, 1888, p 113.

26   Letters, Bishop Rooney, 1909-1912, 44, CAC.

27   Letters Rooney, 1909-1912, 10/13, from Sr Augustine Barry, Woodstock, CT, 17 July 1912, 45, 24A, DAC.

28   Report of Canonical Visitation, 14-16 Oct. 1918, DAC.

29   *Ibid*.

30   Interview, KB with Sr Philomena Mulcachy, 1962, DAC.

31   *Concluding instruction addressed to the Mothers General, Sacra Congregatio de Religiosis, Acta et Documenta, Congressus Internationalis Superiorissarum Generalium,* Editiones Paulinae, Romae, 1952, pp 273-274.

32   Acts of the Fifth General Chapter of the Congregation of Irish Dominican Sisters, Dublin, 23 July- 3 Aug 1954, 25, p 6, DAC.

33   Letter, Mother Benignus Meenan, MPG, to Prioresses, Dublin, 20 Dec 1954, 39, DAG.

34   Acts of the Sixth General Chapter, 1960, 29&30.

35   Acts of the Fifth General Chapter, pp 1-2.

36   Acts of the Third Regional Chapter of the Irish Dominican Sisters of South Africa, 6-9 Jan 1954, DAC.

37   KB, Oral evidence, Sion Hill, Ireland, 1991.

38   *Constitutions*, 1947, 231, p 83.

39   *Ibid*, 235, p 83.

40   *Constitutions, 1947*, 313, (16), p 109.

41   Acts of the Eighth General Chapter, First Session, 12 July - 3 Aug 1967, 38, p 9, DAC.

42   KB, Oral Evidence, Sr Bede Kearns OP, Sion Hill, 1991.

[43] 1924, 145, p 50. Italics mine.

[44] ·*Constitutions*, 1924, 310, p 79.

[45] Dates of birth, profession and death, HRC, 1867-1943, DAC.

[46] C. Owens, Oral Evidence, 5 Feb 1997.

[47] 1908-1993, Necrology, 1928-, DAC.

[48] Sr Gerard Crawford, Interview, KB, HRC, PE, 1991.

[49] Sister Oliver Fearon, 1910-1993; Sister Finbar Lawlor, 1913-1997.

[50] Oliver Fearon, Interview, KB, St Dominic's Priory, PE, 6 March 1991, DAC.

[51] Sr Finbar Lawlor OP, Interview, KB, St Dominic's Priory, PE, 7 March 1991, DAC.

[52] *Ibid.*

Chapter 10

[1] *Saint Dominic*, Éditions du Signe, Strasbourg, p 39, 1995. Italics mine.

[2] W A Hinnebusch OP, *The History of the Dominican Order*, I, Alba House, New York, 1966.

[3] Lesley Brown, (ed), the New Oxford English Dictionary, II, Clarendon Press, Oxford, 1993, p 334.

[4] Hinnebusch, *History of the Dominican Order*, I, p 48.

[5] *Basic Constitution*, VI.

[6] *Ibid*, VI & IX.

[7] Tugwell, *Saint Dominic*, p 2.

[8] Hinnebusch, *The History of the Dominican Order*, I, p 124.

[9] *Book of Annals*, Sion Hill Convent, Blackrock, Co Dublin, Browne and Nolan, Dublin, 1904, p vii.

[10] Sisters M F M Butler, prioress & Anne C Maher, sub-prioress, Cabra, Dublin, 2 March 1831, APF, SOCG 946, f.1170.

[11] APF, SOCG 964, ff.1173-74. Text on f.1173r only. Copies and notes of archival material from the above source were supplied by Father Hugh Fenning OP, and can be found in Dominican Archives, Cabra.

[12] In Memoriam, Mother Columba Maher, nd, pp 26-27, DCA.

[13] Grimley Episcopacy, II, 20a, CAC.

14   In Memoriam Mother Columba Maher, pp 33-34, DCA.

15   Letter, Newbridge, 8 Dec 1893, DCA.

16   *Ibid*, 4 Jan 1894, DCA.

17   Letter, Sister Ignatius O'Doherty OP, Belfast, 12 Feb 1901, DCA.

18   San Michelle, 30 August 1895, quoted in O'Hanlon, *Dominican pioneers in New South Wales*, pp 104-105.

19   O'Hanlon, p 106.

20   *The Rule and Constitution of the Sisters of the Order of St. Dominic, O'Toole*, Dublin, 1843, pp 5-8.

21   Letter, May 9, 1901, DCA.

22   *Constitutions of the Dominican Sisters of the Second Order*, HRC, PE, pp v-vii.

23   *Ibid*, footnotes, p 83.

24   *Ibid*, Introduction, p vii.

25   Letter Book, 1884-1893, Dr Leonard, File 22, CAC.

26   Letters, Leonard, 1886-1900, 35, DAC.

27   *Ibid*.

28   Letter quoted in O'Hanlon, pp 108-109.

29   O'Hanlon, pp 110-111.

30   *Ibid*, pp 114-115.

31   Letter to Cardinal Moran, Rome, 14 June 1902, in O'Hanlon, p 121.

32   O'Hanlon, p 121.

33   Cardinal Moran, nd, file 28, DAS.

34   O'Hanlon, pp 122-123.

Chapter Eleven

1   Interviews, *passim*.

2   Minutes, Provincial Council, 2, 1903-1922, 11 Jan 1913, p 47, DAC.

3   *Ibid*, p 50.

4   *Ibid*, p 48.

5   Minutes, Provincial Council, 1903-1922, p 66.

6   *Ibid*, p 72.

7   *Ibid*, p 71.

8   Minutes, Provincial Council, p 87-88, DAC.

9   Letter, Mother De Ricci to the Prioress, Sion Hill, Port Elizabeth, 10 Nov, 1919, *JSA 2, p 65*, SA Box, DAS.

10 *Ibid*, Port Elizabeth, Easter Monday, [1921].

11 File 58, DAS.

12 Uncl, DAC.

13 Draft letter, 11 February 1920, to Father Louis Nolan OP, DCA.

14 Minute Book, Cabra, 1910-1923, 7, 8, 9, Jan, 1920, DCA.

15 Letters, Galway, 1920-1928, *passim*, DAG.

16 Minute Book, Meeting, 11 July 1920, pp 2-3, DCA.

17 Minutes, Provincial Council, 1911-1922, May, 8, 1920, DAC.

18 *Ibid*, p 96.

19 *Ibid*, 27 Sept 1921, p 99.

20 Letter, 18 Sept 1922, in Council Minutes, 1903-1922, pp 96a-96b, DAC.

21 Misc Letters, 1883-1952, CT, 4 Sept 1922, DAG.

22 Book of the General Council, 1889-1928, 24 Jan 1922, pp 114-117, DAP.

23 Letters, Port Elizabeth, to Mother Prioress, Sion Hill, 5 April 1922, SA Box, DAS.

24 *Ibid*, Letters, Easter Sunday, 1922, Port Elizabeth, to Mother Pius, Sion Hill.

25 Misc Letters, 1883-1952, Grahamstown, April 25 1922, DAG.

26 *Ibid*, CT, 28 April 1922.

27 *Ibid*, CT, 20 June 1922.

28 *Ibid*, CT, 28 June 1922.

29 *Ibid*, CT, July 1922.

30 Misc Letters, 1883-1952, CT, 8 Aug 1922, DAG.

31 *Ibid*, CT, 1 Nov 1922, to Srs Imelda & Gonzalez.

32 *Ibid*, CT, 7 Nov 1922.

33 Letter, Mother Provincial, CT, to Mother General, Cabra, 1931, DAC.

34 *Ibid*.

35 Letters, Port Elizabeth, 4 March 1931, Box 1, DAG.

36 6 Jan 1931, Cabra, DCA.

37 Italics mine.

38 Bloemfontein, 23 April 1924, DAC.

39 Box 122, nd, DAG.

40 Minutes, Provincial Council, 1922-1929, 85 & 88; pp 24 & 26, DAC.

41 Minutes, Provincial Council, 1922-1929, 85, pp 24-25, DAC.

42 Letter, Bloemfontein, 7 Aug 1924, DAC.

43 Minutes, Provincial Council, 28 June 1924, 100-101, p 29, DAC.

44 Letter, 20 June 1924, Bloemfontein, DAC.

45 Minutes, Provincial Council, 31 July 1934, 116, p 33, DAC.

46 Letter, Bloemfontein, 7 Aug 1924, DAC.

47 *Directory and Customary*, Prologue, p iii.

48 *Ibid*, p 70; Italics mine.

49 *Directory and Customary*, pp 70-71.

50 *Ibid*, p 73.

51 *Ibid*, p 77.

52 *Directory and Customary*, pp 86-87.

53 Introductory words of the Apostolic Delegate, Kimberley, July 1924, pp 14 & 15.

54 *Directory and Customary*, p 86.

55 The Provincial Register, 1922-1952, Nov 1926 - June 1927, pp 24-26, DAC.

56 *Ibid*, pp 22-27.

57 *Ibid*, pp 22-23.

58 *Ennius, Annals*, XII.

59 Minutes, Provincial Council, 1922-1926, 21 March 1925, pp 54-56, DAC.

60 Port Elizabeth, nd, DAP.

61 Minutes, Provincial Council, 31 Aug 1926, 263-264, DAC.

62 Minutes, Book of the General Council, 1928-1938, pp 6-7, DAP.

63 Replies on the question of amalgamation with the Dominican Province of Port Elizabeth, 1930, DAC.

64 *Ibid*.

65 Letter, Bloemfontein, 28 Aug 1930, DAC.

66 Letter, Wynberg, Jan 1931, DAC.

67 Letter, Cabra, 16 Feb 1931, DAC.

68 Letter, Bloemfontein, 9 June 1931, DAC.

69 Minutes, Provincial Council, 1930-1933, 21 Dec 1930, p 2, DAC.

70 Letter, CT, 25 Nov 1931, DAG.

71 Minutes, Provincial Council, 1930-1933, pp 35-36, DAC.

72 Oral evidence.

Chapter Twelve

1 Letters, Alberta Grant OP, CT, 25 Aug 1933, *12, pp 15-16*, DAG.

2 Letters, Grant, CT, 31 Aug 1933, *12, p 19; Ibid*, CT, 31 Aug 1933.

3 *Ibid*, CT, Sept 1933, *pp 25-26*.

4 Letters, Grant, PE, 29 Oct 1933, 12, *pp 55-56*.

5 *Ibid*, CT, 17 Aug 1933, *12, p 11*.

6 Letters, Lyons, CT, 14 Sept 1933, *p 34*, DAG.

7 Letters, Grant, PE, 25 Oct 1933, *12, p 56*.

8 *Ibid*, Wynberg, Cape, 14 Dec 1933, *12, p 79*.

9 Letters, Grant, PE, 5 Nov 1933, *p 64*.

10 Letters, Grant, CT, 31 Aug 1933, *12, pp 19-20*.

11 Diary, 1933, Grant, *13, pp 24-25*, DAG.

12 Letters, Grant, PE, 25 Oct 1933, *12, pp 54-55*.

13 Annals, St Dominic's Priory, Emerald Hill, 17 April 1925, p 51, DPA.

14 Letters, Grant, Nov 5 1933, *12, p 64*.

15 Letters, Lyons, CT, 25 Aug 1933.

16 Diary, 1933, Grant, 26 Aug 1933, *13, p 25*.

17 Diary, 1933, Grant, 30, *13, pp 26 & 30*.

18 *Ibid, p 77*.

19 Letters, Lyons, PE, 3 Oct 1933, *p 44*.

20 *Ibid*, PE, 10 Oct 1933, *p 49*.

21 Diary, 1933, Grant, 23 Nov 1933, *13, pp 88-89*.

22 Minutes, Provincial Council, CT, 1930-1935, 22 April 1933, pp 69-70, DAC.

23 Letters, Grant, CT, 17 Aug 1933, *12, p 12.*

24 *Ibid,* CT, 25 Aug 1933, *12, p 17.*

25 Diary, 1933, Grant, CT, 20 Aug 1933, *13, p 17.*

26 Letters, Lyons, CT, 25 Aug 1933, *pp 17-18.*

27 Letters, Grant, CT, 25 Aug 1933, *12, p 17.*

28 Letters, Grant, PE, 26 Sept 1933, *12, pp 37-38.*

29 Letters, Lyons, PE, 26 Sept 1933, *pp 38-39.*

30 Report, T Coleman OP, Regional Vicar, 1947, p 3, DAC.

31 Letters, Grant, PE, 3 Oct 1933, *12, p 40.*

32 Letters, Lyons, PE, 3 Oct 1933, *pp 42-43.*

33 Archbishop M H Lucas, SVD.

34 CT, 29 June 1947, p 3, DAC.

35 Diary, 1933, Grant, 1933, *13, pp 68-69.*

36 Letters, Grant, CT, 14 Sept 1933, *12, 12, pp 28-29.*

37 Diary, 1933, Grant, 8 Dec 1933, *13, p 36.*

38 Letters, Grant, CT, 14 Aug 1933, *12, pp 27-29.*

39 Diary, Grant, Oct 1933, *13, pp 57& 59.*

40 Letters, Grant, PE, 17 Oct 1933, *12, pp 44-45.*

41 *Ibid,* Grant, 26 Sept 1933, *12,* pp 36-37.

42 Diary, Grant, 2-8 Nov 1933, *13, pp 72-77.*

43 *Ibid,* 23 Nov 1933, *13, pp 8-79.*

44 *Ibid,* 23 Nov 1933, *13, p 82.*

45 Letters, Grant, Bloemfontein, 23 Nov 1933, *12, pp 72-73.*

46 Diary, Grant, 24 Nov 1933, *13, p 87.*

47 Letters, Grant, 23 Nov 1933, *12, p 72.*

48 Letters, Grant, 23 Nov 1933, *12, pp 72-73.*

49 Diary, Grant, 24 Nov 1933, *13, pp 91-92.*

50 *Ibid,* p 92. See Cleary, Columba OP *et al, Being Driven forward: An Account of a century of ministry by the Dominican Sisters of Newcastle, Natal,* Dominican Sisters, Boksburg, 1997. This gives a detailed, somewhat different view of the life, character and work of Mother Rose Niland.

51 Letter 245/34, Gijlswijk, Bloemfontein, 26 Dec 1933, *JSA 7, p 38,* DAG.

52 Letter, General Council, Holy Rosary Convent, PE, 4 Jan 1934, DAC.

53 Letter 245/34, Bloemfontein, 15 Oct 1934, *JSA 8, p 7*, DAG.

54 Letter, Cabra, Dublin, 8 Dec 1934, *JSA 8, p 9*, DAG.

55 Letter, CT, 2 Aug 1937, *JSA 8, p 19*, DAG.

56 Letters, M Colmcille Flynn, Cabra, Dublin, 18 May 1938, *JSA 9, p 25*, DAG.

Chapter Thirteen

1 Sacred Congregation of Propaganda, 1923.

2 *Instruction of the Sacred Congregation of Religious re founding of Native Congregations of Religious, p 1.*

3 Letters, Uitenhage, 27 Nov 1940, St Rose's, Misc Papers, 1937-1971, p 4, SA 124, *p 6*, DAG.

4 *Ibid*, Letter, Uitenhage, 27 Nov 1940.

5 'Native Sisters', Mother Felim, Killeshandra, 16 July 1942, St Rose's, Misc Papers, 1937-1971, Box 2, *p 9*, DAG.

6 *Ibid.*

7 Constitutions, Appendix 1, 'The Native or non-European Sisters', St Rose's, Misc Papers, 1937-1971, Box 2, DAG.

8 Letter, Father T Garde OP, Rome, 2 Sept 1943, St Rose's, Misc Papers, 1937-1971, *p 12*, Box 2, DAG.

9 *Ibid*, Garde to Lyons, Rome, 13 Dec 1943, *p 12.*

10 *Ibid*, Mother Teresa Coleman, 'Points arising from discussion on a non-European Sisterhood in the Regional Vicariate', 1942, *p 8.*

11 St Rose's, Misc Papers, 1937-1971, 1944, *p 14.*

12 Reports of Regional Vicars: Mother Teresa Coleman, 1947, p 3; Mother Catherine Dixon, 1954, p 4, in Reports of Regional chapters, 1930-1965, *pp 21 & 29*, DAC.

13 Acts of the General Chapter, 6-17 Jan 1948, 27, p 6, DAG.

14 Annals St Rose's, 1944-1968, *passim*, DAC.

15 Mother Catherine Dixon, 1954, p 4, in Reports of Regional Chapters, 1930-1965, *p 29*, DAC.

16 *Ibid*, Mother Jordan Keary, 1961, 'Congregation of St Rose of Lima', p 4, in Reports of Regional Chapters, *p 45.*

17 *Ibid.*

[18] Annals, St Rose's, 1944-1968, *passim.*

[19] Oral evidence, 1991.

[20] Report of the Regional Vicar, M Damian Madden, Oct 1961 - July 1965, in Reports of Regional Chapters, 1930-1965, *p 51*, DAC.

[21] *Ibid.*

[22] Report, Congregation of St Rose of Lima, July 1956 - Dec 1967, DAC.

[23] Archbishop McCann to Fr Michael Browne, Master General, 31 May 1957, *16, p 7*, DAC.

[24] Letter, CT, 13 May 1957, in St Rose's, Misc Papers, 1938-1971, *16, p 3.*

[25] Minutes, Regional Council, 1963-1964, pp 148-149, DAC.

[26] Letter, 7 April 1956, in Catherine Dixon OP, 1956-1962, *3, pp 5-6*, DAG.

[27] Minutes, Regional Council, Jan 1963 - Aug 1964, 24 March 1964, *pp 148-152.*

[28] Letter, 14 June 1964, Mother Jordan Keary OP, 1960-1968, 14 June 1964, *p 17*, DAC.

[29] Annals, St Rose's, 1944-1968, *2*, p 69.

[30] Minutes, Regional Council, 1964-1965, pp 20-23.

[31] Acts of the Eighth General Chapter, 1967, 18, p 4.

[32] Letter, CT, 4 Oct 1967, Mother Angels Donnellan OP, 1965-1968, *p 34*, DAC.

[33] *Ibid*, CT, 4, 7 & 30 Oct 1967, *pp 35, 37, & 41.*

[34] *Ibid.* CT, 12 Nov 1967, *p 42.*

[35] Mother Jordan Keary, Address, 1968, St Rose's Misc Papers, 1937-1971, *p 59.*

[36] Visitation Report, PE, 12 Sept 1969, DAC.

[37] St Rose's, Misc Papers, 1937-1971, *p 89.*

[38] *Ibid*, 1938-1974, *p 77.*

[39] *Ibid*, Letter, Dublin, 26 Oct 1969, *16, 39-40.*

[40] Letter, Lisbon, 13 Nov 1969, in St Rose's, Misc Papers, 1938-1974, *16, pp 34-37.*

[41] *Ibid*, Letter, Mother Isidore Collins, Dublin, 27 Dec 1969, *16, p 43.*

[42] *Ibid*, 11 April 1970, *p 46.*

[43] Rome, 22 Aug 1970, Pretoria, N.10499/61, in St Rose's, Misc

Papers, 1938-1974, *p 80.*

44 Letter, Isidore Collins, Dublin, 27 March 1969, in St Rose's, Misc Papers, *1938-1974,16, p 53.*

45 Letter, Isidore Collins, Dublin, 22 Dec 1973, *p 89.*

Chapter Fourteen

1 Letters, Teresa Coleman OP, CT, 8 March 1938, 2, DAG.

2 Letters, Finbar Ryan OP, Port-of-Spain, 13 Dec 1938, 7, DAS.

3 Oral evidence.

4 Letters, 1931-1938, Teresa Coleman OP, CT, 1 March 1938, 2, *pp 34-36,* DAG.

5 Minutes of combined Councils of CT and PE, *1, pp 1-4,* DAC.

6 The Regional Vicars from Ireland who served the Region of South Africa for the period 1948-1961 were: Mother Colmcille Flynn, 1948-1951, Mother Catherine Dixon, 1951-1960 & Mother Jordan Keary, 1960-1961.

7 Letters, 1931-1938, Teresa Coleman OP, CT, 23 Aug 1938, 2, *pp 75-76.*

8 Oral Evidence.

9 Letters, 1931-1938, T Coleman, CT, 17 May 1938, 2.

10 Minutes, Regional Council 1938-1943, 14 Jan 1939, *1,* p 19.

11 Letters, 1939-1940, Teresa Coleman OP, CT, 10 May 1940, 4, *p 20.*

12 Rescript 6698, 5 Sept 1940.

13 Letters, 1939-1940, Teresa Coleman OP, CT, 30 Jan 1940, *3, p 47.*

14 *Ibid,* CT, 24 July 1940, *4, pp 38-41.*

15 *Ibid,* CT, 7 Oct 1940, *p 56.*

16 Report of the Regional Vicar, 1947, p 1, DAC.

17 Second Regional Chapter, July 1947; Petitions sent in by the Convents, DAC.

18 Acts of the Second Regional Chapter, 1947, 14 & 15, p 2.

19 *Ibid,* 20, p 2.

20 Regional Chapter 1947, Petitions, 2, v.

21 Acts of the Fourth General Chapter of the Congregation of the Irish Dominican Sisters, 6-17 Jan 1948, 24, p 5.

22 Acts of the General Chapter, 1948, 34, p 8.

23   Acts of the General Chapter, 1948, 21, p 4.

24   *Cape Argus*, 25 May 1957, Newspaper cuttings, DAC.

25   *Ibid.*

26   Letter, Stellenbosch, 27 June 1939, Box 122, DAG.

27   Visitation Report, Stellenbosch, 4 May 1947, DAC.

28   Bernard Delaney OP, 14 Aug 1938, np, DAC.

29*   Letter, Cabra, Dublin, 11 Feb 1948, DAC.

30   Letter, Teresa Coleman OP, CT, 30 Jan 1945, DAG.

31   *Ibid*, 9 April 1945.

32   Letter, Teresa Coleman OP, CT, 17 July 1945, DAG.

33   Provincial Register, 1948-1952, p 28, DAC.

34   Minutes, Regional Council, 1939-1955, 3 March 1951, p 194.

35   Minutes, Regional Council, 1939-1955, 22 Nov 1953, p 264; Acts of the Third Regional Chapter of the Irish Dominican Sisters of South Africa, 1954,17, p 4, DAC.

36   *Ibid*, 18.

37   Minutes, Regional Council, 1955-1957, p 3.

38   For details see Ch 8.

39   Letters, Teresa Coleman OP, 9 June 1956, 1946-1960, *8*, pp 37-38.

40   *Ibid*, p 38.

41   *Ibid*, p 39.

42   *Ibid*, p 37.

Chapter Fifteen

1   Maria Mackey OP, 'Cry mercy', *Grace & Truth*, VII, 2, Sept 1986.

2   Reports of the Regional Vicars, 1973, p 1, and 1976, pp 1-2, DAC.

3   Acts, 31, pp 7-8, DAC.

4   Oral Evidence, Ireland, 1978.

5   'Statement on Race Relations', *Pastoral Letter*, 19, p 5, Press Commission SACBC, Pretoria, 1952.

6   'Statement on Apartheid', *Pastoral Letter*, 2-6 July 1957, pp 13-15.

7   *Ibid*, p 16.

8   KB, Oral evidence.

9   C Owens OP, Oral evidence, Jan 1998.

10 L J Hughes SJ, Treatment of recommendations, NC/ SACES, R, 6, pp 1-2.

11 *Ibid*, 13, p 3, VI, p 22.

12 AWR, Paper for discussion on Catholic schools and apostolic commitments, 1972, p 2.

13 Letters, Genevieve Hickey OP, 28 Nov 1973, DAC.

14 A Survey of the South African Region of the Irish Congregation of Dominican Sisters, First Interim Report, July 1974, 9.6.0, p 7.

15 *Ibid*, Second Interim Report, 21 Jan 1976, p 2.

16 Newspaper Cuttings, CT, Sept 1975, 'Open schools', *p 4*, DAC.

17 *Ibid*, 1 Oct 1975.

18 Education Council of Associations of Religious.

19 Letter, CT, 20 Nov 1975, 'Open schools', *p 18*, DAC.

20 An exception had been made earlier in some schools, in the case of the children of African diplomats, but this was by concession and did not affect the law.

21 Open schools, Newspaper Cuttings, *The Cape Argus*, 1976, DAC.

22 K Boner, Oral evidence.

23 *Ibid*.

24 Commission for Christian Education and Worship (Department of Schools), Minutes of Meeting, Hammanskraal, 19-21 July 1976, p 1.

25 Quoted in Minutes, AGM of AWR, 15-16 May 1976, p 1.

26 *Ibid*, p 10.

27 Minutes, Executive Committee of the AWR, 13 Sept 1976, p 2.

28 *Ibid*, (e), p 2.

29 Acts, 29 Dec 1976-10 Jan 1977, 9, p 2, DAC.

30 *Ibid*, 23 (a), p 5.

31 Newspaper Cuttings, *Sunday Tribune*, *20* May 1979, 'Open schools', *p 76*, DAC.

32   *Cape Times*, 21 Jan 1977.

33   22 Jan 1977.

34   Interview with Paul Goller.

35   *Cape Times*, 26 Jan 1977.

36   Oral evidence, Justina Nutley OP.

37   Open schools, Newspaper cuttings, 24 Sept 1981, *p 94*, DAC.

38   Acts, Interim Regional Chapter, 29 Dec 1976-10 July 1977, Wynberg, Cape, 25, (a) & (b), p 5.

39   Minutes of the Meeting of School Principals, Johannesburg, 8 July 1979, p 1, DAC.

40   Sisters Sheila Mullen, Áine Hardiman, Feargal Cassidy and Caitríona Owens.

41   Elsies River, Sept 1985, DAC.

42   *Ibid.*

43   *Cork Examiner*, 31 Aug 1985.

44   *Ibid.*

45   25 Sept 1985.

46   Oral Evidence, Clare Harkin OP and Áine Hardiman OP, 23-24 Oct 1997; interviewer, Caitríona Owens OP, DAC.

47   Oral evidence, Kathy Gaylor OP, Nov 1997.

48   'A *Call to conscience addressed to Catholics in Southern Africa*', SACBC, Plenary Session, 8-11 Feb 1972 in *The Bishops Speak*, II, *Pastoral Letters and Statements, 1967-1980*, Pretoria, 1980.

49   Newsletter, Justice and Reconciliation, Sister Bernard Ncube and Sister Margaret Kelly, Pretoria, 14 Sept 1982, p 1, SACBC.

50   Newsletter, Justice and Reconciliation, 14 Sept 1982, p 2.

51   Abstract, South African women and feminist theology, unpublished M Phil Thesis, Dublin, 1986.

52   Áine Hardiman OP, Working in an unstructured apostolate, nd, pp 1-2, DAC.

53   *The Catholic Directory*, 1996-1997, SACBC, 1996, pp107-108, and oral evidence.

Chapter Sixteen

1   Pius XII, Acta Apostolica Sedis, *Jubilee allocution: Women in*

the modern world, Rome, 15 May 1943.

2   Victor de la Vierge, OCD, 'The Principle of Adaptation', in *Religious* Sisters, Blackfriars, Oxford, 1950, p 248.

3   *Ibid.*

4   *Acta et Documenta: Congressus Internationalis Superiorissarum Generalium,* English text, Editiones Paulinae, Rome, 1952, p 12.

5   *Acta et documenta,* 1952, p 208.

6   *Acta et Documenta,* 1952, p 23.

7   *Ibid,* Parcadio Larraona, Sec Sacred Congregation of Religious, 'Concluding instructions addressed to the Reverend Mothers General', pp 272-273.

8   *Ibid,* 'Address of the Holy Father to the Superiors General', *p 333.*

9   *Ibid,* 'Concluding Instruction', p 273.

10 Acts of the Second Regional Chapter, Springfield, Cape, 1-7 July 1947, 34, p 23, DAC.

11 Acts of the Fifth General Chapter, 1954, 26 & 27, p 6, DAC.

12 Austin Flannery OP, (Ed), *Vatican Council II, Conciliar and Post-Conciliar Documents,* Dominican Publications, Dublin, 1981, 17, p 621.

13 'Address of the Holy Father to the Superiors General', *Acta and Documenta,* Romae, 1952, p 333.

14 *The Rule of St Augustine and the Constitutions of the Congregation of the Irish Dominican Sisters,* XXIV, 212, p 75.

15 See Chapter 9, *passim.*

16 In Austin Flannery OP, (ed), *Vatican Council II: The Conciliar and Post-Conciliar Documents,* Dominican Publications, Dublin 1981, p 611; See also, *Renovationis Causam,* 6 Jan 1969, and Paul VI, *Evangelica Testificatio,* 29 June 1971.

17 *Ibid,* p 612.

18 *Ibid,* p 613.

19 11 July - Aug 1980, 20, p 25.

20 Acts of the General Chapter 1977, 11, p 6.

21 These were Sisters Bede Kearns, Florence Thérèse Hewson, Sheelagh Wilsdon, and Sister Joan O'Donovan, who was at that time a member of the General Council and worked as co-ordinator for this body.

22 Congregation of Dominican Sisters of Our Lady of the Rosary and Saint Catherine of Siena, Cabra, *Constitutions and*

Directives, I, 1983, p 26.

23 *Directives of the Congregation of the Dominican Sisters of Our Lady of the Rosary and Saint Catherine of Siena, Cabra*, 1983, 'Community', 1, p 7.

24 Annals, II, Sancta Maria Convent, Vanderbijlpark, 1967.

25 *Ibid*, 1969.

26 See Ch 14, *passim*.

27 'Some causes, intellectual and spiritual, of crisis in the life of faith of the religious', in *The Religious woman: Minister of faith*, St Paul Edition, Boston, 1974, p 142. Italics mine.

28 *Theology brought within your reach*, Theology Correspondence Course, Dominican Fathers, Welkom, OFS.

29 Letter, Johannesburg, 8 March 1982, DAC.

30 Florida, Transvaal, 10 April 1974, DAC.

31 Letter, J L Brenninkmeijer OP, Johannesburg, 31 May 1974, DAC.

32 Circular, Federation of Dominican Congregations of Southern Africa, 10 April 1974.

33 Letter, Genevieve Hickey OP, Cape Town, 21 May 1974, DAC.

34 Quoted in Flora Mc Glynn OP, President, Fedosa, Boksburg, 28 Jan 1992.

35 Minutes, Regional Council, 1972-1978, 14-18 Sept & 31 Dec 1972, DAC.

36 *Ibid*, 31 Dec 1972.

37 Oral evidence, Sister Agnes Finn OP, Dec 1997; written and oral evidence, Sister Genevieve Hickey, Dec 1997.

38 Oral and written evidence, Sister Agnes Finn OP, Dec 1997.

39 Acts of the Fourth Regional Chapter, 6-9 Jan 1960, 20, pp 5-6, DAC.

40 Egress, Renewal, 1967-1968; Proposals, 18a, 4, *15, p 57*, DAC.

41 *Ibid*, 4 & 1.

42 *Ibid*, 18a, 2.

43 KB, Oral evidence.

44 Proposals, Common Life, collated responses, 13c, Renewal, 1967-1968, *15, p 45*, DAC.

45 New revised edition, Burns & Oates, London, 1963, p 132.

46 *Ibid*, p 133.

47 Acts of the Sixth Regional Chapter, 6-11 Jan 1967, Wynberg, Cape, 15, xii, p 7, DAC.

48 K Boner, Oral evidence, 1991-1997.

49 Augusta Neal SND, *South African Catholic Education Survey, 1971*; Canon Trevor Verryn, *Cabra Dominican Sisters: Sociological Report, 1976*, DAC.

50 *Letter, Belfast, 10 Dec 1967, DAC.*

51 KB, Oral evidence, 1991-1997.

52 KB, Oral evidence, 1991-1997.

53 Minutes of the Executive Committee of AWR, 29 Nov 1976, p 4.

54 Commissions: Answers to questionnaires and Reports of Commissions, Special General Chapter 1967, *Renewal, 11 & 12*, DAC.

55 Answers to questionnaires, Ireland & South Africa, *Renewal, 1966-1968 14, pp 1, 2, & 8*, DAC.

56 *Ibid*, p 9.

57 Answers to questionnaires, Training of local Superiors, 1, p 33, See also p 35.

58 Commission on Government, 13 July - 11 Aug 1968, p 24.

59 Community, 7.8.1, p 12.

60 Letter, Áine Killen OP & Rosaire Boden OP, Dublin 14 Oct 1997, DAC.

Appendix II

1 Both Mother Dympna and Mother Borgia were appointed "there not being a sufficient number of vocals in the community to have an election"; Annals, St Mary's, CT, 1 Nov 1872, p 9, DAC.

2 It should be noted that Mother Dympna Kinsella, even when not holding the office of Prioress, nevertheless as foundress, played a primary role in all community business, especially in respect of new foundations, the appointment of officials and the admission or dismissal of candidates.

3 Whether this indicates that Mother Dympna was not elected or that after election her appointment was ratified by ecclesiastical authority, is not clear from the text; Annals, St Mary's Convent, CT, 27 Dec 1975, p 10, DAC.

4 Mother Berchmans resigned in 1924 because of ill-health.

5   The 1917 *Revised Code of Canon Law* came into force and each house was to have its own appointed Prioress and Council. The Provincial and her councillors were responsible for "all the management of the important business of the community" with the Provincial having the casting vote; Annals, St Mary's CT, 7 Jan 1924, DAC.

6   Archbishop Gijlswijk presided at the election of the Provincial by the capitulars in the morning of the 16 December 1926, and the Councillors were elected by delegates to the General Chapter in the afternoon of the same day.

7   The title 'Prioress General' remained a matter of contention between the Dominicans of the Western Cape and Gijlswijk . It came into use gradually in the 1930's and by 1936 was the accepted title used in respect of Mother Teresa Coleman.

8   Died in office on 19 Oct 1933.

9   Died on 21 Dec 1936.

10 No precedence is indicated in the records for this or for the 1936 elections .

11 There is no record of an election in 1870; Annals, HRC, pp 5-7.

12 "A dispensation from Rome was granted for re-electing Mother Rose, she being in office twelve years in succession". Annals, HRC, 1 Sept 1880, p 27, DAP.

13 *Ibid*, 4 Sept 1883, p 32.

14 *Ibid*, By special dispensation from Rome, 9 & 10 Oct 1889, pp 60-61.

15 *Ibid*, Owing to ill-health, Mother Catherine Behan was relieved of the duties of prioress and Mother Dominic Housley was placed *in capite* by the bishop. Annals, HRC, 24 June 1899, p 95.

16 Mother Dominic Housley died on 15 Sept 1915; Annals, HRC, p 167, DAP.

17 After Giljswijk held visitation at HRC and its filial houses in 1922, Mother de Ricci Harkin used the title Prioress provincial.

18 "According to the New Constitutions the four Councillors of the Prioress General receive the title of 'Mother'", Annals, HRC, 19 April 1925, p 176, DAC.

19 Mother de Ricci had hoped that amalgamation would be achieved by August 1937 and there would be no need for a General Chapter and elections in that year.

[20] There is no entry in the Book of the General Council for the 15 August 1937, the Day scheduled for the elections . The names of the Councillors are given in an entry of 27 August of the same year.

[21] Mother Teresa Coleman and her Councillors remained in office for three terms, 1938-1948, the last term being renewed by special permission of the Holy See.

[22] Mother de Ricci Harkin died in office on 19 Oct 1950 at the age of 83.

[23] Mother Jordan Keary was elected Prioress General of the Congregation in 1961.

[24] St Dominic's Convent, Falls Road, Belfast.

[25] In 1974 the title 'Mother' was dropped for all superiors with the exception of the Prioress General and the Regional Vicar in South Africa. See Acts of the Ninth General Chapter, 12 July to 23 Aug 1974, 30,1, p 21. The title was dropped completely in 1977. See Acts of the Tenth General Chapter, 12 July to 6 Aug 1977, 11, (vii), p 7.

[26] The Regional Vicar and the four Regional Councillors for the Region of South Africa were elected by the capitulars at the 1979-80 Elective Regional Chapter, held at Springfield, Wynberg. Acts, 16, p 3. For the Cabra Dominicans in South Africa this was the first election of major superiors to take place in the post-amalgamation period.

[27] Sister Majella Keary was elected third General Councillor at the 1980 General Chapter. See Acts of the Eleventh General Chapter, 11 July to 7 Aug 1980, 15, p 3.

[28] On the 12 July 1986, at the Twelfth General Chapter of the Congregation, Sister Marian O'Sullivan was elected Prioress General.

[29] This Chapter was postponed by Rescript 6698 of 5th September, 1940, in order to allow the South African delegates to attend should the war come to a speedy end. See Acts of the Third General Chapter, 23 July- 3 Aug 1941, 13, p 3.

[30] Mother Benignus died in 1960, shortly after her election for a second term of office as Prioress General.

[31] In 1968, at the second session of the 1967-68 General Chapter, for reasons of health, Mother Jordan Keary resigned from office. During the same session Mother Isidore Collins was elected Prioress General. See Acts of the General Chapter, 13 July - 11 August, 1968, 10 & 18, pp 2 & 3.

SELECT BIBLIOGRAPHY AND ARCHIVAL SOURCES

Selected archival sources:

Acts, Reports and Minutes of Chapters:

Acts, reports and minutes of the thirteen General Chapters of the Congregation of the Irish Dominican Sisters, Cabra, 1928-1992, DAG.

Acts and reports of the General Chapters of the Congregation of St Catherine of Siena, Cape Peninsula, 1930 and 1936, DAC.

Acts, reports and minutes of the Regional Chapters of the Cabra Dominicans, Southern Africa, 1940-1998.

Selected Annals.

Convent of Jesus and Mary, Galway, 1929-1970.
Mater Admirabilis Convent, Uitenhage, 1887-1970.
St Catherine's Convent, Florida, Johannesburg, 1957-1991.
St Dominic's Convent, Wittebome, 1937-1991.
St Dominic's Convent, Hammanskraal, 1962-1979.
St Dominic's Priory, Walmer, PE, 1900-1992.
St Mary's Convent, CT, 1863-1972. Annals, 1962-1966 missing.
Sancta Maria Convent, Vanderbijlpark, 1956-1991.
St Michael's Convent, Rondebosch, 1925-1991.
Sint Paulusklooster, Brummeria, Pretoria, 1961-1991.
Springfield Convent, Wynberg, 1955-1991.
Holy Rosary Convent, PE, 1876-1991.
Holy Trinity Convent, Matroosfontein, 1931-1991.

Books of Minutes and Reports:

Chapter Commissions, & renewal: records of proceedings, 1966-1990, DAC.
Book of the General Council, HRC, PE, 1889-1928, DAP.
Provincial Council, CT, 1903-1938, DAC.
House Councils, 1924-1980.
Provincials' Register, CT, 1922-1952, DAC.
Regional Council, South Africa, 1938-1980, DAC.
Visitation reports, Dominican Convents, South Africa, 1, 1926-1943; 2, 1944-1953; 3, 1953-1973; 4, 1979-1983, DAC.

Letters, diaries and miscellaneous papers:

Diary: Journey, Cabra to Cape Town, 16 April-2 June 1903, DCA.
Finance and property, 1, 1867-1965; 2, 1942-1992, DCA.

Grimley, T, J Leonard & M Colgan, Diary records & letters 1861-1896, CAC.
Coleman, Mother Teresa OP, Letters, 1930-1973, DAC & DAG.
Collins, Mother Isidore OP, Letters, 1969-1974, DAC.
Dixon, Mother Catherine OP, Letters, 1931-1962, DAC & DAG.
Flynn, Mother Colmcille OP, Letters, 1937-1950, DAC.
Grant, Mother Alberta OP, Diary of a visit to South Africa, 1933, DAG.
Grant, Mother Alberta OP, Letters, 1933, DAG.
Harkin, Mother de Ricci OP, Letters, 1931-1950, DAG.
Hickey, Mother Genevieve OP, Letters, 1969-1976, DAC.
Keary, Mother Jordan OP, Letters, 1960-1968, DAC.
Lyons, Mother Reginald OP, Letters, 1933 & 1943-1951, DAC & DAG.
Madden, Mother Damian OP, 1963-1965, DAC.
Meenan, Mother Benignus OP, Letters, 1956-1961, DAC.
Miscellaneous letters and papers, 1843-1924, DAC, DAS & DCA.
O'Sullivan, Mother Marian OP, Letters and Newsletters, 1977-1986, DAC.
Roche, Mother Jordana, OP, 1974-1985, DAC & DAG.
Ryan, Dr Finbar OP, 1920-1962, DAC, DAG & DAS.
Whitty, Mother Rose OP, & Srs Thomas Kelly, Baptist Taaffe, Hyacinth Potter, Aloysius Cowley & Michael Morton, Letters to Sion Hill, 1867-1881, DAS.

Personnel Records and Obituaries:

Cotter, Mother Berchmans OP, Necrology of the Dominican Sisters founded from Cabra at Cape Town in 1863, 1872-1934, DAC.
Dates of birth, profession and death, HRC, PE, 1867-1943, DAP.
Dowley, Mother Bertrand OP, Obituaries, Dominican Sisters, Western Cape, 1872-1936, DAC.
Interviews, Cabra Dominican Sisters in Southern Africa, (See Appendix I).
Necrology, Congregation of Dominican Sisters, Cabra, 1928-1998.
Obituaries, newspaper cuttings, sermons & letters, 1925-1974, DAC.
Regional Council Records, Cabra Dominicans, statistics & personnel, 1951-1988, DAC.
Statistics, personnel, schools etc, Cabra Dominicans, South Africa, 1901-1965, DAC.
Statistics, personnel, Dominican Convents, PE, 1867-1969, DAC.

Status, jurisdiction and amalgamation:

Amalgamation, Galway, 1952-1971, DAG & DGA.
Amalgamation, South Africa, Letters, reports & statistics, 7, 1930-1936, DAC & DAG.
Amalgamation, South Africa, Letters, reports and Decree of Amalgamation, 8, 1834-1938, DAC & DAG.
Amalgamation, South Africa, Misc papers, 9, 1934-1945, DAC & DAG.
Cabra, Sion Hill & foundations, Status & jurisdiction, 1206-1968.

Dominican Convent, Cabra, *I*, Misc documents, 1826-1903.
Dominican Convent, Cabra, Letters & papers, amalgamation in
  Ireland, *6*, 1926-1928, DAG.
Letters & queries re amalgamation, Cabra, Rome & Galway, 1920-
  1922.
Lynch, Sister Vincent OP, Letters re amalgamation, *5*, 1920-1929,
  DGA.
Minutes & records of meetings in CT, PE & Cabra, *3*, 1919-1923.
Misc Documents, Letters, Status, jurisdiction & amalgamation, *2*,
  1910-1938.

Congregation of St Rose of Lima

Annals, St Rose's, *1 & 2*, 1944-1968.
Misc letters & papers, *16*, 1944-1974, DAC.
Visitation Reports, Congregation of St Rose of Lima & Holy Trinity
  Convent, Matroosfontein, 1932-1983, DAC.
Council Minutes, Congregation of St Rose of Lima, 1965-1971, DAC.

Education and schools:

Adult Education, Misc records of the Dominican Sisters, Cabra, *9*,
  1970-1979, DAC.
Brendan McGinty OP, 'The Sisters' preparation for teaching Christian
  doctrine, Springfield, Wynberg, *6, 1952*, DAC.
Catholic Education in South Africa, misc papers, *8*, 1965-1981, DAC.
Catholic Schools Association, minutes & papers, *5*, 1954-1976.
Directress General of schools, reports & recommendations, *1*, 1926-
  1938, & *2*, 1939-1943, DAC.
Dominican Schools, Region of South Africa, letters, inspection reports
  & related material, *3* 1868-1980; *4*, 1887-1997, DAC.
Dominican Schools, closure, mergers & transfers, *7*, 1889-1983, DAC.
Dominican Sisters, Regional Advisory Educational Council, 1968-
  1979, DAC.
Open Schools, letters, newspaper cuttings and misc documents, *10*,
  1974-1983, DAC.

Renewal: Miscellaneous documents:

AWR, Maryville, PE, Finance, *1*, 1983-1987; Misc papers, *2*, 1983-
  1987.
Commissions, evangelical life, apostolate, formation & government,
  21, 1971-1974, DAC.
Fedosa, Canoe Renewal Course, papers, 1977-1978.
Questionnaires: Common life, misc papers, *15*, 1967-1968, DAC.
Questionnaires: Formation, education & government, *14*, 1966-1968,
  DAC.
Questionnaires & principles of group discussion, *11*, 1955 & 1966;
  Spiritual renewal, *11*, 1966-1968, DAC.
Questionnaires, 1970; Critique of community life, 1980; Government
  commission, 1990, DAC.

Regular life: Chapter findings & decisions & main topics in circular letters, *2*, 1931-1975. Regular life: Ordinations & visitation memoranda, *1*, 1790-1975.

Renewal: Commissions in preparation for General Chapters, *12*, 1966-1968, DAC.

Renewal: Misc Papers, re women religious, *3*, 1943-1971; *4*, 1949-1946; *8*, 1959-1976; *22 1974-1976*; *23*, 1976-1978, DAC.

Women religious, superiors' retreat, 1968, & misc papers, *9*, *1961-1969*; *10*, 1962-1981, DAC.

Dominican Constitutions and related publications:

Constitutions of the Dominican Sisters of the Second Order, Eastern Vicariate, Holy Rosary Convent, Port Elizabeth, Marianhill, 1888.

Constitutions of the Nuns of the Sacred Order of Preachers, approved by His Holiness Pope Pius XI, Polyglot Vatican Press, 1930.

Constitutiones Fratrum S.Ordinis Praedicatorum, Rome, 1954.

Constitutions and Directives, Congregation of Dominican Sisters of Our Lady of the Rosary and St Catherine of Siena, Cabra, Dublin, 1983.

Constitutions of the Congregation of St Rose of Lima, under the protection of Our Lady of the Rosary and of St Rose of Lima, Cape Town, 1967.

Constitutions and Ordinations of the Order of Friars Preachers, Holy Name Press, 1968.

Gijlswijk, Bernard Jordan OP, *The Rule of St Augustine and the Constitutions of the Sisters of the Third Order of St Dominic forming the African Congregation of St Catharine of Siena*, revised in accordance with the requirements of the New Code of Canon Law, Bloemfontein, 1924.

Irish Congregation of Dominican Sisters, *Interim Directives*, General Chapter, 1967-1968, Cabra, Dublin, 1968.

Potton, Fr Marie-Ambroise OP, *Constitutions des Soeurs Dominicaines du Second Ordre: Traduites et accompagnées de commentaires*, Paris, 1864.

Rule and Constitutions of the Sisters of St Dominic, conformable to the Brief and Decree of Pope Gregory XVI, St Mary's Convent, Cabra, O'Toole, Dublin, 1943.

Rule and Constitutions of the Sisters of St. Dominick, conformable to the Brief and Decree of Pope Gregory XVI, St Catherine's Convent, Sion Hill, Michael Markey, Dublin, 1858.

The Rule of St. Augustine and the Constitutions of the English Sisters of the Second Order of St. Dominic, St William's Press, Market Weighton, 1902.

The Rule of Saint Augustine and the Constitutions of the Congregation of the Irish Dominican Sisters under the protection of Our Lady of the Most Holy Rosary and of Saint Catherine of Siena, Dublin, 1947.

Statute of the Province of Ireland of the Friars of the Order of Preachers, St Mary's Tallaght, 1974.

Statutum pro missionibus fratrum S.Ordinis Praedicatorum, Dominican
    Generalate, Rome, 1958.

Customaries, Directories and Ceremonials:

Ceremonial of the Irish Dominican Congregation, Cabra, 1947.
Directory of the Dominican Congregation of Saint Catherine of Siena
    of Oakford, Natal, nd.
Gijlswijk, Bernard Jordan OP, *Directory and Customary of the Sisters
    of the Third Order of St. Dominic forming the African Congregation
    of St. Catharine of Siena,* Bloemfontein, 1925.
Statute of the Province of Ireland of the Friars of the Order of Preachers,
    St Mary's Tallaght, 1974.
The Rule of St. Augustine, Sedosa, 1980.
Canonical legislation concerning Religious, Vatican, Rome, 1918.

General:

Annals of the Dominican Convent of St Mary's, Cabra, with some
    account of its origin, 1647-*1912,* Dublin, 1912.
Aubert, Roger, *et al, The Christian centuries: The Church in a
    secularised society,* V, Darton Longman & Todd, London, 1978.
Augustine, C A, OSB, *A Commentary on the New Code of Canon Law,*
    III, 4th revised ed., Herder, St Louis & London, 1929.
Beck, George A, *The English Catholics, 1850-1950: Essays to
    commemorate the centenary of the restoration of the hierarchy of
    England and Wales,* Burns & Oates, London, 1950.
Boner, Kathleen, OP, The Irish Dominicans and education in the
    Western Cape (1863-1892), Unpublished Dissertation for the
    Degree of Master of Arts, Unisa, 1976.
Book of annals: Sion Hill Convent, Blackrock, Co Dublin, Browne &
    Nolan, Dublin, 1904.
Bowie, Fiona, (ed), *Beguine spirituality: An Anthology,* SPCK, London,
    1989.
Brothers of the Sacred Heart, *Catechism of the religious profession,*
    Metuchen, N J, 1919.
Christie, Pam, *Open schools: Racially mixed Catholic schools in South
    Africa, 1976-1986,* Ravan Press, Johannesburg, 1990.
Cleary, Columba OP, Eleanora Murphy OP, & Flora McGlynn, OP,
    *Being driven forward: An Account of a century of ministry by the
    Dominican Sisters of Newcastle, Natal,* Dominican Sisters,
    Boksburg, 1997.
Chikane, Frank, *The Church's prophetic witness against the apartheid
    system in South Africa: 25th February - 8th April 1988,* SACC,
    Johannesburg, 1988.
The Code of Canon Law, Collins, London, 1983.
Congregation for the Doctrine of the Faith, *Instruction on Christian
    freedom and liberation,* Vatican City, 1986.
Cotel P, SJ, *A Catechism of the vows, for the use of persons
    consecrated to God in the religious life,* Burns & Oates, London,
    nd.

Daughters of St Paul, (compilers), *Religious life in the light of Vatican II*, St Paul editions, Boston, Mass., 1967.

Davlin, Sr Clemente OP, and Sr Nona McGreal OP, *Concerning Dominican Constitutions*, Sinsinawa Dominican Sisters, General Chapter, 1977.

De Couesnongle, Vincent OP, *Confidence for the future*, Dominican publications, Dublin 1982.

De la Vierge, Father Victor OCD, 'The principle of adaptation', *Religious Sisters*, Blackfriars, Oxford, 1950.

Devine, A, CP, *Convent Life; or the duties of Sisters dedicated in religion to the service of God, intended chiefly for superiors and confessors*, London, 1889.

Doing Justice, Conference Proceedings 24-29 July, 1988, River Forest, Illinois, USA, Parable, River Forest, Illinois, 1988.

Dominican Nun (Stone), *The Conventual Third Order of St. Dominic*, Benziger Brothers, New York etc, 1923.

Dominican Sister, *The Irish Dominican Sisters and their mission*, Standard Press, Cape Town, nd.

Dominican Sister, *In God's white-robed army: The Chronicle of the Dominican Sisters in Rhodesia, 1890-1934*, Maskew Miller, Cape Town, 1947.

Dorcy, Mary Jean, OP, *St Dominic's Family*, Priory Press, Dubuque, 1964.

Dubay, Thomas, SM, *Ecclesial women: Towards a theology of the religious state*, Alba House, New York, 1970.

Elphick, Richard, and Rodney Davenport, (eds & compilers), *Christianity in South Africa: A Political, social & cultural history*, David Philip, Cape Town, 1997.

Fiand, Barbara, *Living the vision: Religious vows in an age of change*, Crossroad, New York, 1993.

Fiand, Barbara, *Releasement: Spirituality of ministry*, Crossroad, New York, 1987.

Flannery, A, OP, (General ed.), *Vatican Council II: Conciliar and Post-Conciliar Documents*, Dominicans Publications, Dublin, 1975.

Frigerio, C, SJ, (Translated by F Loughnan), *Practical manual for the superiors of religious Houses*, P J Kenedy, New York, 1912.

Gouws, Mariette, OP, (compiler), *All for God's people: 100 years*, Dominican Sisters, King William's Town, Queenstown, 1977.

Grant, Judith, *Fundamental feminism: Contesting the core concepts of feminist theory*, Routledge, New York, London, 1993.

Griffey, Sister Nicholas, OP, *From silence to speech*, Dominican Publications, Dublin, 1994.

Hinnebusch, William A, OP, *The Dominicans: A Short history*, Dominican Publications, (with revised bibliographies), Dublin, 1985.

Hinnebusch, William A, OP, *The History of the Dominican Order: Origins and growth to 1500*, I, Alba House, New York, 1965.

Holy Rosary Convent, Commemorative Magazine, 1867-1982, Port Elizabeth, 1982.

Horgan, Sister Dominique OP, (ed), *Weavings: Celebrating Dominican women, Dublin, 1988.*

Huyghe, Mgr Gerard, *et al, Religious Orders in the modern world: A Symposium,* Geoffrey Chapman, London, Dublin, 1965.

Irish Congregation of Dominican Sisters, *Survey of attitudes and opinions, 1974.*

Irish Congregation of Dominican Sisters, *Survey of attitudes and opinions: Supplementary report on education, 1974.*

Küng, Hans, *Christianity: Its essence and history,* SCM Press, 1995.

Lanslots, D I, OSB, *Handbook of Canon Law for Congregations of women under simple* vows, 6th ed, revised & enlarged, Frederick Pustet, Ratisbon, Rome etc, 1911.

Marifont, St Mary's Dominican Convent School, Cape Town, 1948-1949, Standard Press, Cape Town, 1949.

Leddy, Mary Jo, *Reweaving Religious life: Beyond the liberal model,* Twenty-third Publications Mystic, Connecticut, 1990.

Lees, Shirley, (ed), *The role of women: When Christians disagree,* Inter-Varsity Press, Leicester, 1984.

MacSweeny, Rev P M, *Upon good ground: A Centenary memoir of the origin and growth of the Dominican Convent, Cabra,* Educational Co, Ireland, Dublin, 1920.

McDonagh, Sister L M, HC, *Wordless witness: History of the Holy Cross Sisters in Southern Africa 1883-1980,* Marianhill Mission Press, 1983.

Nolan, Louis C, OP, *Canonical Directory for the admission of subjects to the religious life and their departure and dismissal,* Rome, Angelicum, 1931.

O'Driscoll, Mary, OP, *Catherine of Siena,* Editiones du Signe, Strasbourg, 1994.

O'Hanlon, Assumpta, OP, *Dominican pioneers in New South Wales,* Australasian Publishing Co., Sydney, London, etc, 1949.

O'Murchu, Diarmuid, MSC, *Religious life: A Prophetic vision: Hope and promise for tomorrow,* Ave Maria Press, Notre Dame, Indiana, 1991.

O'Murchu, Diarmuid, MSC, *Reframing religious life: An Expanded vision for the future,* St Pauls, Middlegreen, Slough, 1995.

O'Neill, Rose, OP, *A Rich inheritance: Galway Dominican nuns, 1644-1994,* Dominican Sisters Galway, 1994.

Paul VI, Pope, *Apostolic exhortation of his Holiness Pope Paul VI on the renewal of the religious life according to the teaching of the Second Vatican Council,* Vatican Polyglot Press, Rome, 1971.

Peters, Marygrace, 'The Beguines: Feminine piety derailed', *Spirituality Today,* 43, I, Spring 1991, St Louis,

Pius XII, *Jubilee allocution: Woman in the modern world,* Acta Apostolica Sedis, *Rome, 1943.*

Ricaud M -A, OP, *Frère Prêcheur, Toulouse,* 1950.

The Religious woman: Minister of faith, Addresses, First International Assembly *Consortium Perfectae Caritatis, Feb* 23 - March 4, 1974, St Paul's Editions, Boston, 1974.

Riley, Maria, *Transforming feminism*, Sheed & Ward, Kansas City, 1989.

SACBC, *The Bishops speak: Pastoral Letters, 1952-1966*, I, Press Commission, Pretoria, 1966.

SACBC, *The Bishops speak: Pastoral Letters and statements, 1967-1980*, II, Pretoria, 1980.

SACBC, *Inter nos, 1980-1992*, Khanya House, Pretoria.

SACBC, *Justice and peace news*, 1989-1994, Justice and Peace Commission, Khanya House, Pretoria.

SACBC, *Justice and peace in Southern Africa: A Pastoral letter of the Bishops of IMBISA*, Occasional papers No 18, Sept 1988, Pretoria.

SACBC, *Report on police conduct during township protests, August-November 1984*, Pretoria, 1984.

SACBC & SACC, *Relocations: The Churches' report on forced removals*, Randburg, 1984

Sacred Congregation of Religious, *Acta et documenta: Congressus internationalis Superiorissarum Generalium*, Pauline ed., Rome, 1952.

Schema Constitutionum pro Sororibus Tertii Ordinis S.P. Dominici, Rome, Angelicum, 1925.

Silver Leaves: Centenary Issue, 1871-1971, Springfield Dominican Convent, Wynberg, Cape, 1971.

Silver Leaves, Springfield Convent, Wynberg, Cape, 1902, 1908; 1921-1922; 1926; 1930; 1947-1948; 1951-1952; 1963-1964; 1968; 1977; 1978; 1979; 1980; 1981.

Silver Leaves: The Cape Dominican Annual, 1931-1932.

Commins, Rosemary OP & Pia O'Connell OP, (eds), *Springfield: The First one hundred and twenty-five years*, PG & A, Ottery, W Cape, 1996.

Storkey, Elaine, *What's right with feminism*, SPCK, London, 1985.

Suenens, Cardinal Leon Joseph, *The Nun in the world: Religious and the apostolate*, 2nd revised ed, Burns & Oates, London, 1963.

Synod of Bishops, *Justice in the world*, Vatican, 1971.

Tugwell, Simon, OP, *Saint Dominic*, Editiones du Signe, Strasbourg, 1995.

Uitenhage Convent School, 1887-1987, Uitenhage, 1987.

Vicaire, Marie-Humbert, OP, *The Genius of St Dominic: A Collection of study-essays*, edited by Peter B Lobo OP, Dominican Publications, Nagpur, India, nd.

Vicaire, Marie-Humbert OP, *Saint Dominic and his times*, translated by Kathleen Pond, Darton, Longman & Todd, London, 1964.

Ware, Ann Patrick, (ed), *Midwives of the future: American Sisters tell their story*, Leaven Press, Kansas City, 1985.

Weaver, Mary Jo, *New Catholic women: A Contemporary challenge to traditional religious authority*, Harper & Row, San Francisco, 1985.

Weinzierl, Sister Ferrera, OP, *100 Years of evangelisation: Dominican Sisters in Zimbabwe, 1891-1991*.

The Western Wind, Year-book of Dominican Convent Taylor's Hill, I, No
    I, 1921, Educational Co of Ireland, Dublin, 1921.
Wood, Priscilla, OP, (ed), '*Justice and truth shall meet*', Conference
    proceedings, Caldwell, New Jersey, 22-27 July 1984, Parable,
    1984.

Index

Amalgamation xi, 2, 25, 65, 85, 99, 102-103, 143, 173-174, 180, 203, 206-211, 214, 217-218, 221-222, 23 2, 236-246, 263-266,287, 289-292, 296, 298, 304-305,309, 311, 314, 319, 344-346, 352, 354, 365, 367, 371, 412, 424

Aquinas Convent 278, 295, 296, 305-307

AWR 320, 322, 326, 339, 358, 369, 370

Broderick 149, 150, 391

Butler 21, 22, 50, 67-69, 190, 390, 391, 409

Cabra x-xiv, 4, 5, 18, 19, 21-25, 27, 30-39, 41-52, 54, 56-57, 59-61, 63, 65, 67-70, 80,82-83, 86, 89-90, 94, 97, 100, 104, 107-108, 110-111, 113, 117-121,125-128, 134-139, 144, 146, 147, 151, 154, 155, 158-161, 166, 171, 182, 185-187, 189-196, 200-202, 205-214, 216, 218, 220, 222, 230, 232-234, 236-237, 240, 246, 251, 253, 263-267, 270, 273-275, 281-282, 284, 286, 290, 292, 296, 298, 300-302, 307-309, 312, 314-323, 328, 331-336, 339, 341-342, 344-345, 347, 349-353, 356, 358-362, 365, 368-371, 373, 381, 384, 387, 397-400, 403- 405, 407-409, 411- 413, 415, 418, 421-423, 425

Canoe 360

Cassidy 374, 387, 420

Channel Row 21, 30

Choir sisters 25, 27, 37-38, 41-42, 60, 64, 83, 120, 132, 135, 159-160, 165-167, 169-171, 173-174, 191, 218-219

Clontarf 21

Coleman 218, 236, 239, 267, 270-271, 291, 293, 308, 313, 345, 354, 378, 380-382, 392, 414-415, 417-418, 424-425

Commissions 123, 339, 341, 350, 423

Constitutions 18, 95, 100, 102, 104, 105, 107, 109, 158-159, 165, 167-176, 185, 187, 192, 195-198, 201-202, 206-210, 218-225, 229-234, 237, 246, 248-249, 251, 264, 266-268, 275, 281-283, 290, 295, 298, 309, 348, 350-352, 354, 356, 363, 366, 368, 370, 397, 403, 407-410, 415, 421, 424

Cotter 126, 130, 133-134, 146-147, 149, 160-162, 205-206, 212, 215, 221-222, 232, 377, 390, 400, 403-405, 407

Dale 56, 78, 81, 118, 121, 123, 134, 142, 278, 286

Deaf xi, 33, 35, 114, 127, 135-156, 192, 227, 247, 272, 305, 312-313, 337, 342, 406

Directory 221, 223, 224, 225, 227, 229, 232, 403, 412, 420

Dixon 172, 276, 281, 299, 307, 309, 311, 363, 381, 392, 415-417

Dominic ix-xv, 21, 39, 76, 85-86, 90,118-119, 183-184, 186-188, 202-203, 220, 225, 240, 276-277, 285-286, 329, 356, 375, 379, 386, 391-392, 395-396, 398, 403, 424

Donnellan 242, 285, 380, 416
Dowley 57, 130, 163, 377-378,
   390, 392, 404-407

Education ix, xi, 21, 23-24, 26-33,
   36, 39, 42-47, 52, 55-58,60-
   61, 69, 76-85, 87, 89-92, 102,
   107-108, 112-114, 116, 118-
   146, 149-157, 159, 167, 173-
   174, 192, 197-199, 204-205,
   211, 226-229, 239, 247, 251,
   254, 256-259, 262, 270, 272-
   274, 277, 279, 282, 291, 295,
   298-300, 302, 305, 307, 313,
   316, 318-339, 341, 343-344,
   351-352, 354, 357, 366, 367,
   369, 370, 404-406
Egress 34, 82, 84, 250-252, 254,
   256, 262, 265, 267, 282, 296,
   297, 302, 304, 309-310, 346,
   363, 364-366, 422
Elections 166, 169, 296, 341,
   373, 376, 424, 425
Enclosure 21, 25, 34, 43, 52, 56,
   64, 79, 82, 84-85, 89, 109,
   120, 158, 165, 182-183, 187,
   194, 250-254, 270, 282, 296-
   297, 309-310, 364, 366-367

Finance 54, 62, 80-81, 114, 117, 127,
   238, 287
Flynn xiii, 218, 237, 256, 263, 266-
   267, 271, 277, 292-293, 297,
   299, 308-310, 354, 381, 384,
   390, 393, 399, 415, 417

Galway 18, 19, 21, 23-25, 30,
   158, 187, 189, 196, 203, 210-
   211, 397-398, 407, 411
General Chapter 21, 95, 171-173, 187,
   189, 203, 209-210, 238-239,
   242, 257, 64-266, 268, 273,
   276, 284-285, 289, 292, 297-
   302, 309, 348-350, 353-354,
   359, 366, 368,371-372, 408,
   415-418, 421-425

Gijlswijk 109, 170, 175, 204, 212-
   214, 217-236, 246- 251, 254,
   257, 261-266, 269, 282, 298,
   414, 424
Grant 56, 142, 172, 239, 240,
   293, 354, 367, 413, 414
Griffiths 32-33, 44, 69, 155, 386,
   398-399
Grimley 33-34, 36-38, 41-45, 47-
   52, 62, 115, 121, 136, 149,
   151-153, 160, 386, 398-400,
   404, 407, 409

Hardiman 333-336, 374, 385, 420
Harkin 87, 181, 204, 207, 222,
   232, 237, 239, 247, 291, 295,
   308, 336, 345, 374, 379-381,
   386, 393, 420, 424-425
Hickey 195, 289, 307, 323, 327,
   351, 358-359, 362, 369, 375,
   382, 385, 393, 419, 422
Holy Rosary Convent 44, 68, 77,
   78, 80, 81-87, 94, 103, 110,
   125, 128, 132, 160, 164, 177,
   178, 181, 197, 199, 204, 207,
   209, 214, 232, 235, 246, 256,
   267, 295, 299, 327-328,331,
   337, 374, 386, 415

Jurisdiction 18-23, 33-35, 39,
   59, 67, 69, 186-197, 200-203,
   211, 213, 218, 221, 225-226,
   228, 274-275, 287,323, 329,
   358

Keary 279, 281, 283-284, 286,
   360, 364, 381-385, 387, 393,
   415-417, 425
Kelly xiii, 70-71, 75, 81, 132,
   168, 307, 327, 339, 369, 375,
   378-379, 383-385, 390-391,
   393, 401, 420
Kerdiffstown 97, 99, 101, 173, 279-
   280, 296, 298, 300-301, 305,
   310-311, 318-319, 346, 349

King 70, 125, 132, 142, 149,
177-178, 199, 214-215, 220,
233-234, 245, 248, 261, 264, 271,
274, 282, 387
Kinsella 33-34, 42, 45, 52, 59-60,
62, 78, 90, 114, 118-119, 121,
125, 130, 135-136, 153, 376
-377, 390, 423
Kirkwood 271, 277, 296, 318, 374,
387

Lay sisters 25, 28, 34, 37-38,
42, 45-46, 54, 72, 74, 86, 89-
90, 95, 103, 157-181, 218-
219, 237, 248-250, 265, 300
Leahy 51, 119-121, 390, 394
Lennon 286, 288, 394
Leonard 41, 44, 47, 52, 54-55,
57-59, 117, 123, 131, 137,
142, 160, 162, 164, 399-400,
404, 410
Lynch 19, 24, 61, 210, 362,
390, 394
Lyons 172, 221, 239, 244, 274,
300, 302, 307, 309-310, 354,
384, 413-415

Madden 284, 369, 381, 394, 416
Maher 21-23, 33, 36-38, 41,
44-45, 54, 67, 144, 155, 190-
191, 193, 195, 200, 389, 394,
399, 406, 409-410
Maris Stella 82, 83
Marsh 144, 145, 148
McAuliffe 59-61, 119, 205, 241,
377-378, 390
Meenan 313, 318, 384, 408
Moran xii, 64, 69, 71, 79, 193,
200-202, 410
Muir 81, 144, 146, 148, 406

Niland 216, 221, 232, 264, 414
Nolan 19, 209, 218, 236-237, 247,
266-267, 395, 398, 409, 411

Novitiate 39, 46, 51, 55, 57, 62,
65, 77, 82, 85, 87-88, 92-
112, 119-121, 126, 132-134,
150, 160, 173-174, 178, 180-
181, 205-206, 209, 216-218,
231, 233-234, 236, 246, 248-
249, 262, 267, 272, 276-280,
287-288, 296, 298-301, 304-
305, 308, 315, 318, 349, 353,
361, 387

Open schools 299, 321-322, 324-
325, 327-330, 332, 419-420

Perfection 29-30, 88-89, 92-94,
97, 100-101, 105, 109-110,
114, 158-170, 179, 199, 211,
220, 232, 240
Priory 78, 85-86, 177, 179,
182, 254-255, 259, 261, 278,
293, 306, 308, 328, 337, 343,
358, 374-375, 386, 409, 413
Professionals 90, 112-113, 116, 135,
152

Regional Chapter 172, 283, 300-301,
307, 311-312, 316, 320, 327,
331, 349-350, 363-364, 366,
408, 415-418, 420-423, 425
Renewal 104, 202, 285, 287, 290,
309, 319, 331, 343, 348-353,
356, 358, 360-362, 366-373,
422-423
Ricards 54-55, 79-80, 83, 400
Roche 316, 384, 395
Rooney 77, 387, 391, 400, 408
Ross 123-125, 129, 131
Ryan 172, 237-240, 264, 292-293,
308, 343, 344-345, 385,
395, 417

SACBC 317, 323, 326, 328-329,
338-339, 341, 418, 420
Sherwin 56, 126, 390

Sion Hill 18-19, 23-25, 27, 30-32,
    35, 38-39, 41, 46, 64-65, 67-
    70, 72, 74-77, 79, 86-87,
    89-90, 94-95, 108, 111, 113,
    117, 119-120, 125, 127-128,
    135, 159, 185, 187-189, 191-
    192, 196-197, 199-200, 204-
    205, 207-212, 214, 220, 231,
    233-234, 273, 285, 309, 344,
    374, 381, 398-399, 401, 403,
    408-409, 411
Springfield 44, 54-55, 57-58,
    61, 115, 119, 126-128, 134,
    161-164, 169, 172, 176, 258,
    307, 311, 323-325, 327, 331,
    343, 374, 385, 400, 405-406,
    421, 425
St Agnes's 58-59, 133, 148, 160,
    163, 247, 297, 329, 343, 374,
    385
St Dominic's 293, 312, 318, 328,
    337, 341, 343, 358, 374-375,
    386, 398, 403, 409, 413, 425
St Mary's 298, 342-343, 375, 386,
    399-401, 403-404, 423-424
St Rose's 269, 273-275, 277-290,
    309, 415-417
Struggle 25, 91, 94, 187, 203, 240,
    253, 271, 314-316, 319, 321-
    322, 334-335, 338, 340-341,
    347, 350, 373

Teacher training 102, 118, 122
Tugwell 183, 186, 409

Uitenhage 83-84, 132, 164, 249,
    256, 270, 277-278, 286, 337-
    338, 374, 387, 404, 415

Vatican II ix, 107, 173, 290, 314,
    319, 343, 348-349, 351, 353,
    357, 368-370

Whitty 70, 77, 79, 81, 85-86,
    90, 114, 125, 130, 132, 196,
    378-379, 391, 401
Wittebome 143, 151-152, 154, 156,
    163, 272, 276-277, 332, 337,
    341, 375, 386, 407
Women ix-xv, 18-19, 21, 24-30,
    32-33, 39, 41-43, 45-46, 50-
    52, 60-61, 63, 65, 72, 74, 77,
    87, 89-92, 94-95, 99-102,
    104, 106, 108-109, 111-117,
    119, 122, 129, 131, 135, 150,
    155-157, 159, 161-162, 164-
    165, 168, 171-172, 174, 177,
    179, 182-189, 197-198, 203,
    205-206, 210-213, 216, 217-
    218, 221, 223, 225-226, 228,
    231-233, 238, 240-241, 243,
    254, 255, 264-265, 267, 271-
    272, 275, 277, 280, 283, 285,
    290, 295, 297-300, 306, 309,
    311, 318, 321-322, 324, 326,
    329, 335, 337, 339-341, 343-
    348, 350, 352-354, 357-358,
    360-362, 365-371, 373, 397,
    420